Hans Joachim Schrö

Through Difficult Times

The Life of
Erich and Ursula Spickschen

Hans Joachim Schröder

Through Difficult Times

The Life of Erich and Ursula Spickschen

Published by
Positive Imaging, LLC
http://positive-imaging.com
bill@positive-imaging.com

Alles Liebe & Heil Hitler! Wie Falsche Hoffnungen Entstehen

(German book: Concept and Design by **Carsten Kraemer)**

English Cover design by **Carley Marie Metzger**

Translated by: **Bergild Thyra Spickschen Neary**

Edited by: **Marilyn R. Simpson**

ISBN 9781944071325

Acknowledgments

First and foremost, I want to thank Dr. Hans Joachim Schröder for writing his book about my parents and our family and for conveying such empathy, compassion and depth of understanding of our struggle to survive. He graciously sent me a copy of his original manuscript titled “Durch Schwere Zeiten - Das Leben von Erich und Ursula Spickschen“ (Through Difficult Times – The Life of Erich and Ursula Spickschen) and I kept the title for this English translation. While translating his book, I strived to do his work justice.

Dr. Schröder‘s book was first published in Germany in 2012 under the titled “Alles Liebe & Heil Hitler! Wie Falsche Hoffnungen Entstehen” (All our Love and Heil Hitler! How False Hopes Arise) and is currently available in German on www.Amazon.de. The German version features the actual letters written by my parents instead of excerpts in the English version. The English version also does not contain the Notes, Bibliographies, Publication Registers and Geographical Registers given in the German version of the book.

My gratitude also goes to several other people.

To Marilyn Simpson, who helped transform my translation from German to English into a more readable version by spending not only hours but days and weeks reading and modifying my script.

To my granddaughter Carley Metzger, many thanks for the wonderful, beautifully designed and appropriate cover for our book.

To my publisher A. William Benitez, who made it very easy to disseminate the book to the public. He was very patient with my novice attempt to get things right. I am very grateful. Many thanks to him.

And last but not least, to my long-time companion and husband, Richard Phlegar, who gave me almost constant moral and technical assistance and support and without whom my translation of the published German book into the English version could never have been realized. My deepest gratitude!

Contents

Introduction

Everyone, whether man or woman, old or young, has a unique life. And yet some biographies are certainly more interesting than others. The story of Erich Spickschen's life and that of his wife Ursula (nee Dietrich) which is told in this book is unique for various reasons. Erich Spickschen lived from 1897 to 1957 and Gerda Ursula (Ursel for short) was born in 1903 and died in 1981. The fact that these lived during the time of two world wars with all the changes, revolutions and catastrophes of the era may not seem very important because there have been numerous biographies and countless stories written to give a nearly comprehensive picture of the first half of the 20th century. However, the unique qualities that identify the character and lifestyle of the Spickschens make their lives both unique and typical.

As regards the uniqueness, it will be fully revealed only after one reads and becomes familiar with the stories and all documents. Some prominent occurrences can be listed in advance to pique the curiosity of the reader. Consider the fact that Erich Spickschen became Landesbauernfuehrer (Minister of Agriculture) of East Prussia during the Nazi time. This is the most striking feature of his biography and is by itself already remarkable enough. But it becomes even more remarkable when one considers the fact that through the determination of Erich and his wife Ursel they were able to establish a stable existence despite much opposition. A detailed view of their lives, beliefs and motivations reveals how the Spickschens, after having to fight many years of setbacks before 1933, saw their careers suddenly take off during the mid- and late 1930s.

The rapid ascent Erich experienced during the NAZI era was similarly experienced by Ursula when she acquired a public position in the "Landesfrauenbewegung" (the Countrywomen's Movement). Ursel proved to be a very efficient, imaginative and resourceful woman whose talents were both in practical matters and as a narrative and poetic writer.

As regards the background, it does not only include the childhood and adolescence of the Spickschens. Also included are the stories about the varied and often amusing ways of the parents, grandparents and many ancestors. The family tree of the two Spickschens can be traced far back in history but this information should not be seen as dry genealogy but as a living series of stories.

The family Spickschen was unusual during that time. From a sociological viewpoint one can say that while on one hand parents Erich and Ursula held prominent positions and won considerable prominence during the Nazi era while on the other hand at the same time they remained unassuming members of the middle class. Because they were also part of the rural population it can be said that strictly from a sociological perspective they maintained somewhat unusual positions in their society. Being part of the middle class and also having prominent positions in the Nazi government created various interesting facts that give new insights into their lives.

The life of Erich and Ursula – (or Ursula and Erich, since neither of them is more important) – is unusually open and transparent for readers because of the wealth of source material and actual witnesses that are available as references. The most important witnesses are the six living children of the eight that Ursula brought into the world between 1924 and 1943. Starting in the early 1920s (or perhaps even earlier) the family showed a strong awareness and appreciation of their history. This is particularly evident in Ingolf Spickschen, the first son who was born in 1935. He is a dedicated historian who not only collected photographs and documents but also used a tape recorder starting in 1965 to capture his mother's detailed stories about her ancestors and her own childhood. In the same year he contacted Tante Martha Seelig (Erich's only sister) to learn from her about Erich's childhood and the origin of the Spickschens. Again in 1967 he recorded accounts and descriptions from his mother and also Tante Käte, a cousin of his mother. Tante Käte knew additional facts about Ursel's and her ancestors because she was a few years older.

Ursel herself was always active in documenting the family's historical events. One of her most exciting stories was about her escape from the East Prussian estate to the west of Germany with her seven children and several accompanying adults but without her husband. She wrote a tightly spaced, typed diary of 550 pages during the escape which serves as a living testimony of that astounding journey. Around the year 1979, she spoke with her grandson Erich Hart and told him her life story covering the years 1903 to 1948. That conversation is also on tape. About two years later, a few months before her death, Ursel spoke again in detail on tape with her son Thorlef and his wife Brigitte about her ancestors and her own life. So there are many taped documents in addition to the escape diary that allow us to show a wide ranging and diverse picture of the various aspects of the life of the family Spickschen.

The above mentioned recordings and documents are by no means the extent of the resources. Extremely important is also the large collection of letters that Erich and Ursula wrote in the years 1921-1948. Most of them are addressed to Erich's mother, Maria Spickschen (née van der Mark, b. 1868 – d. 1948) who lived in the Niederrhein, the far North West of Germany. It is a stroke of luck that Maria Spickschen kept the letters and saved them for posterity. The letters that she wrote in response to her son and daughter-in-law have been lost. The surviving letters can be regarded as particularly valuable not only because they offer an authentic insight both into the external circumstances but also show the beliefs and opinions of Erich and Ursula. Most of all, they are written in a style that shows rich insights. On one hand their basically factual style is not all colorless and bland but on the other hand they show intermittent blatant sadness which was typical of the time. The letters are written so that they can still be read today with great interest. Since the letters have great value as a source they are quoted extensively in the book.

Finally, in 2009 and 2010, all surviving children of Erich and Ursula were questioned with the help of a tape recorder so that they could contribute to the life story of their parents. In addition, there was a lively exchange of e-mails and phone calls, which allowed for ongoing additions and corrections to the double biography. Overall, the available source material is so plentiful that one can hardly think of more diversity.

For all that, it should not be forgotten that the life history of the parents can by no means be "completely" told, because of two reasons. First, it is basically impossible to tell a life completely since all the reality of life has an insurmountable lead on its description on paper. Second, even with the outstanding source material some events and individual stages of life remain inevitably undocumented so that little or nothing can be told about them. A careful reader will notice at a first glance that the table of contents lists only a single chapter for the tales of Erich's ancestors and his childhood while the equivalent for Ursula's are compiled into two chapters. This imbalance is directly attributable to the nature of the sources. Ursula left a broad biographical trail behind through her stories and explanations regarding her ancestors and the first decades of her life. Unfortunately we had to learn about Erich's ancestors, childhood and youth from relatives and outsiders. For example, there is comparatively little to be said about Erich's experiences as a soldier in World War I.

As for life during the years between 1933 and 1945, the story (enhanced by many surviving letters) provides a detailed and always very interesting description of certain aspects of life. However, Erich's political and administrative actions as "Landesbauernfuehrer" in East Prussia cannot and therefore is not shown in detail. An accurate analysis of these activities in the nationalistic "Reichsnährstand" must receive its own research project.

One cannot look past the fact that even the most detailed biography can only show pieces and excerpts of a life. Regardless of the shortcomings of the information, one can still find an unprecedented wealth of insight in spite of the inevitable limitations.

Hans Joachim Schröder

Foreword

The fascinating stories my mother told us and our often very emotional conversations about Vati's and her personal duties and activities in the National Socialism (Nazi) era, were part of my formative years. The study of the many preserved documents, such as the private letters of my parents since 1918 as well as the many tapes and cassettes of talks with my Mother and other relatives gave me the idea to have a memoir written. With the help of my siblings and other witnesses I wanted to have the life of our parents summarized for our children and grandchildren. By chance I was able to read the biography about the father of a friend, written by Dr. Schröder. The work was impressive and I decided to go ahead with the project. It was a sign of fate that it turned out that Dr. Schröder's mother worked two years for my parents' very close friend Adelheid von Kannewurff in East Prussia – we called her Tante Adelheid – and they remained friends. After the war and the flight from East Prussia, the Schröders welcomed the whole Kannewurff family for several months in their home.

At the suggestion of my brother Ingolf I instructed Dr. Rohrer, a historian specializing in the National Socialism (Nazi) era in East Prussia, to research the public role of our parents during the period from the Third Reich through the denazification. His findings, the additional archival documents, as well as the many outstanding, critical issues have been included in the biography of Dr. Schröder.

Our life since 1945 has been a rare period of peace, the democratic maturing of our German Republic and our generally growing prosperity. The involvement of our parents' generation with the National Socialistic Party can only be understood by future generations if one considers their historical situation and the philosophy of life (Weltanschauung) of that era. Our parents had a sheltered middleclass childhood during the Kaiser Reich, the German Empire under Kaiser Wilhelm. Then in 1914 my father left school at 17 and volunteered for service as a soldier in World War I. The four years of gruesome fighting helped form his life. The end of the war and the revolution that followed aroused his first doubts about the democratic system that was formed by many political parties. The few years that our parents spent in Denmark before their marriage greatly influenced both of them and they often spoke about this wonderful time in their lives. Inspired by ideas of the "Grundtvigianer" (a group of Danish freedom seeking ministers), they were idealistic supporters of a "Volksgemeinschaft", a community of people without any class distinction who believed in providing equal opportunities through public education. They were excited about the Christian-Nordic philosophy of life they found in the Youth Movement. They read together Nordic literature and Goethe's Faust and wanted to improve the world. But the Grundtvigianic ideas, which even now are present in some democratic parties of Scandinavia, became an entry portal for the "Blut-und-Boden" ideology of the National-Socialists, or better known as the Nazi Party.

The excesses of the Weimar Republic – major inflation and the great depression - brought millions of people, including our parents, in need of even the most essential sustenance for an ordinary life. This was in no way conducive to bring democracy closer to them. Fear of the Soviet Union and communism strengthened the desire for authoritarian leadership with the goal for a "Volksgemeinschaft", or "Community of the People". Both parents willingly accepted duties in the Agricultural Ministry of East Prussia during the Nazi regime. The promotion of my father to the office of "Landesbauernfuehrer" (the equivalent of Secretary of Agriculture) of East Prussia brought him increasingly into conflict-prone participation and involvement with the criminal Nazi system.

During the denazification procedure, Vati gave the reason for his remaining in his leadership position by saying, "he wanted to prevent a worse intervention of the Nazi party authorities". His statement was similar to one given by Ernst von Weizsäcker regarding his role in the Foreign Ministry. (**Ernst Heinrich Freiherr von Weizsäcker** served as Secretary of State of Nazi Germany from 1938 to 1943. His son, Richard von Weizsäcker, served as President of the Federal Republic of Germany form 1984-1994). This attempted but in reality ultimately overwhelming moral balancing act is today hardly imaginable for us. Many opponents of the Nazi era confirmed Vati's defensive statement after the war, including Countess Schulenburg, widow of Fritz-Dietlof Graf von der Schulenburg, one of the July 20, 1944 resistant movement participants who was executed by the Nazis. (**Fritz-Dietlof Graf von der Schulenburg** (5 September 1902 – 10 August 1944) was a German government official and a member of the German Resistance in the 20 July Plot against Adolf Hitler [https://en.wikipedia.org/wiki/Fritz-Dietlof von der Schulenburg]). The Schulenburgs were good acquaintances of our parents. The Denazification Committee noted that Vati "performed his duties in a proper manner and he stayed clear of the prevailing evil machinations of the Third Reich". However, many critical questions remain unanswered.

Today, I personally feel that I had wonderful parents who gave my life a lasting foundation of security, confidence and trust in God. They had a deep love for each other that was based on partnership and they complimented each other. Mutti was highly emotional and spontaneous and we often argued with her when we children were young, but we made up just as quickly. Her imagination and fantasy, her great gift of storytelling and love of adventure, her constant struggle on behalf of her children and the demands she made of us were immensely formative to us. Vati was more reserved and cautious. He controlled his temper, was loving and served as our role model in matters of education, morality and justice. He wrote his poems in impressive humanistic style and they were the highlights of our family celebrations. After his return from captivity in Russia, Vati suffered not only from many physical injuries but he also had serious psychological issues. Therefore - I as a child and teenager and all of my siblings - tried never to hurt him.

Goethe called his memoirs "Dichtung und Wahrheit" or "Fiction and Truth". Please note that all of these stories are subjective. So some memories of the siblings contradict one another. But we all agree that our parents embedded in us children a particularly strong sense of family which has been transferred to their grandchildren and great-grandchildren - as we notice time after time with great joy at the family festivals and reunions.

To this day I am very glad our generation was spared the horror and grief of having to live through the extraordinary existential and moral challenges that our parents went through in the early 20th century. Reflecting on the entirety of world history during that time, a final assessment of our parents' generation is difficult. Gerd Traube, who for us siblings was more than just a "brother-in-law" and who himself was a victim of the Nazi regime because of his Jewish ancestry, had a wise outlook on life. He counseled never to condemn anyone outright and always to believe in the good even in a bad situation. He ignored the "Nazitreue" (trust in the Nazis) philosophy of my parents. Instead he stood by their side, gave them a helping hand and thereby enabled all of us to experience a new beginning after the war. His forward looking and open-minded philosophy, together with his generous actions based on his belief that individuals should not be categorized as victims or perpetrators embodies for me the epitome of "Nathanian" tolerance. (Per Wikipedia - **Nathan the Wise** (original German title: **Nathan** der Weise) is a play published by Gotthold Ephraim Lessing in 1779. It is a fervent plea for religious tolerance).

Thorlef Spickschen

Haus Spickschen / Vluyn 1952

I

Erich Spickschen: Ancestors, Childhood and Youth.

In addition to the sources mentioned in the Introduction, a paper by the regional historian Hermann Thelen is available with the title of: "The Spickschen Family; Vluyn, District of Moers". It is an unpublished, typewritten study, which was probably completed around 1959. According to the subtitle it was prepared "from archival sources". Thelen's descriptions provide further insight into the origin of the Spickschen family. The following account uses only a limited amount of the genealogical details since the original material is dry and perhaps in some ways a bit confusing.

Thelen writes that the name Vluyn describes a large, charming village west of Moers, which now is merged with the neighboring town of Neukirchen to form the city of Neukirchen-Vluyn. According to Tante Martha in a 1965 interview, at that time Vluyn had 2,600 inhabitants. This number is no longer current and might relate to the period around

1900. Now (2006) Vluyn has well over 13,000 inhabitants. The town is situated west of the Rhine River in the Lower Rhine Valley close to the Dutch border. This fact is important for the Spickschen family. Vluyn still remains an important location and reference point of the Spickschens even though most members of the family no longer live there today. It is where Friedrich Erich Spickschen was born in Vluyn on July 23rd, 1897.

In Hermann Thelen's study of the origins of the Spickschens he reports that the Spickschenhof (the Spickschen homestead) was located in the eastern part of Vluyn. The name "Spickschen" can be traced back to the 15th century. However the spelling of the name was not uniform. The records show "op der Spicken" or "opm Spiecken". Only since the end of the 18th century is there proof of the spelling "Spickschen". The terms "Spiek", "Specke", "Spike" or "Spich" can mean various things, such as "fish pond", "damming of water with wooden boards", "Faschinenbridge or way", a "dyke clad in wattle" or even "a causeway". Apart from the meaning "fish pond", the name can be traced to damming waterways or to paving roads.

Thelen explains that the name "Spickschen" was not passed on consistently by the males of the family. For example, Thelen documented that the heiress Metgen Spickschen (or Metgen op der Spicken) who was the ninth generation of Spickschens, married her third husband Heinrich Schroers in 1760, after her two previous husbands died earlier in quick succession. Schroers took his wife's last name which was at the same time the name of the homestead. The marriage of Heinrich and Metgen produced only one son, Derk Spickschen (1766 - 1843). Derk Spickschen married the heiress Trintgen Kerskamp (1763 - 1805) of Vluynbusch (or Vluynbosch) in 1789, and thereby laid "the corner stone to a new family homestead."

The Spickschenhof itself was inherited by the oldest daughter of Heinrich and Metgen, a woman named Merken or Maria (1761 - 1800). She married Jan (Johann) Deckers in 1782, who also adopted the name Spickschen. The marriage of Maria and Jan produced five children - but the line that leads to Friedrich Erich Spickschen runs through Derk Spickschen, who left the Spickschenhof after his marriage to Trintgen Kerskamp. According to Thelen, this means that the original Spickschenhof, which "at the present time (around 1959) consisted of 30 acres of farmland and meadows", was first in the possession of a childless daughter and then went completely into foreign hands.

Derk was the tenth generation of Spickschens and he was followed in the eleventh generation by Henrich or Heinrich (1794 - 1864) and in the twelfth generation again Henrich or Heinrich Spickschen (1816 - 1880). The latter was Erich's paternal grandfather. Erich's father, the younger of two sons, was named Gerhard. This Gerhard, who was born on June 6, 1854 in Vluynbusch and died on December 12, 1918 in Vluyn, has a special significance for Erich and his children.

Memories are very important in documenting a family's history even if proof has not been found to substantiate them. Even uncertainties voiced by the immediate family have explanatory value. Such is the case with Erich's two oldest daughters. Helga, who was born on May 30, 1924, and Karen, who was born on June 13, 1925. In a conversation with them on July 20, 2009, they made statements about their ancestors and the Spickschenhof that cannot be proven to be true but which should not be ignored. Karen, who married Gerhard Traube in 1949, said that she remembers that the Spickschens previously owned a farm whose name has changed several times. The homestead was situated near a dead branch of the Rhine River and its present location is still known. The estate featured a large boulder with a coat of arms but Karen does not recollect exactly where the stone was located. She also remembers an aunt who told her about an ancestor, possibly a great-grandfather, who was very lazy. Many people thought that his laziness was the reason that the farm had to be sold. Later it was discovered, that the great-grandfather's tiredness resulted from a liver disease. Karen suspects that the reason for the story about the great-grandfather's laziness was to hide the fact that he had run into financial difficulties and therefore had to sell the farm.

The often uncertain and unclear family memories about the great-grandfather's role in the farm's sale are inconsistent with Thelen's explanation that the loss of the farm was due to the departure of Derk Spickschen. While Karen herself is aware of the vagueness of what she remembers, her memories should not be considered inaccurate. These stories are evidence of how the Spickschenhof remains a significant reference point by which the Spickschen family seeks to identify and understand their history. Moreover, since Karen has at least two paternal great-grandfathers it may be that in this case the ambitious family researcher has discovered more details about their ancestors than a non-family historian.

These explanations can be clarified by evidence given by Ingolf Spickschen. The great-grandfather, who was often tired because of his liver ailment, is the aforementioned Heinrich Spickschen, who lived from 1816 to 1880. In a birth certificate, he is referred to as "Ackerer zu Vluynbosch" or "Farmer of Vluynbosch". The farm, which he had to sell, was not the original Spickschen farm, as one might infer from the statements made by Karen Traube, but the "new" Spickschenhof, which Derk Spickschen had taken over in Vluynbusch with his marriage to Trintgen Kerskamp.

There are few details available about great-grandfather Henrich Spickschen who was born in 1816. In the family tree prepared in the 1930s, his occupation is listed as farmer and it can be assumed that he owned land in Vluyn. More can be said about Henrich's wife Sophia (nee Tangen), who was born in Vluyn in 1826 and died there in 1906. Tante Martha remembered Sophia. Martha, the oldest sibling and only sister of Erich, was born on October 6, 1890 in Vluyn and she knew her grandmother Sophia as a child and adolescent. Martha described Sophia as a woman who worked very hard all her life. However, in her later years she was so crippled by gout that she had to walk bent over at a 90 degree angle. In the small town farming world of Vluyn with its tensions between individual farms and conflicts between the few Catholics and the many Protestants, Sophia had experienced a lot of life. She developed a philosophy which was revealed to her granddaughter around 1902, when she advised Martha against reading a book which she had picked up. Martha remembered Sophia's words, "I'll tell you something. You don't have to read novels. As crazy and mad as life is, no one can adequately write about it."

Gerhard Spickschen / Erich's Father

In her old age Sophia had trouble with her teeth. The tasty rabbit which was often roasted on Sundays had to be cut into small pieces for her. With it she ate apple sauce. Probably around 1895 she was diagnosed with a cancerous tumor on her gums. Per Martha, the growth looked like an eye. The tumor was successfully removed in a hospital in Krefeld (the county seat). Initially, the wound was open so that Sophia had trouble even sipping liquids. However, the doctors predicted that she could live about ten more years. In fact she recovered very well and lived until 1906.

For granddaughter Martha, it was important that her grandmother always had a bag of candy in her pocket. She loved the nice malt balls that were cut from a roll of brown malt sugar.

The family stories Martha told her nephew Ingolf on October 23, 1965 when she was 75 years old were important only in part because of the specific details of the life of her grandmother and - Ingolf's great-grandmother - Sophia Spickschen. Martha's descriptions are important because they make life in Vluyn and the world in which Erich grew up come alive in all of its facets and in full color. Many things are mentioned which do not directly concern Erich but because the stories are about the people and surroundings of his childhood, he always remains indirectly in the center of that world.

Erich's father Gerhard was a successful businessman in Vluyn and he held a number of honorary positions. He was respected, popular and had an engaging personality. He was chairman of the volunteer fire department as well as the local choir. Before he founded his own seed shop, he worked in the business of his sister Margaretha (1847 - 1914), who had married Peter Minhorst in 1873. Martha speculated that tensions must have been created between Gerhard on one side and Margaretha and Peter on the other when Gerhard opened his own business. It was said that Gerhard stole customers from the company owned by Peter and Margaretha.

Martha knew Margaretha and Peter only as Tante Gretchen and Onkel Peter. Every Sunday after church the local farmers came to their shop in Vluyn. Farmers from other towns arrived in wagons. After buying and packing the groceries needed for the coming week they drank a cup of coffee, - "e Koeppke Koffn" -, and they probably ate a piece of cake.

As a small child, Martha was always over at the house with Onkel Peter. Because he had tuberculosis, he drank fresh hot goat's milk with sugar every morning. Martha always begged for the same drink. Tuberculosis was widespread in the Lower Rhine around Vluyn and Borken. Martha recalled that there were many tuberculosis cases in the right-bank district of Borken and the left-bank district of Moers. Later, when Erich's daughter Bergild (born 1936) was sent to Borken for recuperation in 1947, they had to send her right back because a doctor told the family that the risk of her catching tuberculosis was too great. The locals in the Lower Rhine were likely to be more immune to tuberculosis but children from outside the area could too easily be infected.

Whether Martha's story about the year 1947 can be reconciled with Bergild's memory is difficult to decide. In a March, 2010 interview Bergild reported that in 1947 she was sent to Vluyn with her brother Thorlef (born 1941) for fourteen days. She fell ill with tuberculosis in 1948 and she was not allowed to go to school for six months. During this time she visited Tante Martha and her husband Onkel Guste in the mountainous region of the Sauerland to recover.

[THE FOLLOWING IS NOT IN THE GERMAN VERSION]

Addition by Bergild: There exists a photo of Thorlef and Bergild in the Vluyn garden. There is also a letter from Onkel Alfred sent in September 1947 – see Chapter VI – reporting the visit of Thorlef and Bergild.

Maria Spickschen / Erich's Mother

Martha did not elaborate much on the layout of the Vluyner home and garden where Gerhard lived after his business flourished. In her memoirs she assumed that the house and garden where the children grew up were well known to everyone. However, she remembered a little room off the kitchen particularly well. This later became the private office. Most of their childhood happenings played out in this room. The family ate and spent their evenings in this room, especially in the winter. The adults, Father Gerhard, his wife Maria and Uncle Kluthen, who apparently lived in the neighborhood, played a lot of "Skat" - a German card game – in that room. Who was Uncle Kluthen? Martha also left that unanswered. She had a vivid memory of him sitting in a Worpsweder chair that stood in the corner of the little room. Martha embroidered a black linen pillow with a floral wreath for that chair. Not only this pillow but also a second one was completely worn through by Uncle Kluthen because he sat on it day after day. Scarcely had the last bite of lunch been eaten when Uncle Kluthen appeared from his own house by walking through a dividing hedge, entered the little room, said "Guden Dag" and sat down in the Worpsweder chair. He must have sat there for an inestimable number of hours.

Martha told her memories as they came to mind in no particular order. On July 11, 1889 Gerhard married Maria Emma Katharina Amalia Elisabeth van der Mark (born on August 7th, 1868) in Roermond. When Hans, the younger brother of Martha and Erich and the last of the four children, was born in Vluyn on April 22nd, 1900, Martha and Erich were sent to their maternal grandparents in the town of Roermond in the Netherlands so that their mother could devote herself undisturbed to the newborn baby son.. Roermond lies a short distance southwest of Vluyn in the Dutch province of Limburg just on the other side of the Dutch border. No mention was made of where Alfred, the second oldest, was during this time. The two children stayed in Roermond for several months with their grandparents. Erich, who was three years old at that time, very quickly learned to speak Dutch. When he returned to Vluyn, he continued to speak Dutch with his mother.

Karen, Erich's second oldest daughter, remembers a tale regarding Erich's return to Vluyn from Roermond. When little Erich saw his mother again he asked, "Who is this strange woman?" Maria was very shocked and saddened. Karen and her older sister Helga agree that they always felt that their grandmother favored her son Erich. Maria Spickschen had four children who were all born in Vluyn. Beside Martha, the oldest, Alfred, the second child (born on March 8, 1893) became important to the family. Erich arrived about four years after Alfred. Hans, who was born on April 22, 1900, was the youngest.

In a conversation on August 14th, 2009, Ingolf Spickschen reported some important history about the view of the van der Mark family ancestors. In the 16th century there was a Count Wilhelm van der Mark, who was a friend of the famous Count Egmont (Edmond). Both played prominent roles in the war against Spain for the liberation of the Netherlands. Wilhelm was a "Haudrauf" (an "aggressor") and was called the "Wild Boar of the Ardennes". – History records a Willem van der Mark (Wilhelm II van der Mark) who lived from 1542 to 1578. It is written that "he fled to William of Orange and swore not to cut his beard and hair until he avenged the deaths of the Count Lamoral von Egmond and Count Philippe von Hoorn." Count Lamoral von Egmont who has only a slight connection with Goethe's Egmond figure, - was sentenced to death by a special court of the infamous Spanish Duke of Alba (1507-1582) and beheaded in 1568 at the age of 45 in the market square in Brussels. William of Orange, - more precisely, William I (of Orange-Nassau), (also called William the Silent), - lived from 1533 to 1584. As a spokesman for the Dutch opposition, he turned against the terror regime of Alba.

Ingolf also reported that more recent ancestors of the van der Mark family were still counts and owned sailing ships. Maria's grandfather, Jan van der Mark (1798 - 1885), was a director of the Dutch "Treidelfahrt" (or towing company). This means that Jan van der Mark was the head of the government-organized towing service that used ropes to tow larger vessels upstream on Dutch rivers to their destination ports. Cables were stretched from the ship to the towpaths along the river and were pulled by humans or by draft animals.

According to Martha and Ingolf, Maria's father Meyndert Jan (Johannes) van der Mark (born in Leiden in 1835 and died in Roermond in1918) was a bank official. His granddaughter Martha remembered him well when she spoke with Ingolf in 1965. Martha said that he was typically Dutch - very self-contained and always distant. Unlike his wife Emma Amalie, (nee Lühl) (1836 - 1912) he did not participate in chastising or correcting the children. This meant the little ones adored him. If Jan was in Vluyn for a visit, he smoked his white clay pipe. Otherwise, Martha knew him only as having wrapped up legs. After getting up in the morning he wrapped his legs in bandages because his varicose veins gave him a lot of discomfort. As an official representative of a bank he was careful of his appearance. He was always immaculately shaved, regularly used eau de cologne and always wore a neat shirt and tie. For Sunday morning church service he used special cufflinks. The grandchildren gave him only one minus point and that was that he never read to them as his wife, their grandmother, did.

The historian Emil Kubisch published an article about the family Lühl under the title: "Bilder aus der Geschichte der Familie Lühl" (Pictures of the history of the Family Lühl). He wrote that Emma's great-grandfather Johan Derik Tee Lühl, born in the year 1737, date of death unknown, was an established patriarch of the Lower Rhine Farmers' communion. His son, Johann Diedrich Lühl (1779 – 1818) lived in the city of Wesel and farmed his fields outside the city walls. In 1803 he married Johanna Schlarhorst (1769- 1853), whose family were also farmers.

Their son Ludwig Bernhard Lühl (1808 – 1888) was an imposing person. He developed a talent for salesmanship early in life. After a four-year apprenticeship in an iron factory and a 3-year stint in the military, he founded a textile company in Almelo in the Netherlands in 1835 and married Amalie Feldhoff (1816 – 1857). He sold velvet, silk, cotton and cloth of other materials, also ready to wear garments like pants, shirts, shawls, overalls and other clothes in his store. His company was so profitable that he was to expand it to include a weaving factory. He opened the factory in 1838 with 38 looms, one of which was called "the Grand Machine", came from England and apparently was a steam-operated loom. But Ludwig Bernhard was not satisfied with his success. In 1845 he moved his large family, which after the death of his wife in 1857, consisted of 14 children, to the town of Gemen in the western Münsterland. There he founded another textile factory in 1856; it was the first factory in the whole district and he was held in great esteem by all.

As reported by Ingolf (the great-grandson) the marriage style of Ludwig Bernhard's oldest daughter Emma and her husband Jan van der Mark was that she patronized him in a very determined way. For example, when the family sat together at the dinner table and the servants served the main course, each family member took his or her share. After that, everybody could ask for a second helping. But when it was Jan's turn his wife Emma, who was seated next to him, declared: "Johannes says no thank you!". With this statement, the issue was settled for the great-grandfather. The women were in charge in that family. It may be that Emma was looking out for his health, so that he would not gain too much weight.

Everything went by the clock with Jan van der Mark. At an exact time each day he would push a black damask upholstered chair in front of his armchair, put up his feet, read a bit and fall asleep. While he was sleeping, his right hand would open and a bunch of keys would fall to the floor and wake up Meyndert Jan. Then he read some more. This short cat-nap was enough for him. He said that if you fall asleep even for a short time you will feel refreshed.

Jan always had to work late every Christmas Eve and New Year's Eve. The Dutch did not celebrate Christmas at that time. St. Nicholas Day, (December 6?), was the day when gifts were exchanged by the family. Everyone would go to church on Christmas, but Christmas trees were not known in Holland.

Emma Amalie Van Der Mark, nee Lühl / Erich's maternal Grandmother

Jan Van Der Mark / Erich's maternal Grandfather

The word Christmas awoke many memories in Martha. The festival was always beautiful in Vluyn. Christmas Eve was not celebrated, but the Christmas tree was decorated on that day. The children finished their last secret presents and the parents and Uncle Kluthen were busy in the Christmas room. The fir tree was covered with non-flammable cotton wool from top to bottom and white candles were attached so skillfully with pins that it looked as if they grew out from the branches. In the kitchen, the banquet was being prepared.

On Christmas Day morning, the Dutch grandparents came to Vluyn. In the late afternoon coffee and cakes were served. In the Christmas room all was ready for the festivities. Only now and then someone slipped in to organize the last little things. Then in the evening everyone gathered in the living room. This room, which later served as a private office, was "cold beauty" in 1900, as Martha put it. Unnoticed by the children, Uncle Kluthen disappeared and secretly lit the numerous candles on the Christmas tree behind closed doors in the Christmas room. In the living room, Christmas songs were played on the piano to accompany the singing. Suddenly the doorbell rang. This was the signal to open the door to the Christmas room. The sight that now presented itself was so overwhelming that the children almost burst into tears with joy. There was a large mirror placed in the window behind the Christmas tree so that the radiance of the candles was multiplied. Everything was incredibly impressive - almost like a miracle. The children had no idea that Uncle Kluthen had silently staged the big surprise.

Henrich Spickschen / Erich's paternal Grandfather

On one Christmas Eve little Erich peaked through the keyhole of the Christmas room while his parents and Uncle Kluthen decorated the tree. Someone caught Erich spying and everyone found out. His father Gerhard said in a deep, thoughtful tone "Well, it is questionable if the Christ child will still bring you gifts". Later, when all entered the Christmas room, everything was prepared and all had their places with their intended gifts. Only Erich's was not there. One of the children recited the customary poem and Erich had to apologize to baby Jesus, (or maybe he did it on his own). Then someone picked up a cloth, and underneath it were Erich's gifts. But before that, he was very sad and depressed!

It was said that Erich was a little clumsy as a child, - that he had two left feet. Around the year 1904, the family was about to take a long walk. No sooner had Erich stepped out of the house when he stumbled and fell into a cartwheel rut. There was no actual water in the track but it was muddy and Erich wound up quite dirty. Erich's younger brother Hans had on a fine velvet suit with a lace collar but out of sympathy and camaraderie with Erich he laid down beside him in the muddy rut. He received a smack on his bottom for that. Hans started to scream and became angry. So Uncle Kluthen took him by the hand and said: "Oh, come on, let's go look for deer!" Hans replied "I don't want to see any deer". A little further on some deer actually appeared in the distance and Uncle Kluthen lifted Hans onto his shoulders to show him the animals. "I've already said on the road that I don't want see any deer" the little guy yelled. This was quite a sentence for four-year old Hans and it became popular with the Spickschen family from then on. If someone wanted to have his own way he would shout, "I've already said on the road..."

Gerhard always liked to go hunting and once he was no longer a toddler, Erich was thrilled because he was often allowed to accompany his father. Gerhard always rented a hunting ground somewhere. Frequently he was invited by a farmer in the neighborhood or Mr. Erk, the forester of Baron von der Leyen. The von der Leyens owned the "Leyenburg" and the castle "Bloemersheim" and also large estates near Vluyn. Rabbit and deer were hunted in the area. The rabbits that were served for Christmas dinner were shot on these hunting trips. Martha believed that the often told story that a rabbit was placed as a Christmas gift at the door of the poor in Vluyn was more of a legend than fact. However, Gerhard's wife Maria helped many of the poor. She carried baskets of food around and each of Gerhard's workers actually received a rabbit. But what could the poor of Vluyn do with a rabbit? Roast rabbit was an expensive meal because grease, which was very expensive, was needed to cook it since the rabbit meat is almost completely fat-free.

While Gerhard was sociable, relaxed and liked a good joke, his wife Maria always insisted on good behavior. She was, as her daughter Martha remembered, "almost always a bit strict." Martha recalled a prank Gerhard pulled one morning at the breakfast table. He ate his soft boiled egg, punched a little hole in the bottom of the egg shell so that the egg shell was open at both ends. Then he blew air into the kids' faces. Maria had no patience or appreciation for such jokes. She scolded her husband and sat there showing her "Pränumerando-face," (a reproachful face).

When macaroni was served for lunch, Gerhard would suck in each tube of pasta and let it slurp smoothly into his mouth. Maria would reprimand him every time. As well, she got upset each time Gerhard came home late on Sunday evenings after visiting the local "Stammtisch" (- the table for "regulars" at the local guesthouse). The Stammtisch was the only opportunity for him to get out once a week. When he would arrive home late as usual she would be angry as usual. She showed her displeasure with stony silence or she knitted intently until it was time for bed. The next morning all was back to normal. Martha said explicitly that her parents never argued in front of the children.

Maria could be very strict, but she loved to go bowling every Tuesday evening with her husband, children and some other ladies from the neighborhood. She used the left alley and Gerhard, who was chairman of the bowling club, used the right alley. He bowled left handed. He slapped with his left hand, too. His slaps, which came unexpectedly from the left so you could not turn away quickly enough, always hit their mark. Maria also slapped the children often but she used her right hand.

Martha recalled the last slap she received from her mother. She was seventeen and the year was 1907. The house was full of visitors - the grandparents, the Erk family and many of their relatives. At noon, everyone went to the Bloemersheimer pond for rowing and to celebrate. August Mercker, a cousin of the Erk-girls, was also there. He was a theology student and was as interested in Martha as she was with him. (In retrospect Martha said: "I would not have known what to do as a pastor's wife.") That day Martha had to stay home in the kitchen and help make supper. Food had to be prepared for about thirty people and mother Maria usually did not bother with cooking. Martha said: "I grumbled because I had to stay in the kitchen and then wham, I had a slap in the face. We were both shocked." Martha remained in the kitchen, the guests returned to the house, and it turned out to be a really nice evening during which Maria not only made music but she, like the grandparents, even danced the waltz. Maria van der Mark could be a very cheerful woman.

Sophia Spickschen, nee Tangen / Erichs paternal Grandmother

On other occasions it was all very cheerful. For example, the relatives on Maria's side of the family were invited to a punch bowl evening. Gerhard prepared a hoax. He told everyone that the bowl of punch, which stood near the pond under a large tree, had been provided by the Baron von der Leyen and that, no doubt, he would arrive any minute. "But we'll try out the punch now", he said. The punch was drunk and when no one else appeared they finally realized that Gerhard had fibbed.

Martha pointed out that she and her brothers had a very good life. Since she was the eldest, she had to supervise and care for her three younger brothers. She was more or less the governess of the younger ones. Martha looked back critically on her role. It was not good to be the only girl in the family and to be the oldest at that. It is easy to begin imagining that you have authority and wisdom and you get a completely false picture of yourself.

However, she and her mother did not have sole responsibility for the three boys. There was Marieken who sewed, embroidered and mended the children's clothing. Marieken later became Mrs. Handik. There were also two girls and a young Fraeulein (a young lady). Until 1900 when Martha was ten years old, she and her brothers were not under the supervision of a nurse maid but instead they had a nurse man - which was very uncommon. Mother Maria stated that one could do much more with a boy nurse maid than with a girl. The boys were 17 or 18 years old and came from the town. They did not live in the Spickschen house, but they ate there. They were probably given some money. They came from poor backgrounds. Once one of them was so hungry and so obsessed with fat that he drank the rancid fish oil that was used for polishing shoes. To remedy the possible ill effects, he was immediately given cod liver oil. When their time in the Spickschen household was over the boys probably went to work in a factory.

Marieken was the factotum, the manager of the family. Her mother had been with Martha's grandmother van der Mark as a maid. Her mother died early and Marieken took her place. Then she came with Maria to the Spickschen household. She embroidered all of the linen and sewed everything for the children. Later, while Martha and her brothers were still at school, a baker from Vluyn fell in love with Marieken. Sometimes to the amusement of the children, Marieken was seen with a white flour paw on her bottom. Baker Handik married Marieken and they had several children.

Maria Spickschen did not like sewing and mending, but knitting became one of her favorite activities. She also did not like housework. However she worked diligently in the family business. Martha reported that several relatives claimed that she often sat at the desk in the office until just before midnight doing paper work. Gerhard did none of that.

Gerhard took care of their business needs in his own way. For example, he regularly went to the stock market in Krefeld and the afternoon when he returned from there, always became a gala event for the children. The maids bought fresh bread at the bakery and the children were allowed to participate in drinking the afternoon tea. The bread with the creamed cheese on it was wonderful. Gerhard also always brought some kind of candy for his children, and sometimes he made them especially happy when he surprised them with a small toy.

Despite the domestic workers and staff, Martha said that the children never felt neglected by their mother. Every night before going to bed they would sit in the little room on either side of her on the sofa and she would read to them. Very cleverly Maria knew how to be independent from her children but also remain indispensable to them. She carefully ensured that everything was fair. None of the children could eat candy or a bar of chocolate all by themselves. Maria took the gifts that businessmen occasionally brought with them and placed them in a round tin. Before the children were given a treat they had to take some to the domestic helpers.

The kids never received money in order to buy sweets. While Grandmother Sophia supplied them happily with malt bonbons, they wanted to buy something little in the shops around their school. For two cents they could buy a handful of "Salmiakpastillen" (a kind of liquorish candy). The kids were very rarely given some money for sweets. After all, giving the kids two pennies to buy something was not pampering.

From the very beginning the children had been taught to play independently. They did not need care or guidance from the adults. For example, they built a cabin near the chicken house with rooms that were separated with boards from a crate. Sometimes they went into the fields and picked primroses and other wildflowers. The children often came home from the fields soaking wet after one of them might have fallen into the water. They even played with the workers' children for which they needed no special invitation. Someone would simply call: "Come with me" and then they would run to carpenter Geldermann's shop and play on the wood stacks. Vutz's had a fabulous backyard with a kind of orchard that ran up to Kramer's factory and the children liked to play there. On some days father Gerhard made time for them and went with the children outside to play with them.

Martha and Alfred Spickschen / 1898

It was especially nice on Sunday mornings in the summer when father and Uncle Kluthen went fishing. First, the children had to catch flies and then they went to the Leyenburg pond. Often the bait had to be reattached and the fishing poles prepared anew so the children had to catch more flies on the bank of the pond between the grasses and colorful flowers. In the spring the pond was stocked with pike from a boat with a flat bottom. Some of the fish thrived and got huge.

In the summer everyone went swimming. There was a sandy place near a bridge where the water was easy to reach. They also swam in the Small Parsick creek. Then there was the Leyenburg pond on the right side of the road to Krefeld, or you could go to the Great Parsick River. But Martha was not allowed to take part in these fun outings, especially when she became a little older. It was not proper for girls and boys to go bathing together even if the girls were wearing a suit.

The parents Gerhard and Maria had their own fun and relaxation by taking trips without the children to places such as the Eifel and Hunsrück mountains or into the mountains on the right Rhine riverbank. In July 1914, shortly before the outbreak of World War I, the parents went on a trip with their four children to celebrate their silver wedding anniversary. They went by rail to the Salzkammergut, Berchtesgaden and Salzburg.

How Gerhard and Maria experienced the outbreak of the war in 1914 is unknown. Martha reported that they always voted for the National Liberal Party. Germany declared

Erich Spickschen / 1899

war on Russia on August 1, 1914 and on France on August 3. This created immediate and drastic changes in Vluyn. Erich turned seventeen on July 23 and as his sister said, he was still a real adolescent lad. Without hesitation he wanted to go to war. His parents were convinced that he would not be accepted as a volunteer but then came the telegram: "... your gunner Erich." On August 17 he drove off. His parents gave him some money before he left so he could look around southern Germany and have a few nice days. Martha did not remember whether he was able to come home before being inducted into the army. Anyway, he left Vluyn immediately after his high school graduation. His diploma from the humanistic Royal Adolfinum Gymnasium in Moers is dated August 4, 1914.

Martha said that it was immaterial whether his parents' consent was needed to allow Erich, young as he was, to report immediately to the military as a volunteer since his father and mother would not have had the opportunity to raise an effective opposition. Erich was determined to be a soldier, especially since his older brother Alfred had already served in a regiment from Württemberg. Even younger brother Hans went into the military. In Ingolf's discussion with Martha in 1965, he said that he believed that Hans, like his two older brothers, served in the war. However Martha insisted that boys like Hans who were born in 1900 were not sent to the front lines. Hans had indeed asked his parents to give him permission to serve at the front but they had refused it outright. According to Martha they said: "We already have two sons in the war. A third one – no way!" So he remained in a Belgian training camp.

In recognition and even in admiration Martha recounted the activities in Vluyn to support the German war effort. The Leyenburg was turned into a hospital with forty beds, a physician, nurses, paramedics and a fully equipped kitchen including an experienced cook and servers. Prior to that, the palace building and the park had been carefully repaired and renovated. Martha still remembered that she together with other school children knelt in the palace square and tried to remove the grass from the cracks in the pavement with an old knife. Everything was renovated into tip-top condition by volunteers and then made available to the army.

What Erich saw and experienced in World War I is given only in hints and bare outlines. It is known that he was sent to the Western Front on October 22, 1914, and that he became a petty officer on Christmas, 1914. In May, 1915 he was promoted to sergeant.

He attended a course in Beverloo (Belgium) from August 22 to September 19, 1915 and after completing the course, he was promoted to lieutenant in the National Guard.

Erich was deployed in the Vogesen (Vosges) until the end of 1915. Beginning in the summer of 1917, he participated in heavy fighting. It is certain that he participated in fierce battles from June to September, 1917 - first on the battlefield at Verdun. From then until July, 1918 he was in the Argonne. In July, 1918 he fought at the Marne (Meuse) and later in the Champagne region. During September and October of that year he was again in the Argonne and the Meuse. In November, 1918 he was finally deployed near Metz.

Erich in the Trenches / WWI

Additional details can be found in Erich Spickschen's "soldier pay-book". On the first page of the note book - about the size DIN A6 – is stated: *"Pay book for Spickschen", National Guard Lieutenant in the 1st Replacement Division of Field Artillery Regiment No. 13 "Issued by the treasury department, 1 October, 1915"*. The signature and stamp are illegible. On the next page of the document amid superfluous notations is Erich's religious affiliation: Erich Spickschen is Protestant. At this point it should be mentioned that all of Erich's ancestors who are listed here and on the family tree belonged to the Evangelical Church. The van der Mark line affirmed their belief in Calvinism, - which explains why Maria disapproved of any form of inactivity.

As for "Personal Information" of Erich, the pay book says on the third page among others items: "*Height: 1m 76 cm, Shape: slim, Hair: blond, Beard: none. Special features: none.*" A seal is at the bottom of the page and also another indecipherable date. Up to a point the book can be read fairly well and it says: *"4 (F.) Batterie Württ. Landw. Feldart. Regiment. No. ..."*. Based on other information the statement can be completed. Since December, 1915 after a regrouping of troops, Erich was part of the Württemberg Reserve Field Artillery Regiment. No.2. In October, 1916 he was transferred to the staff of the Second Division. On August 15, 1917 he was assigned as aide to the artillery command 148th.

Many pages of the pay book show what Erich received as "battle field pay". Until the end of 1917 he received 310 marks every month. Then from January through December, 1918 (November is missing) he was paid 370 marks per month. Further records show that he already received the amount of 310 marks in September, 1915 as battle field pay. In addition, he received 250 marks for mobilization and 300 marks for uniforms. From this dry data it can be discerned that at least part of the war was an administrative matter with considerable red tape.

In an interview that took place on December 18, 2009, Erich's son Thorlef stated that his father likely spent most of the time in the devastating struggle in the trenches of Elsas-Lothringen (Elsas-Lorraine). As a young man of nineteen or twenty years, he commanded a troop of soldiers, who were around forty years old. According to a story Thorlef's mother told him, his father once rescued a wounded comrade from the battle field under life-threatening danger and handed him over to the paramedics, an action that saved the wounded man's life. This act was probably the reason Erich received the highest Württemberg Orden (or Medal of Honor) for exceptional bravery. His mother also claimed that with the receipt of this medal Erich could have been granted personal nobility and to be allowed to place a "von" before his last name. But Erich did not want nobility!

Thorlef's statements are confirmed by his oldest sister Helga. Their father received a placement in the Württemberg Regiment Horse Artillery. He probably did not have much to do with horses since his main duty was fighting in the "trench warfare" for two years. In addition to the Orden of Württemberg he had also received the EK I (or the Iron Cross I). In later years around 1930 when he dressed to attend a "Stahlhelm" (Steel Helmet) Assembly, he sometimes talked about the First World War. For example, he described how the soldiers were full of lice because in the trenches there was no hygiene, no way for the soldiers to take care of themselves, no showers or baths. After the war when he was at dinner with his children, the effects of the war experiences were felt when he paid close attention to ensure that everything on their plates was eaten. No piece of fat or bacon could be laid on the side. He said that it is a sin not to eat the bacon because by the end of the war in 1918 the soldiers had almost nothing to eat.

Martha's stories revealed what the end of World War I meant to the Vluyner Spickschens. The general assumption was that father Gerhard died from the joy of the fact that his three sons returned home safely from the war. But Martha said that this is only partly true. It is not quite accurate that Gerhard drank a few glasses of red wine with his three sons who had just returned home and that they found him dead in bed the next morning. Instead, Martha remembered that he had a massive heart attack. The doctor came and stayed with him for an hour or so. Because Gerhard was feeling better, the family all went to bed. Maria and Martha were with him again just before six o'clock in the morning of December 12, 1918. The boys came in a little later. Gerhard said that he was so happy that all was well with the children now. Then he took a deep breath and died.

Martha said that everyone was saying that she should be blamed for the death of her father because she had violently argued with him in November. Neither of them gave in. She does not remember the reason for the fight, but it was a very serious argument.

Erich Spickschen / Lieutenant 1915

Gerhard was short tempered, a real hot-head at times. Erich shared this trait when he was young. On one occasion, perhaps because Maria annoyed him, Gerhard threw a stack of dishes on the floor in the kitchen. On another occasion when Martha was quite young, she found herself suddenly air-born, flying to the ceiling after being launched by her father. Her pea soup splashed all over the room.

However once the anger cooled all was well again. Martha concluded that Gerhard had a good and full life. He was a man happy with himself and with many good qualities - someone who knew no envy.

Erich soon disappeared from Vluyn after he had returned from the war. Why? Martha said that she is pretty sure that he had his eye on another, younger Martha, namely Martha Erk, and he wanted to spend the evenings with her. That was in 1919 during the Belgian occupation of portions of Germany. However, there was a curfew in the occupied area. No one was allowed on the road in Vluyn in the evening after 21:00 hours (9:00 pm). One night, Erich rode his bike after 9:00 pm along the road to Leyenburg and was just going to turn off to Martha Erk's home when a Belgian soldier stopped him. Erich crashed sideways into the bushes and in a flash he was gone. On reaching home, he told his parents what had happened, then gathered up a few things and left. The Belgians ordered an intensive search for him. No one knows how he got away from Vluyn and traveled to the east. An identity card or passport was required in order to get across one of the Rhine River bridges because they were guarded. It is possible that Erich had one. In any case he travelled to Pommerellen, a small town on the Weichsel (Vistula) River delta near Danzig. This was an 1100 km trip (over 680 miles). He stopped at the first farm he came to and stayed there to work. Originally, he did not want to be involved in agriculture and perhaps planned to become a chemist or physicist. But he remained in agriculture.

While it is not known what profession Erich preferred, Thorlef declared in 2009 that his father was originally planning to become a professional officer at the end of the First

World War. How long and how strong this wish persisted is not known. However when the Treaty of Versailles was signed limiting the Weimar Republic to a *one hundred thousand*-man army, it was impossible for Erich to become a professional officer.

Martha, Erich, Alfred's fiancée, Alfred, Maria, Hans and Gerhard Spickschen

II

Ursula Spickschen: Ancestors and Parents

Gerda Ursula Spickschen was born on February 8, 1903 in Berlin and she was an excellent storyteller. On several occasions she spoke extensively not only about her own life but also about her ancestors, especially the life of her parents. Her father Ernst August Dietrich lived from 1860 to 1943 and played a dominant role in her life. Ursula remembers her father so well that her biographical description of him almost comes to life.

Ursula's stories, mentioned in the introduction, were told during long interviews in each of the years 1965, 1967, 1979 and 1981 that were recorded with a tape recorder. In addition, there are numerous letters and a 550-page typewritten diary of her family's escape from East Prussia. Therefore, in contrast to the life of Erich, there are very rich sources of material. However, since the descriptions and memories are told at various times, there are not only some repetitions but also many additions and the details do not always match exactly.

The interviews during the years 1979 and 1981 set a crucial basis for the following narratives. Since the timeline between these years is very narrow, there are virtually no differences in the description of the details. Greater differences are seen with the talks of 1965 and 1967, not only in factual details but also in the assumptions. For example, in 1965 Ursula believed her father, Ernst August Dietrich, was significantly more critical than she remembered fifteen years later. The critical assessment of him is reinforced by stories told by his niece Käte Rehfeld, (nee Hahn) and recorded on tape in 1967. The different opinions are documented in context later with notations as to the time of each remark.

In 1981, a few months before her death at the age of 78 years, Ursel told the following stories in a conversation with her son Thorlef and his wife Brigitte:

My grandfather was able to find out a lot of history about the Dietrich family by searching through the "Märkischen Archiv", the archives of the district of Brandenburg which is south of Berlin. Unfortunately his papers, which were in my possession, were lost at the end of the Second World War. These records were handed over for safekeeping to some of our friends who lived on an estate in the Neumark. We hoped that they would be far enough West to escape the Soviet hordes. But their property was overrun and occupied by the Russian army while I was fleeing with my family from East Prussia. However, I memorized much of what my grandfather found out.

The Dietrichs landed in the Spreewald (the forest by the river Spree) while the Ascanians ruled in Brandenburg around mid-1150s and perhaps even under "Albert the Bear" who became the first Duke of Saxony in 1139. They were hired as "Wildnisbereiter". The "wilderness riders" were employees of the prince who had police powers and were also the tax collectors. The Spreewald was inhabited almost exclusively by the Wends. There is a large gap between this early origin and later generations. For several centuries, we know little about the names and dates of the Dietrichs. In our research we discovered that a church book which could have given us more insight was no longer available since it was destroyed during a church fire.

The next information I have is about my four-time great-grandfather who was a small farmer in Kolkwitz near Cottbus. Listed in the church book in Kolkwitz we find his name – Georg - and in parentheses the word “Juro” which is the Wendish word for Georg. One of this farmer’s sons studied at the “gymnasium”, a secondary school that prepares students for the university in Cottbus. Every day he had to walk thirteen kilometers each way to reach the city of Cottbus from Kolkwitz. He received his high school diploma at the age of sixteen and then was hired as a teacher in the Spreewald town of Byleguhre. In the beginning he was a substitute teacher working for the principal who was certainly a very experienced man. After some time my triple great-grandfather married Anna Maria Pfeifer, the daughter of the head teacher. Out of this marriage came Karl Christian Dietrich, who came into the world on September 17, 1771 in Byleguhre. My great-great grandfather Karl Christian also became a teacher, first in Byleguhre, then in Niewisch am Schwielochsee (Schwieloch Lake). Both of these places are near the lake and not far from the Spreewald. In Niewisch was a small church. Vati (Erich Spickschen) and I drove through the town in 1938 and we saw the grave of Karl Christian. We dug up a small wild rose bush from the grave and planted it at our farm in Woydiethen, East Prussia.

There was no minister in Niewisch so my great-great grandfather started a “reading church service” every second Sunday. This strengthened his position as a teacher. He was also called the "French-slayer". He must have been a big, strong man with black hair and blue eyes. The Napoleonic Wars began in 1800 and between that year and around 1807, French marauders wandered through the area and demanded valuables. Karl Christian gave them all his silver pieces. After that, other looters came and wanted more valuables. Because there were no more silver pieces, they threatened to kill the German and his whole family. My great-great grandfather grabbed two Frenchmen by their necks, one with his right and one with his left hand, and strangled them. The story that he beat the heads of the two Frenchmen together and cracked them is not true. Per the writings of my grandfather, he strangled them.

Of course, French soldiers pursued him after that affair. He was forced to hide in the reeds of the Schwielochsee (Schwieloch Lake) for several weeks in a row boat. Obviously he was very popular in his village and no one betrayed him. In fact, the people of Niewisch would row out to him at night to bring him food and drink. Unfortunately he was only able to save a small treasure - a tiny silver sugar spoon. This old spoon, which we had in Woydiethen, suddenly disappeared one day. We never found out what happened to it. So even the last valuable relic that my ancestor saved was lost.

Ernst Heinrich, the son of Karl Christian, was born December 26, 1806 and he was also a teacher in Niewisch. He wrote a confession that was put into a container and soldered into the tower of the church in Niewisch. In the document he says that he was plagued with strong sexual desires but that he learned to control his drive through fervent prayers so that he was and remained a decent and honest man. His wife, Auguste Ernestine (nee Kieschke) died a few days after giving birth to my grandfather, Ernst Gustav Dietrich, on September 28, 1831. The women who were supposed to care for her were drinking coffee in the next room and did not notice that my great-grandmother bled to death. So my grandfather did not have a particularly rosy youth after his father married a second and eventually a third time. I myself did not know him but as my mother told me, this grandfather was nevertheless a very kind and friendly man, always optimistic and cheerful. My mother also told me that she had rarely met another person as loveable and joyful as he was. Whatever happened to him in life he always tried to make the best of everything. My mother loved him very much.

Ernst Heinrich, my great-grandfather, was indeed a fair minded man but was unpleasant and not very nice. My grandmother Sophie Wilhelmine (nee Breithaupt) in whose house he later lived, suffered a lot under him. He probably would have preferred it if his son had married a tough farmer's daughter. He did not really like that his daughter-in-law was delicate, educated and intellectually interesting. My father told me that when he was a small boy he noticed how his grandfather mistreated Sophie Wilhelmine. He constantly nagged her and was dissatisfied with everything she did. Also he had no sense of humor. The bad treatment by her father-in-law perhaps caused my grandmother to suffer from a nervous illness. On top of that, her father-in-law was not only frugal, he was stingy. Only once did he give my father, his grandson, a Taler (a silver coin from that time). The rest of the family was almost in shock because such a thing had never happened before!

In contrast to the Dietrichs, the family Breithaupt, from which my grandmother Sophie Wilhelmine originated, was an old established family with many branches and genetic lines. Many of the family were pastors. Wilhelmine belonged to the so-called "Johanniterorden" line. Several family members were influential and wealthy and it can also be said that it was a noble family. Again and again, probably for the last 400 years, the family produced academics and officers. The origin of the Breithaupts is somewhat vague. In all probability, they can be traced to a Southern German knight family. It may be that they once owned a castle in the southern Lower Saxony town of Dransfeld. But originally they came from southern Germany.

My grandfather Ernst Gustav Dietrich studied theology and became a minister. At first he was a tutor in a noble house, as was customary in that time. I believe that he got his first job as a vicar with his future father-in-law, the Rev. Breithaupt, somewhere in the Neumark or in Prignitz. After marrying, he became the associate pastor in Arnswalde in

Pomerania. There my father Ernst August was born on August 15, 1860, the eldest son of several brothers and sisters.

Cunow August Breithaupt and Dorothea Sophie Breithaupt / Ursel's paternal Great-Grandparents

Originally Grandfather Ernst fell in love with Elizabeth, the youngest daughter of pastor Breithaupt, and she with him. But the oldest daughter of the pastor, the afore mentioned Sophie Wilhelmine (called Minna) was also in love with Ernst. Minna had a very serious nature and was probably always a bit melancholy. So when Ernst asked Pastor Breithaupt for Elizabeth's hand he said, "My dear Dietrich, I cannot give you my youngest daughter to be your wife because my oldest daughter also loves you very much. She is a very sensitive person and since she is a little inclined to melancholy, she would not get over it if you married her youngest sister. Elizabeth is a happy and well-adjusted person and she can surely find another man who will marry her." Unfortunately, Pastor Breithaupt was wrong about that. Tante Elizabeth never married although she certainly had a lot of suitors. She was good-looking, intelligent and, as I said, she had a happy and cheerful nature.

At this point I want to add that Pastor Breithaupt's first name was Cunow August. Together with his wife Dorothea Sophie (nee Stammer) he headed a generous, hospitable household. My father often raved to me how great a time he had with his grandparents Breithaupt when he spent his summer vacations with them. In earlier times it was customary that a small farm was part of the manse (the pastor's home) along with servants, maids and farmhands, horses and wagons. Since Cunow and Dorothea were wealthy, they did not have to save money so they always spent plenty for food and drink. They also lavished gifts on their grandchildren. The two had far more than ten grandchildren - I think it might have been almost twenty. Amazingly, they left each of their grandchildren, including my father, the huge sum of 6,000 gold marks.

As for my grandfather Ernst Dietrich, he later received a position as associate pastor in a small town in the Mark Brandenburg. I can't recall the name of the place. It was difficult to find suitable living quarters in this small town, but eventually they found a large house that was the former home of a rabbi. The large ballroom in the house previously served as the temple. The Jewish community became so small in the village that it no longer made sense to support a synagogue with a rabbi.

The house was rented and a very strange story is handed down concerning this residence. My father told me the story and it was confirmed by his sister Tante Maria. The large room, the former synagogue, was used by Ernst Dietrich as a confirmation hall and also as the formal dining room.

On Christmas Eve the gift giving was also held there and for Christmas dinner the table was beautifully decorated. On one such occasion, the family was gathered around the table when the serving girl walked into the room with the festive roast. Suddenly a figure appeared in the doorway. The figure, or rather a dimly visible silhouette, raised a threatening arm so the scared serving girl dropped the tray with the roast. The family cried out and then the ghost disappeared. Everyone looked through the whole house for the figure after the scary event was over. She had to be hiding somewhere. The ballroom was on the second floor of the house so the figure could not have disappeared out of the windows. All were baffled. A day later it was said in town that it must have been the wife of the former rabbi, or the ghost of that lady, who could not tolerate a Christian ceremony being held in the old synagogue and therefore wanted to interfere. This is the famous ghost story of the family Dietrich.

My father, who was a pretty sober and down-to-earth man, swore that he had witnessed the whole thing and that it happened exactly as just said. All those present saw the figure and all cried out at the same time. And as I said, the girl who stood beside the figure was so shocked that she dropped the Christmas roast.

Later, my grandfather Ernst became First Pastor in Pritzerbe near the town of Brandenburg. From the large family that he founded, only his daughter Maria survived my father, who died on September 14, 1943 in Lindow. My father's second sister Käthe died as a child. His brother Konrad, whom he loved very much, died at the age of twelve of diphtheria. Then there was also the little brother Martin, who I believe died immediately after birth.

Just as with his parents-in-law Breithaupt (my great-grandparents) a real farm was part of the pastorate that belonged to my grandfather Ernst in Pritzerbe. So my father grew up as a country boy, which probably explains why he had a life-long interest in agriculture. As a minister and farmer, my grandfather Ernst was extremely fond of animals. If he had to hold a Sunday church service in another town, still wearing his good black Sunday suit he always went back out to see the horses that the coachman had just unbridled after coming home. He spent time with the horses and always got his clothes dirty. His future second wife did not like this at all and she constantly asked him reproachfully if he would change his clothes before going to the horses.

My grandmother Sophie was always very weak after the births of each child. She must have been sickly. Perhaps she felt that the man she loved deeply did not really return her love and that made her really sad. Per my father, she possibly also suffered from a gynecological problem that was not recognized at that time. Anyway, she spent a lot of time in the Kneipp health resorts (known as cold-water spas). But all this was of little use since she died young. When she died my father was still a high school student or maybe a first year university student.

As for my father, I can tell very much about him. After studying at the village primary school he was inducted into the Military Academy in Brandenburg, a distinguished old school. From this academy he graduated and finished his "Abitur" (final exams). At the special request of his mother he then began to study theology in Greifswald. During this time he finished his Hebraicum (a language test in Hebrew writings) with "blaze and glory". This is not meant sarcastically. He sat himself down and crammed and later he was extremely proud to have gotten an "A". However he soon realized that he was not suited to be a theologian. His great interest was in medicine and so he switched to study medicine. On the advice of his uncle August, the youngest brother of his mother, he joined a fraternity during this period. I knew the theologian Onkel August Breithaupt. He was last on the island of Rügen as a Superintendent. My father joined the fraternity Borussia Corps "The Prussians", in Greifswald. Later he studied medicine in Würzburg, located in southern Germany. I do not know whether he joined a fraternity with ties to the Borussia Corps or if he entered into a new organization. In Würzburg he became very good friends with a man named Riedinger, a professor of orthopedics, who later became my godfather. Riedinger died very young.

My father passed his medical board exams at the University of Erlangen, a city north of Nuernberg in Bavaria. He probably also received his doctor degree there. When he was in Greifswald he served one year as a soldier in the Bismarck-Hunters. After graduation he became an assistant physician at a hospital in Wittenberg, a town southwest of Berlin. During that time he became friends with an active duty army captain named Theodor Hahn.

Partly supplementing and partly with different details, Ursula Spickschen gives a somewhat different account in an interview in 1965.

After attending the University of Greifswald, my father (Ernst August Dietrich) began studying in the city of Halle, near Leipzig. My grandfather Dietrich previously studied theology there. Since his father (that is my great-grandfather) could not afford to send his son to the university on a teacher's salary, my grandfather earned his stay by becoming a teacher at the Francken Foundation where he could live for free. He earned the money for tuition and other required fees by giving private lessons and tutoring. My father met the officer Theodor Hahn in Halle.

Friedrich Theodor Hahn and Maria Hahn, nee Hintze / Ursel's maternal Grandparents

Later my father studied medicine in the city of Erlangen and he liked it there very much. He passed his final exams probably with a "B". After graduation he remained in Erlangen for half a year as an assistant to a professor of internal medicine. I forgot the name of this man but he was very encouraging and helpful to my father. The professor told him: "Dietrich, stay here!" But that was not what my father wanted for various reasons.

One day Theodor Hahn asked my father if he would like to visit his family in Schwedt on the Oder. His father had a factory there and he also had a cute sister. This invitation suited my father very much because he could combine the trip with a visit to see two unmarried Breithaupt great-aunts who lived in that city. This way he could say that he wanted to see the great-aunts and at the same time he would have the opportunity to meet Theodor Hahn's sister.

My father drove up to Schwedt, visited his aunts and then was invited to the Hahn house. To make a long story short, Theodor's sister became my mother. She told me later that my father "came, saw and conquered", or in Latin, "veni, vidi, vici"! My mother was very young. I think she was not yet eighteen. She had just graduated from her boarding school and sometimes she even still played with a large doll.

At this point I would like to speak briefly about my mother's ancestors. My great-grandfather Karl August Hahn came from a non-commissioned officer's family - not from an officer's family. But because he distinguished himself with his bravery, he was promoted from sergeant to major. He married the daughter of a postillion (a mail courier). Later after he received his discharge, he became a tax inspector in Berlin. My grandfather Friedrich Theodor Hahn (the son of Karl August) studied chemistry but had to discontinue his studies because he was almost deaf as a result of scarlet fever.

My grandfather completed two semesters when a distant relative who owned a soap factory asked him to come to Schwedt, a town northeast of Berlin on the Oder River. These relatives came from Polish nobility and they had no children. They probably had learned from other family members that Friedrich Theodor could not continue his studies. He was told that if he was willing to marry a niece of the relatives he would inherit the soap factory. The niece was born Hintze, my maternal grandmother. Friedrich Theodor took over the soap factory and over the years expanded it into a large concern. He was a very clever and capable chemist who was producing mainly medicinal soaps. Formisol, the product that later was sold as Lysoform, was developed in his factory. Later the patent for the soap was sold to a soap factory in Stettin.

Important information about the history of the factory in Schwedt is found in Tante Kaete's interview in 1967:

Maria Henriette Luise Hahn (nee Hintze) was a feisty and extremely capable woman. She decisively contributed to the development of the soap and perfumery factory in Schwedt. It became a large company with sales in the millions. As a small child I spent a lot of time in Schwedt and have many memories of it. The factory became well known throughout the country as gauged by the good relations it developed over the years. Large important merchants from Stettin (a large city at the Baltic Sea coast) had great connections to the Schwedt factory and made generous gifts, as was customary among businessmen at that time. I can remember that once a large package arrived which contained an aluminum pot that was filled with wonderful candied fruits. On top were candied violets. I was amazed at the pretty colors and the beautiful arrangement and the smell was exquisite. I had never experienced something like that before. I stood in front of these delicacies and felt like it was Christmas. The package was sent by a company in southern France that supplied our factory with perfume ingredients and the like. The Hahn's factory had a considerable reputation which I already was aware of as a small child. It is a pity that the company came to a sad end. This occurred before the end of 1903, when Ursula was born. I'm nine years older than she.

Tante Käte continued her story.

Grandmother Hahn (nee Hintze) impressed me immensely as a child of five. My sister was maybe three years old when we were told, "Oh go over to grandmother and pay her a visit". She lived alone in a house in a lovely ground floor apartment. When we appeared she was busy doing something but immediately, one two, three, she could find something to do for us children in a most skillful manner. She brought out a basket that contained pieces of cloth and made a patchwork doll out of patches. First the head was made by filling a patch that was tied up and so on until the doll was finished. To my sister she said: "Honey, here's a small broom, you can sweep the kitchen", or "Here's a scoop and that's where the bucket is." There was no plumbing in the house. She continued, "You can pour the water into these containers". We were very busy. Grandmother was just very practical and we never felt bored around her. She was always loving and kind.

She thought we were sweet and sunny because we were blond - unlike the rest of the Hahns who all had dark hair. One day she sat in front of a mirror and said, "Today I have a wreath on my head". She had wrapped and unwrapped her hair with papillotte (what would later be called curlers). We stood by in awe. We were extremely thrilled with our grandmother when in the afternoon she appeared in a beautiful black silk dress with a wide sable fur inset at the hem. We were immensely proud of her.

She took walks with us, too. Wherever she went she was respectfully greeted with a low bow. "Good day, Mrs. Hahn; good afternoon, Mrs. Hahn; how may we serve you?" they would say. She was highly regarded by all. This suggests that she must have been a very capable woman and much more efficient than I could determine at the age of five or six years.

Grandfather Hahn was also enormously hardworking and very efficient. With him everything revolved around income and profit and the expansion of the factory. But it was also important to him that the children were well behaved. Several of their children lived only a short time.

Besides the three children who came of age (Theodor, Gertrud and Hans) there were probably at least three other children who died young. I saw several children's graves at the cemetery in Schwedt of whom it was said, "These are the little Hahns".

What happened soon after the death of Grandmother Hahn (who died in 1900) and Grandfather Hahn (who died in 1895) was catastrophic. My father Theodor, who now became the head of the factory, experienced difficulties caused by his younger brother Hans. Onkel Hans was very spoiled in his younger years. As an officer he later contracted syphilis. Although that was cured in Aachen, a city in the Niederrhein (lower Rhine valley), a certain brain disorder developed that affected him something like schizophrenia. His behavior was very strange. He always tried to bully my father in matters concerning the company and portrayed himself as the one that knew and could do everything while telling my father that he knew nothing. One day my father had enough and told his brother, "Well if you want to run the company alone then take it". I do not know how much my father got paid since I was only nine years old but my parents lost a lot of money in this disaster.

The factory went rapidly downhill after the takeover by Onkel Hans. A little later he shot himself while he was in the bathtub after he took the drug Veronal. Before he committed suicide he wrote my mother a card. "Maria, forgive me" it said. Although my mother was only a pastor's daughter, she owned 40,000 marks and had put it all into the factory. She inherited the money partly from her grandparents but partly it was the inheritance of her mother (a born Breithaupt). Because of the large losses that Onkel Hans had inflicted upon us, we were not thrilled with him or his closest relatives. Tante Lotte (wife of Onkel Hans) did not listen to any advice on how to run the factory and later sold it at a big loss. She squandered the company away.

Ernst Gustaf Dietrich and Sophie Wilhelmine Dietrich, nee Breithaupt / Ursel's paternal Grandparents

Ursula Spickschen's interview continues below.

Back to my father. Apparently he very much liked Marie Anna Gertrud Hahn, Friedrich Theodor's daughter. It is also fair to say that he was not indifferent to the fact that she would bring a fortune into the marriage. As a pastor's son he did not have much money and during his university and fraternity time he had to make do with one hundred marks a month. That amount was all that his father could afford to give him so he had to go into debt.

One day my father got engaged to Theodor's sister. Her name was Marie Anna Gertrud Hahn (she was also called Trudchen) and was born on April 11, 1869 in Schwedt. My parents got married in this city on July 5, 1888 when my mother was just nineteen years old. What should I tell about my mother? In her way she was like my daughter Bergild who was born in 1936. If something did not fit her or her feelings were hurt, she would "mucksch"(pout). Otherwise she was a happy and contented person. My father, in contrast, was quite different in character. He could quickly flare up and get very angry; he had quite a bad temper. The fits of rage occurred mainly within the family where he did not have to keep his temper in control.

With his tendency to tolerate no opposition, he was extremely intolerant. If my mother or I had an opinion that was different than my father's, he would begin to shout and swear so much that, just for the sake of peace, we would finally say "yes and Amen" to everything. When my mother later began to rebel and assert her own opinion, there was a continuous row between my parents. That was anything but beautiful.

Why was my father such a tyrant? Perhaps because he had lost his mother relatively early in life. He loved his mother very much and was also her favorite. After the death of his first wife, my father's father (Grandfather Ernst) could now have married his wife's youngest sister Elizabeth, the woman he originally loved and who loved him. But instead he married his housekeeper, a friend of his deceased wife. This step-grandmother of mine did not love my father (her step-son) at all. I believe that she must have treated him quite badly and she probably told my grandfather lies about my father to get him into trouble. As a young man my father did not have an easy life when he was with his parents. Whether that is the reason that he became so uncontrolled is any man's guess.

The following information is from the conversation with Ursula in 1965.

Within the family, my father was a tyrant. The worst thing about him was the volume of his tirades. While my mother was self-control personified, he would raise his voice many times every day because of some little things that annoyed him. Once he flew into a rage he began to bellow literally like a bull so that everyone in our house jumped. Normally he would speak in a quiet tone. Because of his frequent shouting I have developed a special aversion to loud voices. My mother did not dare to stand up against him.

Otherwise he had very different likes and dislikes than my mother. For my father, there was nothing more beautiful than to hike with a backpack somewhere in the lonely mountains. He would stay in simple guesthouses and sit in simple taverns where the farmers got together. In contrast, my mother loved to dress up, put on fineries and stay at fine hotels. She loved parties and going to the theater while my father couldn't care less about any of that. He might go to a concert, occasionally the opera, but the theater was not for him. The two were extremely different.

It used to be that couples had little opportunity to get to know each other before they became engaged and were married. There were always others present when they met. In the time around the 1890s, it was taboo for an engaged couple to go for a walk alone. Walking together could only take place if a third person was present. Couples were never left alone before they were married. Also it was not in fashion that women went on hikes. Around the turn of the 20th century, the emphasis was on a pale complexion for women. They wore gloves and carried umbrellas outside the house. Not until much later was it no longer unseemly for women to take walks. I was born in 1903 and did not have an opportunity to join the Wandervogel (migrating bird) club, a club where boys and girls traveled to different places together and played guitar and sang folk songs. The club was founded in 1896. Times had changed a lot.

My father got a job as a miners' doctor in Rüdersdorf near Berlin. Many miners and their families lived in the area where the local government limestone mines were located. Miners' physicians received a fixed salary and therefore they had to treat the workers without extra remuneration. In addition, my father also had a private practice and often drove across country to visit his patients. He drove two horses but he had four horses because he often had to take long trips in the morning and again in the afternoon. There were only a few paved roads and the country lanes were hard on the horses.

He talked a lot about a Polish coachman who handled the animals. He drove with this man to Hungary and Poland where he was able to buy wonderful horses in the markets for less money. He learned a lot from the coachman so he soon understood much about horses. As the son of a country pastor he always had to deal with horses but the right "horse knowledge" he learned from the coachman. For example, he learned the difference is between coach horses and riding horses.

Gerda Ursula Dietrich / 1903

Unfortunately, shortly before my father left Rüdersdorf in the 1890s he lost this good man. During one vacation he appointed a substitute doctor to take care of his practice. This doctor also used my father's coach and driver for his travels in the country side. But that doctor was a drunkard and he offered the coachman drinks. He drank to "brotherhood" with the coachman and talked about personal matters with him. However, Polish coachmen are used to maintaining a respectful relationship and distance between themselves and their masters. When the driver lost respect for that doctor, he no longer obeyed him and did whatever he wanted. Through this substitute doctor the coachman learned that even with doctors a subordinate can be on a first-name basis.

The coachman soon became fresh and insubordinate to my father so that he had to dismiss him. The driver was called Thors, I remember that.

At this point I want to tell a story that I have told many times before. This also happened in Rüdersdorf. My father liked harness racing and on such occasions often talked with the trainers. One of the trainers once said to him, "Doctor, don't you want to buy this horse? You can get it very cheap because it is going to be butchered and made into sausage. The fact is that it always starts to gallop and cannot be used as a trotter. Otherwise, it is a great horse." The horse was in fact very good. My father bought it very cheaply and had it shipped to Rüdersdorf. It was probably transported by rail.

At home he harnessed the horse to a light dog-cart and wanted to try it. A pharmacist from the neighborhood came up and asked, "Can you take me with you? I want to experience the initial ride!" My father said, "Of course. Sit down next to me." The two drove off without a coachman even though there was a coachman's seat in the back of the dog-cart. As soon as they reached the street, the horse was no longer controllable. It ran and ran and ran like it was crazy. My father tried everything to get it to stop. Even though he yanked on the reins as hard as he could, the horse pulled into the bridle and ran blindly along. Finally the two men came to a cross road with the cart and my father pulled on the reins with all his power and managed to pull the horse into the cross road. As soon as the horse left the paved street it stopped with a jerk. It no longer felt the hard asphalt beneath its hooves but only the unfamiliar sand. During the wild romp the pharmacist thought that his last moment on earth had arrived and said to my father, "If you survive me, please get my will and take care of my wife's and my daughter's inheritance". With the sudden jerk of the horse stopping, the pharmacist was thrown from the cart. Luckily he landed on soft sand, so that nothing happened to him. When my father brought the horse to a halt he had another problem. Now my father could not move the horse from the spot where it stopped. The animal knew only the solid harness track and not the soft sand. I don't know how the cart was returned home. To my father's sorrow, the horse was slaughtered soon after that.

Another story concerns the medical work of my father. In Rüdersdorf there was a herring merchant, who didn't like doctors and was convinced that Herring marinade would cure everything. This man came to my father one day and said that his son was seriously ill. Treatment with Herring marinade, although thoroughly applied, was of no use. His son had a swollen neck and could barely breathe.

My father was very open to all new medical innovations. He not only received and read a medical journal but also kept in touch with other physicians who he knew had experience with ground-breaking developments. So he had knowledge of a serum which the pharmaceutical company Behring had recently discovered. Most doctors viewed this serum still with great skepticism because they feared the side effects. My father immediately guessed that the son of the herring dealer was ill with diphtheria. At the time a lot of children died, particularly of diphtheria. So my father immediately purchased the diphtheria serum from the above-mentioned pharmacist and injected the merchant's son. The child was so severely ill with diphtheria that my father had to perform a tracheotomy to keep him from suffocating. Initially the fever went down but then rose again. So the serum had to be injected in such an increased dosage that was so high that the pharmacist did not want to deliver it. However my father was able to change his mind when he told the pharmacist that the child would otherwise certainly die. The high dosage was his last chance. The child recovered and the herring dealer now sang great praises of my father and he won many new patients.

In Rüdersdorf my parents had a nice circle of acquaintances. They included the director of the limestone mine, a man from Braunschweig and a family named von der Decken. My mother felt particularly at home in that town. However my parents went through hard times in Rüdersdorf. They had a daughter born 1889 who they named Ilse. Judging by pictures, she must have had a great similarity to my daughter Runhild. Ilse must have been very clever, very reasonable for a child of her age. She used words and expressions that were not usually heard from a child. Runhild also exhibited this amazing trait as a child. Ilse's godfather once told me that she was a very strange child. At the age of four years she had an almost philosophical discussion with him by asking, for example: "Where do we come from and where do we go when we are dead?"

My parents were delighted with their small Ilse. One day when she was not quite seven years old she had a baby tooth pulled. A few weeks later she became ill and nobody could tell what was wrong. Even my father did not know what to do for her. He took her to the best hospital that existed at the time, the Charité in Berlin. Even there no one could figure out what was wrong with the child who was becoming weaker all the time. My mother told me later repeatedly in tears what Ilse said in the last weeks of her life. She said, "Mother, I know I am going to the Lord God, so please do not cry." As I am telling you this, I am almost crying myself. At that time a professor from Munich came for a short visit to the Charité hospital - perhaps to study something. He saw Ilse and explained, "The child has actinomycetes". This is a fungus disease that occurs typically in beer brewers. If brewers put barley corns from which they make the malt for beer in their mouths to taste, they could easily come into contact with the fungus that is stuck to the barley grains. Bacteria of the actinomycetes can get into a wound in the mouth and can gradually spread throughout the body forming puss in the internal organs. My sister was beyond saving and died in Rüdersdorf. Fourteen years after the death of Ilse, after two miscarriages, my mother brought me into this world. (Note: actually, Ursel was born 7 years after Ilse died. There were 14 years between their births from 1889 to 1903.)

One day my father decided to take the medical administration exam for a public health official. He applied to take the course and passed it with flying colors. As was customary, the candidates who had recently passed the examination were transferred to places where no one else wanted to go, such as one of the eastern provinces – Posen or East or West Prussia. In Posen there were several places to which candidates were being sent who had not done well. For example, assessors who were drinkers or district judges who had some other flaw. To be transferred to East Prussia was not the worst. My father was sent to the county and city of Gerdauen where he became the district physician. There he was not only responsible for official state medical concerns but he also had his own independent practice and was chief of the district hospital.

As chief of the hospital he once had a serious situation. After his studies he spent half a year in Erlangen or Würzburg and was an assistant to an internist. He therefore had some practical experience in internal medicine but he had no knowledge of surgery. It so happened that a farmer's wife was admitted to the Gerdauen hospital with acute appendicitis and she needed immediate surgery to remove it. My father said that he "sweated blood and tears". The night before the operation he was engrossed in a textbook and he looked at and tried to remember every single cut as well as he could so that he could perform the surgery without doing any damage to the patient. Thank God, he managed to remove the appendix without any mistakes. During the entire surgery he was under the observant gaze of the surgical nurses who were all deaconesses from Königsberg. The senior nurse was well aware that he was untrained in this procedure but he got it done and he was very happy about it. Even later he never lost a patient during surgery. Difficult cases were routinely taken to the University Hospital in Königsberg.

In Gerdauen my parents felt extremely comfortable. Initially the owners of large estates in the district treated my father very condescendingly. He was regarded by them almost like a kind of servant. The district physician was responsible for everyone, including the farm workers and the serving staff. He received an annual fee from the estates and did not get any additional payment for individual treatments. If a female farm worker had a difficult birth that the midwife could not handle alone, he had to be there. The landed gentry were accustomed to inviting the doctor alone - without his wife - to their functions. However my father would say to them, "Thank you for the invitation but I cannot accept without my wife". Soon after that the "Sir District Physician" Dietrich was invited along with his wife.

Should I tell you the story that my mother experienced with a manservant? She was a kind-hearted woman, but she was not very good-humored. No one would dare to take the butter off her bread. The coachman had a young apprentice who my mother wanted to talk to in the stables. As she spoke, the apprentice remained sitting on the fodder bin with his legs dangling. It never occurred to him to get off the box and show respect. He even gave my mother a snotty, brash reply. She bawled him out and even gave him a slap. From that moment on she was recognized as "gracious Lady". That is how conditions were at that time.

My father made many reforms in Gerdauen. Again and again the people came down with typhoid. This was because of the often contaminated wells in the area. On the estates there usually was only one well from which all water was drawn, including the water for the squire's estate which was carried in buckets to a barrel in the kitchen. It could happen that the animal urine from the manure piles ran or seeped into the wells. Since my father had a very good relationship with Count Klinkowstroem, the district administrator, he was able to get an edict issued that only deep wells would be allowed to be built.

In addition, the Egyptian eye disease, a condition which was caused by dirt and uncleanliness, was widespread in the district of Gerdauen. My father did a lot to counteract this disease. Hygiene was usually unsatisfactory because of the poor wells. I had a funny experience later in the 1930s as the department head of the Reichsnaehrstandes, the country's food supply agency that shows some of what my father did to stop the eye disease. After a lecture that I gave in the district of Gerdauen I had a conversation with the local department head, an elderly woman. I asked, "Can you remember the district physician Dr. Dietrich? I am that doctor's daughter". "Lord God, yes", she answered and then said, " Oh God, no!" I questioned her, "Why are you so shocked?" "Well, you know," she said, "he had to come to every village because of the eye disease. We were told to meet in the school, which we did. But we did not know that we had to undress and be completely naked in front of him! And then he scolded us if we were not clean or if our underwear was dirty! He told us, 'You have the eye disease because you are such pigs'. He was very rude!" I had to laugh out loud at that. The department director had obviously met my father as a young child.

Several people in Gerdauen wanted my father to stay there permanently. My father was always interested in agriculture and dreamed of owning some property. In Gerdauen people tried to talk him into buying some property there. A count from one of the local estates said to him. "Listen Doctor, if you buy this estate I'll see to it that you will be elevated to the nobility". The property was a knight's estate that was on the market for a good price. As much as my father was dreaming of something like that, his wealth and money was more important than nobility and a feudal estate. In 1902, he accepted an offer as a district medical officer in Rixdorf near Berlin. With that promotion he became a full government employee and no longer needed to keep a private practice. His practice in Gerdauen became increasingly stressful because of the many trips to the various towns that were part of his responsibility. He had been there at least seven years.

At this point some remarks from family members characterizing Ursula's parents are added - first by Ursula Spickschen, then by Tante Käte and finally by Tante Martha.

My father, Ernst August Dietrich, had a two-sided nature. On the one hand he was romantic, soft and sentimental. On the other hand he was hard, made lone decisions and unwaveringly followed his goals without worrying about others. At the same time he was very helpful to others - as long as it did not cost him any money. In lieu of a more drastic expression, he was "extremely thrifty". If he would have been even a little bit generous, he would have been able to do a lot of good. The contrasting traits within him are difficult to reconcile - the strong willingness to do good and work for others versus the determination to keep the money bag firmly closed. About my mother I can say that she was an excellent cook, even though she did not work in the kitchen herself. She was able to cook many savory dishes with just a few ingredients. Early on she showed a special interest in vitamins and was all for healthy meals. My father was equally interested in healthy eating. He followed the trade journals closely and the progress made in the development of healthy nutrition. Preparation of food containing vitamins was one of the few things in which my parents agreed.

Marie Anna Gertrud Dietrich, nee Hahn and Ernst August Dietrich / Ursel's Parents

Tante Kate was very critical about her uncle, Ursula's father:

Ernst August Dietrich was a very punctual, reliable and industrious man. Those were his good qualities. His not-so-good qualities were exceeding avarice and his self-centeredness. He only thought about himself. From the beginning he treated his wife, who married him for love, in an unwise and psychologically inept manner. I am sure that this girl who was so young at the wedding, dreamed of something much better for their marriage. She was wealthy and was probably spoiled by her father. After her marriage she had to live with a man who treated her without kindness.

I will give you an example. Gertrud was working with the maid in the garden. Ernst August looked out the window and said, "You go ahead and work hard, but the overseer is better than ten workers." That was very typical of him. Unfortunately it was not said in jest. This was his attitude - let others work hard. But one cannot deny that he worked hard in his field.

Käte Rehfeld, nee Hahn / Ursel's Cousin / 1967

He lacked a sense of friendliness, a certain goodness and commitment. He had no idea why he was in this world. I asked him once, "Ernst August, why are you in this world? We are here to love each other and you don't". He was wealthy and he could easily give some love. But that idea never came to him. I frankly told him my opinion.

I observed an occasion when he was very ugly and mean to his wife. When consequently she had a heart tremor, he got terribly scared and excited, jumped back and forth and cried, "Trudchen, Trudchen, Trudchen!" I told him, "Ernst August (I did not call him 'uncle'), you must consider the consequences before you act! You have a great brain, but you also have to have a heart. And you don't! "

Their marriage was not good. Whether he married her for love or mainly for the money I do not know. But she loved him for sure. At one time she asked my mother, who was Ernst August's sister, "Would you have advised me to marry your brother?" My mother answered, "Never, I would not have had you married him".

Gertrud was a very beautiful woman. She had naturally curly hair and a complexion like milk and honey. She also had many talents. She painted and drew very well and she was otherwise artistically gifted. She was a very good housekeeper and a great cook who tried out all sorts of recipes. In the Neukölln house she set up a carpentry workshop. She dismantled many of her furniture pieces and then she carved the different pieces of the wood, stained and polished them and reassembled them so that they looked grand and perfect. The oak leaves and acorns that she carved were beautifully done.

On the other hand she had, to say the least, a lot of fantasy. She should have married a man who could slow her down by saying, "Slowly, Trudchen, you probably don't see this in the right light." But no one ever told her that. However she had no musical talent, quite unlike her father-in-law, Ernst Gustav Dietrich who was highly musical and had a wonderful voice. Ernst Gustav's wife Wilhelmine (nee Breithaupt) also had a good voice and the same was true of Ernst August.

To conclude this chapter, Tante Martha, Erich's sister, discussed Ursel's parents in a 1965 interview with Ingolf.

Martha Spickschen /
Ursel's Sister-in-Law / 1924

Ursula's mother was a warm, very humble woman. She remained in the background when her husband was around. But often she quietly got her will. Ursula's father was a tyrant. Everyone had to dance to his tune. I noticed this once when I was a guest in their house. He had an unshakable self-confidence, saw only himself and nothing or no one else. However Erich, his son-in-law, knew how to handle him well - actually better than Ursel. All in all, Ernst August was an impressive figure. Perhaps he became such a difficult person because he blamed himself because he, who was such a good doctor, was unable to save his daughter Ilse's life. Then it is possible that he questioned his decision to become a farmer in his old age on top of being a physician. Others, and in the end even he, had to ask: Can this go well?

Dr. Dietrich's Home, Rixdorf-Berlin, Kanner Street 39

III

Ursula Spickschen: Childhood and Youth until 1921

Ursel will be speaking exclusively in this third chapter. No additional explanations are required.

Ursel / 1913 ?

"My grandson Erich Hart and also my children want to learn more about the first decades of my life. I was born in Berlin on February 8, 1903 late one afternoon about 4:30pm. My father had just been transferred from East Prussia to Berlin and therefore my parents initially only rented an apartment there. My father was the new medical examiner of Rixdorf, a borough of Berlin which was later renamed Neukölln.

After my birth my parents bought an old farmhouse in Neukölln. We moved in after it was renovated. Everything was very nice. The main feature was a large garden in which my father and mother spent a lot time gardening. The former stables and barn were partially used as a chicken coop. The other sections served either as a tool shed and machinery shed or remained empty. The new chicken coop had a small shed on the side that was reserved especially for me so I could keep two chickens there.

Our property was located in a small subdivision outside the town of Neukölln. It was somewhat remote and as a result I had no playmates as a small child. I felt pretty lonely there. There were no children my age in the whole neighborhood. Even though I always had a nanny – (a girl or young lady) - the feeling of loneliness remains as a dominant experience in the memories of my early childhood.

A farmer who had a few cows lived in the neighborhood on the other side of the street. So when I was only five years old I learned how to milk a cow. I was very proud. I have been interested in farming and agriculture from a very early age.

On the other side of our property, which was about a half-acre in size, there were summer houses and community gardens that belonged to the Social Democratic Society. At that time the citizens of the colony knew that my father was the chairman of the Conservative Party in the city council of Neukölln. To annoy my father they loudly sang socialistic songs, especially in the summer during their garden festivals. In addition, they broadcasted speeches with loud-speakers close to our property so we could not miss a word that was said. My father was angry about it and duly berated the “Red Brothers”. Neukölln was a real blue-color workers' town. One could say that it was a city of poor people.

My mother worked with the Red Cross and was also active in the Women's Aid Society. When I was still quite young she often took me with her to visit poor families to bring them needed clothing and food. I therefore learned early in life the difference between rich and poor. Sometimes I would ask my mother why this is so, “Why are some people so poor and others rich?” She could not give me a good answer.

This reminds me of something else. There was a swimming pool not very far from our house where at the age of five I learned to swim and received my certificate, an accomplishment of which I was very proud. Across the street from the swimming pool was a corner bar that was called Zur Stolperecke (The Stumbling Corner). One day I asked my mother, "Why is it called Stolperecke?" She replied, "Don't you see the drunken men who come stumbling out of the door? That's why it is called “The Stumbling Corner." We also witnessed the parades of striking workers and that experience made me very afraid. The people were marching through the streets singing songs, screaming and yelling, waving red flags and carrying banners. At such times my mother would quickly pull me into a shop to buy something to escape the unrest.

I remember a funny incident that happened during one of these shopping trips. I had a nanny who took me on errands when I was perhaps four years old or less. She was in love with a merchant who had his own shop. I can see everything in front of my eyes as if it were happening today. Four or five stone steps led up to the store front. Once when no other customers were present, my nanny and the merchant were engrossed in talking to each other and I was very bored. In those times, the shopkeepers had large bags in their shops that were filled with sugar and malt coffee. The bags stood on the floor and they were open with the tops turned inside out at the edges. Because the time that those two spent together seemed so long, I started to mix the sugar in with the malt coffee. When the two finally realized what I was doing they were shocked. I don't remember how much I ruined.

For domestic help we had several girls working for us. One worked as a cook in the kitchen and the second cleaned the rooms. My nanny sewed, mended clothes and ironed when she did not have to take care of me. My mother spent a lot of time with me and was very kind. But in addition to her intensive work in the garden, she was heavily involved in the Red Cross. My father also was always very nice to me when I was little. However,

I hated that I had to help him constantly in the garden. In the winter when it was cold and he pruned the fruit trees, I had to gather up the branches and cuttings and carry them away. My fingers were hurting and my feet were freezing, but it was customary that the children did what their parents wanted them to do.

When I was six years old, I started school at a lyceum (a type of secondary school). I had a very long way to go because the girls' school I attended was far away from my home. I had a twenty minute walk just to get to the streetcar stop. Then I had quite a long ride on the tram until I finally arrived at the school. It was very hard on me but it was also inconvenient for my mother because either she or my nanny had to accompany me to school. In a large city like Berlin small children like me were not allowed to walk alone on the street or take the tram. After a while I was taken out of that school and given private lessons. Twice a week I went to a teacher named Mrs. Volgenau. She and her sister (daughters of a district magistrate) were both teachers from Prenzlau. I don't know how my parents knew the ladies but they were quite friendly with them.

During my early school years, we had a girl working for us who was not older than fourteen or fifteen. Her name was Anna Finsterbusch (dark bush) and strangely, she came from a town called Finsterwalde (dark forest). Her father was a miner and she came from a large family. She was very nice and loving but also terribly dirty. My mother had to constantly remind her to wash herself. Every morning Anna had to show her hands to my mother who checked whether they were clean, even under the fingernails. Anna and I loved each other. In particular, I was pleased when she taught me some naughty little rhymes and verses that, of course, I would have never gotten to hear otherwise. I will not quote them here so that my grandchildren, if they read this, don't get shocked.

One day there was nobody in the house; even my parents were gone. My mother had not given Anna any chores to do, so she could spend uninterrupted time with me. We played a lot of games and then, when we started to get bored, we remembered that there was a sack full of walnuts in the pantry behind my parents' bedroom. These walnuts came from a large walnut tree on our property. "Should we crack some walnuts?" asked Anna. "Oh yes," I replied, "but what if someone finds out"? Anna said, "Oh, nobody will notice! The bag is so full, that if a few nuts are missing, it won't make a difference."

So we picked walnuts out of the bag - but it did not stop with a few nuts. We cracked and ate a lot of them. But now we wondered what we should do with the walnut shells. If we just threw them into the trash, my mother would probably know what had happened. “Oh," said Anna, "we better burn them in the stove”. I also thought that this was a very good idea. In our house were a few ceramic great stoves that were heated with briquettes. Once they were lit it was important that the briquettes were fully burnt until only embers remained. Only then could you safely close the flue. Why this had to be done I did not know at that time.

We then stuffed all of the nut shells into the stove in which some embers had remained.

We were convinced that they would all burn well together. We talked for a while - until we heard a muffled bang. Suddenly we were enveloped in a cloud of black dust. It immediately spread and covered all the upholstered furniture in the room. The stove had collapsed. Only a sad pile of rubble remained.

While we were still helplessly staring at each other, we heard the key being turned in the front door. My parents were home. We did not have the courage to run away so we just stood there like wet poodles. My parents came into the room and saw the mess. My mother was speechless and my father said nothing at first, which was rare. But then he started yelling with a voice like thunder which I have not forgotten to this day. It took days to clean everything up. Then the master potter had come to build a new stove.

I have a clear recollection of the youngest sister of my paternal grandmother, Tante Elizabeth. I saw her often as a child. When my parents were traveling without me, she would come to take care of me. But even when I went with my parents, she came to keep the household going because our cook, who would normally be in charge, was not very reliable. Tante Elizabeth played the piano very well and often liked to sing short devotional songs with me like "Weil ich Jesu Schaeflein bin" (because I'm Jesus' little sheep). She especially liked to sing a hymn called "Let me go, let me go, that I might see Jesus." I always found that horrifying because it is a song of death. I asked her not to sing that song with me because I did not find it beautiful and it made me so sad. Then she answered, "It does not make me sad at all when I think that I will see Jesus!" That was Tante Elizabeth Breithaupt, a tremendously energetic woman. Later she lived as a spinster in Neuruppin.

At this point I want to mention that I always had a special love for horses. I do not know if that had anything to do with my grandfather Ernst Dietrich who, as I mentioned before, was very fond of horses. My mother was also a horse-friend. Even though she did not ride herself, she was happy when I started riding. At first I rode a "doublepony" bareback. A doublepony is larger than a pony but smaller than a horse. Later I took riding lessons at a Berlin Tattersall (all riding academies in German were called Tattersall). I kept on riding horses as a means of transportation up to approximately 1927 - often with my father.

When I was nine years old I entered a girls' school, the private high school of Miss Gunkel. This school was not far away from my home. It was located in the Richard's Square in Neukölln. But it was still a walk of half an hour and most of the time I was accompanied by one of our young ladies. The road that ran from the development in which we lived to the City of Neukölln went by community gardens, meadows and open fields. It was often very cold in the winter, especially if a sharp wind blew. Therefore I will always remember that as a school girl I always had cold hands and freezing feet. I got on well in school and I liked it there but again, I had no real friend since we lived too far away from the other girls. None of them wanted to visit in the afternoon if they had to walk about half an hour to get to our house. And the same was true for me, especially since I was not allowed to be on the road alone in the big city. So I was always lonely. However I was never bored when I was home alone. My favorite game, and I remember it well, was playing with my grocery store. I owned a large play grocery store and whoever was in the room where I was playing or in the adjoining room sewing had to buy products from me. I was the merchant who weighed the groceries, gave them to the customers and wrote the bills. That was a lot of fun. Another of my favorite activities was playing "post office". I always loved writing - even in my later years. But today I no longer like to write because I had to do too much of it during my life time.

I cannot forget that as a child I loved to play "doctor". I had my mind set on becoming a doctor. Our helpers had to let me bandage their fingers and the dolls had to get splints on their legs. Later I was excited because my youngest daughter, Astrid, was exactly like me as a little girl. She also wanted to become a doctor. In preparation for a future in the medical profession, both my father and I agreed that I should attend the gymnasium (grammar school). After a time of intense preparation which I believe took half a year, I was actually accepted as a student in that school. Before I go into details, I must come back to talk about my father.

As I already indicated, he had a prominent position in Neukölln. He was not only the county medical examiner but he was also an official of the Conservative Party and had an important position in the city council. Later he was actually elected into the Mark Brandenburg provincial parliament. In general, I must reiterate that he really helped many people – as long as it did not cost him any money. If he received petitions he would write letters and lobby for the concerned people. Sometimes he asked acquaintances and friends to help (e.g. to give them a job). But as I said before, this help could not cost him any money. If relatives were in trouble, he gave them no money.

Even the Social Democrats, who were his political enemies, respected and liked him. I suppose it was because he was fair in all matters. There was a bicycle dealer who was a staunch Social Democrat. Sometimes we bought small items from him and he was always extremely polite and kind. Apparently he was extremely happy if my father appeared in person in his place of business.

Different circumstances, of which I shall talk later, ensured that my father was quite well-to-do, so that we could often take trips. I traveled a lot with my parents. We went to the Ötztal Alps, the Riesengebirge (which is situated southeast of Dresden on the border of Czech Republic and Poland) and the Harz Mountains, where we often stayed in Bad Sachsa. Near Garmisch in Bavaria we trekked over a remote pass. In June 1912, we visited the Bavarian forest, a spot where my father usually liked to hike alone or with a friend.

We also went to Sweden several times. My father was particularly fond of Sweden. It was his great desire to buy an estate in Sweden and to live there permanently in his old age after retirement. In fact, he bought a small estate in Västergötland, not very far from Goteborg. There was very little arable land and only a few meadows, but it had a big forest.

I believe that it was 500 hectares (about 1,350 acres). Several small lakes that were full of fish also belonged to the manor. My father originally wanted to become a farmer but my grandfather said that it would be useless to study and learn about agriculture, because he, the grandfather, did not have the money to buy him a farm. Therefore to become a farmer, my father would have to work all his life as a manager on estates owned by others and that would indeed be no fun.

In the summer of 1914, we again went to Sweden and stayed with Dr. Aurel. When we visited Sweden in previous years my parents always arranged to stay for a while as boarders at various estates. This time we stayed with Dr. Aurel whose estate was very close to the farm that was for sale – the one my father wanted to buy. The farmer who lived there agreed to stay on the farm as manager. My parents wanted to visit there on vacation as often as possible. They intended to build a new house for themselves next to the existing farmhouse. Everything was settled. Dr. Aurel was going to take care of business matters, find a contractor and so on.

During the return trip to Germany on the ship after our stay ended, the passengers suddenly became anxious and excited. The captain received a radio message stating, "We are at war!" We knew nothing of the murders in Sarajevo. The news did not reach us since we stayed in the countryside where newspapers came only irregularly. The postal service was not yet as organized in Sweden as it is today and the mail was delivered to the estates and farms only once every eight days or so. Therefore we had heard nothing about world events.

I will never forget how a group of older German boy scouts on the ship broke out in cheers at the captain's message. The young people believed they would soon be able to prove their courage and bravery as soldiers by defending the Fatherland. They immediately began to sing patriotic songs. What today is barely comprehensible to most was typical of that time. Not only the Germans, but the French and British soldiers all went to war with joyful anticipation.

I cannot remember exactly what happened in the following days. I only know that the German Kaiser made a speech that became very popular. Standing on the balcony of his palace in Berlin he gave a great speech in which he declared, "I no longer recognize parties; I only know Germans!" Everyone was thrilled and excited - from the simple working man up to the highest aristocrats. All felt that they were brothers.

Then the war began. My father was already over fifty years old and therefore he did not have to join the army. He became a "reserve doctor" in the medical corps with, I think, the rank of captain. He did not have to go to the front but instead had to take over the responsibilities and supervisions of two of his younger colleagues in two districts. One district was Berlin-Charlottenburg and the other - as far as I remember - was Berlin-Lichtenberg. So he had an enormous workload. The work became even heavier when he had to deal with the fight against various diseases, especially infectious diseases. As a medical officer he was not treating patients himself but he had to ensure that all regulations were observed and followed.

There was compulsory military service in Germany. For example, university students had to go to war. However, only healthy men were deemed fit for war. Other people who worked in economically important jobs in factories and plants and butchers who were indispensable for the food supply were excused from duty in the Army. Something terrible happened concerning the university students who volunteered during the first few months of the war. There was a great battle near Diksmuide in Belgium and many of the German regiments that fought there where made up of those young volunteer university students. Without adequate artillery protection, these volunteers ran into enemy machine guns and suffered cruel losses. Most of them were killed at that time. The top army management had failed!

I learned of such happenings as a child. Since I was an only child my parents almost always discussed everything openly in front of me. They also discussed the events of war. Part of the reason I heard about the war was that many of the soldiers who were sent to the front had to march past our house to the railway station in Johannisthal. From there they were sent to the different war theaters. In the beginning, as I said before, everyone was excited. Our servant girls threw bouquets to the passing soldiers; the men sang and were merry. I still remember that the railroad cars that transported the soldiers to the western front carried slogans like "We'll be home for Christmas!" and "The French, we will send them running!" and the like.

My mother, who was working at the Red Cross, had to organize the training of young girls who wanted to become nurses' aides. She also had to ensure that the properly trained Red Cross nurses were utilized correctly in the field hospitals. Therefore she had to do a lot of paperwork. But she liked doing it.

Initially we did not notice much of the war. We had one victory after another and the people thought that perhaps by Christmas the war would be over. I can still remember Christmas, 1914 when we stood around the piano. My mother played Christmas carols and the words "Peace on Earth" were in one song. In my childish mind, being eleven or nearly twelve years old, I thought that peace would now come really soon. But it did not. As we know, the war was not over until 1918.

For my father, who was indeed no longer young, the work soon became too much. He became very nervous and thought that he would have to retire prematurely. He would have gladly retired to the Swedish farm but when the war broke out, he rescinded the purchase of the property. In retrospect that was a big mistake. He told himself that as long as the war lasted, he would not be able to vacation in Sweden. He knew that he would have to travel to the farm often - perhaps every three months or so - to make sure that the former owner, now the manager, was properly taking care of the farm. Such trips would have been impossible because my father could not take vacations during the war. So he decided to buy an estate in Germany instead.

He purchased the estate Jeserig, which was located between Potsdam and Brandenburg on the Havel River, very close to Berlin. It was easily accessible by taking the local train that ran frequently from the Potsdam railroad station. There was an old manor house on the property that was called the "castle" by the village people. The estate was situated on the edge of the village Jeserig, close to the church. Four hundred hectares (or 1,080 acres) of land belonged to it. The soil was mostly poor but it had a forest with a mixture of young and old established trees. Only about 240 acres could be used as arable land and grassland. In front of the house was a beautiful forty-acre lake. Unfortunately there was no swimming in it because it was marshy and surrounded by reed beds. It was a great place to take out a boat though.

While I really do not care very much for pine trees a lot of them grew in the dark, peaty soil. But at least the soil was adequate for growing vegetables. And there was a beautiful grove of acacia trees that smelled wonderfully when in bloom. The manor house and the apartment for the inspector needed a lot of repair and also the stables had to be put in order. Overall it was a beautiful piece of property.

My father had not used all of his money to purchase the property. Materially, he was a wealthy man. He owned over half a million marks before the World War I and during the war years. He inherited some money from his parents and grandparents but mainly it was my mother who was considered to be a very rich woman under the conditions at that time. She brought 60,000 marks as dowry to the marriage and my father knew how to manage and increase the capital. First, he made a lot of money buying and selling land. In Neukölln he bought cheap farmland that he then sold as expensive building land to developers. Secondly, he was always lucky in buying and selling stocks. He was also very frugal, which helped him to amass a great amount of money.

At this point I would like to mention something that concerns both my early childhood as well as my father's relationship with money. We had a relative who visited us almost every Sunday in Neukölln. He was my uncle second-grade, the son of the youngest brother of my paternal grandmother. That means he was a grandson of superintendent Cunow August Breithaupt. The uncle's name was Georg and he studied economics in Berlin under the famous Professor Damaschke, the land reformer. I loved my uncle dearly because he spent a lot of time with me. He put me on his shoulders and galloped through the garden with me; he played hide-and-seek and catch with me. Because I had no other playmates, I appreciated this greatly.

One Sunday my mother suddenly told me that "Uncle Georg will no longer come for a visit. Father has kicked him out." So I asked my mother, "Why has Father thrown him out?" She replied, "I am also very sad that he will not come any more but Father and he had a difference of opinions." I later learned that the two clashed because of different views on the issue of taxation of profits in land speculation. The land reformer Prof. Damaschke was committed to charging a value-added tax and Uncle Georg supported his arguments to justify this form of taxation. One can imagine that my father had a totally opposite opinion because he made a lot of money through land acquisition and land sales. Father responded to this opinion in such a harsh way that he became completely estranged from Uncle Georg.

My father earned a lot of money not only through land transactions but also as the medical officer. He not only received his regular salary but also had other income. For example, he had to examine teachers who wanted to go on sick leave. He had to give his expert opinion before they could leave. Once a governing board accused him of being too lenient with some teachers because he sent them on vacation or to a rehabilitation facility. But my father insisted that he was very careful with his findings and he determined that someone was sick only if they desperately needed the rest.

He also had to examine individuals who were allegedly mentally ill. When someone was arrested because the police thought he or she was mentally ill, he had to determine whether the person was actually sick or faking. Most of these cases turned out to involve drunks who had beaten their wives and the wives then alerted the police claiming that their husbands were mentally ill. My father had no patience for police officers who brought drunks in for a second time to be examined. He would ask them reprovingly whether they were unable to distinguish a drunk from a madman. Those occasions most often occurred late at night and he had to take a taxi to the police station.

There were other things for him to do, too. He was also the district physician which meant that he had to examine the prostitutes in his district once a week for sexually transmitted diseases. He must have treated these women decently because I remember a comical incident that happened later. After my father no longer practiced his profession as a doctor and had retired to the Jeserig estate, he continued to do his banking in Neukölln at the Commerzbank on Hermann Road. He sometimes took me with him to show me how to clip coupons off stock shares and other securities like bonds. On one such occasion, as we left the bank, an overdressed person flung herself at my father, hugged him and said, "Ah, Your Excellency, that I see you again, no, no, this is overwhelming! You always treated us so decently and honorably that I could never forget you. In your eyes we were still people." When I asked my father later who that was, I received only a brusque reply. Later I learned that it was an old prostitute from Berlin-Neukölln who had welcomed him so warmly.

Besides all that, my father had to determine whether persons who applied for early retirement were entitled to do so. He was also employed as deputy medical examiner by the homicide division in Moabit. He would work there when the responsible physician, who I believe was the medical officer of Charlottenburg, went on trips, took a vacation or was sick. – For all these jobs, tests and expert opinions, my father received payment.

Unfortunately no car came with his positions so my father always used a taxi. He did not even have a secretary or a typewriter available like today's doctors. Since he had to write all opinions and certificates by hand, he often sat at his desk until eleven o'clock at night. At that time in our history it was not common for a physician to employ assistants to do the paper work. Because the work became too much for him, he retired in 1917 and we moved to the Jeserig estate which he acquired in the previous year.

Around that same time something bad happened. My mother became very ill in 1916 and we found out that she had colon cancer. Professor Silex was a famous surgeon at that time and he worked at the Charité in Berlin. He knew my father very well. He successfully operated on my mother but she had to remain in the hospital for several months because she did not want to put up with a colostomy. She then needed a second operation which was also successful. After that my mother was again a very healthy woman.

In the fall of 1916, I started high school. This change of schools again brought difficulties because I had an extremely long journey to school. I had to walk almost half an hour to get to the train station from our home in Neukölln. Then came a half hour train ride. After that there was about a ten minute walk to the school. The long round trip was very tiring for me. When I got home I was so tired that I had to force myself to do my homework.

When my mother became ill, I was sent to a boarding school - to a Miss von Lindeiner-Wildau in the Martin-Luther-Straße in Berlin. I liked it there. At first I felt a little lost and a little sad. I was not homesick but I guess it was a little strange for me to be dealing with so many girls that I was not accustomed to. These girls were mostly older than me and they had received private tutoring at home. They never attended a regular school as I had. To finish their schooling, these girls had to get a so called "Selekta" – (or high school equivalent certification) as proof of the completion of their private tutoring. Mademoiselle von Lindeiner had some professors on hand who gave these girls the finishing touches on how to write German essays and they also instructed them in art history, etc. At thirteen, I was one of the very few girls who was still a child and who had regularly attended school. There was just one other girl my age, Piene Kien, who was a few months younger than me. The older girls were between fifteen and eighteen years old but one was already twenty. She previously visited the Lette-School. These schools were very popular because there girls learned sewing, cooking and housekeeping.

I found a girlfriend there after all, Gundis von Eberstein. This friendship continues to this day. After many escapades and misfortunes she now lives in Michigan in the United States. However, at that time she was particularly interested in navy solders. We were allowed to go home every other Saturday and her train left from the Anhalt train station and mine from the Potsdam station. But both stations are fairly close together. My train left a little later than hers, so that I could always take her to her train. That was probably what Miss von Lindeiner intended because when Gundis saw a cute naval officer walking on the other side of the street, it was hard to stop her. She would yank me by the sleeve and urge. "Come, let's go across the street; come on, let's go over there!" But I was always very good and answered, "What are you thinking! That's impossible! Stay here!" It often happened that she grumbled, "Oh, you dumb goose!"

I found a second friend at the boarding school, a Polish girl named Yvonne Countess von Podulitzka. I had a funny experience with her that I remember well. One night we woke each other up, pricked our little fingers with a needle and let some blood drip into a glass of water. Then we emptied the glass by taking alternate sips. We now had formed a solemn blood sisterhood! Unfortunately, I do not know what happened to Yvonne Podulitzka. The correspondence which we started in later years soon stopped and I never heard from her again.

When I think about it, I made other close friendships. For example, there was Huehnchen Herzberg. Her first name was actually Anita but because she was so small, she was called Huehnchen (or Little Chick) by everyone. I only lost contact with her after World War II. Why, I don't know. We corresponded for many years and then one day I received no answer to my letter. She became a nanny and then married a railroad president who soon was devastated by a terrible disease that begins innocently and then at the end movement is impossible. (Lou Gehrig's disease?) So her husband died quite early and Huehnchen went to live with her mother.

Ursula / 1918

Shall I tell you what happened to me with Renata von Schehlie? When I first came to Mademoiselle von Lindeiner, I was put in a room where a girl named Louise von Behr- Negendank from Mecklenburg was the room elder. She did not like me. She was always nagging me about something or laughing at me or making me look ridiculous. The only one who defended me in that room was Renata von Schehlie and I loved her dearly for that. But her support helped me only a little. Finally I went to Miss von Lindeiner and told her that Louise von Behr-Negendank constantly annoyed and pestered me. I then asked if it were possible to move me to another room. So I moved into the four bed room where Huehnchen Herzberg also slept. Later I was able to move again when Madame von Lindeiner asked me if I wanted to move to a two bed room. I liked that very much because my roommate was Yvonne Podulitzka, who was only a few months older than me. I was soon very close to her - one heart and one soul, as we used to say. She always told me strange stories that I did not really understand. I grew up very sheltered at home and in many ways I was very naïve. I was awed by what all she had to tell me.

By 1916, the gradual effects of the war's evil fallout were noticeable; food and clothing were getting sparse. In the winter of 1916-17, the "turnip winter" began. This was the start of a terrible famine that occurred because apparently the harvest was very bad. In Berlin, food was scarce and we had hardly anything to eat. I often felt faint from hunger. To get to the boarding house of Madame von Lindeiner, we had to climb the stairs up to the fourth floor. I had become so anemic and so exhausted that climbing the stairs often got to be too much for me. From Jeserig (my parents' farm) we received almost no food because my father - always a good Prussian - promptly delivered all produce to the authorities as required. - After my mother was well again in 1917, we sold the house in Neukölln and my parents moved to the country estate with all the furniture.

After I left the boarding house of Madame von Lindeiner and the secondary school in Berlin-Schöneberg – (where I had spent a whole year), - I was sent to Rostock, a city on the Baltic Sea. The first reason for moving to the north in Mecklenburg was that the food situation was much better there. The second reason was that my father felt it was important that I learned Greek. At that time there were very few humanistic girls' schools like the one in Rostock and it was uncommon for girls and boys to attend high school together. I liked the school very much - better than the one in Berlin. But I did not like the boarding house since I was quite bored there. I very much liked the boardinghouse mother, a pastor's widow named Mueller. She was smart and interested in everything. But again, I did not have a girlfriend. I was not really shy; I just had a difficult time connecting with someone. It took a while for me to trust someone - probably a consequence of the fact that I had grown up so lonely.

At least I found a friend for life while living in the house where only six or seven other girls roomed. My friend (with whom I still correspond today) is Karl Warnecke. His father previously owned an estate but then bought a villa in Rostock where he retired. I met Karl Warnecke because his sister was a close friend of the oldest daughter of my boardinghouse mother. We always sat together and read poems or a book - but we never kissed - not even once. That was out of the question for both of us.

At war's end in 1918 a revolution broke out in Germany. Around the end of October, I went home to Jeserig for a prolonged fall vacation. Packing my suitcase was always a terrible thing for me. I would start to pack the night before I had to leave. Then I would repack the suitcase again and again and again to get all my things into the suitcase. I would be half dead before finally making it to the train station.

The estate of Jeserig is situated on a broad highway that was built by Napoleon and runs from the West of Germany to East Prussia. This main road was only about 300 meters from our farmhouse. On it we saw columns of German soldiers carrying red flags and singing Communist songs as they marched toward Berlin. Most soldiers had torn off their insignias and epaulets and they looked pretty scary. We were afraid that they might hurt someone. But they always marched by without giving us any trouble. Without exaggeration I can say that we experienced the revolution first hand.

One day though, a lot of workers from the Brennabor factory in Brandenburg an der Havel came onto our estate and demanded that my father give them food. As I said before, my father always delivered all of his excess crops to the state as required and we only had enough food for ourselves and our farm workers. Farmers were only allowed to keep a very small portion for their immediate needs.

My father was not afraid of the workers. He stood at an upper floor window and cursed and screamed at them. He had a powerful, loud voice that thundered across the yard. He threatened that he would shoot and defend himself before anyone tried to shoot him. He said that the people should leave his farm and go home. He told them that he had faithfully delivered all the food to the state. He asked them if he should let the Russian prisoners-of-war who worked on the farm starve? After his tirade, the workers demanded nothing more and left one by one.

I was supposed to return to Rostock because in that city the revolution was not quite as dangerous as in Berlin. But to get to Rostock I had to travel through Berlin. So I could not leave and my autumn holiday lengthened. Finally, we heard that the shootings had stopped in Berlin and it was safe to leave. My uncle Hans Hahn (my mother's brother) and his wife Lotte lived in Berlin. Her real name was Hedwig but every one called her Lotte (or Tante Lotte). They were the parents of my cousin Gudrun Brausewetter (nee Hahn). So my parents said, "First you go to visit Onkel Hans and Tante Lotte and when those two believe that it is safe enough, you can continue on to Rostock." To be able to get to Rostock I had to travel across the entire city of Berlin. This meant that I had to go from the Stettiner railroad station in the south-east of Berlin to the Rostock station in the north of the city. Berlin at that time was still very dangerous with shootings and fights happened there constantly.

Finally, we heard that people could dare to travel. My cousin Horst Brausewetter, a young military officer who had just come home from the war and who later became the husband of Gudrun, wanted to accompany me in a horse-drawn carriage to the train station. We started out early in the morning but we soon ended up in a shootout. The driver whipped the horses to make them run as fast as possible. Fortunately, no bullet struck us. In Rostock everything was quiet and still. I only saw soldiers who were missing all medals and insignias.

At that time, my father began to fear that the Communists could become a direct threat to him. He saw coming the events that actually happened after the World War II. He was encouraged in his fears by his good friend, the famous pastor Conrad of Berlin's Kaiser Wilhelm Memorial Church (where I was confirmed). The two believed that the Communists, who were then vigorously opposed by the German "Freikorps" (or Freedom

Party), would take over the whole of eastern Germany. They feared that the Communists would oust the estate owners and appropriate their land holdings. Whoever did not agree with the Communist ideas would be either imprisonment or execution. So in the spring of 1919, my father decided to sell the estate Jeserig. He wanted to move to Augustenburg, the city on the island of Alsen in Schleswig-Holstein, where he had previously purchased two houses as an investment.

It was no longer possible for my father to retire to Sweden. The land and estates had become very expensive. The exchange rate for the Swedish kroner was so very high that the purchase of land was no longer possible. The two houses in Augustenburg, which now belongs to Denmark, were rented to two ladies. They were boarding young female students at the local seminary in the castle Augustenburg who were in training to be teachers. A sudden announcement had been made that the teachers' seminary would be closed. The two ladies realized that they would get no more boarders and therefore they terminated their tenancy. My father then explained, "This is a sign from heaven; we move to Augustenburg!" And we did!

For me this move was very unfortunate. I wanted to finish high school with a diploma and then study medicine. As I mentioned before, even as a child I wanted to become a doctor. Around 1920, it was no longer a problem for women to get a high school diploma and go to college to study. It was still a rarity when my mother grew up but in my time it was not unusual. Women who were born after 1900 frequently continued their education to get a high school diploma. My father said to me, "I have to take you out of school. You cannot stay in Rostock when we live so far north. It is too dangerous during these troubled times. You cannot get your diploma; you have to leave school and go with us to Augustenburg." On the one hand, I was very sad but on the other, it was exciting to see and experience new things.

So in the spring of 1919, I had to leave school. We moved to Augustenburg and into the beautiful, large villa. The house was equipped with every modern convenience. For example, it had a large bathroom. At that time only a few houses had an inside bath and toilet. In addition to the main house, there was a Zweithaus (a second house) next door. But after a while my father became bored. He thought about opening a medical practice again. But at that time there was a suddenly announcement that the island of Alsen and the northern part of Schleswig-Holstein would again become Danish. The Danes demanded a referendum by which it would be decided which part of the country should be returned to Denmark. The Danes were quite right to demand this because Bismarck apparently cheated them previously. After the Danes were defeated by Prussia in the War of 1864, it was agreed in the peace treaty that the counties in Nordschleswig would vote on whether they wanted to be German or Danish. It was said that this was written in paragraph 5 of the peace treaty. But the treaty was not signed until after Prussia's victory over Austria and Bismarck was said to have crossed out that paragraph 5 so the referendum never took place.

This vote was now to take place in 1920, and it was clear that the people of Alsen would choose Denmark because they had a great majority. However it did not matter to us what decision was reached because the laws were different from today. Then, if a possession, an estate or a home came under the rule of a new country, those possessions and property were not taken away and remained the property of that owner. So we had no fear.

But then my father noticed that the German mark suddenly lost much of its value. "Inflation" was an unknown word until then. While the word might be found in a lexicon or dictionary perhaps, no one really knew what it actually meant. We experienced the devaluation very directly. There was a captain who would always come across from Denmark on a small boat. He offered coffee or soap - things that were long gone from the markets in Germany. These goods were getting more and more expensive in a short period of time. When my father asked him, "Why are things getting so expensive?" the captain replied, "The German mark is losing its value." The value of the mark continued to fall quickly. Since my father still had a lot of cash, he realized that he urgently needed to buy more land in the area. However, to acquire an estate he would have to use all of his assets. This he did not dare do because he was not a professional farmer. So he decided to buy a farm on Alsen that had only 125 acres of land but with first-class soil. Each "morgen" (about 2/3 of an acre) cost about 4,000.00 marks, which was about four times what it cost before the devaluation.

So my father bought this farm just in time - which was good because the rest of the cash he owned became completely worthless. We estimate that he lost half of his fortune. The farm we bought was called Tordengaard, which means "Donnerhof" (Thunder Farm). It was just outside the village of Lamberg. At first we still belonged to Germany, but after the vote we belonged to Denmark.

The homestead, which was just outside the village, was beautiful. But when it came to agricultural use, it was quite inconvenient. The twice angled building was huge and very pretty. Everything was under one thatched roof. In front of the section of the building that served as the residence there was an attractive little garden with a pond in the middle. Joined to the house were the cow barn, the feed room, the horse stable and the barn. Off to the side was a modern pigsty with an addition for poultry.

In the meantime, I had taken a Red Cross course in Sonderburg and also worked as an aid in an orphanage that took in infants and children up to age three. There I worked together with the daughter of a German who was the medical officer in Augustenburg. My parents socialized with some resident doctors, including a German named Sarau who was leaning more toward Denmark than Germany. However, it was really pointless to distinguish between Danes and Germans because the differences were only in the individual's views. Doctor Sarau was an avid fraternity alumnus. He was very happy to find out that his own fraternity and that of my father, the Borussia Corps of Greifswald, had a close, friendly relationship.

Ursula / 1920

The course I took in the children's home was six weeks long. When I came home one day I felt miserable and sick. My parents were traveling that day and when they returned in the evening they found me with a high fever. It turned out that I was suffering from nasal diphtheria. A few months earlier there had been several cases of diphtheria in the children's home and the night nurse was found to be the carrier of the bacteria.

My parents moved to Tordengaard, but my father kept the houses in Augustenburg. The second house was rented to three tenants but the villa where we previously lived was no longer used. The house was by no means empty however. It was full of furniture. My father had purchased several particularly beautiful old pieces at an auction so we could not move all of our furniture to Tordengaard. Therefore the villa was fully furnished with the furniture we left behind. That is where the wonderful inlaid "Schrank" (armoire) that later stood in the "Herrenzimmer" or gentlemen's room (Vati's office) in Woydiethen was from. The large trunk that stood in the dining room in Woydiethen; the old, richly carved arm chairs in the Herrenzimmer as well as the real gate leg table all came from Augustenburg. The antique grandfather clock that I had in Woydiethen in the "Damenzimmer" (or ladies parlor) also came from there. That clock was made from ash wood that was inlaid and it had a painted face of a seascape with a boat that threatened to capsize in a storm. I have a very clear picture of it in my mind and if I could, I would paint it."

IV

Erich and Ursula in the years 1921 to 1931

1. The Time in Denmark

This chapter portrays a dual turning point in the lives of Erich and Ursula. On one side the lives of Erich and Ursula are now united while on the other side, beginning with the year 1921, letters exist that give insight into what moved them and shaped their lives. As in previous chapters, this chapter has descriptions contributed by Ursel herself as well as others expressed by the children, from their respective memories.

First Ursula tells her story.

"In Tordengaard I found life very interesting. My mother was to be pitied although I did not realize it in my youth. Our home was moved from the beautiful modern villa to an old farmhouse with no bathroom or shower. The toilet was located in an outhouse behind the barn. There was no running water, only a pump in the kitchen. That was a hard transition for my mother, who had been accustomed to modern comforts from her childhood on. She was no longer a young person; born in 1869 she was fifty years old in 1919. So it was asking a lot of her to live in such primitive conditions. I, on the other hand, thought that life was wonderful and increasingly began to discover my love for agriculture. But I did not really like the tedious work in the sugar beet fields, like hoeing and thinning the plants. The rest of the field work, such as the binding and unloading the grain sheaves during harvest, I liked a lot and often helped. I also regularly fed the pigs.

My interest in farm work was also made more intense by the fact that we now employed some German "Eleven" (agricultural students), with whom I had to work a lot. The first apprentice who came to us was Fritz von Borcke. He had been a cadet at a military academy and just received his diploma, I think. Since the war was over he was not able to become an active duty officer. He was my ideal of a man. He was tall and slender with blue eyes and light blond hair. We immediately fell in love with each other. Later a second apprentice arrived. He was older than the first and his name was Erich Spickschen. He went to war in 1914 as a volunteer and returned as a lieutenant of field artillery. He would gladly have remained an active duty officer but after the war the newly established "Reichswehr" or National Guard, could employ only a few officers. So he decided to become a farmer.

Before I say more about these two men, I want to mention a few more workers we employed. For a short time we had a third agricultural student, a pastor's son named Schulze who was from Burgdorf near Hanover. We also had a German speaking Danish superintendent who was in charge of the eleven. As for Schulze, he soon left us and we were glad because he was stupid, lazy and had a voracious appetite. We also had a young girl with us for a short time. Her name was Esther von Kayser. I told my mother that she should place an ad for a companion for me in the paper so I would not be alone all the time. Esther was the niece or great niece of the famous Westphalian Baron Romberg, also known as "the Mad Bomberg". We could not keep her very long because she was man-crazy and on top of that acted like a lunatic. My mother could not and would not take responsibility for her. I liked her and got along well with her, so I was very sad when she had to leave us.

Erich Spickschen previously worked as an apprentice on an estate in Pomerania. He did not like it there because the estate was so large that he hardly came in contact with any physical or practical agricultural work, so he did not learn anything. His main job was to supervise the workers. A newspaper ad for Tordengaard, near the town of Lamberg, caught his attention. When he came to us, I was very amused because he was wearing a stiff bowler hat like the British wear. Such hats were not completely out of date but they started to become unfashionable. A year later, no one wore that kind of hat anymore. Sometime later he told me that he fell in love with me the moment he first saw me. In Vluyn, his home town, there was a girl that he thought he would marry someday, Martha Erk. But when he met me, it was immediately clear to him that he would never marry Martha. Unlike him, I did not immediately fall in love with him.

For the time being, I only had eyes for Fritz von Borcke. I even got secretly engaged to him, but with my parents' knowledge. We did not tell anyone else of our engagement. However, our friends and acquaintances noticed how things were between us. But then, as time went by, there were more and more disagreements between Fritz and me and finally we realized clearly that in many ways we were very different. Oddly enough, Erich was my confidant during my disagreements with Fritz. If I was angry at Fritz, I went to Erich and consulted with him. I must say he impressed me every time the way he responded with fairness and thoughtfulness. He never just sided with me and told me what I wanted to hear. When I was right, he agreed with me, but also told me when I was wrong.

One day I became convinced that Fritz and I were not compatible. I frankly told him that. He was very angry and very sad at the same time and tried to dissuade me from breaking off our engagement. However he failed. By that time Erich was no longer with us in Tordengaard but he lived about twenty kilometers away on a farm in the Sundeved-region. This is the peninsula that lies opposite the island of Alsen. Fritz von Borcke soon left our farm, and Erich very often came to visit us on Sundays. That is when I started to fall in love with him. One day - or more precisely one day in March 1921 - we got engaged, and this union had substance!

What I remember about the time that Erich and I got to know each other in Denmark is that for a few months we joined a little dance circle in Augustenburg. Once a week we walked there together to meet with about ten other couples between the ages of sixteen and forty years. For example, we met the purchasing manager of a grain company who wore a suit with a high collar and carefully parted and heavily pomaded hair. We invited a few couples from our dance circle to a small dance festival at our house. It was during this event that I realized that I definitely wanted to break contact with Fritz von Borcke.

Erich and I immediately told my parents that we were engaged and both my father and mother agreed to it wholeheartedly. They liked Erich very much because they already knew him in Tordengaard as an efficient eleve (agricultural student) with the best certificates. We definitely wanted to wait to get married, because Erich first had to complete his training in agriculture. This raised a question for him. Should he continue with his practical experience or study agriculture at a university. What would be better? But first, our official engagement was celebrated on June 24, 1921, St. John's Day. For this occasion, my future mother in law, Maria Spickschen, traveled to visit us in Denmark together with her daughter Martha.

My father made sure that during Maria's visit Erich's future would be discussed to clarify with her what options were open to him. For example, if Erich would not get any money or an inheritance from Vluyn, he should study agriculture and then try to get a seat on an Agricultural Council somewhere in Germany. But if he could get some money from Vluyn, he wanted to become a practicing farmer.

Maria told my father that Erich would get 250,000 marks. At that time, the money in Germany was becoming more and more worthless so my father anxiously asked, "That's hopefully not inflation money"! "No, no," declared Maria, "that is solid gold marks". It was therefore decided that Erich would not go to university to study but instead he would complete his practicum, his practical experience. We wanted to try to purchase our own property. Maria clarified her previous comment that she could not give Erich the entire amount at once. But if my father would chip in with a share, the amount of money Erich would have by the wedding date would be sufficient to buy an estate."

The first preserved letter makes it clear that Erich and Ursula not only knew each other well, but it also shows that Ursula made the acquaintance of several of Erich's close relatives. As an eighteen year old, she writes on November 4, 1921 from Tordengaard to Erich's older brother Alfred in such a familiar way that one could assume that they had known each other and exchanged views for many years. Detailed plans were obviously made from the beginning by Erich and Ursula, especially about the important issues. Ursel wrote of "cognitive work" – or what must be considered in order "to acquire a property". Ursel's thought process need not to be detailed here, but it is probably explained by Ingolf's remark that as a young child his mother had to learn how to deal with stocks and bonds under the supervision of her father. In fact, financial transactions were not strange to Ursel. In the letter to Alfred, she refers indirectly to the problem of the incipient inflation.

She wrote of her father "he is opposed to any speculation and has little confidence in the German mark."

Speaking about Erich she continued in the letter dated November 4, 1921:

"He is completely absorbed by his new job. He works from 4:30 every morning to 6:30 at night. That is a long day. He wrote me that his forearms and fingers are stiff from milking the cows. I know from experience that milking cows hurts. But the people seem to be well educated and they are nice to him. That makes me happy."

The workplace to which Ursel makes reference is no longer the farm in the Sundeved area but a new farm, as is evident from a letter Erich wrote to Ursel which will be cited later. In the meantime another passage from Ursel's letter from November 4:

"Here at home I am having a difficult time. Erich is gone and it really is not good when an engaged couple gets along as well as we do because then the separation is twice as hard. Especially when you are the one who is at home. But this only means: buck up!

"I have a feeling that [your] mother is worried. Probably less about money matters than other things. First, she is worried about my father's nature and that I might have inherited it, but I don't think so. Although some of his traits might be found in me, one can always realize a fault and can deal with it. And I am sure that I have not inherited "Muttels", my mother's, congeniality. I might have lost some of my own self-confidence while living at home, but I am sure that it will come back when I'm somewhere else. I definitely know this and I don't tend to overestimate myself. In Lysholm and also in the orphanage they praised my sense of order.

"Just because of the time I've spend here I am a little down - no wonder! You can be a good judge of that if you are living the life, as I am. It is not a lot of fun. Calm "Mutterchen" (Mother-Dear) and tell her not to worry! Well, I sometimes get the idea that she does not like my style. I never gave it much thought in the spring, but now in the fall it is different. I'm different from you guys, I know that. I've also learned a lot of good things from you, even if it was sometimes difficult. But the heart remains the same and that is as it should be. If all of you continue to treat me like a daughter and a sister as you have, I could imagine nothing better."

With amazing self-assurance, perhaps even with a bit of precociousness, this eighteen year old judges and speculates here about herself and her relationship with others who will soon officially be her relatives. The subject of the speculation is the universe of feelings, which was probably more important to Ursel around the year 1921 than anything else. The significance of Lysholm and the orphanage can perhaps no longer be clarified in detail. Her letter of 1921 makes references to training facilities that Ursula does not mention sixty years later and perhaps at that late date she did not even remember them.

Erich wrote a letter to his mother on the same day as Ursel, on November 4, 1921. Almost six years older than his fiancée, and undoubtedly matured a lot by the difficult and multi-year experience of war. The tone of his narrative is much more matter-of-fact but it also comes from the heart, as Ursel's did. Erich writes from Tommerupgaard near Haarby (Harby), a farm on the island of Funen (Fyn).

Erich Spickschen / Ursula Dietrich / 1921

"Now about this place. Tuesday Ursel accompanied me in stormy seas to Faaborg [Fåborg]. We had nice hours together before we had to say good-bye, which was pretty hard because we have become very accustomed to each other. Added to this was the feeling of uncertainty about how I would like this new place of work and for Ursel, the thought of having to live again with her father for a long time. On the other hand it is good for both of us to start working hard again.

"I arrived here at coffee time and was very warmly received. He (farmer Fenger) is the son of a farmer from Vestjylland (western Jylland) and she is from Copenhagen where she was a nurse for twelve years. In addition, there are two well-behaved nice boys of seven and nine years. I went to work immediately to help with milking the cows from 4:30 pm to 6:30 pm. I finished four cows; he milked the other twelve. He does this every day, quite an accomplishment! Milking is the only sore point with me at this time. I only milk one or two cows now because I hurt my left hand. The tendon of the little finger is sore. The farmer does not want me to do more milking, so that I don't get tendonitis, however he also does not want me to get out of practice. The day starts at 4:30am. After milking, first there is breakfast with beer bread (bread cooked in beer) with hot milk and white bread (tastes great). Then the feeding starts (16 cows and 20 heifers), mucking out the stable, and then washing the milk cans. After that we have a second breakfast (a mountain of sandwiches), pig sty mucking, livestock grooming and other hands-on work. Noontime break is from 1:00 pm until 2:00 pm. After that, again there is feeding, mucking out and milking until 6:00 – 6:30 pm. As you can see, it's a pretty long day. But it's fun for me, especially since the people are so nice. I will take over the feeding of the pigs as soon as I master the milking. He is very happy with my work, but of course it is hard on him that my milking skills are so poor. Let's hope for the best!

“The food is very good and the evenings are very sociable and comfortable. First, the boys, who helped all day long, are read a story. Then we have a very lively conversation. They are really solid and well-educated people. The rooms are very cozy and warm. Tonight he started reading the book "Gosta Berling" out loud and it will be continued every evening from 8:00 to 9:00 pm until it is finished. I think I will be learning Danish very quickly. I can already understand a lot, but speaking is my weak point. I started going to evening school for 1 hour from 7:30 – 8:30 pm every Monday and Wednesday evening. I already spoke with the teacher and it costs me nothing.

“Last night the Fengers suggested that I should have Ursel come for a visit sometimes on a Saturday so that we can go to the theater in Odense on Sunday. All that after two days! [...] My room is quite bare but, after all, I only sleep in it. I can learn a lot here, I believe. The farmer is extremely efficient and he works from early morning to late in the evening. Most of the time I look like a large cow patty! I can’t wear clean clothes every day. Naturally we change our clothes for the meals. I seem to have had great luck. Here one is treated as a human being and not just considered a working machine. Unlike in Lei, working here is a downright joy. The day comes and goes in a flash."

Who or what Lei was remains a question. It maybe the employer that Erich worked for on the farm in Pommerellen in the region that encompassed the Polish Corridor since 1919. The letters written by Ursula and Erich, which are quoted below in great detail, do not always require comments as they speak for themselves in vividness and realism. But it should be noted that the "near-perspective" of the letters and the "remote view" of the life histories are often quite different in a backward-looking view as is demonstrated here in the juxtaposition of the more recent commemorative narrative and the older letter-stories.

In a letter dated November 15, 1921, which is addressed to "My Dears" in Vluyn, Erich describes again how he fares in Tommerupgaard:

"I'm here now fourteen days and it seems to me as if it were months. I feel like part of the family here. Day by day I like the Fengers better. They are really charming. After work they try to make my time enjoyable and comfortable. If one could only have a little more time for oneself, then it would be great. [...] Sunday night he invited me to a small sleigh ride party so I would have a change of pace. It was a wonderful experience. The snowy landscape in the clear moonlight! On that occasion he asked me if I did not want to stay with him through the next summer to do the tilling and planting of the fields. We both work well together, he said. [...] Mr. Fenger spends a lot of time with me and teaches me a lot. He is an ambitious and capable man and nice guy, as well as his wife. His grandfather was a pastor and a farmer in West Jutland.

“The milking is now getting somewhat better after having severe pain from my tendons in my right arm all of last week. Yesterday I finally managed to milk six cows but my hands look terrible. They are full of cracks, because of the constant change of wet and dry from washing the milk cans, etc., then being coated with dung and earth. I am constantly lathering them with glycerin and fat.

"Yesterday, your dear letter from November 11 arrived, my dear Mother. I was really surprised to learn that you got the idea that the two of us got together because of the Mammons (gods of material wealth or greed). Have I lived for 24 years and you still know me so little? "

Erich's glib question was followed by monetary considerations because of the possible purchase of an estate or other landed property. Erich then made a brief critical comment about his future father-in-law:

"I am sorry for poor Ursel who now constantly has to be with the crotchety old guy. Though currently, it seems to be peaceful. If that man would once and for all finally know what he really wants!"

One day later, on Wednesday evening, November 16, Erich found time to finish the started letter:

"That is as far as I got yesterday. Just now I finished a fine dinner. Here is the menu from this week: meatballs in a celery sauce, chicken with a spicy mushroom sauce, cold pork ribs with red beets and fresh white bread with pear sauce and tea. You see, we do not live badly. Now and then coffee is served in the evening with fresh cookies or sweet rolls. The idiotic practice from Alsen of eaten cake all day long is not known here, thank God! Mr. Fenger said that practice occurs in areas where the soil is good. He comes from land with sandy soil where the people only get by if they work hard. Great financial benefits are not possible there. Here the people are much more helpful to their fellow men and the morality and ethics are much higher. You will find true piety here, which is put into practice. This is what Mr. Fenger is like, a really fine man, who always looks for only the good traits in a person. I can only say again that I am very glad to have come here. Also, I enjoy the animals. They are state-of–the-art standing in their stalls all healthy and brushed clean. Order also reigns here, nothing is wasted. Anyway, there is a really solid spirit here. So much of this life reminds me of our youth at home.

"Ursel is looking for a job for January 1, (1922) and she will try to find one here on Fuenen. Hopefully she will find one as good as mine is and one that is close enough so that we can see each other off and on."

In the letters that Erich wrote from Tommerupgaard – where he stayed for half a year – he described not only his circumstances but he also highlighted the friendly character of the Danes. The letters also show very clearly what is important to Erich, what standards he judges and what matters to him are his apparent principles: true piety, frugality, the renunciation of "Kuchenfresserei" (the gorging on cake), order and hard work.

In one of her letters Ursel described one of the most beautiful islands of Denmark, the island of Mon. In retrospect, she summarizes and comments on it in the conversations that took place in 1979 and 1981:

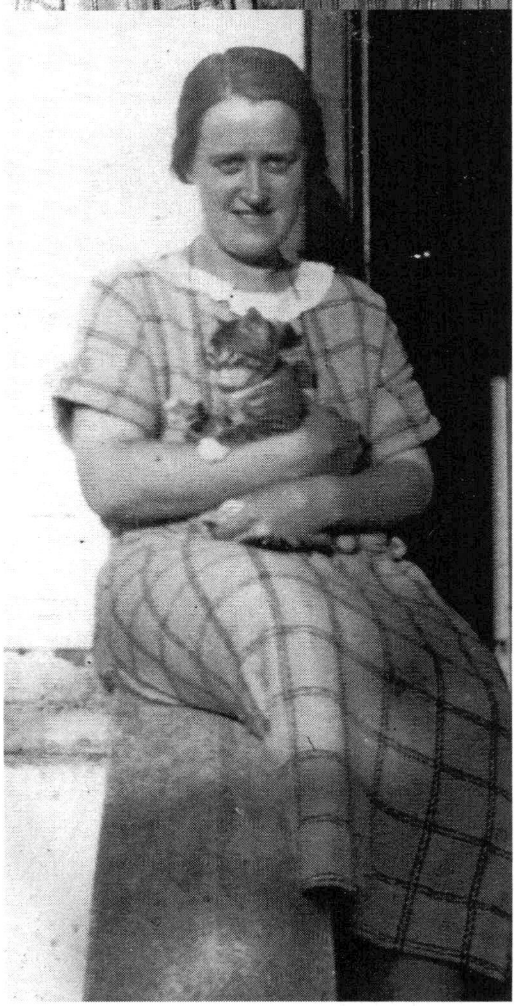

Karen Abrahamsen

"During my time in Denmark I did not only live in Tordengaard. Even before our engagement I worked a few months as a home economics apprentice for a Danish couple on the estate of Lysholm, which was also situated on the island of Alsen. It was not very enjoyable for me there because they did not like the Germans and made me feel it. I also spent several months working in a vicarage in Stege, the largest town on the island of Mon. I corresponded with the pastor's family for many years until the death of the lady of the house. After that I attended the Danish prep school Askov for three months and there met my girlfriend Karen Abrahamsen. We visited each other several times and wrote letters until she died in 1946 from lung cancer. It was a very close and loyal friendship and she was also the godmother of my second daughter, Karen."

From Stege on the island of Mon Ursel wrote another letter on January 23, 1922.

"My dear Mother,

Today I received your dear letter from Erich, and now hasten to answer you immediately so you finally know where I have been since January 15. I am with a pastor Kring here in Stege, the only town on the beautiful island of Mon. Stege has 2,200 inhabitants and the parsonage is located in the suburbs so conditions here are very rural with small animals, etc. I got the position with the help of the local high school principal. Mrs. Kring usually does everything herself with only some help from a young girl. But now she wanted some additional help for two to three months so that the piled up darning and mending could be done. I left home on the 13th and traveled first to the Fengers, where I again spent a few nice days."

Ursel followed with a detailed description of the trip to Mon.

"Pastor Kring picked me up from the station – he is a giant in his forties. In ten minutes we were at home. Frau Kring was not feeling well and was in bed so a beanpole-thin Fraeulein Anderson, the thirty-year old "young girl", received us. The next morning I slept in and was then warmly welcomed by the pastor's wife, a woman from Hadersleben. I had a good impression of everything and hopefully that will remain so.

"The family consists of eight members. First, Pastor Kring is a vivacious, very pleasant, intelligent man. Frau Kring, a former teacher, is also lively, very capable and intelligent and seems to be a good person. Then there are three boys. Stefan - 16 years old, Asger - 15 years, Bent - 13 years. The eldest is already quite grown up, but the other two are still pretty much adolescents. But both of the younger boys - each in his own way – are trying to impress me. Sometimes this is hilarious. Then there is Rachel - 9 years old, Bøgild - 8 years and Dortee - 6 years. These little girls, mostly the latter two, are in my care. Especially little Dortee, a nervous little thing, has won my heart. Rachel is a little too precocious for me. All the children are probably quite clever because they usually achieve the top three places in the school.

"As for the work I have to do, it is quite easy. Although Fraeulein Andersen, an educated teacher's daughter, who was totally overwhelmed, wants to push off a lot of her own work on me, I don't have any rough or strenuous work to do. The day starts at 6:40 am. At 7:00 am, I'm downstairs cleaning the large dining room. Fraeulein Andersen cleans and prepares the stove. At 7:45 am the little girls appear so they can be dressed and have their hair combed. That takes till about 8 – 8:15 am. Then the porridge is eaten and the morning tea is drunk. After that I dust in the parlor and straighten my room. Before that, I clear away and wash the dishes. Then I do some sewing or darning until it is time to set the table for lunch. After lunch I clear the dishes and dry them. I then go upstairs to change my clothes and then set the table for coffee. We drink coffee at 2:00 in the afternoon. After that, Fraeulein Andersen and I wash the coffee cups. Until it is time to set the table for supper at 5:45 pm, I help Frau Kring with the mending or sometimes I take a walk outside to enjoy the fresh air. This is my daily routine.

"I think that this place is good for me because Frau Kring discusses everything with me such as what she is planning to do in the household each day. I have to help her think things through and, as I mentioned before, I have to take care of the little ones when they are home. If an unfamiliar dish is prepared, I help so that I can learn how to cook it. This is also true when something different is being baked, etc. I always thought that managing a household with so many children would be more difficult than it really is. If you just start doing it, everything is only half as bad as it looks. That is what Frau Kring also says and as a teacher she had no great experience in financial matters. Her household is probably not praiseworthy, but just what one might call a well-ordered one. How could a big household like this be so admirable with only one helper and a once a week cleaning woman? However everything is clean and tidy - just very simple from clothing to living habits. The food is good and plentiful.

"I have full and complete connection to the family. Unfortunately this comes at the expense of Fraeulein Andersen who is not particularly liked by Frau Kring, while I am probably favored a little more. So I am now trying to be especially nice to Fraeulein Andersen, a reserved Jütin, (not a Jew!), from Jutland, with whom I get along very well. We quite often go to lectures at the high school in Rødkilde in the evening. Once, Frau Kring gave me a ticket to one of the four winter concerts in Stege. A Finnish singer and a Danish pianist were performing - it was wonderful."

Less than a month later, on February 16, 1922, Ursel wrote a letter to her mother. She had been taking piano and singing lessons and again had effusive praise for Frau Kring, a woman who was almost sacrificing herself to provide for Ursel, the young helper from Germany:

"I really admire Frau Kring that she, a busy housewife and mother, is almost adopting me - a stranger. Any work or meal preparation that I do not know how to do, she shows and explains to me until I can do it myself. I am really learning a lot here, also in other respects. Take Frau Kring's self-control and self-education as an example - not only her efficiency. Often the three of us, Mr. and Mrs. Kring and I, sit at night when everyone else is in bed and philosophize in the dining room. I think it maybe in a different way from how the Fengers do. The Krings rely more on reality which is tangible, and take practical life into consideration. This is probably good for me because I may be a bit too sentimental. The Krings are Grundtvigianer who are liberal, but not too irrational Christians, whose goal is to love life and the world and the people in it. They spiritually strive to help their fellow man. They are optimists and that is good for me.

"I am really dreading the time when I have to leave because there is something special about the people here. They have a very admirable educational talent that you can recognize not only with the children but also I feel it myself. They are teaching me by praising me. When I sometimes say that I'm not as "sød" (sweet) as she said or not quite as capable, then Frau Kring says, "No, no, that's not true, I know this too well." After that, of course, I try twice as hard to be nice, reasonable and efficient, so that she keeps a good opinion of me. And then there is something else. Here I have the feeling of being regarded as an adult. This is not only in relation to pots and pans and clothes but also when they talk about politics or anything else. At home I am expected to do the work of an adult, but as for my opinion about all sorts of things, I am still the child and will probably remain that forever. I almost believed that on Als [Alsen] I turned into a country bumpkin but they talked me out of that here. No, the Krings are not half-Germans, they are solid Danish Stock.

“But that reminds me. Father wrote today that we are all registered as Danish citizens. Now I am curious if Erich will hear something soon. I am very happy that I am now a Dane. Why? I feel at home and well here in the Danish spirit and I feel like I belong here with my views, my ideas and my feelings. I no longer feel like a stranger here like one usually does in a foreign country."

Ursel never became a Dane, but she always retained a special love for Denmark and the Nordic countries for the rest of her life. The Nordic names that she gave her children in the 1930s and early 1940s are an expression of that love. At the same time it has to be added that this also reflects the fact that Erich and Ursel's regard for the Nordic ways coincides with the Nazi thinking.

As Ursel explained above (from the recordings from 1979/81), after her stay in Stege she attended the community college in Askov where she took a summer course. From there she wrote a letter to her mother on June 29, 1922. But she did not go into details about what she was learning in Askov. (Later she mentioned that attending the school at Askov enabled her to master the Danish language also in writing.) In the letter, she answered a question her mother had in her search for a new housekeeper. She wanted more information about a woman named M.R. and Ursel replied in her letter.

"I cannot really judge M.R. because I've actually worked with her only a little. That first winter I worked one month in the nursery and then spent a long time in bed with diphtheria. After that I had to take it easy. Then in the summer I worked a lot outside and in the end I came to Lystolen in the fall."

This short passage is instructive insofar as it refers to circumstances – the time in the nursery and her illness with diphtheria - about which she revealed very little elsewhere. In the letter dated November 4, 1921 there was a place called Lysholm and Ursel later in retrospect recalled a town named Lystolen. It may or not be the same place. Whatever the case, it's all about the places where Ursel had her training and learning. How much it meant to Ursel to thoroughly educate herself and how much she was always seeking advice, is shown in the continuation of the letter.

"I have thought about my education in detail and sent Erich your letter, with some notations. I agree with you regarding the first-aid training, Mother. I believe that a six-week course would be a good idea, even if one only learns how to properly wrap bandages, for example. I realized after my infant-care course that I learned to handle babies very different from the way I did before. And I completely agree with you that the nursing staff is usually exploited and that at this time I do not have the requisite make-up like strong nerves etc. But I recently read that certain hospitals will give free Samaritan courses for certified housekeepers. That may perhaps be the appropriate step after I complete the examination.

“Well, Mother, I would really like to take the housekeeping course and I will try to convince you today by listing all the benefits of taking it, because I don’t like to pursue this without your consent.

“You see, Mother, I have always had the desire to have something solid to depend on, and to take an exam may provide me with a job. Since I am now engaged to a man who wants to be a farmer, it is a given that I choose something that I will be able to use later on. I am well aware that an internship at an estate would be extremely useful, but there would still be plenty of time for that after graduation. It seems quite improbable to think of a marriage before the summer of 1924.

“I have corresponded with the head of the school Beinrode in Leinfeld. I gave her detailed information about my educational background and she replied that I could easily learn to tailor, sew and mend during the long winter hours and that gardening played an important role in Beinrode in the summer semester.

“I believe, Mother, that a stay in such a school would not only fill in the gaps in my education but also teach me and give me insight into the very different conditions of a large German household. It would make it that much easier and better for me to run a medium sized estate. I would also be a bit older by then and maybe more physically suited.

“Something else should be added. Father wrote to me recently that he wished that I learned a profession. He also informed me that Erich had decided to go to the agricultural college Wolfsanger near Kassel. Then it would be suitable that I go to Beinrode near Leinfeld, which is probably not more than 60 km away from there."

Two days later, on July 1, 1922, in a letter written to his mother, Erich also mentions the problem of professional training, both for Ursel and himself. Again from the perspective of a man who already had gained some experience, he advocated that Ursula should make a change and attend the Home-Economics School in Beinrode, which belongs to the Reifensteiner Association. Erich was no longer in Tommerupgaard but was still in Denmark working on a farm called Majbollykke. The owner’s name was Blom. (In an interview in 1981 Ursel said that the “meadow architect” Jørgen Blom and his wife were a very nice childless couple. Erich worked for Mr. Blom as the farm administrator.)

"So, after all these inquiries by Ursel, I believe that the Reifensteiner School would be very practical and advisable. For her to manage a household on her own at this time is not to my liking. At her age she should not have to accept such a position. She would be trying to do too much and I know how she is. In a group of young people, she can enjoy more of her youth instead of being put into a position of responsibility. I also would like to see her there for the very reason that she once again will get to know a wider circle of educated German girls. She has had no chance of that since her mid-teens. That has to be taken into consideration if you want to understand her fully. It would be great if she could start in the fall and I am anxiously waiting for the response from Beinrode.

"I do not know what else she could begin in the spring. Under no circumstances should she live at home. To be a nurse here in Denmark, where the working hours are set and which pays about 40 kroner pocket money, she is unfortunately a little too young at 19 years. In Germany, she would only be exploited. Father Dietrich wrote that she should learn something that would give her a chance to support herself later on. A choice may be either the Home-Economics Teacher's Exam or a course in purchasing or business with a double in bookkeeping. The former requires three years and the second is useless, so both are out of the question. Ursel wrote that perhaps she should take a course in typing and shorthand which would probably be useful to her later if she were to assume a position as a household accountant. I doubt it though. But time will tell. So far everything has worked out to everyone's satisfaction. One should not worry so much about things."

Following, Erich comments on his own situation. His future father-in-law, Ernst August Dietrich, had contacted the renowned agricultural economist Friedrich Aereboe (1865 -1942) and asked him what he would recommend to ensure a qualified agricultural education. Ernst Augustus acted quite arbitrarily. Erich writes, again referring to Ursel first.

"I'm just happy that we will be fairly close to each other near Kassel, the area is very pretty and not so far from you. That should be quite satisfactory to you, right? Father Dietrich has probably told you the "how and why" by now. After such a great recommendation as that of Aereboe, [Wolfsanger] must be the best such institution there is, and I am pretty excited about this coming year.

"Father Dietrich must have greatly finagled things to have Aereboe take an interest in me. Now I just hope that I will do well at the school. After that, having Aereboe on your side will be of great benefit, because he is one of the first, if not the first, leader of German agriculture. On the other hand, the old gentleman seems to think that he now has the right to force me to make "my luck" according to his terms. He simply said to Aereboe that I want to become an "agricultural operations consultant". For him it is already a done deal and everything else is out of the question. He went so far as to tell me that I need to write him a thank-you letter. And since the letter is of immense importance, he would like to see a draught of it first!! (His taste would probably be crawling politeness.) At first I was mad as heck, but I soon had to laugh at myself and felt sorry for the guy who has a view of life, where money and reputation are most important. I will send him an answer soon after I have time to think and reflect. He is probably slightly mentally ill, and I have to keep that in mind.

"In the end he lamented over his wayward daughter. He does not agree with our fall trip to Vluyn, because it would cost him significant money. I am supposed to stay with Blom until the last possible day to be able to read as much as possible. And Ursel must learn to contain her selfishness, to be less demanding of her parents, etc. He owed it to her to ensure that not everyone (!) of her wishes gets fulfilled. –

"I'm just thrilled about Blom. If he had received some academic training, he would have become a great man in his field. – It is fabulous how he handles any situation, he is very practical. To be honest, an agricultural operations consultant career would be excellent on its own; it expands the view and experience like no other and it gives you the first opportunity to choose a suitable property."

This last sentence of Erich's makes it clear that his intent to make himself independent by acquiring an agriculture estate remains a high priority. Of particular interest is the letter because it is the first time that comments are made about the political situation in Germany. On June 24, 1922 the industrialist and Foreign Minister of Germany, Walther Rathenau (b. 1867) was murdered by members of the National-anti-Semitic organization Consul.

Erich commented on this in his letter.

"I was stunned for several days by the terrible murder of Rathenau. How people who consider themselves educated and informed can stoop so low as to become murderers and bandits is a boundless shame. They have greatly harmed our cause."

One must attach great importance to these three sentences. They show that Erich leans toward the "right" in a conservative and a nationalistic sense, as can be concluded from the last sentence, but that he rejects violent actions with the utmost determination.

Erich once again commented on the political situation in Germany in a letter written a short time later, on July 16, 1922, in Majbollykkke, to his mother and future parents-in-law. The relatives were gathered together during a visit:

"My Dears!

If only the conditions in Germany were not so sad. According to the Cologne Gazette the situation looks just terrible. How blind are these people? Everywhere you look, crass selfishness, both the right and the left, and what view of life they have. Usually the saying is that "need brings people together" - but now it is just the opposite. The Reichstag scenes are downright disgusting. But where is there a way out? As long as the Versailles Treaty is not changed, there is no hope. Don't you think that it might be advisable to change everything into kroner, dear Father? - Here we have begun to harvest grass seeds (10 acres of meadow fescue and orchard grass). Of course, it had to rain again today (Sunday)."

The negotiated terms and conditions in the treaty of Versailles at the end of World War I were very harmful to Germany in a broad and devastating way. They gave Hitler a reason to argue again and again that the position of Germany in a geopolitical and geostrategic, "revolutionary" sense was unacceptable and that a change was needed. It is certainly striking and typical of the time, that Erich blames the plight of Germany primarily on the "Schanddiktat (shameful dictates) of Versailles" in 1922. - Suddenly, he changed the subject, which is normal for him as for other letter writers, by going back to the subject of agriculture.

2. Wolfsanger, Beinrode, Bonkow, Schwesternhof

Later in the year 1922 drastic changes happened for Ursula and Erich and also for Ursel's father. Ursel told this story in retrospect collectively in her interviews of 1979 and 1981.

"Before Erich and I were married, we had the intention to buy a farm. My father was willing to give us money, and also Erich's mother wanted to support us financially. At that same time the work on Tordengaard was getting too much for my father. He wanted either to move with my mother back to the villa in Augustenburg or settle into the "old-folks" section of Tordengaard. But it turned out that Erich's mother was unable to keep her promise to help us monetarily with buying a property. That made my father angry; so he also no longer wanted to give us the money he had promised. He was very stubborn in such matters and did not even realize how much pain he was causing me.

"Unfortunately, my father sold the beautiful farm Tordengaard. Erich and I continued to try to buy another farm, such as one located south of the Danish border in Angeln for example. However, all efforts failed because of the lack of money. Finally, Erich decided to attend the Agricultural College in Wolfsanger for a year to get a degree and certification in agriculture. I myself went to Germany to the home-economics school Beinrode, a training institute, which - as already mentioned – was part of the Reifensteiner Association. There, I wanted to get my certification as housekeeper.

"In the meantime, my father bought a small farm called Bonkow in the district of Stolp in Pomerania with little money, perhaps 10,000 Danish kroner. The Danish kroner had a lot of value during this time of high inflation. The estate of about 300 acres of land consisted mainly of deforested woods. The farmlands, like the meadows, were pretty bad and were located 3 or 4 miles from the farm. The great distances were naturally unfavorable because tractors were not yet available and everything had to be done with horses and carts.

"My father tried to bring everything into working order as best he could but because he was already older and not much of a farmer he was totally unable to accomplish this. Suddenly he demanded that Erich leave the agricultural school and come to Bonkow to take over the operation. When Erich refused, my father said, "Then I forbid you to marry Ursula". He was always very direct in his statements and freely declared his will. Erich then gave in and left the school in the spring of 1923. He found Bonkow in sad condition. Neither feed nor straw was available for the cattle. Because of the inflation both could be obtained only with difficulty. That springtime Erich had only his bike available. So he cycled all around the area to purchase the bare necessities. He often got soaked by the rain and soon he caught a cold and eventually became ill with pleurisy and pericardial inflammation. He had to stay in bed in Bonkow where my father treated him. My mother also came from Denmark to take care of him."

Ursel remarked in an interview with Thorlef in 1981 that her father, Ernst August Dietrich, threatened that if Erich's illness caused permanent damage, he would not allow her to marry him even though they were already engaged.

Erich described the circumstances and conditions he found when he first came to Bonkow, a former knight's estate located near the county town of Lauenburg (Pomerania), in a letter to his mother on November 28, 1922.

"So on Friday I arrived in Lauenburg by train at 3:30pm and then walked the eight kilometers with my heavy suitcase. Luckily I found the farm by randomly following paths through the woods in the dark of night. It was already dark by 4:00 in the afternoon. I arrived at Bonkow in the middle of the predecessor's moving mess without finding the new owners here. They will be arriving on Saturday. I was shown where to find a bed, got a mattress and blankets and slept soundly. I had time the next morning to look around by myself. The estate has 282 acres, including 56 acres of forest which unfortunately has been sold to a lumber company. Hopefully we can buy back a portion. The buildings are mostly new with some still under construction. The house itself is perfect with twelve rooms, a kitchen, etc. It is delightfully located and I believe that especially in the summer it must be wonderful here. But there are hardly any livestock (2 cows, 2 heifers, 2 calves), 11 horses that have seen better days and above all, no supplies or feed and sandy soil. One will have to put a lot of money into this operation until the next harvest but with proper management one could make a good living here.

"The predecessor has done a fantastic job here although for many years he was also an administrator for other estates of up to 1,200 acres. Above all manure is needed here and that means buying livestock; but only later when there's feed available. The fact that the predecessor only harvested 3-5 zentners (100 pound) per acre is significant.

"For the above reasons, I said "no" when father asked me if I wanted to start working the farm immediately. I want to first finish my training at Wolfsanger to be able to get my certification and complete my education. Since he did not feel like working the farm by himself we came to the decision to resell it immediately. This could possibly bring a profit of 1 - 2 million (marks?). To hire a manager would be too much of a gamble. Then this morning he told me his latest plan. He now wants to keep Bonkow so that we will have a place to call our own in October and be able to get married soon after that. He believes that it is very questionable that he could still buy another property by the end of the year. And the future of a job for an agricultural government official is too hopeless. But I have to come here on vacation and relieve him of as much work as possible. That's very nice of him and he deserves our thanks. He will have a lot of toiling and hard labor here and hopefully he will not regret it. Of course, I fully agree with his plan. This way I can finish my studies from which I am expecting a lot, get my certification and know what I have accomplished. No one can take that away from me!

"I have to stay here for the next fourteen days to get things going and come up with a business plan. I really enjoy it and if it were not for Wolfsanger, I would start immediately and without hesitation to show people how you can make this farm work and be profitable with good management and the blessing of God Almighty. I can work here in one of the empty buildings along with a representative of the previous owner who we will probably hire. There is also the housekeeper who already works for us. She is an older, clean, modest and frugal woman. The maids, who are dirty and thieving, will not be hired. But we don't need any maids until the furniture arrives here from Augustenburg. There are very beautiful large tile stoves in all the rooms and a large brick oven stands in the kitchen. We also acquired a large topical coal mine. Ursel will come Saturday for a few days and she will be mightily surprised.

"I'll have mountains of work in front of me because father does not want to be bothered with the big purchases that are necessary. I will take care of as much as possible right now, of course, but there will still remain many things that will emerge only over time. I can see already how much the training at Wolfsanger has done for me because of the knowledge I am able to utilize here."

Ursel told about the conflicts that arose with Ernst August Dietrich in the interviews from 1979 and 1981 but her surviving letters do not give any details. Initially, Erich continued to study in Wolfsanger - where he had a friend named Dettmering - and he travelled to Bonkow as often as his time permitted. The letter he writes to his mother from Wolfsanger bears the date of March 16, 1923.

"Ursel was here a few days ago and we discussed the whole situation. I have to go to Bonkow as soon as possible, probably on Thursday. They are messing everything up and the manager is failing completely and is totally incompetent. Right now it is very important to get the seeds into the ground. We can't miss a day. I still have to take some of Kassel's beauty with me so I was just in the picture gallery. Tonight I will see the "Götterdämmerung" with Dettmering and tomorrow I will tour the Wilhelmshöhe and Hercules. And please send 85,000 marks for room-and-board to the Institute, Frankfurt postal account No. 84 023."

The huge amount of money attests to the galloping inflation, a catastrophe to which Ursel retrospectively reported in 1981.

"When we started in Bonkow, inflation came in increasingly worse forms. After the first harvest had been reaped we were able to do all kinds of shopping in town because we had grain to offer. Rye and wheat were indeed stable currencies, whereas the Reichsmark rapidly lost value from one day to the next. The loss in value was so rapid at the end that those who received their wages in the evening - which was perhaps enough to buy two loaves of bread – found that the next morning they would just get *one* loaf of bread for the same money. - The inflation significantly harmed my wealthy father Ernest August Dietrich."

On March 30, 1923, before the harvest, Ursel wrote to her future mother-in-law from Bonkow:

"Of course, we again found a lot of excitement here. My parents have a lot trouble with the people who cut down the forest. They illegal use our roads and fields that are now totally ruined by the heavy wagons. Then they still want to cut down some of the underbrush and clear the stumps, although they have to be off our land by April 1! Yes, it's always something. At least it is good that Erich is now here and can manage the farm. My father is no longer involved. And Erich can manage the farm as he sees fit. It is indeed very difficult for him to bring these acidic fields to a state were a good harvest is possible. But the difficulty of the task excites him and it is also guaranteed that he learns from it.

"The things we have corresponded about recently will now probably become reality. We have debated several times back and forth and then again came to the conclusion that it is best if we get married during the first days of July. The household management is far too much here for Mutteln (my Mother). The combination of household problems and all the stress and excitement in the running of the farm is doing her in and is too much for her. It is better for her and for the whole business that a young person takes over the task.

"It certainly will not be easy for me to be to thrown into such a mess, but it will be instructive, and I believe that I will be able to handle it. It will also be much better for my parents to be out of this dirt and mud and mess when we get married.

"Hopefully I will get my dowry out of the occupied territory; otherwise it would be very bad. But I do believe that you can get personal property out, especially household related items. People who move from western states to the Reich can also take their belongings.

"I'm going back to Beinrode on the 9th."

A day later, on March 31, 1923, Erich also got in touch with his mother with a letter from Bonkow:

"The departure from Wolfsanger was very nice even though it was hard. We had a good time, looking back, full of beautiful memories and camaraderie. Maybe I will take my exams in the fall. I will get directives from the professors. Dettmering accompanied me to Hanover.

"A week ago tomorrow we arrived here a little exhausted in the morning after three almost sleepless nights. Here everybody's nerves are pretty much shot and I don't have to complain about not having enough work. First, it was time to get the lazy manager back into shape. That meant that I had to get him out of bed at 4:30 every morning. Now everything is working quite well with him and he knows he can not fool around with me.

All the people are really trying. But during the current situation I can keep only two of the families who work the fields. The others I may be able to employ for a little while longer. With the former, I have just completed very favorable contracts and they are quite satisfied. Tonight is the final payday and then the new fiscal year starts.

"Two days ago I sowed all the oats (9 ½ acres). The unaccustomed work was hard on my muscles. Right now I am in the process of sowing some of the fields with Seradella, which I have inoculated (grafted) for green fodder. I cannot think about working on the stable buildings this year. That would use up too much capital. I will temporarily rebuild part of the barn with my people. I hope that God may spare us with a drought until at least 1926. Now I have an urgent request that Alfred cash out as much of the money that has been invested for me as soon as possible. I will then change the money into kroner to have a large amount available in case a good opportunity comes my way, for instance a good buy for sheep, cattle or other livestock (as soon as I have fodder for them). "I will probably lease Bonkow, the first year completely free."

In her narrative of September 1981, Ursel clarified Erich's financial situation, which she earlier implied to in a general sense, in more detail. She described the help, actual or potential, that Erich originally expected from his mother and brother Alfred.

"One day we received a letter from Alfred in Bonkow in which he informed us that the inheritance issue, which remained open after the death of his father Gerhard in December 1918, could now be settled. Alfred asked his brother Erich to grant him a general power of attorney to simplify the procedure. Vluyn, where Alfred was living, and Bonkow where we lived, were very far apart, so a power of attorney would facilitate the inheritance issue. Erich gave him the power of attorney. For months nothing happened and then we received an official letter which was unexpected and quite devastating for us. The letter said that we would get only 25,000 marks.

"This amount was a tenth of what Erich's mother originally promised us and also what she talked to my father about. We had expected an inheritance of at least 100,000 marks. Instead, now 25,000 marks. – There was no way that we could even think about purchasing a farm or other property with such small amount. The whole matter was complicated by the major currency uncertainty in 1923. With the introduction of the Rentenmark (a devaluation), one could hope that the money would finally regain stability.

"We finally learned that the inheritance value was based only on the house, outbuildings and gardens in Vluyn. The value was estimated at 100,000 marks which was divided between the four siblings - Martha, Alfred, Erich and Hans - each receiving 25,000 marks. I was surprised that the seed company that Gerhard had left to Alfred had not been calculated into the value. It was a well-established company with a solid customer base, a large turnover of goods so it had to have some value! I spoke to Erich about it and he then wrote his mother. She took Alfred's side by declaring that if Alfred would have had to pay out a higher inheritance he might come into difficulties, possibly losing the company's good credit rating with the banks. However, Alfred intended to support us later, she said.

"I did not like the word "support" at all. It was not about support. We were entitled to the payment of the inheritance even if the payment was made gradually. Erich finally settled for the verdict and I gave up arguing about it because I did not want discord in the family. My father Ernest August, however, was furious when he learned of this turn of events. He had a tantrum and shouted that Erich's mother had lied to him. So now he also would not give us any money to buy a farm. The sum of 25,000 marks was ridiculous. Later we received a message from Vluyn that we would get an additional 7,000 marks. Not until the 1950s did I learn how the 7,000 marks came about, but to explain that here would lead us too far off the track. But it was clear that even with an amount of 32,000 marks we could not be independent!

"The future was very dark in Bonkow and we did not know what to do. We had to see how to get by on the farm. Somehow we were able to make it, even after the introduction of the Rentenmark. Alfred sent us a small amount from Erich's inheritance. I believe it was 2,000 marks. The principal amount we would receive only when we were ready to buy an estate. We were young and inexperienced and had no high expectations, so we were able to live frugally. Most of what was placed on the dinner table was provided by the farm. Clothes were darned and patched but hardly ever purchased new."

The letter that Ursula's father wrote to Erich's mother on May 6, 1923 from Bonkow addressed nothing about the conflicts that were ongoing at that time or perhaps occurred only a short time later. While Ernst August Dietrich sought to be pleasant to his future relatives he also seemed to see himself in the role of "paterfamilias", one who stands above the daily problems and who wants to send an evaluation report of sorts on his future son-in-law.

"Dear Maria!

After having worked together with Erich for six weeks or at least having given him a free hand with the farming, I am compelled to write to you about how things are going. It is working out as I always assumed - everything is going well. Erich has not only remained a very sensible man, he also shows such an intense interest in his job that his professional interest together with his innate common sense and excellent skills that he acquired, guarantee his own future and the future of his subsequent family, no matter what comes his way. You see, my confidence in Erich is stronger than ever. He is also a really good boy but when needed he has the necessary skills to control the farmworkers. He is working well with the people. He is quiet, determined and able to get things done. Of course, the dear boy also has some weaknesses, like all us humans, but they are not such that they affect the overall picture or are even worth mentioning. In short, I congratulate you and us on our dear Erich! You can be proud of him as a mother, and I am as a father-in-law. Erich and Ursula have gotten to know each other so thoroughly over the last several years and nothing thus far has disturbed their harmony. Now that Ursula has attained a thorough knowledge for her job as a rural housewife, there should be nothing more that stands in the way of their marriage. They will certainly have to live through a few lean years. Bonkow has been devastated for 30 years, thoroughly devastated, and therefore the land will not yield anything. But afterwards, how much greater the satisfaction will be when all the work pays off! The children want to marry in July. That will probably work. It is more difficult to say where the wedding should take place. That must still be thoroughly discussed. In light of all circumstances, of course, the wedding will be small and simple, because Erich will need all available extra money for Bonkow."

From the descriptions that Ursula gave in interviews in 1979 and 1981, it is clear when and how the wedding was celebrated in Bonkow - not in July but in August 1923. However, first Ursula spoke briefly about her time in Beinrode. She previously reported that Erich became ill in Bonkow with pleurisy and pericardial inflammation.

"I was able to take the theoretical written test for the certificate at the home economics school in the spring but the practical examination was supposed to take place

Wedding / Bonkow – 08.12.1923
Foreground: Ernst August Dietrich, Ursula and Erich, Gertrud Dietrich
Background: Martha Spickschen, Herta Winblad,
Karen Abrahamsen, Maria Spickschen

in September. My father was anxious that I get to Bonkow and that Erich and I, who was well again in August, should get married and start managing the farm. I was able to take a reduced practical exam earlier and therefore was able to get my certificate as home economics teacher and housekeeper. We were married in Bonkow on August 12, 1923. It was a very modest wedding in the mansion, no church wedding. Only a few guests were invited because we did not know anyone in the area.

"Attending the wedding was Tante Lotte who was the wife of Onkel Hans, the second brother of my mother who had died a while ago. I liked Tante Lotte very much. She is the mother of our Tante Gudrun Brausewetter. My Danish friend Karen Abrahamsen was also there. We went to the small seaside resort Kolberg on the Baltic coast for our honeymoon and it was very nice. Once we were back in Bonkow, my parents soon returned to their house in Augustenburg."

Six weeks after the wedding, on 22 September 1923, Erich wrote from Bonkow.

"Dearest Mother!

This will no longer reach you by tomorrow, Sunday, but working on hay and seradella in this weather will tell you all. The former is now happily in piles. I have decided not to mow the meadows by the river. We finally snuck in the last of the seradella yesterday, even though it was not quite dry. The barn, which will hold ten large wagon loads, is already steaming this morning but I have cattle salt between the layers. Of course, all the seed will be gone from the constant turning and spreading apart. Too bad! But better that way than letting the entire crop turned to manure with all the rain we have had. If only we would get a few dry weeks. Monday I may start with potatoes. With favorable weather they may bring in a nice seed crop. Quite a lot still needs to be harvested. The spring rye, which I have sown between the potatoes, has not suffered at all. The rows are tremendously full.

"One of the six piglets has died, the smallest and the only sow of the litter. The others are healthy. - The cow barn is getting the new roof today. Now you can see just how high this thing is. Then at least there will be enough space and room for everything. If only the craftsmen were gone from the farm. It will be too much for Ursel now that the potato-gatherers are coming and there is no meat in the house. We can't kill the pig and there has been no luck with hunting. I went hunting a few times with the workers but we got nothing. The deer and elk only come out in the night. There are enough does, but no bucks.

"Ursel would like to write to you, but on Saturdays everything comes together. Yesterday and the day before, instead of working on laundry and canning, Ursel and her girls helped with turning the seradella and bringing it into the barn because the farm workers were in the meadow. Today the chores in the house have to be done. Her pantry is her pride and joy. With justifiable pride she showed me the canned jars. Recently we purchased a number of cheap ceramic pots of different sizes and 37 canning jars. It is very gratifying when you gradually get all this stuff together. By the way, regarding the preserves, to my great joy when it was my time to try the canned goods I discovered that everything tasted like you make it; the sour- and sweet pickles, onions, tomatoes, cranberries, etc.

"Here everything is calculated in gold. Who can afford that? We started out in an unfavorable time. The result of high wages and prices is high unemployment and starving people."

Bonkow estate / decorated for the wedding on 08.12.1923

To a crucial event, the birth of their first child, Ursula expressed herself briefly in her later interviews.

"On May 30, 1924, Helga, our eldest, was born on the estate Bonkow. Tante Martha Spickschen, who was still unmarried at the time, was a midwife and she helped me during the birth. In addition, I asked my mother to come and help me in the household. A little later, my mother-in-law also announced her visit. Unfortunately, it soon became apparent that the two mothers did not get along. My mother was a quiet, friendly person but my mother-in-law was not afraid to attack her openly and directly. Mother Spickschen took over running the whole household and my mother had no say in the matter. I remember that my mother took long walks alone in the woods and was always a bit sad. I don't like to think back to those times."

At a later date Ursel expanded on what happened to her at the birth of their first daughter. On the morning of May 30, 1924 she had fed the chickens and then felt her fist labor pains. During the actual birth, not only Martha Spickschen, the midwife was present but also her father, Ernst August. Whenever Ursula had to contend with a particularly painful contraction, she grabbed her father's arm and squeezed him with all her might. Many years later, Ernst August told everyone that at the birth of Helga his daughter squeezed his arm so hard that her fingernails dug into his skin leaving deep impressions. At birth, Helga had a rosy complexion with blond hair and she was very alert.

In the letters there is nothing to find about the birth of their eldest daughter. Seven months later, in a post-Christmas letter Erich wrote on December 28, 1924 to his sister Martha from Bonkow and mentioned Helga.

"The holidays were nice and quiet with us. Karen [Abrahamsen] is such a pleasant and unassuming housemate and guest. She is taking care of little Helga with real enthusiasm. The little sparrow is getting sweeter every day. For Christmas, she stretched her arms out in delight but otherwise she did not make any fuss."

Ursel und Helga / 1924

Ursel summed up their plight in Bonkow and their leasing a new farm in her interview sometime in the year 1980.

"Bonkow was not an estate from which you could make a livelihood. Actually it was a place great for hunting and suitable only for people who had enough money to live without being dependent on the farm. We were looking for a farm that could feed us. An opportunity offered itself through our neighbor, a very nice gentleman named Herr von Massow in

Langeboese. He owned an estate in East Prussia but the tenant was a bad drinker who had neglected the estate and had not paid the rent. Mr. von Massow dismissed the tenant and then offered us the lease. The estate was called Schwesternhof in the district of Labiau. It was 1200 morgen, about 749 acres in size, with very good first and second grade soil. The inventory was available to us but we needed some money for a security deposit for Mr. von Massow. The fundraising was very difficult but after much pleading and arguing, Erich's brother Alfred Spickschen paid him a part of the legacy. I think it was 25,000 marks. In addition, my father gave some money. So we rented this beautiful estate.

"The house in Schwesternhof was primitive, similar to Bonkow. There was no electricity in either farm - we had kerosene – and it also lacked plumbing. But here there were several water wells while in Bonkow there was only one well that had to supply us, the kitchen and the animals. We were used to all of that so we were not upset.

"What we did not know and even Mr. von Massow was unaware of was the fact that the drainage system no longer worked in the fields. The clay pipes which were laid perhaps thirty to forty years before were mostly disintegrated. In the relatively dry years before we came to Schwesternhof no one had noticed anything. Ironically, in the year we got there, it rained constantly. I believe that it was on May 15, 1925 that we were supposed to take over the estate. My parents were then going to move to Bonkow. In the meantime I was expecting our second child and accomplished the move to East Prussia in the last stages of my pregnancy. Karen, called Hase, was born at a clinic in Königsberg on June 13, 1925.

"I want to point out that the second birth was much more difficult than the first. During the move I had physically worked very hard and it adversely affected the baby's position in the uterus. The doctor predicted that it would be a premature birth. But then I had to lie for three weeks in a hospital in Königsberg waiting. The birth was very difficult. I was in labor for a long time and lost a lot of blood and needed a transfusion. Even now, when I think about it, my veins start to cramp up. The newborn was a long, thin, shriveled up little person. When Erich came and saw her he said, "She looks just like a hare." So now she had her nick-name.

"In Schwesternhof everything started out great in the beginning. The crops flourished thanks to the good soil and we were hoping to finally have a care-free life. But it ended up differently as I already explained. When we were ready to start the harvest of winter rapeseed, which was always the first crop to bring in, it started to rain. It rained so horribly, so unendingly that we could not even start to mow. Because rapeseed falls out of its husk very easily, it has to be carefully bound by hand. Even that was hardly possible, let alone using a binding machine. I still remember exactly when Erich, an apprentice, and I ate our lunch sandwich in the morning on the veranda under the tin roof. The weather had just cleared up a little and Erich hoped to be able to start work in the field at noon. While we were still eating, the rain started to drum again on the roof. It was hard to listen to.

Erich threw his napkin on the table and shouted, "For God's sake, we have been looking forward to be able to get some work done this afternoon and now it starts to rain again!" Then the apprentice said dryly, "Mr. So-and-so from the neighboring estate has already committed suicide because he saw that his whole crop was spoiled!" We had to laugh after that.

"With the unending rain we found out how useless the drainage system had become. We had no fields around the farm, only lakes. The sheaves, if we could tie them, swam in the water. It was a complete catastrophe. Mr. von Massow realized that and forgave us the lease so that we were spared the worst. He now wanted to try to sell the property. We were able to stay at the farm for the time being and use the sparse income to pay for operating expenses. And that is what we did. At the same time we looked around for a new estate to rent or buy. Once Schwesternhof was sold, we received the deposit back that we had paid Mr. von Massow."

In a letter that Erich wrote to Alfred on January 6, 1926 from Schwesternhof, he wrote in a little more detail about the Christmas holidays of 1925 and talked about his two young daughters. Please note that the second daughter got her first name "Karen" later on and that she was originally named Evamaria.

"Our two little ones were too cute. Evamaria lay quite raptured in her carriage and soon played enthusiastically with a rattle that the Christ Child gave her. You can hardly get it out of her fingers. Helga quickly got over the impressive sight of the tree lights and soon occupied herself with some other details like blowing out the candles and tearing down the ornaments. The toys made no impression on her. Constantly running around like a weasel, taking everything in her hand and carrying it around - mostly three things at once - is her latest thing. Grandmother is now taking charge of her, thank God, and we can take a little breather. It is a lovely picture of her as she sits in her new little chair across from her sock-darning Omi playing with all sorts of things and often taking dangerous items in her hand like needles and scissors. Off and on she attempts an escape but is soon captured. It is just too funny when suddenly liquid splashes through the slats of the chair in front of Omi's eye. One just stands there helplessly vis-a-vis".

An additional glimpse of life in Schwesternhof can be found from a letter written by Ursel on August 23, 1926 to her mother. She sent a detailed report about a trip to Königsberg, the development of the two daughters and the work involved in home and garden. Because Ursel was sick in bed, the letter was written from dictation by Karen Abrahamsen – who had been staying in Schwesternhof probably for some time -.

"Yesterday we visited the agricultural exhibition in Königsberg that was combined with the Eastern German Fair. We saw a lot of interesting products there but more of that later. Already in the morning I felt pain in my legs and my back, but I thought that it came from standing a long time in the train and walking around in the exhibitions. By the afternoon the pain was almost unbearable and I also got a headache. I began to shiver and was extremely relieved when we finally got home in the evening. My temperature was 38 degrees Celsius (100.4 F) so I took some aspirin to be able to sweat it out. Today I have no fever, just a little back pain. Hopefully I can get up tomorrow.

"But now let me tell you about the fair. There were some wonderful items to see such as the nice hand-woven fabrics that are back. I bought myself fabric for a dress with money that I made from the last three hatchings of my "Nackthals" (bare necked) chickens. The material is a wonderful delicate, hand-woven woolen cloth. The blouse is green, the skirt green with stripes of various shades of yellow and brown. - There were many agricultural machines, chickens, pigs, horses, etc., and whatever else belongs to a fair. In addition, there was also a major scientific and statistical exhibit of the Chamber of Agriculture and the University. A beautiful flower exhibition was particularly notable.

"But now I want to answer the questions you asked in your dear letter. Helga has been completely potty trained for the last few months but just last week she had another relapse. Her panties were wet two to three times a day. Yesterday and today went ok. Evamaria is much better than Helga was last year in this respect. But of course, if she is not put on the potty in time, her panties will be wet because she still does not ask herself. But at least she does not wet her pants every five minutes and she does her business quickly when you put her on the potty. She is not as wild as Helga and probably will learn to speak faster than Helga. She babbles quite cutely but of course it is mostly nonsense. But sometimes one can understand what she means.

"It's a shame that Helga is not a boy. There is nothing better for her than to gallop on Mausi with her father to visit the pigs and cows and romp around. We will probably never be able to make a demure little girl out of her. Evamaria will probably become the little 'housekeeper'.

"Here we are still working on canning the vegetables but the garden is full of weeds since we just have not been able to work on it in recent weeks. We also have quite a bit of fruit in the garden; but unfortunately the village children stole so much this year. They tear down whole branches of the trees and trample down the lettuce and cabbage. Last week I delivered 14 ducks to the women's club and this week I will send another 11. These are the last fattened ducks. I also have a lot of orders already for breeding poultry – (Nackthals roosters, turkeys and Aylesbury ducks). The ducks that I can't sell as breeding stock and no longer need for us I will fatten up and use for Christmas as gifts. The ducks which we determine from the outset to be fattened have to be sold within ten weeks otherwise they start to molt and lose all their fat. If later on you try to fatten them again you lose money because they have eaten so much. I have earned quite a bit of money with my fattened ducks."

The letter proves that, despite the great difficulties and setbacks in Schwesternhof, there were always bright spots. The daughters made visible progress and were a constant source of happiness. Also in poultry breeding Ursel could report successes. In the long run however, the situation in Schwesternhof proved to be untenable.

From the stories that Ursel told in 1981, in addition to her girlfriend Karen Abrahamsen, a woman named Emma Laser came from Bonkow to Schwesternhof. Miss Laser became part of Ursel's household for a number of years. She cared for Helga and Evamaria and she took care of the clothing and linens. Later, Emma met a young farmer while vacationing in Bonkow whom she married and with whom she had four children. She lived on the farm that her husband bought until 1945 when the Russians came. What happened to her then upset Ursula very much when she heard about it. Emma Laser, a good woman, as Ursula says, was brutally raped several times by the Russians. After that happened she took her children and walked into the Leba, a river near Bonkow, and drowned herself and them."

Ursula and Erich with Maria / Schwesternhof 1923

3. Woydiethen. Emigration plans

Looking back at the troubles of a fresh start at a third farm, now in East Prussia, Ursel reported in retrospect from around 1980.

"Our limited funds made it very difficult for us to find a suitable small estate. Finally, we were able to buy Woydiethen, an estate of about 500 Morgen (about 309 acres) on the Samland peninsula. Again it was an operation that was completely neglected and run down because the owner was a drunkard. We bought the farm in November 1926 and wanted to take it over in January. There was very little grain available for the late autumn sowing and distribution to the workers. Each month the workers were given their allotment of grain for baking bread and to feed their pigs and cows. We were not able to find a better operation because of the small amount of money we had. After all, the price of 230 marks per Morgen was favorable. However, because we had only about 30,000 marks for the down payment, the farm was heavily mortgaged and we had to pay very high interest.

"Around that same time something very sad happened. My mother died in the spring of 1927. During our move to Woydiethen my mother took Helga and taught her to speak. Hase was left with a nanny, a farmer's daughter from West Prussia whom we met in Bonkow. When my mother brought Helga back in early March, the little one told me all kinds of things on the way from the train station in Warnicken to the Woydiethen farm. She even recited a cute little poem, "Timpe, Timpe, Timpe Te, Fischlein, Fischlein in dem See, myne Fru, die Ilsebill, will nich so, as ik wol will." At the age of three she had learned all that! - Unfortunately my mother died in April of blood poisoning soon after she left us in March. I was not able to see her alive again.

"A second misfortune came to us with the dilemma of grain and milk prices. As I said earlier, we found very little grain and therefore had to buy more at a price of 12 marks per zentner (hundredweight), I believe. The price per liter for milk was 14 cents. When we harvested the first grain in the fall, the price of grain had fallen to 6 marks and the cost per liter of milk to only 11 or as little as 9 cents. I do not remember it exactly.

"In addition, we purchased some pigs for fattening. The animals had the sniffing disease and grew very poorly. On top of that pork prices fell considerably. Initially the cost per pound of pork was 90 cents and soon afterward only 57 or 54 cents. Under these circumstances, we slaughtered the pigs for ourselves, made sausages, smoked bacon and ham, and sold everything in the Hausfrauenverein (housewives' club). At least that way we had no loss.

"The first years in Woydiethen were very, very difficult - especially since we had to pay such high interest rates. We hired apprentices and I established a poultry farm with ducks, geese and chickens. After all, breeding poultry and selling the eggs and young birds brought in good money. Our female and male apprentices also paid money to learn on our farm but it was still very difficult to make ends meet. We literally dragged ourselves through each day and month."

The bleak picture that Ursel paints here is not excessive according to the writings in the letters from the following years. It can be stated that initially the efforts of Erich and Ursula to start their own business in agriculture during the 1920s garnered almost no success. Especially from the letters it is clear beyond any doubt that these two with their tireless hard work and ambition left no stone unturned and tried every conceivable way in order to gain economic security. But the "external conditions" – including the adversities on the home front and the general economic situation (for example the miserable prices for agricultural products that they had to deal with) – left them no room to expand.

Erich and Ursula / Woydiethen 1929

However, and this is another characteristic feature, the letters don't dwell much on the misery. The following is a brief excerpt from a letter that Ursel wrote to her mother-in-law on May 9, 1929. The Spickschens had been living for two years in Woydiethen. Ursel provided further proof of the untiring zeal with which all their work was undertaken.

"All of us now work in the garden from dawn to dusk. Even I don't mind getting up early this time of year when it is so nice and warm outside and the sun is shining. We get up at 5:00am. Everything is coming to a head. Three-quarters of the garden has been turned over and has been planted but in the flower garden just the beds have been laid out. The lawn and pathways have to be worked on. The vegetable garden alone is almost ⅓ acre."

In the letter that Erich wrote on the same day to his mother, Ursel's optimism is not only confirmed but also his joyous feelings even offer cause for cautious anticipation. Much more crucial is the description of a Stahlhelm event in which Erich took part. The "Steel Helmet, League of the Soldiers of the Front" was a paramilitary armed organization in the German Empire which was founded in December 1918 shortly after the end of World

War I by the Reserve Officer Franz Seldte (1882 - 1947) in Magdeburg. Seldte was Chairman of the Association with Theodore Duesterberg (1875 - 1950). This group was generally regarded as the armed wing of the German National People's Party (DNVP). Erich's letter described to a certain extent a new level of politicization. It revealed a commitment which before probably did not exist - even if the opinion on the assassination of Walther Rathenau (1922) makes it clear that he followed political events for a long time with great attention.

In general in Germany in the late 1920s politics came to the forefront. As a result of critical events, this led among other things to the weakening of the political center which in turn led to a growing polarization of the Communist Party on the one hand and the Nazi Party on the other. Even Erich's mother Maria, who certainly was not just a silent spectator, is likely to have been following the political occurrences with growing interest particularly regarding how they related to her son's position. – Unfortunately her response letters have not been preserved.

On Ascension Day, the 9th of May 1929, Erich wrote to his mother.

"My dear Mother!

Today I'm sitting outside on the lawn in the warming sunshine whose power one hardly dares even to think about. How wonderful to once again feel like a man to whom nature is no longer the enemy but a giving friend. How a little bit of warmth can raise hope and joy in us. But even the practical success is not missing. Since Sunday we have 66 to 68 degrees F in the shade. The grass in the pasture is practically shooting up so that we should be able to drive the cattle out early next week if the weather holds up. Yesterday I drilled the first crop. The workload is now very heavy. I don't know how we can handle all of it. The rutabagas will last only until Saturday even though we have cut back the feeding as much as possible.

"The "Stahlhelmtag" was Saturday and Sunday and we had great weather. I can tell you that really was an experience! On Saturday 22 comrades, including myself, drove to Königsberg at 5:00pm where a big rally was held at a large sports field. About 30-35,000 people were there. The place was mystically illuminated by 37 large torches placed on catafalques. First came the entrance of 400 musicians, then a concert, then everyone participated in calisthenics and finally 150 flag bearers entered. First 100 torch bearers marched in, then the flag bearers and at the very end again 200 more torch bearers who formed a square around the flags. Finally "taps" was played. The enthusiasm was unprecedented. At night we all laid on straw in mass-quarters, 6 km away. On Sunday we were represented with 30 men which was by far the strongest representation of the whole district. More than 6,000 comrades came from Danzig-Pommern, the border districts, Brandenburg and Ruhrgebiet. But over 10,000 from East Prussia. I had a good seat with the flag bearers. Our flag was consecrated by the first "Bundesfuehrer" (president of the Association) Seldte, so we stood the whole time in front of the lectern. The parade, which was also attended by Prince August Wilhelm, took two hours. The march through the city was calm. The enthusiasm of the citizens of Konigsberg was significantly greater than in the previous year, while the Kvzi [socialists?] were not visible thanks to the excellent police protection. Only individual members of the Steel Helmets were accosted. In the afternoon another large concert was held in the exposition hall where both Bundesfuehrers spoke. Approximately 15,000 people were in attendance. You probably were able to read the speeches in your newspaper. They were accepted with thunderous applause, particularly when Franz Seldte said Sahm-Danzig would have to answer to history one day because of his cowardice. [Heinrich Sahm was a politician from Danzig without party affiliation.] And then Duesterberg shouted that it is high time that the weak guys of today need to have their backbones straightened, and that we want to have the military service re-installed. - In the morning I met Berich, my "Vorknecht" (lead farmworker from Schwesternhof) who left there on October 1. There was nothing more going on at the estate and the "Red Front" had the dominant position."

Erich Spickschen was greatly impressed by the Stahlhelm convention which is clear from this letter. He was very impressed by the huge display and effort and the massive number of participants. The swaggering tones that were struck by the speakers led him to use barracks language himself. But all the rhetoric and staging did not help him out of his difficulties, as the next letter reveals. On July 6, 1929 he presented his older brother in Vluyn with an idea that should free him from his misery.

"My dear Alfred!

Thanks very much for your nice letter and the blank check that I immediately filled out for the required amount of 600 marks for the mortgage and interest that are due and sent it straight on. I'm really grateful to you from my heart and only hope that you will not get into trouble because that would really make me feel bad. It was a very big help for me considering the various interest payments, taxes, wages and insurance premiums for fire and hail due and no other income right now than what I receive for milk which brings in only 12 ½ (cents per liter)!

"Now you better sit down first. We are seriously looking at ways to sell the property even though, albeit temporarily, there is little chance for it to happen. This decision is not a sudden idea but it is well thought out. The entire political atmosphere and from that the resulting economic conditions simply force us to do this. Here in Germany one can calculate that in a short time everything will be lost and there is little or no prospect for a speedy recovery. Who could justify that to his family? Even if the sales conditions improve a bit in the future, we would perhaps be able to get along but there will be no guaranteed opportunity for advancement. Today, despite all our work, effort and thrift, the farm has been a constant loss for years and this is ultimately no longer acceptable. I can already hear your angry reply, "nonsense" - "idiotic" - "giving up for no reason," etc., but it is not so. We have informed ourselves about the situation in the whole Reich. Everywhere we find the same picture, though not quite as bad as here in East Prussia. Everywhere you look there is a growing indebtedness except for a few of the best companies.

"It should also be noted that in the long run one does not only invest money but also ones nerves and eventually one's life's energy and that is not even the worst case. Each effort is doomed to unprofitability. How that wears one down in the long run, you can perhaps imagine. For six years we have been independently self-employed, and yet not a penny earned. Please!

"Of course the latter would not matter if there were a prospect of improvement. You will ask why we bought Woydiethen. Well, if we were as smart then as we are today we would not have done it.

"Mother often writes that she hopes that better times will soon come to East Prussia. From that and from her other comments I see that she, and perhaps all of you, are of the opinion that farmers are better off in the empire, especially in the Western states. But that is a crazy view. We have heard that already from various quarters, especially from Mr. Wichmann, who met with men from all corners of the Reich in Munich at the DLG. Of course even here there are some establishments that do very well, but they either have no mortgage to pay or have only a very low debt load and they have been operating for many years or are very conveniently located. But those who had to buy property with a low down payment or whose debt is very high will slip ever further downhill. And this happened to us even though we are located in one of the best areas of East Prussia! It is the same in the West.

"Also, government harassment, fiscal and social burdens and the precarious, constantly deteriorating labor problems are the same throughout the empire. As long as we are slaves of the Entente, and have to annually pay these enormous sums of money, I see no way to improve. And I don't believe that in the foreseeable future our nation will be able to raise itself and shake off these shackles.

"So we need to get out of Metz! But where to? To - Africa. You may think that there the situation is not much better, and that this abrupt change in my situation is nonsense. You will cite as an example brother-in-law Gust's live, but ..."

His sister Martha married Gustav Adolf Seelig on April 10, 1925, in Tanga, German East Africa (now Tanzania). Gustav Seelig obviously ran into financial difficulties there. In the course of the letter Erich referred to many voices which tell of successes overseas.

"Seeligs would like to buy a neighboring farm for us but that makes no sense before we get rid of this sweatshop here. If only they would have given us better information to our questions about East Africa when we contacted them a while ago. We would have sold

Woydiethen with a considerable profit and been there long ago. I still hope to some extent that we can get out without a loss. Of course it cannot happen overnight. Father (Ursula's father) wants to come with us when we move down there. He has a buyer for Bonkow but we advised him not to sell until we get away from here. Where else should he stay?

"Yesterday we hired a young Swede for the summer who wants to learn about the German situation and help with the farm. His brother is in Markehnen (a neighbor estate). A few days ago the 14 year old son of a sharecropper had an accident here. He was helping to take the horses out to pasture when he fell off the horse he was riding and the horse fell on his head. He lost consciousness for only a short time and seemed okay the next day. Of course, looked like hell, but he appeared to be okay. Then day before yesterday in the morning he suddenly began to hallucinate and was dead within a few hours. He was such a nice, kind boy. You don't find them like that too often."

Apart from the letter's introductory and ending paragraphs that concern the reality in Woydiethen, the letter dealt exclusively with the new plan for the future that should lead Erich and his family to a better life. In a letter dated July 19, 1929, addressed to "My dear Vluyner" Ursel addressed the emigration plan issues that were raised by either her mother-in-law or Alfred:

"Now to your questions: 1. To lease in the West (of Germany). We do not expect the situation there to be any different than here. I especially emphasize, that it has nothing to do with the fact that I do not particularly care for West Germany. If you have toiled and worried for six years for absolutely nothing, one is beyond such prejudices. No, agriculture is not a good field at this time in Germany. The burden of high interest rates, social war debts and taxes, which the tenants must pay as well as the owners, is just too high. My friends in Mecklenburg, the Dreitens, say that the tenants there are worse off than the owners, because the former can get only personal credits from the banks which have a higher interest rate. Johanssen from Hannover to whom Erich wrote, confirmed that the entire German agriculture is in bad shape.

"2. Today you cannot find a lease with an iron inventory (machinery). Therefore, we would need all kinds of money in order to buy the machines, more than the deposit for a purchase would be. The entire risk would be ours.

"3. It would be very difficult to find a lease that is a running concern; and one with acceptable terms.

"And finally, the 4th reason: We, especially Erich, are sick and tired of the whole situation here and he is very pessimistic regarding Germany's future. He does not believe that we, Germany, will succeed to get rid of our war debt payments in the foreseeable future. The constant haranguing with the burocrats who are getting more and more aware of their power are making him sick and tired and he is utterly exhausted. And this is no different here than in the West, as one hears and reads everywhere.

“We recently received a letter from a former estate owner here from the Samland, who emigrated two years ago to German Southwest Africa (now Namibia). He wrote the following among other things. ‘When you get here it feels as if all the pressure has been lifted from you. You feel free and happy almost immediately. The old Sou'westers, people who have lived here for years and decades, do not feel this freedom because they don’t know the situation of post-war Germany. But all of us who have come to this place breathe a sigh of relief here.’ These sentences show everything!

“Southwest or East Africa - it is a difficult question that still needs to be carefully considered. The climate issue is not very important. It is absolutely not the way we think here in Germany, that Southwest Africa is healthy and East Africa is unhealthy. For example, there are some districts located in the north of Southwest Africa where you do find dengue fever, even though the majority is fever free."

After further consideration Ursel reached a preliminary conclusion.

"The most promising colony now is supposed to be Portuguese Angola. You hear and read this again and again.

“Where we will end up has to be seen but the question is ‘when’! At this time no one buys any goods except for a greatly reduced price. Everything is so depressed and hopeless. In my humble opinion the only way to sell this place is to divide it into various poultry breeding partitions because land developers don’t pay anything right now. Poultry farms can make a go here because there are very few of them here and the demand is always good. The long winter is offset by higher prices for everything from eggs to chicks to hens. The more sturdy coops that are needed are offset by lower wood prices and low wages. The pastures are ideal for chickens and ducks and also geese. The marshy areas would be great for duck farmers.

“We made an offer to a poultry breeding-and development company, but [?]. We must receive 350.00 RM (Reichsmark) per Morgen if we want to come out ahead and 70,000 RM minimum down payment. But that would include the full harvest. Would you also help by putting out feelers? The whole West is crawling with poultry farmers. Poultry farming is now really the only business that pays for itself and will pay off even in the foreseeable future.

“Perhaps one could still find a fool who would buy this sweat-shop, but certainly not an East Prussian. They emigrate or move to the city if they have the cash."

The letters about the intention of emigrating to Africa provide the proof of how serious Erich and Ursula were with their plans. The East Prussian estate Woydiethen, on which the two have toiled, is now only disparagingly referred to as a "sweat-shop". - However, in hindsight in later years, the unpopular spot that they desired to leave was transfigured into a small paradise. While forging these complicated plans, Erich and

Ursula always kept in view the realities of the situation. Only if Woydiethen could be sold at a fairly reasonable price would the project be put into action.

These letters also show that in addition to a main topic - the desire to emigrate – there are always "side issues" which in turn would temporarily become major subjects. In a letter written on July 29, 1929 in Woydiethen to her mother-in-law, Ursel vividly and engagingly describes a spontaneous trip they made, that cannot be dispensed with.

"I hope that you don't think that we were too frivolous by taking the trip to Visby, (capital of the island of Gotland). We already feel terribly wasteful. We don't even dare to write my father about it. But it happened like this. We read the brochure and Gotland (island in the Baltic Sea) has always been our dream since we read about it earlier in the Swedish Baedeker (Baedeker is the official European Tourist Information Guide) and in Selma Lagerlöf's story, which we read together with you in Schwesternhof. And 30.00 RM per person is also very cheap. Then there suddenly arrived the 60 RM from you. The beautiful coat, for which it was meant, is already paid for and we actually had expected only 30 RM from you. Then suddenly the 60 RM arrived - just the exact amount of money we needed for the trip. That seemed like a sign from heaven so we went on the cruise tour. It did Erich a world of good to just let go of everything for 48 hours and see something totally different. It was enchantingly beautiful. The ride on the ship "Prussia" was interesting but the first night not so great. There the seas were very rough and the ship had only a shallow draft in order to be able to stop in the small ports. But it was top heavy with three decks so it swayed back and forth. Of course 90 percent of all passengers were seasick. Everywhere you went people were throwing up. We did not, thank God, but were close to it because of the gagging sounds around everywhere. It rocked so much that the entire top deck was awash. But afterward we slept wonderfully on our deck chairs.

"When we awoke at 3:30 in the morning, we first went to the communal bathroom. We had already arrived at the 150 km-long island and Visby is half way up the coast. We sailed between two small islands, the large and the small Karl's islands that were quite bare and formed from craggy limestone and sandstone. On the great Karl's Island there is a lighthouse and also a cottage for the Gotland's hunting club. The cottage is used by hunters because there are lots of rabbits on the island. Little Karl's Island is uninhabited. Countless birds live there and semi-wild sheep that belong to some Gotland farmers. They run around free all year and sleep in huts in the winter.

"At 8:00 am we arrived in Visby. We took a short tour of this interesting city. There is an almost completely preserved town wall with 10 or 20 watch-towers and church ruins in wonderful architecture whose inside walls are now covered with ivy. Many great fine old houses were there and many, many roses. The brochure said that it is "a rat castle in ruins". Visby was an old Hanseatic city founded by merchants from Lübeck in the 12th century. After that the Hanseatic League, the Danes, the Swedes and the Russians have constantly fought over it. Today it is a small village. We went to the museum. There was beautiful old furniture, jewelry, coins from Arabia which were found there, ancient altars that were artistically carved and painted. We also visited an old patrician house which was furnished exactly as it was 300 years ago. It is completely overgrown with ivy outside. The garden is managed by a hotel and we ate there.

“After visiting the city we all drove in a rental car through the country called "the fruitful Gotland”. The fields are generally much worse than here even though the climate is much better! Last winter the lowest temperature was - 25 ° C (-12 degrees F) but no fruit or walnut trees froze. It is the sea air! The houses and stables were freshly painted and many of the small farmers had cars parked in their open barns. Everywhere the roads were paved. You can really see now how hard we have to struggle - mostly for the enemy governments and the socialists. What good is our better harvest? Nothing! We cannot afford to make even emergency repairs to our buildings. We can’t even think about such luxury as we saw there. Two estate owners from the Samland, who were in the car with us, were actually saying out loud what we were only thinking when we saw it. In Sweden the standard of living is worse than before the war but they are still far better off than we are and it shows. By and large there are only farmers on Gotland with 50 to 300 Morgen [1 Metric Morgen = 0.61776 Acre] of land each and some forest. However there are bad pine and fir forests on the stony heather soil, which runs in strips through the island."

The love for northern European countries is expressed by the fact that the Spickschens always acquired their temporary help for Woydiethen by getting Swedish eleve (agricultural students). Erich added to the letter from Ursel. He comes back to talk about his intentions for the future.

"We have not yet found a serious buyer. It just does not happened from one day to the next. Everyone who orders poultry for breeding also comes and buys it. All the other inventory stays here to help elevate the price. The fields are in good shape on average except for a small lot of barley and one of rye. The fact that our Swedish eleve had to leave so soon was sad for him and for us. He was a fine man, quiet, humble, hardworking, a world of difference from our bully Kress. The other one, Sudan, is also quite nice. The hay harvest went great except for the first lot and it is now all in the barn.

“No, we are only interested in Africa. We have letters from East Africa, Kenya, Angola and Southwest. Everywhere the people are satisfied. They all write of good prospects for the future and strongly recommend that we immigrate. So there is no longer any doubt, only the question of “which country” remains. If only we could sell."

The hope of being able to emigrate remained the dominant topic also in the coming months. In between, the subject always goes back to the farm, as shown by a letter from Ursel dated September 6, 1929 to her mother-in-law.

"It has been raining without interruption since Monday but it came after all the nice weather we had that lasted for weeks during which we were able to harvest all the rye and barley. Some of the fodder is also harvested but the bulk is still out there. Hopefully it will soon dry out again. The mood among the farmers here is getting gloomier."

Exactly one month later, on October 9, 1929, Ursel wrote to her mother-in-law from Woydiethen.

"Today we had a very gloomy message. The East Prussia Financial Help we sought has finally been rejected "because it was Wiemann (the previous owner) who suffered the loss and not we." They did not take into account the fact that we paid him in full for that loss. Now all we have is the expense of 500.00 RM and Erich has wasted so much time and effort that was all in vain. It seems that nothing we do is meant to succeed. Now we have to figure out how we can meet our obligations. It will be difficult. I guess that we will have to sell more cows. It would be useless to ask Father for some help because he has stated very explicitly that he would give us no more money because it would all be lost anyway. He has no ill will towards us since he is usually very sweet and nice to us. But he is in constant fear of losing everything again and then he would not be able to leave us anything in his will. He just cannot differentiate any more between when it would and would not be prudent, in pecuniary terms, to contribute to help us. He believes that he has to "hold on" to everything. It would have made much more sense and been more practical if he would have co-signed for our debts so that we would not have to pay such high interest rates. But he just couldn't see it. It must have something to do with his age because he cannot be convinced. To keep pestering him is entirely useless and makes no sense and in the end he will just turn against us. He was always strange when it came to money matters and it is getting even worse now as he is getting older. No one can do anything about that. For me personally, it's all twice as bad and is very depressing but I can't change it nor is it my fault. But it is unspeakably sad.

"My nerves are pretty shot right now. Last night I had a nasty gall bladder attack, the first one for a long time. This is nothing more than nerves and I am quite convinced of that. One is simply not up to the constant daily problems. Every little thing is turning into an un-climbable mountain. If only the Lord God would arrange that we could sell this place. So far, there has not even been a buyer to look at the farm. I am at least glad that everything is in working order in the house.

"If only we were at the point when we would be boarding the ship in Hamburg! Hopefully we won't have to sit around here until all our energy and courage is gone. It's a miserable time in which we were born! But at least we have one hope now - Africa!"

The "East Prussia Help" was an aid package from the government with which Erich and Ursel were trying to obtain relief to counteract and mitigate the agrarian crisis since agriculture was regarded as the "problem child of the times" of the Weimar Republic. The East Prussia Help was founded on May 18, 1929 and composed of the so-called "Hindenburg program" and the "Law on economic aid to East Prussia". The man called Wiemann, who is mentioned in the letter, was the previous owner of Woydiethen. The Spickschens got the short end of the stick in the disputes with him.

Especially important is Ursel's depressed state of mind. She wrote, "It is as if nothing is meant to succeed". In addition, Ursel's father created ever new difficulties. He possessed the money to help, but nothing could convince him to abandon his rigid principles and his fear of getting old and having no money left. When Ursel wrote that she was "quite down with her nerves," one can hear it in the tone of her letter. In contrast to the callousness of her father, she shows remarkable understanding and flexibility.

One month later on November 11, 1929, in a letter to his mother, Erich was fully consumed with the idea of selling Woydiethen as soon as possible and emigrating to Africa.

"With longing we await the day when we can leave here. Several real-estate agents have already called a number of times, but no one actually comes here to look at the place, although I have already calculated the selling price at a significant loss. On top of that, the fields and the buildings are in perfect order now. We have a lot of turnips for fodder (all stowed away in piles), most of the fields are plowed and everything is ready for the winter - but still no buyer. I believe that people just do not want to buy. Whatever other farms they have seen and visited are devastated. Tomorrow I will go back again to the agents. The sad thing is that the prices are falling more and more for agricultural products. Yesterday one farmer got only 7.20 RM for a 100 weight of rye. Of course at those prices, no one has the courage to buy a farm. But I have to sell! The longer we remain here, the more of the value is lost. Therefore it is better to get away with some loss. Then, in East Africa, we will be able to gradually pull ourselves up again. The day before yesterday I received a letter from the Africans (Martha and Gustav Adolf Seelig) who warned us again to hurry. But I cannot leave Ursel here alone until Woydiethen is sold. Here, even the two of us together are getting gray hair. With joy I'll shake the dust of Germany from my feet, even though much love will be left behind. Certainly one will feel uprooted, but if the roots are permanently in water it is impossible to grow, and that is most important thing that has to be guaranteed."

As much as he contributed to the difficult life that his daughter and son-in-law had to go through, Ursel's father was in his right mind and not senile, as is shown by the following letter. Medical Examiner Dr. Ernst August Dietrich wrote on December 29, 1929 from Bonkow to Erich's mother. Dr. Dietrich's letter is hard to read because it is written in a very accurate Sütterlin font. [Sütterlin is the name of the calligraphy used in Germany through the first part of the twentieth century. It is often seen by readers of older German manuscripts.]

"Dear Maria!

They have it pretty hard in Woydiethen. But it makes no sense to help them out of their difficult situation. Meanwhile the government, to which inexplicably even the People's Party belongs, seems to have a plan to destroy the local economy in favor of international high finance. The latest tariff increase does not give even the slightest compensation, especially since the modest improvements offered by the "Green Front" have been blindly accepted by the powers that be. One can see how catastrophic the prices of grain are. When I look at my old books from the years 1888-96 in Rüdersdorf when I was a general practitioner, I paid an average of 8.00 Marks per hundredweight of oats. And now I am offered a mere 7.00 Marks for my impeccable oats. At that time everything else cost half as much as now, and health insurance and disability insurance did not even exist. If you look at the proper ratio, oats should cost 15-18 marks today. Under these circumstances, it is right for the children to sell, albeit at a loss. They are young and have a chance to show what they can accomplish in East Africa. I hear that Martha is planning to come back to Europe soon for a visit. Please be so kind as to let her know that I certainly expect to welcome her here for a few days in Bonkow.

"So Bonkow is not as bad as one thought. But if the kids can get away from Woydiethen, I do want to sell and go along to East Africa with them. Otherwise I would be too lonely here. It is bad enough for me here now. (E. A. Dietrich's wife died on April 28, 1927 in Bonkow.)

"But I have another interest since a few days ago which somewhat fills my days. I am now a National Socialist with all my heart and soul and see with delight that this party, which alone can save Germany from the mess that it is in, is growing in this area from week to week. If the rest of Germany could see the benefits, the Reds,(communists), and their followers would be overthrown in no time. For example, a former social democratic teacher is now going from farm to farm with the latest Nazi brochures. Recently in a village near Lauenburg, a party group was formed which now has more than 180 members. Hopefully, "Masten[?]",who previously has failed the people, will not leave us in a lurch."

This letter is revealing, especially the last paragraph. Considering in addition to this the "history" as it can be deduced from the first paragraph and from all the previous "emigration" letters, it is not very surprising when people like Erich, Ursula and Ernst August sought their rescue in the National Socialists Party with more and more determination. As these last three chapters have shown with numerous authentic letter testimonies, their misery deserves special attention because it illustrates in a very concrete way, what caused the decision to join the Nazis party. The plan to emigrate to Africa can be interpreted as an attempt to escape, as a desperate attempt to evade the obvious path to a disaster for the German States. None of the letter writers, neither Erich nor Ursel or Ernst August, can be viewed as people who blindly followed or were influenced by propaganda or even tended to talk big words or trusted people with big words. The letters seem rather more persuasive because they are guided by reason almost continuously, in a positive sense. They are down to earth and simple, without false pretensions or exaggerated expectations. They illustrate - and this is scary at the same time - how serious and good people who are caught up in ever increasing difficulties, were basically forced with a certain inevitability to become members of the Nazi Party.

4. The Years 1930 and 1931

Even in the letters that were written in 1930, the hope to start a new life in Africa is still not buried. Next, in a letter that Erich wrote to his mother on March 3, 1930 from Woydiethen, he talks about symptoms of growing distress, including a growing willingness to resist in East Prussia.

Woydiethen Farm

"Yesterday we received an emergency notice here, or rather an emergency church service for the rural population in St. Lawrence where Priest Willigmann from the

Königsberg Cathedral preached a brilliant sermon. The church was full to bursting. We had to stand like many others. Beside the altar stood the black farmers' flag, which was also consecrated. Next Sunday emergency church service is in Thierenberg."

Fourteen days later on March 17, 1930, Erich, in his letter to his mother, again referred to demonstrations of the rural population. In addition, he talked about political policies that do not bode well.

"Here everywhere are now large emergency notices and emergency church services. The rural population walks behind the black farmers' flag into the church. Because of the treaty with Poland, which Hindenburg will probably sign, East Prussia is completely betrayed and screwed. During the last few days we can no longer sell our pork and rye. In Konigsberg there are around 200 railroad cars full of rye that is unsalable because of the accumulated storage fees! The latest price was 6.30 RM, as were all other grains. Our government should be fired! The treaty with Poland reads that the 200,000 (and now 350,000) pigs that are available there cannot be imported by East Prussia. This is the same rule that forbids some foreign wines to be shipped into the Rhineland, in order not to endanger the German wine industry. When will the Lord God relent and do away with the ignorant politicians. It seems as if Berlin is giving up on East Prussia. We are moving toward serious times but at least our health is still intact. The good Lord will take care of it all, even if the political sky is getting blacker by the minute."

On March 12, 1930 the Reichstag, and on the following day the Imperial Parliament, adopted "An Act relating to regulate the agreements of Part X of the Treaty of Versailles". The most important part of this edict was the so-called "Polish-German Liquidation Agreement" of October 31, 1929. Reich President Paul von Hindenburg signed the bill on March 18, 1930 and at the same time he sent a letter to the German Chancellor in which he emphatically ordered him, "to help our East Prussians and all our other brothers in Eastern Germany in their trouble, which is at its height, and to preserve their land which is their life line!" It cannot be ignored that when Erich was fighting for survival in Woydiethen, countless other farmers were in the same situation and many were even worse off. Looking back in 1981, Ursel said that in 1930 around 85 percent of all farmers in East Prussia were doing badly. Only those who owned land that had been profitably farmed for generations and only had debt that they deliberately kept for tax purposes, did not need to fear falling into bankruptcy.

The letters continue to describe on one hand the direct juxtaposition of reactions to the overall political situation and on the other hand observations of the situation at the home front. Ursel wrote on March 18, 1930 to her mother-in-law.

"Yes, I also want to learn how to cut out patterns, and I thought that I should sew some dresses at Karen's [Abrahamsen] since she is perfect in sewing and tailoring. She was always the councilor for tailoring in Askov for everyone. I have some knowledge of sewing because of the course I took in Beinrode, but I lack practice. If working with Karen doesn't work out, I'll do it in Königsberg and live with Mrs. von Nathusius who lives not far from the railroad station. She already invited me to stay with her."

Ursel's reaffirmation of their strong intention to sell Woydiethen and move to Africa need not to be quoted again because Erich mentioned it in the letter he wrote to his sister Martha on March 27, 1930. However, it seems that doubts were growing in him whether Africa could actually be the salvation for him and his family.

"Before we finally say goodbye, I have to ask for your opinion of something. I've thought time and again about the Africa predicament in light of the uncertainty of whether and for how much we will be able to sell here. If I more or less break even and am left with only a little of my own money and if Alfred wants to get his money back, will it still make sense to travel to East Africa? I don't want to be separated from my family for more than a quarter to half a year. If the four of us have to live on my salary, we would not be making much progress. With the money needed for travel and associated expenses one could buy a small business here near town to sell eggs and milk and live modestly.

"Now looking at the other side, should we make a small profit and given the fact that under those circumstances Father would not want to contribute anything toward a purchase in Africa, would Kauffmann's plantation still be available? How much would it cost and how big is it? Have they already planted kapok and how much? Kapok seems to be the most promising crop based on market reports. I assume that a sale here is hardly possible before July. We are expecting to have considerable economic upheavals here in May which are supposed to improve the situation and no one will commit to buy before that happens. I recently offered this place to the East Prussian homestead, which declined because they only take hopeless enterprises. My debt was too low!

"Please, don't misinterpret this letter again and assume that I think that I am too good to take a job as a civil servant but that is not really me. According to your letter, it would pay about 500.00RM. That is hardly enough money to put some aside for the trips to Europe that one has to take every 4-5 years. And we also have to think about the expenses needed for the education of the children. One would probably find employment faster in the unhealthy areas where Sisal is grown. Or do you think you can actual save some of the money?"

On the same day, March 27, 1930, Erich also wrote to his mother from Woydiethen.

"Now, Martha's days here are numbered. How quickly these four months have gone by. It is great that she has accomplished so much here. Those two deserve it after all the drudgery they had to go through. Here, the prospect of a sale has not improved. You really do learn patience! But we are thankful that we can still muddle through and we can continue as long as no great misfortune happens. I was able to pay the past due taxes by selling a truckload of stones for 500.00RM. In addition, I delivered stones to Pressmar (owner of the nearby dairy) for 600.00RM to build a new pig sty so that the interest I owe to Wiemann are covered for April. To cover some of the minor debts I will deliver another 50 cubic meters of gravel. Thank God last week I discovered a valuable gravel pit in the marshy portion of our land. I hope to be able to deliver gravel to the highway department to cover the taxes owed to the Department of Interior but for now the county has no money. Well, until now the good Lord has been supplying us with patches which allow us to plug the holes.

"Hans writes confidently about operations for great assistance to East Prussia. I don't believe it. At most they would fizzle out like the last one. What we need is profitability. We will have to help ourselves. Probably in May the bankruptcy of the entire East Prussian economy is to be announced (but don't talk about this in public). Then the government has to act because they cannot take over all local operations! Otherwise, everything will slowly be going down the drain. After that, people will probably start buying again, at least for a short time.

"So we continue to hope for better things and enter springtime with hopefulness. By the way, two Swedes will come here on April 1st. Hopefully they are worth more than the son of an estate owner who I have now. To you and all the dear Vluyners, warm greetings and kisses, your Erich."

Once more it is clear from this letter that Erich, even though he is serious with his emigration intentions, is always at the same time a sober and forward-looking farmer who explores and exhausts all possibilities in order to make ends meet. Once again the talk is about Wiemann as the letter from Ursel dated October 9, 1929 indicates but now the amount of money that has to be paid to him is no longer perceived as a heavy burden. There are constant ups and downs with hopes and fears, but still the very precarious situation is unchanged.

The gravel pit that Erich discovered on his estate offered him the opportunity to earn some extra money. Every penny was badly needed. In an interview from 1981 Ursel said that the stones that were sold were dug out from a boundary ridge. There was some trouble with the neighbor who did not agree to the dismantling of half the ridge but it was clarified in a legal process that found that the border was exactly on the crown of the ridge and that Erich Spickschen was entitled to do with and dispose of the "half" which belonged to him. Ursel explained that the ridge was about two feet wide and contained stones that were partly used for road construction and partly as foundation for houses.

She added, "If we were unable to sell the stones back in 1930, we would have been bankrupt. We constantly trembled and worried whether we could hold on to the farm."

Ursel also explained in 1981 that the Woydiethen property consisted of the nearly 500 Morgen (309 acres) of land of which about 250 (155 acres) were used as arable land

and approximately 200 Morgen (124 acres) of meadows for grazing. There were also 40 Morgen (25 acres) of forest, a few Morgen of bog (or marsh) and then the courtyard and garden area. The main crops were barley and clover and also on a larger scale rutabagas and fodder beets. It was not worth it to plant wheat. In later times, in a field behind the garden, kale, cabbage, celery and other vegetables were planted.

An additional more detailed and precise description of Woydiethen, that was located in the county of Fischhausen in the Samland, was described by Ingolf Spickschen (with his mother) and the writing was published in 1974. Because the property (the exact official name was "farm Woydiethen II", total 121. 88 hectare) is still an important place of identity and memory to most of Erich and Ursula's children as well as Ingolf himself and all his younger siblings who were born, grew up and lived there until they had to escape at the end of January 1945. It is a good idea to list some of the finer details about Woydiethen from that writing.

"The local and more distant roadways were good. A 200 m paved road went to the dairy and it was 5.5 km to the train station at Thierenberg and 35 km to Königsberg. 75 hectares were located in a plat around the farm proper with the rest in three plats up to 2 km distance from the farm. The land was divided into 70 hectares of arable tracts, 28.5 hectares of pasture that was subdivided into 15 paddocks, .6 hectares of meadows, 1.5 hectares of garden and 12.5 hectares of forest. The remainder consisted of water, peat, gravel pit, the farm yard etc. The soil consisted of 70% sandy clay with a good base and the rest was loamy sand. The crops consisted of 50% grains, 30% of root crops and 20% clover and grass seeds. The grain yields were 6000 lbs. / hectare and 56,000 lbs. / hectare for potatoes."

The year 1930 produced more testimonies. The juxtaposition of statements about the situation in Woydiethen and then the political situation is particularly evident in a letter from Erich dated April 30, 1930.

"Dearest Mother!

It is lousy cold here again since yesterday after a long period of temperatures in the 70s which made the pastures grow enough so that we had the horses out overnight since Saturday. Now I'll probably have to bring them back in again. I wanted to take the cattle out on Friday but nothing will grow when it is this cold. Last night we had 1* C (34* F). Oats and barley are starting to grow and the vetch is already up. But now everything will stop. Rye is already 30 cm high in some sections. Usually it is mid-May before it is high enough for a crow to hide in.

"Father (in-law) writes quite happily. He is working hard for his Nazis with enthusiasm for the cause. We are very happy, because now he has an interesting job that leaves him no time to indulge in stupid and gloomy thoughts. By the way, many of the landowners in Pomerania have gone over to the Nazis after Hitler published his agricultural program. I am personally opposed to this whole party business and still hope that we eventually get a national committee, which will partly be based on National Socialism. We need the laborer! He has a right to see the legitimate aims for his life fulfilled and he must enjoy the respect of the other classes. But he has to work to improve himself by taking a professional approach so that he deserves that respect. Marxism and Bolshevism will try to eventually reduce him to a work animal. In the Stahlhelm organization we work in the above described way. My O.G. (local group) continues to grow. Now we are 60 and most of them are laborers. This is very encouraging."

Helga and Karen / 1935

Since on one side Erich's letters tell of National Socialism's outreach as an encroachment, maybe even something that appears compelling, clearly on the other hand the letter shows that even for a right-wing, clearly anti-Communist aligned representative of the rural middle class, the voters' options remained intact (albeit only in a narrow frame). In the spring of 1930 Erich had not yet become a supporter of the Nazis. The "whole party business" displeased him and he saw his father-in-law work for "his" Nazis. On the other hand, his membership in the local group of the Stahlhelm shows that he was not only thinking about politics but that he actively participated to further its interests.

All the letters quoted thus far are in a chronological order. This allows for continuity in developments and at the same time it also permits for some variegated views, a back and forth in the change of topics. Clearly the difference of the perspectives of Ursel and Erich are shown again and again both in content and style.

Ursel wrote a letter to her mother-in-law on April 30, 1930.

"Helga does not like school at all. But so far she does her homework very carefully. They only draw on their tablet until it is full, nothing more.

“The bankruptcy case will probably not go through because the Reichstag is deciding on an ‘Aid to Eastern Germany’. Hopefully they will really do something."

The "Aid to Eastern Germany" was initiated as the "emergency decree to cover the financial, economic and social emergencies” on July 26, 1930 by the government. Whether this help caused an easing of the problems for the Spickschens in Woydiethen, cannot be found in any of the subsequent letters. In the next letter from Erich dated June 3, 1930, the experiences with the children are important. In addition, he recapped and renewed his political considerations.

"My dear Mother!

The father of Frau v. Nathusius died on Wednesday. He was as old as Father. The poor man was bedridden for almost nine months and must have suffered a lot in the end. How good our dear father’s passing went. He did not have to experience all the misery since no one was aware of the seriousness of our misfortunes at that time and no one knew what was yet to come. How beautiful was our father’s life. At 16 years old, as an almost grown man, he experienced the ‘happy war’ of the 1870's, the founding of the Reich, Germany's frenzied rise and its peak. Then the Great War came, one of the most heroic achievements of a people since time immemorial and he did not lose a son. And then, when fate turns into tragedy, death takes him away gently and painlessly. A lucky man whose life was showered with success. Misfortune and sorrow stayed away and good fortune blossomed for all his loved ones. Truly, the dear Lord God took good care of Father and he deserved it. He really was as good and noble as rarely another person.

“Helga's birthday was very nice. She invited several children and Mr. Smith was here with his three boys. His wife is in Carlsbad due to a gall bladder problem. The games you sent are very nice and caused great joy. We are saving the “connect” game for Evamaria. Sunday we went to the beach for the first time with all the young men. We spent two hours in the sun and it was glorious. The children enthusiastically played with a celluloid duck that the Swedes gave Helga for her birthday. It was repeatedly thrown into the water and floated back to the beach on its own.

“I am now reading Hitler's "Mein Kampf" with great interest. I must say that the man really is a genius. Deep and serious thoughts logically developed. I am one-third through and can only say that I agree with most of it. And if you want to be honest with yourself, you have to take part in this fight, so that our great nation will not die. And that will happen quickly if the demoralization continues on as before. It does not matter that his thoughts are noble but that they are true. In order to understand him completely you must be studying the book from the beginning. Then one sees that this has nothing to do with National-Bolshevism. You may think that the effect in practice is bad because the Nazis are fighting with everyone. Well, should they just let themselves be massacred by the red hordes? One thing is sure, they are never the aggressors. They get into fights more frequently than the Stahlhelmer but they're also a lot more active in public. I am writing this as a Stahlhelmer who often and recently has been attacked by the Nazis. But that does not matter; that is shaking us awake. I still hope that the "Stahlhelmer" and "National Socialism" will soon start to work together again. Then we will achieve something. The objection that France will not allow this development is not valid. We will immediately have Italy on our side and the English have no interest in further strengthening the French. But enough of politics."

This three sectioned letter shows three different perspectives that are of fundamental importance to Erich's self-knowledge. In his reminiscence about his father one may see a noticeable rise of an exaggerated tendency to pathos, a trend that has something formal to it and reminds us of dinner speeches or public appearances. The middle part of the letter deals with observations about the family and household members. These remarks appear relaxed in comparison to the first paragraph. In the final paragraph Erich makes committed statements about politics. Only in some testimonial letters from the years 1925-1945 will you find such an open confession to the "genius" of Hitler. Historically these are typical ideas that must be understood in order to understand the causes and the pre-history of the Nazi era. It should be noted that Erich's assertion that it is an undisputed fact that in fighting, the Nazis were "never the aggressor" is historically not sustainable. This shows a clear bias by him. This bias is also visible when he speaks of the "red hordes". His mother seemed to be critical about the "practice" of fighting because of political differences.

In the same letter Ursel turned to a fourth priority which dominates the content of the letters again and again - domestic issues and agriculture.

"We have a lot going on here again because the oldest of my ladies, who I already taught how to cook some meals, came down with measles and she has a pretty bad case. So now we have lots and lots to do and some things just have to wait. The doctor hopes that Maria can get out of bed before Pentecost. We now have 230 head of poultry in the garden. The oldest of the ducklings are in the furthest meadow garden where they are supposed to feed at the pond in which Erich suspects that lung worms and liver fluke larvae that infest the cattle live. It takes us about half an hour to take the ducks there to feed and back again because these small ducks cannot exist eating only these vermin and they need something more substantial to live on."

In an interview from 1981 Ursula said that she was also in charge of the poultry farming in Woydiethen since she already had achieved such good results in Bonkow. Initially there was only a small chicken coop at the farm but later a large poultry stable was built in back of a barn. The young ducks she raised were Indian Runner ducks. These birds love to feed on a particular kind of slug that can act as an intermediate host that transmits the lung worms and liver flukes to the cattle. So the ducks eliminate the source which may end up in the stomachs of cattle when they feed on the grass in moist meadows which may contain the dangerous slugs. Ursel discovered this relationship between the cattle disease, slugs and ducks in an article written by a “Gutsfrau”, a lady of the manor from the Havelland, near Berlin, in the journal “Die deutsche Landfrau”, "The German Country woman."

The main part of the letter written by Erich on June 25, 1930 addressed to his mother is his fourth priority - house and farm. The final paragraph contains political statements which - possibly provoked by his reading Hitler's "Mein Kampf" - correspond perfectly to the Nazi jargon.

"Today we finally got the first rain. Since April we have had a few drops now and then, just enough to settle the dust but not a drop for the last five weeks. The ripening of the grain has suffered and the stalks are still quite short. The oats even turned brown in some places. Maybe this rain is coming in time so that we will at least have enough straw for feed. In Masuria and Pomerania the fields also look pitiful. Father also writes sadly about the drought. He may visit us this coming Sunday.

“This year for the first time we have a great strawberry harvest. We sold the first ones in Rauschen for 80 pennies per pound. Ursel is canning and making jam today. One night all of us ate strawberries with milk until we almost burst. I diligently watered them while we had no rain. Every second day I watered them with a large vat of pond water. I'm done with the clover harvest, but there are about 30 cartloads of timote (grass?) left, but it is not dry yet. With this drought we still have not been able to plant rutabagas. Last year I only had five acres planted. Now, everything is going at high speed. The heat was magnificent for the pastures and rye. The rye is really doing well since I gave it 30 pounds of saltpeter per acre.

“If the battle against the general demoralization which was fostered by Marxism is to be successful, it can only be done with the strongest measures such as against the Jewish finance system. Certainly this will be repulsive to some, but the final result is the justification."

In no case could Erich have been aware of what was meant with the invocation of "strongest measures” in the mid-1930s. It was a manner of speaking which was taken up by the National Socialists (Nazis) and later on by the army until the war ended in 1945. Not only by word of mouth but it was cruelly put into action. In the last four lines of Erich’s letter he used language that is hardly found in any of his other letters. The introduction said that Erich’s letters were readable "with great interest". This is the case because they normally just do not fall into the jargon of ideological rabble - rousing - but the exception is characterized by the last four lines of this letter.

In his letters to his mother who lived in the far west of Germany, he was first of all "Erich" the son who gave his political opinions in a decided form. Ursel on the other hand, left it rather to hints or hoped for "fate" to interfere when she looked into the future. At least this is what can be read in the notes added by her to the last - mentioned letter.

"Yes, it really seems to go uphill with the Africans. That's great and one less worry for you. How it will end up with us, only Heaven knows. To sell now at a heavy loss is also a serious decision since we are still hoping that we will be able to keep our heads above water for the time being. And the general view is that either this year or the next, something will happen that will improve the agricultural situation. Prices should rise then. I am determined that I will not spend the rest of my life in this little house in Woydiethen where you cannot even invite guests. In Africa it is quite different. There people live mainly on the porch and only need bedrooms in the house and a living room. Well, we certainly must calmly wait where fate will lead us."

By saying "the Africans", she meant Martha and her husband. The intention to emulate these two and head for Africa was still there. It should be noted that in Ursel's memories when she was interviewed in 1965 and1981 she almost never spoke of the plans for moving to Africa. This is a striking example of how something that was so important and had great significance at a time, - as reflected in the letters, - can become almost nonexistent in later biographical retrospective.

In a letter dated September 17, 1930, Ursel again talked about the children,

"Little Evamarie is sick with tonsillitis again. Today she is much better. Since the measles, her tonsils are swollen, but did not hurt and they were not even red. The doctor said that if she got tonsillitis frequently, the tonsils should be capped. Helga has no school today and she is happy. She doesn't like school very much, but so far she keeps up with the other children."

Two days later, Erich writes his mother.

"One could go crazy during this time. Our primary task is and remains to make a change as so as possible and that can only be done by completely changing the Marxist democratic system. That only Hitler can do. It is completely useless now for the private sector and for all professions to deal in politics. This is evident in the agricultural program. Right now we are told to call for new elections in Prussia where the Nazis are expected to be the largest party because "red" Saxony and "black" Southern Germany are eliminated. And who wants to accomplish something in the Reich must first win Prussia. The Reds also know that. The center parties have to be wiped out altogether. Why should it not work here with two or three parties as in England or America? The ones who are afraid that Hitler might be too forceful and alienate the foreign powers should read the Italian and Swedish newspapers - even the Manchester Guardian. England and Italy have no interest in letting France get even greater. Of course we are only able to form alliances if we seriously try to defend ourselves and not cower down with a slavish mentality to the requirement of others. Then we can have hope again. The first breach is plugged and for the first time the growth of the Red Tide is being halted. They were even pushed back considerably in relation to the large number of seats they previously held. East Prussia is the leading example. There is something to the saying 'ex oriente lux' (light from the east)."

Again and again, Erich takes a clear stand against the Communists. They are mentioned by him as "red hordes" or "the red tide" and painted as a hotbed of general demoralization which is in line with the Nazi arguments. He probably did not see that which now, in retrospect, is obvious - the many corresponding schisms, the oppressive similarities between Communists and Nazis in occurrences as well as in objectives. One need not be a follower of a theory of totalitarianism to identify the convergences between the two extremes, - even with all the differences in the details.

Another characteristic which is of fundamental importance to the world-image as well as self-image of Erich and Ursula is evident in the fundamental openness to non-German, foreign situations and conditions. This is shown largely (certainly not always) by their writing style which is independent from the current Zeitgeist (spirit of the times). These two are not fanatical German nationalists. Erich has Dutch ancestry and grew up on the Dutch border. Ursel developed an early love for Sweden and Denmark. The two met in Denmark. Both had a long standing wish to emigrate to Africa. The openness and willingness to look beyond the German borders is again shown in the letter that Ursel wrote on November 14, 1930 from Woydiethen to her mother–in-law.

"I can believe the fact that the Dutch farmers also can't get their money's worth- given these world market prices. Nevertheless, like the Danish farmers they can survive more easily than our farmers because they have or can get labor-saving machinery and other new equipment and systems to provide them with better crops and yields. Only a few areas of Germany have that benefit. Also they do not have the enormous fiscal and social burdens, heavy freight costs etc. under which we suffer.

"It is true that this inflation has made us all poor. Many became accustomed to living the good life that they did not deserve while others who had well-earned savings and other assets lost all or most of it.

"I did not make much of a profit from my canning this year. Last year got 2.00RM per glass jar; this year I could get only 1.00 to 1.50RM. It is a very modest profit for all the hard work that went into it. But what else could we do with all the fruit? We would not have been able to sell them fresh because the price was running around 10 cents per pound - if you could find a buyer. There was too much of it this summer."

Between this and the following letter is a period of several months. One must not forget that the biographical reconstruction is dependent upon the help of letters with a certain degree of coincidences. Especially when there are many letters in very close succession, any gaps that arise "suddenly" or in spite of everything are especially conspicuous. From the period between November 14, 1930 and April 3, 1931 (Good Friday), no letter is received. However, the letter that Erich wrote on Good Friday shows that there is no break in the story. It should be mentioned now that there is a very noticeable gap with the complete absence of letters from the year 1932.

"My dearest Mother!

As always, we send an intimate Easter kiss from us – today from the Prussian Siberia. We just drove to the church in a sled. Cold and gray are the skies and the sermon. The snow is old and dirty and where you see bare spots the winter crops are so gray, so dead. The deer are hungry and stand shivering at the road side, the lapwing (bird) is desperately looking for worms on the frozen ground, humanity looks around dark and cheerless - Good Friday -. Everyone longs so much for spring and sunshine. And Easter is so close. It already feels like everything wants to break through. The warm sun just has to break the spell and that must come soon. Only the snowdrops were helped by their internal drive to sunlight. When we dug through the snow, the flowers were already blooming. It's wonderful. At night we still have -6 to –8 degrees C (18-20 degrees Fahrenheit). When will we be able to start sewing the crops? You really don't know what to do with the help. We can't even clean the yard since everything still frozen."

Two days later, Easter Sunday, Erich changed the perspective by turning to politics in detail.

"Dearest Mother!

Despite everything, let me take you firmly in my arms and wish for you, which we all hope for from the bottom of our souls, the resurgence of our poor people. With it we would have everything. We also have our robust health. Then we will feel like the angels, freed from the oppressive anxiety about an uncertain future. The good Lord cannot let a nation go under, a wonder of the world that for over four years was able to resist overwhelming powers, which only broke down by discord of the insiders and thereby became an easy prey to the international capitalists. Nothing can annoy and anger me more than this frivolous talk that we were "defeated" - even if the French are constantly yelling it. If America would not have joined the fight, we would have taken care of all of them like we did Russia - France, England, Italy, with all their vast colonial reserves and all the other little yappers. You have to continually remind yourself of this to realize that all this is no worse than a serious illness that has to be overcome. Naturally this will not happen quickly if it is the life of a people. Of course, valuable parts and forces will be destroyed. The recovery process is moving forward with increasing speed. The 9th of August will show whether the patient got up too early and will have a bad relapse. Now we wait in silence, the world is listening. Even the emergency regulations and frantic action as the Reichsbank discounts, etc. are perceived as stop-gaps. Now it's about Marxism as a fighting force of international capitalism. - We cannot complain now, dearest mother. Blessed is he who is able to go into the new campaign with healthy limbs. Because it will not be easy even with a national win. We must move slowly forward, albeit at great hardships, otherwise, we will be doomed to certain destruction."

Erich, an active soldier in the First World War, followed the much-discussed thesis that Germany was "in the field undefeated" and in connection with that the legend of the “saber thrust”. The view today of who was the victor of World War I is different from what it was in the 1930s. Erich’s views were in line with the Nazis. Ursel also places her hopes in the views and policies of the Nazis, however, she remains much more restrained in her statements than Erich in the letter she wrote to her mother-in-law on Easter Monday, 1931.

"Otto Rohn has been working for a few weeks now with his uncle in Königsberg. He was here for the holiday and we have little good news from the city. Due to the high unemployment everywhere you see the greatest need and the greatest misery and most of the workers are now more or less Communists. Even the artisans and tradesmen, for example his uncle, are Communists. I believe that we will see sadder times. If for example the farmers have to lay-off more people, unemployment and misery will just be getting bigger.

“If you think about Germany and our own future, it can be really frightening. Now when no farmer has any grain left, you can get a good price for seed. Mrs. Hauffe, whose brother is a wholesale merchant in Riga, recently returned from there and said that the people there assess the German situation very seriously and believe that it will be a long time before Germany will be able to recover. The whole world is worse off than it was before 1914. It would be wonderful if we could soon recover after having been defeated and forced to give up many of our dominions so that the motherland is overcrowded. An ascent would only be possible through a great revolutionary act like Hitler is planning - by the abolition of the gold coin and generous settlement of the unemployed in the country side. But if the conditions in the city are like Otto Rohn is saying, Hitler will probably not come to rule. If only we had taken the 1000 RM offered for the farm just last summer and gone to Gotland! Who knows if we will be able to rescue anything from here? But who could tell! Everything is destiny!

“God, I am sorry I am making your heart heavy with my complaints, Mother. But today Erich is so desperate and down that he has infected me. It seems as though everything has conspired against us: nature, the weather which is obstinate, the people and more. At least the children are healthy and won’t remember anything about all the troubles around them. They are happily playing outside with the village children.

“Erich has to make a lot of preparations for the referendum. Will something come of it? I have my doubts. The general public has too much hate.”

For the Nazis, the threat of overpopulation of Germany and the lack of "living space" became a central idea, almost an obsession. Since the Germans lost their colonies and many border areas with the Treaty of Versailles, Hitler was able to convince many people of the idea of a problem of not having enough "living space". Ursel also followed this view but apparently when she said that Hitler would perform the "great revolutionary act" she did not think that it may mean a coming war. Thinking about the “overcrowding” in Germany, Africa was placed into the background. Instead, the North and Scandinavia were again favored.

In a letter to her mother-in-law of April 28, 1931 Ursel again switched subjects and wrote about the "outrageous" reproaches of her father.

"My dear Mother!

Well finally many heartfelt thanks for your nice letter. Now everything is happening at the same time - garden, house cleaning, teaching the new girls - so I never got to answer it. Spring has arrived here all at once! It is very nice and warm and the meadows are turning green already. Hopefully we can drive the cattle out to the pastures in fourteen days because the straw is awfully scarce. The egg hatching business is slow since no one has any money. I have several turkey hens sitting on different kinds of eggs.

“I have no idea where father is. I don’t know whether he is in Berlin or again in Bonkow. He sent us 600 RM for the 15th of the month for Wiemann plus two hundred more. And then the following day we received a terrible letter from him, peppered with the grossest insults. He may well have considered that he has given us 4000 RM since July 1930 and that he is now sorry about it or something. He had previously asked in the letter, what we intended to do - if we could sell here – and he probably expected the response that we wanted to come to Bonkow and run his 54 acres for him in place of his manager and housekeeper. Since that was not the case, he apparently was very angry with us. He wrote that we should stop writing to him for the time being as our letters only upset him. That note was totally unnecessary because I really would not know how to respond to that. If we contradicted these outrageous things, as we would have to, it would only bring a lot of anger and heartbreak. – God knows that it is terrible and degrading for us that at our age we have to depend on our relatives to keep us afloat. But God also knows that it is not our fault. We have always done what we could. Many thousands of others who started out with much less debt than we did are now broke. Father could really show a little more love in his last years."

In subsequent letters the conflict with Ernst August Dietrich is not mentioned but a few months later, in September 1931, the tensions increased. But first, Ursula was happy about the season in an undated letter written in the spring of 1931.

"The warmest spring weather is here. Everything is beautiful outside. If it were not for the terrible financial difficulties and the disaster of winter crops, one really could be perfectly happy here. The Samland really is a delightful spot of earth! The whole air is full of sweet scents and the sky is wonderfully blue. If we have good weather on Pentecost we want to go to the seashore to swim."

In a letter from Woydiethen on July 8, 1931 Ursel wrote familiar topics to her mother-in-law.

"What do you say about our high politics? With the new loan they bring Germany into such high bondage to foreign countries that Hitler will probably no longer be able to improve the situation if and when he comes to power. I believe that it will be another year or two until the Nazis come to power and by then the others will probably have run this land into the ground. Bleak prospects!

"We have no strawberries this year. Someone ripped them all out during one night, even the little green vines are gone. We strongly suspect a family that moved here from Klycken-Steinhaus. They are "halb Pollaksch" (half-polish) and have two young hoodlum sons that are unemployed. So now all the hard work was for nothing. The raspberries don't look good because too much of last year's new growth froze in the winter. Only a few currants are on the bushes while last year we had vast quantities."

It is hard to determine what ideas and prejudices might be hidden behind the name "pollaksch". Again and again there are details in these letters which may seem strange or biased to today's readers – but once the letters are analyzed in their overall tenor based on the times of the 1920s and 1930s, they are strikingly moderate and therefore untimely. They are written by two people who came to support National Socialism between the years 1933-1945 and yet they never descended into extremes in their remarks as a whole. Erich wrote a letter to his mother on August 28, 1931 that demonstrated his moderation. He did not comment on "the political event of the day."

"Of course you cannot change things in one day even when the right person comes into power. But at least there is a chance that one will be able to slowly better oneself, albeit under many hardships. The politics of Stresemann has finally collapsed. Who cannot see this? After the last rantings of France, it can't be helped. The fact that Hitler is gaining ground in the totally conservative Münsterland is good news and of great importance. - Strange how the current administration uses means which the Nazis have long proclaimed. Only now they have done only halfway and adjusted to the old regime. Where is the sacred democracy - nothing but dictatorship -. Capital flight law – it's too late. Before, we were called disaster politicians. Now we are also playing with the idea of a German mark.

Luther's chair is wobbling. The capitalistic system has run to a halt. In any case, we will all be completely exhausted if the change is not coming soon."

In a letter to his brother Alfred, written in Woydiethen on September 15, 1931, Erich wrote that there is now a serious conflict with Ernst August Dietrich. Ernst August was obviously making financial demands and said that Alfred should help. The details are not quite clear. Among other things, Erich wrote.

"You see what a man can demand, who has made Mammon his god". [Mammon, in the New Testament of the Bible, is material wealth or greed, most often personified as a deity.]

Once again, Erich discussed that he was still considering selling Woydiethen. Shortly afterwards, Erich told his brother that Ursel was currently writing her father "for the umpteen's time to make it clear to him that with a bankruptcy everything will be gone except for the cattle."

"After the sale we would of course first go to Bonkow where we could calmly consider what to do next."

Any efforts to settle the strife that were made in other letters after September 1931 are not documented here.

On September 29, 1931 Erich wrote to Alfred.

"Have many thanks for your dear letter and the promissory note. If I had known that you would be so upset about Father's letter, I would not have sent it to you. We just don't notice any more how offensive he is and how the facts are often distorted by him. But maybe it's good that you got a look at what we have had to endure many times in all these years. One can only pity the man. It will remain his fate until his death to make himself and others unhappy and to leave no friends. How nice and quietly he could live, despite the difficult times. Now he will certainly loose his cool again because of the dive of the Danish crown, particularly since Ursel advised him over six months ago to cash in his Danish money and to take it to Sweden and buy some property there. The Danish krone traded Saturday at .92 while the Swedish krona is still 1.12. Ursel often has a good feel for such things which she inherited from her mother. But actions were rarely taken and the predictions came true.

"Major Sodau [?] wrote me the day before yesterday that my application is now in perfect order and the sanitation restoration plan, which is now complete, was sent to the industrial bank. Hopefully the payment will be made pretty soon. I am basically in a vice because nothing is salable except for milk. The price for cattle is 20.00RM per hundredweight! What are we coming to? The Reichsmark is keeping its value."

The last paragraph referred back to the situation that has made life almost unbearable for the Spickschens in Woydiethen for many years.

In a letter dated October 18, 1931 Erich wrote more.

"The situation in agriculture is getting more disastrous on a daily basis. If there is no change by the spring, general bankruptcy will occur."

In a last letter from 1931, written on October 20, Erich once again indicated what he was doing specifically in political and agricultural organizations to improve his situation. After that he gave his views on the general world situation.

"It was crazy. Everything was coming up at the same time. On top of that there was a lot to do with the Stahlhelm and the agricultural association and federation.
I wonder how the Africans are doing now. We have not heard from them for so long. Hopefully the market situation for kapok is not as bad as it is for cotton, which is being burned in huge quantities in order to keep the price to some extent stable for the rest. In Australia, sheep are not sheared at all and in others countries the poor do not know how to dress. Coffee and wheat is burned, but tens of millions are starving. Gold is piled up unproductively in America and France while there is endless impoverishment on the other side. Crazy world economy! The Nazis are right in that this capitalist system must be run to its death."

A summary review of Erich and Ursula's life between 1921 to 1931 can serve as a transition to the next section. Ursula provided this in her escape diary on March 14, 1945. The estate "Schwesternhof" had been sold.

"Erich toured the province to buy another farm. At last he found Woydiethen. It was certainly not the ideal. The ground was neglected and not particularly good, the buildings were old and the inventory was dilapidated. There was no grain in the barn for the animals and it was just January. The horses were old and poorly fed; the cows were few in number and not good quality. But we had to make do with this property because we had very little money and in 1927 there was not much to choose from. We made our calculations again and again and again. We figured in small harvests and low yields and used current prices in our calculations. It must work if we live and work economically!

"But serious concerns started already in the fall. A sudden collapse of prices in the grain market was to blame. In addition, the harvest was lower than estimated. Our predecessor had been a drinker. He had let the farm go to pot in recent years and had no longer worked it. Everywhere we found only disorder, decay and neglect. Agricultural prices fell rapidly in all sectors. We saw certain ruin in front of us. But we did not want to give up and we certainly did not feel like losers. Erich took in paying farm apprentices (eleven) and I taught paying home-economics students. We both worked from dawn to dusk. Every penny was turned around three times before we spent it. I wore hand-me-down clothes contributed by my better-off sister- in- law. The children wore donated clothes from other relatives that were altered for them. How often did I stand outside a shop longing to buy them a pretty new dress, - but it could not be. We could not go to a movie or theater and we never could afford a bottle of wine. Only our love made us strong enough to give up everything.

"I can never forget the many hours of fear for our property. When the enforcement officer came to the yard and wanted to impound the farm for taxes I thought that I could not bear the disgrace! On another occasion the government seized the grain on the stalk. I never passed by that piece of land without a sense of shame and fear. But we were able to sail safely around the rocks and keep our farm intact despite many setbacks in the economy and so many misfortunes that hit us.

"Then came the 4th of April 1933. Our house burned down. Many valuable family pieces and a lot of memories were lost forever. The magnificent damask table linen from my grandmother - all gone. The oil paintings that hung in the upper floor, the beautiful old armoires – all gone. Then we learned that the fire insurance for the old building had been too low. Again, new worries and new debts had to be made. But we survived even that, though not without fear.

"Then came the much needed construction of a new barn, new agricultural machinery, the replacement of the threshing machine. Erich had gotten the job with the Reichsnährstand, (The Reichsnährstand, or National Food Estate, was formed in 1933 and served to oversee producers, growers, distributors, and sellers of foodstuffs during the Third Reich). Thus, we were monetarily a little more independent. But still I often sat looking over the books, pondering our fate because often we did not have enough money. Finally in 1938 we had it pretty much made. With a frugal lifestyle we could now live without worries. The operation was now in such good order that we made small profits. We could breathe again. Five healthy children we called our own. But sadly, one little boy had died. Then came the war!"

Woydiethen House and Driveway

V

The Time of National Socialism

1. The years 1933 - 1939

Much of what was quoted at the end of the last chapter is a prefix to what is described in detail in this chapter. This might lead to unavoidable repetition in some places. As before, different sources tell their story.

As already indicated, no letters are available for the year 1932 so that no "direct authenticity" exists as would be found in letters or diaries. Instead, the recollections of Ursula Spickschen in her detailed discussions and stories between 1979 and 1981 have become very valuable even though they don't always establish the precise timeframe and sometimes vary in detail.

In 1979, during an interview with her grandson Erich Hart, Ursel explained by summarizing:

"Given the fact that we were always on the verge of bankruptcy in Woydiethen, it was no wonder that we soon liked the ideas of the National Socialists and joined them. They promised better times for agriculture and saved us from the prospect of one day having to give up the farm and being penniless with two kids to support. The Nazis promised a lot, and with the Reichsnährstandsgesetz (National Food Distribution Law), many of the promises were actually kept. For example, a 'freight compensation" was established. That meant that we no longer had to pay for transportation of farm machinery and fertilizer, which had to be bought in Central Germany and was shipped to East Prussia – that was sort of an island in the East. That also meant that we no longer had to spend extra money for necessary purchases. Because of the freight charges that we had to pay before 1933, the price for everything we sold in East Prussia - the grains, livestock and milk - had to be reduced because most of it was not used in East Prussia, but was shipped to Central Germany.

"With the law of 1933, a balance of cost was established and thus East Prussian agriculture gradually faired significantly better. At first, we did not notice much of the changes but then it became apparent. At first one noticed that the number of unemployed was reduced because large projects were started for which many workers were needed. I don't know if the construction of the Autobahn was immediately started but at least the unemployed largely disappeared from the streets.

"In the spring of 1933 we met with another disaster when our house burned down. Back then there was no replacement insurance for homes. At 14,000 RM we received only the actual value of the old house and the new house cost about twice as much. Since the original house was very old, a low value was assessed. But even this shock we dealt with because we were able to get a small, low-interest loan for the new building and also received a construction bonus. These benefits were also listed in the new regulations of 1933. So we built a new house, which satisfied us and felt comfortable in it. It had running water, a bathroom with tub and toilet, a comfort that we were used to from earlier times in Denmark. The old house did not have these facilities, which today would be unthinkable."

During an interview with Thorlef and Brigitte (1981), Ursel went into more detail about the circumstances of the fire:

"The house we moved into in 1927 was built about 1840. The walls on the ground floor consisted of unfired mud bricks dried in the sun. A second floor did not exist, only a finished attic with sloping walls in the rooms. The rooms where the apprentices and eleven (agricultural students) slept were heated with iron stoves that allowed them to regulate the amount of heat they needed. I repeatedly admonished one of the girls, not to set the heat of her stove too high because sparks could fly which could be dangerous under the old roof.

"April 4, 1933 was cold and stormy. We were sitting downstairs in the parlor when I heard a strange crackling. Suddenly the lights went out. We ran into the hallway and Erich tore open the door to the attic. Everything around the chimney was in flames. We were not able to save anything on the top floor. The large linen closet which I had up there was lost and much more. It took quite a while until the firefighters arrived. By then much of the ceiling had fallen down so that much was ruined on the lower floor. Later, one of the girls admitted that she had forgotten to set the stove on low.

"For a while we temporarily lived in two rooms in the house of our friendly neighbor who owned the dairy. The eleven (boys) had to sleep in a stall in the barn. The new house had to be built on the foundations of the old building and that created great difficulties. But we were able to give our input to the layout of the rooms in the new building and also had a decided advantage in that we were able to build cost-effectively since the state took over all accumulating interest and had also launched a job creation program for the builders.

"We also got running water in the kitchen with the new building. Before that we had only one pump. After a second water pipe was installed in the cow barn we suddenly realized that our well was no longer sufficient. A new deeper well had to be drilled which cost a lot of money - 7500 Reich Mark. A motorized pump was necessary to get the water to the surface, a depth of 75 meters (248ft).

"By the later 1930s things were improving for us in every way. We were finally able to bring the farm into good working order after taking it over in such poor condition. We soon possessed a very good herd of registered cattle, the fields were largely drained and the crops were satisfactory to very good. We were even able to sell heifers (young cows that had not calved) at the auction. Also the milk receipts were very profitable because we had such a good herd. Finally our money worries were gone. We built a large new barn so that we could now protect our grain from the rain and we did not have to leave it out in the open. A little later we started to plant seed potatoes and seed grain. We were able to buy high quality, first choice, super-elite seed from a certified grower and then were able to sell the grain and potatoes as seed after the harvest. That meant that we received a lot more money for our quality summer barley than if we would have had to sell it as feed. The same was true for the difference between hybrid and ordinary potatoes. So, all in all, economically we were doing well now.

"To better understand our political situation in the early thirties, I (Ursel in 1981) have to tell you how and why I joined the Nazi Party. I joined already in 1929. We had a farmer's son from the Samland as an eleven (agricultural student) who we particularly liked. He was kind, efficient and responsible. He told us that by chance in November 1923 he witnessed as Hitler tried to usurp power with his march to the Feldherrenhalle (the Generals' Hall) in Munich. The behavior of Hitler's followers so impressed him that he immediately became a Nazi party member and an SA man. This eleve constantly talked and raved about the Nazis to me and what they would put into motion to fix our problems. He confirmed and supported me in my interest in the Nordic culture. I remembered that the University of Askov in Denmark often mentioned our old Norse ancestors and we had already read the "Edda" (Old Norse *Edda*, which applies to the Old Norse *Poetic Edda* and *Prose Edda*, both of which were written down in Iceland during the 13th century in the Icelandic language). The eleve stressed how important all of this was to the Nazis. When he brought me written proof that Adolf Hitler "stood on the foundation of a positive Christian" and after imploring me that he wanted to convert at least one person for the Nazi Party, I could not resist. He brought me an application and I signed it. Erich did not decide to join the party until 1932.

"Although I am getting ahead of myself with this I will add what I experienced later with this eleven. He married and became a soldier. When he visited me in 1943 or 1944 I saw that he had lost a leg. He said to me, 'Ma'am, I made a big mistake at that time'. 'What mistake?' I asked. 'That I persuaded you to join the Nazis.' He was cured of it."

This description should be supplemented by an explanation that Thorlef provided in 2009. As his mother often told later, she was involved, impressed and inspired with a youth movement in Denmark. Ursel could be very romantic on the one hand while on the other hand she was a practical person. The members of the Danish Youth League (part of the Grundtvigs) always sang songs during their meetings and they were accompanied by a guitar. Status differences had no importance there. Workers' children came together with professors' kids and with nobles. The discussions revolved around a lot of Norse myths and about the nature of northern life. One focused on Scandinavian literature, such as by Knut Hamsun. The community spirit in Denmark, probably in all of northern Europe, had a special character, which is true even today. People have a natural, open-minded way of dealing with each other, which is much less common in Germany.

It should be noted that the influence of the Grundtvig and Grundtvigianer was of utmost importance for Ursel, especially in terms of their attitude toward National Socialism. In her letter dated February 2, 1922 she spoke about Grundtvigianism. Hopes of a better society was the leading theme of the Danish youth organization and the idea of a "people's community" was the guiding principle for Ursel and she referred to that principle again and again. It was a crucial reason for her to join the Nazi party in 1929.

Thorlef remembered that his mother's party pin had a membership number under a hundred thousand – and that won her an additional safety status. For instance, she could dare to go alone into the harbor area in Konigsberg, a district that was completely dominated by communists in 1930. She could be sure that there was always a "brown Nazi" to be found among the "red communist" stevedores who would protect her if it came to a conflict. These experiences, in addition to economic and political considerations, encouraged her afterwards to justify her decision to join the National Socialists Party.

The strength of Ursel's dedication to Nazism was such that she soon began to publish numerous articles in various high-circulation newspapers, such as in the "National Socialist Landpost", in "Georgina", in "The German Woman" or "Weekly Newspaper of the Landesbauernschaft" (ministry of agriculture) until well into 1943. In the course of twelve years, she wrote well over thirty articles, some of them quite long. She proved to be an active journalist and not merely as a country woman who once in a while found an opportunity to work for a newspaper.

An example of Gerda Ursula Spickschen's immediate and emphatic support for the Nazis is found in one of her first articles. The following two sentences are quoted from an article she published on July 17, 1932 under the title "Why the German farmer's wife chooses the National Socialists" under the caption "The German farm-wife" in the "National Socialist Country Post".

"The elimination of all harmful foreign influences that have come to us in recent decades and have threatened to poison the soul of our people, reviving old, Nordic folk culture and Christian schools will make our children free and healthy people who, in the Third Reich, are firmly rooted in their land, their nationality, their Christian belief and Nordic world view.

Every German mother who does not want the red hordes who are guided by their invisible rulers, to scourge our country in the foreseeable future, by murdering and burning; who does not want her children to become soulless work-machines and slaves of the United Jewish capitalism; who does not want her children to live without their Christian religion, grow up without joy, without hope for the future, she will vote for the Nazi party on July 31!"

This appeal, which is permeated with ideological clichés that were used prolifically until the end of the war years, appeared before the so-called seizure of power. This whole language has become obsolete and intolerable to modern ears. One has to wonder what significance should be attached to the term of "United Jewish capitalism" or that of "management of international Jewry". This expression was used by Ursula Spickschen again in 1942. These expressions which had already become worn out and hackneyed in the thirties and forties because of overuse probably belonged to the compulsory exercises and basic equipment of every "upright" Nazi. It is doubtful whether Ursula Spickschen despised Jews personally or would attack, pursue or even kill them.

The language and style that Ursula used in her newspaper articles are significantly different from the style of the letters that have previously been quoted here extensively. You have to call it a strong contrast, almost a break from the norm. What caused this difference cannot be examined here. Presumably, the "National Socialist Landpost" (Rural Mail) was already a tightly managed body in July 1932, where rigid propaganda was encouraged and required. Ursel made this tone her own, obviously with fulfillment and conviction as attested by her voters' registration which is signed with her full name.

Thorlef indicated that for Erich Spickschen, among other things, the objective of the Nazis to disperse large estates, to parcel them out and convert them into smallholdings, was important and plausible to him. The idea of strengthening the small farmers appealed to both Erich and Ursel. He actively supported the dispersion of large estates when he was the Landesbauernfuehrer (Minister of Agriculture) in the 1930s and helped that thousands of new farms were created. In addition, the general promotion and support of agriculture by the Nazis, as the aforementioned freight equalization promoted the purchase of goods from Central Germany and the transport of grain there, was a change of vital importance to the Spickschens.

The first authentic preserved evidence of 1933 is a picture postcard that Erich wrote to his mother Maria in Gemen at the beginning of September. Maria Spickschen, née van der Mark, was living in the town of Gemen at that time and later resided north of Borken, Westfalen, the place where her parents were married in 1864. Her son Alfred had built her a house there, which was soon entwined with roses and therefore was called "Rose Cottage". Emblazoned on the face of the card is a huge martial eagle hovering over hands that are clasped in a strong handshake. Under the hands, against the background of the cityscape of Nuremberg, a giant emblem of the swastika appears. To the right and left of the swastika emblem reads: "United the people, strong the country." On the left of the message side of the card the "sender" address is given as: "Feldpostkarte. Reichsparteitag der N.S.D.A.P. in Nuernberg 1. – 3. September 1933". (Field postcard: Party convention for the N.S.D.A.P.[National Socialist German Workers Party] in Nuernberg 1. – 3. September 1933)

Erich's message:

"Dear Mother.

I was ordered to come here all of a sudden. Arrived Thursday, should be back home Saturday evening. It is gorgeous here. One swims in a sea of old architecture, flags, enthusiasm and beer. The roads are brown with brown-shirts. We will take in as much as possible of the beauty here. Alfred must bring you here some time. Everything seems doubly impressive in the new abundance of power; you do not have the impression of vanishing splendor."

Ursel explained why Erich had been "ordered" to Nuremberg in a conversation with her grandson Erich Hart in 1979.

"Both Opaps - as Erich was called by his grandchildren - and I took over responsibilities within the Reichsnährstand organization, the National Food Distribution office. Opaps was the Kreisbauernfuehrer, the county agricultural-representative, at that time. That position was corresponding to the former county farmers' representative. He was thus the chairman of the Agricultural Association for the county. However it was a semi-official position since the Reichsnährstand was a self-governing body. Later he was called to Königsberg, at first as the head of the Division I in the Landesbauernschaft (Ministry of Agriculture). This department had two main responsibilities: one, the question of labor relations, (i.e. the relations between employers and employees) and the regulation of cultural interests (e.g. preservation of old customs). After that, Erich became State Chairman, the deputy of the Landesbauernfuehrer. In 1937 or maybe 1938, he eventually became the Landesbauernfuehrer, the Minister of Agriculture.

"I, myself, was involved with the Landesbauernschaft since about 1935 as the Head of the Department for Women. Again, the main task was to preserve the old customs. For example, folk art was actively promoted through the establishment of courses in spinning flax (linen), wool and weaving. We also helped with the preparation and conducting of exhibitions. Additionally, during the war I also worked in the Division II, where the main focus was on the education of young girls in the agricultural trade, especially in rural home economics.

"Because Opaps was now very often on the road - almost every day dealing with the business of the Ministry - we had to hire a manager to run the farm for us. We had no luck with the first manager but the second one, a Mr. Nolting, was excellent. Unfortunately he was killed later in the war. I worked two or three days a week either in the Landesbauernschaft in Königsberg or traveling in the provinces to give lectures. I had a lot to do. At home I had to take over some of Erich's work, especially at a time when we had the incompetent manager. I had to do some of the bookkeeping including the bill payments and the cash book. Opaps kept the books for the stores and the animals. While the incompetent manager was with us I also had to worry about some of the stores because he often forgot to write things down. It was very important to keep the books accurate so that we did not get into tax difficulties. In addition to all this, I had to work for the Landesbauernschaft and last but not least, I was responsible for the family!"

It should be noted that the "Farming Community" became immensely important to National Socialism based on the September 13, 1933 "Blood and Soil" ideology and the establishment of the "Reichsnährstand" - the "State Food administration" - and the establishment of a "Reichsbauernfuehrer", a "Secretary of Agriculture". While the latter was also in charge of the Reich Ministry for Food and Agriculture, he became a central part of the Nazi agricultural policy. Erich and his wife Ursula Spickschen experienced a sudden and steep climb up the social ladder and the feeling of increased value and esteem in the community.

Ursel wrote a typewritten letter to her mother-in-law on November 17, 1933, the year of the "seizure of power" by the Nazis. At the beginning of the letter she once again talked about the consequences of the house fire. In the second half of the letter the talk was of the political duties that both Spickschens had taken on once Hitler came to power.

"My dear Mother!

I am in the process of getting all the keys replaced for the wardrobes and closets that were lost in the fire. This is not so easy. Much of what Erich usually took care of, I now have to do. That takes a lot of time.

"My new apprentice (she is paying a training fee) is very nice and efficient. She is a teacher's daughter from the Allenstein (Olsztyn) area, Catholic, but not fanatical. I no longer have my maid. She packed up and moved out after I gave her notice for the first of November. So now I again took in an apprentice in her place, against my initial intention. But I seem to have made a very good choice because up till now the girl has a very pleasant manner, is clean, albeit slow, and is not stupid. Previously she worked on a farm where she milked cows and has no idea of how to clean. But she is learning. Mademoiselle, the cook, is efficient and fast, but moodier than ever. She must be handled with kid gloves and rules the kitchen with a dreaded iron hand. The apprentices are all afraid of her. And I have to turn a blind eye to the disorder in the pantry. She is certainly eager, economical and works like a slave. Everyone has his or her faults and I can live with hers. But if she is already so moody at twenty years, I want to know what she will be like when she is thirty. She obviously has a "Küchenfimmel" a kitchen craze, which many farmers' women supposedly get after working at the hot stove in the kitchen all day. We have both been on good terms so far because, as I said, I handle her with kid gloves and reprimand her in a "most gentle, amiable" way, which is not always easy for me in my current nervous state. But it certainly makes me practice the gift of self-control! Yes, yes, we have to have fun.

But at least she is honest and hardworking and gives her best and gets things done. That's worth a lot.

"The little Swedish girl is very nice, does not do much, but the 50 RM we get for teaching her is quite nice. She does not eat a lot. The other girl, the apprentice, pays only 30 RM. This is appropriate since she pays less according to her performance. On April 1, we will probably have to take in a teacher for Helga. Hopefully we will find a nice girl who will also look after the children when the school hours are done. When you get a good tutor, the training is often better than in school.

"Erich is in Königsberg again today. He had to take over Division I of the Landesbauernschaft on a substitute basis. On top of that, he still has his job as Kreisbauernfuehrer, local farmers' leader, and as consultant to the farmers' university. It is a bit much, but the Landesbauernfuehrer thinks very highly of him. He simply gave Erich the order to take over the representation, so he had to do it. So now he gets paid expenses and a mileage allowance, which are often more than his actual costs. So he has a little something left over and it can be regarded as a replacement for his lost labor at home. Tomorrow he will be in charge of the meeting that the Ancestral Estate Representative Sauer usually chairs at the city hall in Königsberg. He had to get all the information from the Landesbauernfuehrer today because he has to represent him in the proceedings. He has to go to Berlin to the Ministry tomorrow. We will probably also get an official car, but we don't know yet where to park it. The shed where we keep the carriages is not secure enough and the good new car will get scratched up. We are thinking of maybe building a small Quonset hut to put it in.

"Yes, I sometimes have to laugh – a lot of honor – but little money! But one must also realize that if you actively assist in the construction of the new Reich, the new country, the New Germany, you do the right thing. It will benefit us and our children in the long run, that we sacrifice our time today. Through Erich's efforts many "bad characters" have already been eliminated from the apparatus that otherwise may have remained in the system and could have caused a lot of damage to a good thing. One sacrifices time and energy now not just for the general public but also for oneself. If the Landesbauernfuehrer values Erich's work as much as he seems to then he won't find anyone else who could do the work as well. And I also believe that Erich is now internally a Nazi and that is very important now. It is not enough to have expertise and efficiency; you have to have the spirit. Otherwise some of Hitler's thoughts and plans would be implemented in practice in a much diluted manner.

"But now I want to ask you for something before I forget. In our woman's club there is a woman who is pregnant and is supposed to deliver in early January. She does not have much money and I wanted to ask you if you want to donate six baby pants for her. We will provide shirts and jackets and also diapers. The girls of the BDM (Bund Deutscher Maedchen – Club of German Girls) are making them. It is too bad that no one in our women's organization has any money. We can't get any assistance from the Winter-Help for our people (PGG and NSBO and Frauensch.? women) because that is only for the poorest of the poor. And the farm-laborers, who are on fixed wages and get bread, only qualify in exceptional cases. But there are many laborer families that have many small children and are very poor. If they belong to a party organization, we jump in to help in these cases; otherwise it is the Help-for-Women organization. But without money, it's bad."

The next-to-last paragraph especially gives explanations and meaning to Erich Spickschen's actions in 1933. But what does it mean when Ursel writes that Erich now also was "internally a Nazi" together with reference that he had ensured that "many bad characters were eliminated from the apparatus"? Ursel's hints remain too vague to draw far-reaching conclusions, especially with regard to the question of what people were considered as having a "bad character". Did she mean they were "deviants" of the Nazis within the party apparatus or did she refer to Nazis that had an evil or sinister character? Did they display corrupt or greedy behavior? It can be assumed with certainty that Erich made every effort to perform his duties as a National Socialist in his political thinking and acting in an ethically correct manner, which even from today's perspective would be in a positive sense. We have to assume that he was probably an "idealistic" Nazi who, for the sake of the "structure" did not betray the party values.

In his final handwritten letter in 1933, sent on November 28 from the railway hotel in Ortelsburg to his mother, Erich provided more interesting information about the tasks that he had taken on and his attitude towards these tasks.

"My Dear Mother!

"I am looking at the stationery here in my room and it reminds me to write a full page to you today because lately you have been neglected by me. I still have a quarter of an hour until the others go to breakfast. Currently, on top of being the county representative for the farmers, I am also in charge of a major department at the Landesbauernschaft (Ministry of Agriculture). It is great to have the trust of my superior but at home I'm just a guest now. However, I am usually at home in the evenings - just not today. We, the State Chairman, my "team leader" (a kind of manager) and the director of the accounting departments, are on an inspection tour of Masuria. We are visiting all 37 district offices. Hopefully we will be done by next week. After this trip I will have learned all about tariffs and lease terms, rural traditions, estate-inheritance laws and will have visited farm women's clubs, agricultural schools, etc. It really is a very interesting position. Hopefully I can do a good job - however the responsibility is great. God knows I'm not a career opportunist but one job after the other is handed over to me. I originally refused this one but then came a direct order from Otto. He said that I should give up the post of

Kreisbauernfuehrer (county representative for the farmers) but I am not going to do that since the work is very rewarding. In September, I am supposed to report for the Reichserbhofgericht, the Estate-Inheritance Court, in Celle against my will. East Prussia demanded to have a representative at the Court. Confirmation has not come yet. What can one do? To go against fate is futile. We do our duty in the position to which we are elected, and ask God's blessing to do it well.

Erich Spickschen

"So far the economy is coming along. Eisenblätter is proving himself. I have given Björkman the supervision of the farms and stables. Poor Ursel has a lot to do and has to make decisions by herself in my absence. I am so grateful to have such a splendidly knowledgeable and capable wife. We are growing closer and closer together. And we really have to start thinking about producing a boy to inherit the estate. Everywhere you look you see hopeful faces. I exchanged my old Putt Putt (clunker car) for an Adler Trumpf convertible. It is a great ride with front wheel drive. I paid for it with an advance from the Kreisbauernschaft. And now I have to go to breakfast. Yesterday we were in Allenstein and Neidenburg, today it is Ortelsburg, Johannesburg - Sensburg. In the evening I'll be at home. A speedy recovery to the dear aunts and best wishes.

To you a kiss from your Erich."

Ursel's letter written on November 17, 1933, confirmed that Erich had to take over numerous functions as the Kreisbauernfuehrer and that he did not totally agree to the extra assigned functions. Working as a farmer on his Woydiethen estate remained the main concern for him and the need to be constantly on the go did not make him happy. Clearly he was not a "career opportunist". At the same time he saw it as his duty to work for the benefit of the public. His readiness to fight for the interest and wellbeing of all the farmers and not only for his own benefit is admirable even though his association with the Nazis has to be critically evaluated.

Erich's mention of a car ("Putt Putt") was already of the utmost importance in the daily life in the country not only in later decades but also in 1933. In a 2009 interview Helga and Karen talked about the purchases of the cars even though they may not have remembered the exact sequence and dates after all the years that have passed.

"It was probably in the early 1930s that Vati fulfilled a dream and bought an old Opel. That was something extraordinary - a bright red car with a black retractable roof. It was called "the Red Menace". When this car went downhill, maybe in a trip to the Teutonic Knights castle Balga at the Frische Haff (Vistula Lagoon), it could reach seventy kilometers/hour. We thought we would die! Uphill it was the reverse and it was with great difficulty that the car managed to go twenty kilometers/hour. This made us very proud. Once in late fall, Vati showed one of our interns a bit of the East Prussian countryside with the Opel. We had frost early that year. They hit a patch of black ice and the car slid into the ditch and was totaled. No one was injured, but the Opel was gone."

Sometime later, a Wanderer was purchased. This is a car company that is long gone and nobody knows of it anymore. It was a very nice car, but we only had it until it was "drafted" in the war. Ingolf explained that the Wanderer was a convertible which the Father only used privately. Later, as Landesbauernfuehrer, he had two official cars. The first one was a Mercedes and the second one was a Horch, made by the Auto Union Company. It was a special treat for the children when they were taken for a ride in the six-seater Horch. There were two folding seats behind the rear seats of this car from which you could look out the back window.

Erich wrote a letter to his mother from Woydiethen on February 11, 1934. Only in the short second paragraph does he talk about farm management issues. The rest of the letter is dedicated to describe a trip and meeting at which the official duties are always combined with fun activities. In the meantime, on July 1, 1933, Erich joined the SA (**SA,** abbreviation of Sturmabteilung "Assault Division"). His enthusiasm for the activities and beliefs of the Nazis seems boundless.

"My Dear Mother!

I just took Ursel to the train. She has to be in Berlin by tomorrow morning to participate in a workshop for the Farmers Women Club, which will be opened by Darré and will last for three days. She left the house and kids with a heavy heart and a lot of sighs. But this seminar is extremely important and will give her a lot of joy later on. I was also supposed to go to Berlin but I have too much to do this week in the province.

"Currently I am in the process of choosing an official. Hopefully I will find the right one for the job. Eisenblätter is not able to run the "store" by himself. Here, one often has to be able to work independently. I also have to hire a new head milkman by April 1. The current one is not up to job and for me to have reliable people working for me is priority one. I'm going to start with seed potatoes this year. Grain yields are not up to par - even when the fields show a lot of promise. Root crops are almost always rewarding.

"Speaking of Berlin, I have to tell you about my last trip. There was a meeting of all department heads in Berlin on December 19 and Darré was one of the speakers in the afternoon. Before that we met with the Reichshauptleiter (T) and State Council named

Reinke, a fabulous guy. He is the son of a farm laborer and he himself was the village blacksmith. He will be the main person I will have to work with in Berlin.

"Exactly one month later the Weimar meeting began. All the East Prussian Kreisbauernfuehrer and Landesbauernfuehrer Otto (28 years old!) traveled by train on the 18th via Allenstein (Olsztyn), Thorn, Posen and Bentschen [Zbąszyń] to Berlin. We wanted to get to know this old German colonization area. The atmosphere was great. We were all in uniform; we are all in the SA. The Polish military on the platforms got big eyes when they looked into the dining car which was filled with only "brown". The activity was quite intense because no alcohol was served in the dining car long before the arrival. We arrived in Berlin at 7:30 in the evening and we all stayed at Schmidt's hotel. Then we all ate dinner together at the Baiernhof after changing into civilian clothes. Then on to the "Vaterland"(?), which got its distinction through us. I was elected the morality commissioner and had to make sure that everyone was in bed soon after midnight. Darré was riding in our train the next morning and, of course, we had to make a good impression. But Otto and I didn't get back to the hotel until just before 2am and that's when I made the bed-check. I was severely criticized by the good men in the morning because I disturbed their beauty sleep. In Weimar we department heads all stayed in the modest Hotel Reichshof. But the people were nice. The beds did not get much use during the conference. Before the opening meeting in the evening I went sightseeing with some comrades in the city, especially the Goethe House. How small and insignificant one feels in front of this man whose genius is exuded here by all things and spaces. One cannot fathom how so much spirit, energy, knowledge and diligence could be enclosed in a human body. How did he manage to divide his time between procuring and gathering together the collections and putting them into order and, on top of his official activities, also creating the great literary works which gave our whole country its character? Not to mention his extensive social activities.

"On the second day at lunch time we toured the castles of Thiefurth and Belvedere with all their treasures. In the former, I was most deeply impressed by the magnificent bust of Goethe, this glorious clarity of craniofacial formation. In Belvedere, the lay-out of the park and buildings with the wonderful view of Weimar is impressive and reminiscent of Kassel-Wilhelmshöhe. In all of Weimar one encounters Goethe memories and some of the details we already knew but only now are combined into a single image. The biggest surprise for me was the unprecedented simplicity of the office and bedroom of the great man. I had expected the opposite. But the feeling has stayed with me despite everything. It may be that one can capture too little because one is not sufficiently familiar with everything and too involved in the present time. But I can't help myself, our leader Adolf Hitler is still greater. And I see this greatness in addition to the tremendous capabilities and absolute purity of character and selflessness.

“But back to the meeting in the Weimar Hall. The impression was overwhelming. You've probably read the excerpts of the speeches. The best and most impressive was the large-scale statesmanlike speech of Darré. We were deeply moved for hours afterwards - probably just because the solid unity of hearts and minds of the entire German Bauernfuehrer were spontaneously expressed.

“The favorite inn of the East Prussians was the Fuerstenkeller (Prince’s cellar), which remains to us all a most pleasant memory. The State Secretaries Backe and Reischle, and Ministry Secretary Dr. Saure (the Erbhofmann, whose family can prove to own the same land Detmold since 1241) can sing a song about our “Gemuetlichkeit”. There are no titles used, only Pg (?) - So I made some interesting acquaintances that are very valuable for me. It might make my work in the office easier because I can contact people by phone on important matters. On the last evening Otto and I went to a wine tasting in Weimar, hosted by the Landesbauernschaft Hessen.”

Erich offered the following explanation about the visit of his friend Dettmering near Kassel:

“I actually want him as the dean of an agricultural high school. But the ownership of the school is not quite clear and I am fighting with the bishop about it. Therefore I will probably have to use him as an editor for rural traditions of the province or somewhere in the Country Women department.

“On January 29, Ursel and I drove to attend “Green Week” and to discuss various issues and negotiate with the different locations.”

Erich Spickschen’s interest and thirst for knowledge is revealed in the effusive praise of Goethe which in his attempted pathos seems somewhat awkward in parts and became almost comical when, in his final evaluation he compares the greatness of Goethe with that of Hitler. In the year 1934 - and probably until 1945 - Erich was convinced not only of the "tremendous skills" but also of the purity and selflessness of the "Fuehrer". It is obvious that Erich’s National Socialism is decisively idealistic with a tendency to exaggerated enthusiasm. His great admiration for Hitler was additionally disclosed in a letter he wrote to his mother on October 21, 1934.

"I have been constantly on the go. Even Sundays I have to work and later (Sunday evening) it's back to Berlin (NAT session) [?]. Tuesday morning I'm back in Königsberg for some important meetings and Wednesday back to Celle. This time I will not be able to visit you all.

“Now to the details. Saturday the 29th I arrived on time at 7:30 pm in Goslar after an insanely hot train ride and got a hotel room in the Achtermann. I immediately met Otto, Reinke, Kanne and Willikens for supper. The other East Prussia representatives arrived later. We then went into town and came back around 11:30 pm. After our return we sat together in the lounge with Darré and his secretaries (Backe, Reischle) and his aides, as well as Meinberg and the Landesbauernfuehrer of Hanover, von Rheden. A little later, Himmler (SS), and Hierl (Labor Service) came down and also Goebbels with his followers, who lived in the same hotel. The latter does not make a particularly sympathetic impression. Black piercing eyes, animated facial expressions, a big mouth. He shook our hands while providing us with a stereotypical friendly smile. Apparently the crowd outside had previously called out for him for hours with great patience. He first looked out from a window, but eventually had to come down to street level.

"We honored guests had free quarters and meals. The next morning at breakfast I wanted to persuade Otto to come with me in one of the cars that were made available to me. He took his time and then did not come to the Kaiserpfalz at all because he did not get his badge. Ursel had forwarded mine to me and it arrived Sunday evening. Nevertheless, I entered with the rest of the delegates. In the Palace we waited quite some time for the Fuehrer. When the Fuehrer greeted us with a handshake, everyone felt the greatness of the moment. This is a wonderful person. Whoever looks into those gorgeous eyes is lost in him forever. I've often seen the Fuehrer before, but here you got a very different impression. None of the previous condescension or of being dealt with on an assembly line was apparent. Everyone had the impression that the Fuehrer was impressed by his personality and was concentrating just on him. One did not feel self-consciousness at all but totally free. This is by no means a supposition but simple fact. The Fuehrer is marked by humanity. His eyes are full of goodness, love and energy at the same time. The best thing was the casual conversation that lasted about half an hour which followed the greetings. He turned away the microphone and just spoke. You clearly felt his common sense. One could tell that even he had fun and was disappointed when Goebbels approached and reminded him that it was time to leave. Have you seen my picture in the Landpost and in the Munich Illustrated # 41? I might enclose the latter if I find it.

"From Goslar we rode in buses as guests of the Fuehrer via Hildesheim to Bückeberg (108 km). I'm glad that I was able to participate in that. SA men stood every few steps along the whole way. Dozens of triumphal garlands were held up. Each of us had a food bag: several sandwiches, apples, pears, one-half of a roast chicken, a bottle each of milk and sparkling water, and not to forget the paper napkin. The view from the rostrum of the Bückeberg over this incredible mass of people and the beautiful Weser valley was immense. We arrived back in Goslar at 10 pm in the evening and at 3:10am in the morning we left for Berlin and then home. Thank God, everyone and everything was well at home.

"Here there is a big to-do about the farm workers question in respect of which we will meet in Berlin tomorrow. The labor leaders are all behind me in the battle with the DAF. We are in the fortunate position of not having to rely on advertising because our membership process is legal, to guild standard.

"Tomorrow the last of the rutabagas are being harvested and then the 30 Morgen have to be plowed. After that the freeze can start! By the way, this time the beet harvest is almost twice as high as that of the rutabagas."

It was with a great deal of pride that Erich reported to his mother that he now has encountered various top Nazi figures and with some of them he had a more or less intimate association. Even though he unreservedly admired Hitler, he expressed his adversity to Joseph Goebbels. This shows that his critical consciousness is not completely suspended. "Great impression" – similar to the Stahlhelm meeting described in the letter of May 9, 1929 – was to him the celebration of the Reich's Thanksgiving (at the same time "Reichsbauerntag"), at the Bückeberg near Hameln. These meetings, which were held annually between 1933 and 1937, together with the yearly National Nazi Party conventions in Nuremberg and the May 1 celebrations in Berlin, were the largest mass gatherings of the National Socialists. On September 30, 1934 about 700,000 people gathered together at the fairground in Bückeberg at noon.

For the years 1935 to 1937 no letters from Erich and Ursula addressed to the mother/mother-in-law were preserved. Therefore other sources such as surviving sound recordings provide reports on life in Woydiethen. These reports are not primarily about political issues or to assess the question of Erich's work in the Landesbauernschaft. Descriptions found in the personal letters of Erich and Ursel and what Ursel later adds from memory are all that remain. Ursel's comments about herself and the Nazi period remain sparse. As mentioned in the introduction, Erich Spickschen's "political" activity is discussed in detail in a separate study. In a 1981 interview, Ursel told Thorlef and Brigitte about her activities and her actions as a Landfrau (a farm wife).

Poultry farming received special attention. Ursel sold breeding eggs, chicks and adult poultry in a poultry market with the help of advertisements in the "Ostpreussische Zeitung" (East Prussian Newspaper). Then the eggs and animals were processed and shipped according to the orders. In an average year Ursel earned an average of 1,000 RM which Ursel emphasized was a lot of money and indispensable to the family's finances.

Additional money came into the house by the apprentices who Ursel trained as teachers or mistresses in different ways (see above the letter of November 17, 1933). During the first year in Woydiethen she had no apprentices. In the second and third year apprentices were slowly hired. Later on there were usually at least four of them in the house, two to train as housekeepers and two who wanted to become agricultural teachers. Apprentices who sought to become teachers had a high school diploma or an associate's degree and paid 50 RM a month. They had to pay this money because they had to get more theoretical training even though they were doing less practical work.

In addition to the apprentices or in their place, young Swedes often came to Woydiethen in order to learn German agriculture and to acquire language skills. Sometimes they did not have to pay anything and sometimes they received a small amount of pocket money. Apprentices and the Swedish boys were put to work in the house, in the garden, on the farm or in the field. Ursel, in her 1981 interview, could not remember many details about the number of apprentices, their payment or the money they paid for room and board. The apprentices and Swedes were a significant help to Woydiethen and many of them became close personal friends.

It should be noted that much (additional) effort was required to deal with these students. For example, the feed for pigs or chickens had to be accurately calculated, compiled and mixed together. Some of the "simple" apprentices were initially not able to distinguish between grams, kilograms and pounds. The lack of knowledge was, as Ursel said, sometimes terrible. In contrast, most of the male apprentices possessed better education. All of the men, no matter if they came from well-to-do families or not, perpetually left piles of dirty clothes to be washed, dried and ironed. Some pieces had to be patched or mended. Ursel remembered that this was a terrible job.

So, when some unknowing outsider thought that life was simple with a lot of staff, they were correct with the "lots of staff" but the simple life part of the idea was entirely wrong. Ursel did not have to constantly worry about the children because she had help. But where the housekeeping was concerned, there was more than enough to do. In the summer, for example, alongside all the normal jobs, large quantities of jam were cooked. The mistress often stood in the kitchen until ten o'clock at night and told the trainees to go to bed. She would say "You don't need to help any more, I'll finish it." However the apprentices would say, "No, we'll stay with you". After the work was done, stories were told and songs were sung and it was all cozy. Life with the many eleven and the young girls was never boring.

From today's perspective, it is amazing how much Ursula Spickschen accomplished since her marriage. The descriptions above show that she was constantly busy with various activities. As she told her grandson Erich Hart, she also worked in the Landesbauernschaft starting in 1935 - in addition to everything else. Since the early thirties she became involved with lectures, presentations and publications in various Landfrauen organizations. She headed the Department of Landfrauen in the Ministry of Agriculture of the Province of East Prussia until early 1945.

The following is an example of Ursel's publishing activities during the mid-1930s:

On May 24 1936 she wrote an article entitled "Thoughts on Hospitality" in the periodical "The German Country Woman; Bi- monthly News for the Woman in the Reichsnährstand" under the heading "The Country Woman in her Home". The article is about the conflict that some hosts feel when they make "many donations to women's organization, public welfare and other charitable institutions on the one hand" but on the other hand they want to generously entertain private guests in the sense of hospitality "of our Nordic ancestors." Ursel calls for generosity in moderation because "hospitality should benefit both parties - guests and hosts – to give them inner enrichment and that can be done even with fried potatoes and homemade sausage."

Ursula Spickschen also belonged to an agricultural housewife club that was founded in 1898 by the East Prussian Gutsfrau Elisabet Boehm. Frau Boehm recognized that many things grow in gardens which cannot be wholly used on the farm and therefore would be suitable for sale. According to this idea Ursel offered eggs for sale in the Baltic Sea spa Rauschen, which was a twelve kilometers journey from her home. Inns, hotels and private people purchased many of the farm products. The eggs, which had to be sold within three days, were sorted according to size, divided into different classifications and were stamped with the quality mark of a bee. Ursel also sold flower bouquets. She was a member and later secretary, of the Housewife Club. When they had to go to a meeting she got a ride from the chairwoman, a Frau Wiegers, in her little rattling car.

Ingolf Spickschen recorded an interview on February 10, 2001 with Doris Vahlbruch, nee Thiesse (1915 - 2010) who was known to everyone as Dodo. She was an apprentice in Woydiethen during the 1930s and the connection to the Spickschens had remained over the last seven decades. Dodo told a strange story whose meaning cannot be completely explained.

During the new construction of the house in Woydiethen, which was built after the fire in the spring of 1933, the chimney builders had done a poor job of laying bricks for the kitchen chimney. The chimney's oven vent functioned poorly which had to be cleaned periodically because a lot of soot formed. This task was to be done by the apprentice who had kitchen duty for that day, and could not be done until late in the evening, or the whole operation would be messed up.

It was the procedure that before the cleaning started the apprentice had to put on an old work coat that had to be long enough to cover the shoes and reach to the floor. Under no circumstances should the sticky soot come into contact with the skin. The wrists of the gown were tied up with rubber bands, the rubber rings used in jar canning. The neck and waist were wrapped tightly with a strip of cloth. So in this disguise the solitary apprentice went to work when everyone else was asleep. All panels of the oven and all the rings had to be lifted out and cleaned. The inside of the oven had to be scraped and brushed to dislodge the large amounts of soot. Two buckets full of soot had to be carried out. The soot was buried in the earth in case it contained toxins.

Dodo told the following, "So here I was almost at midnight, brushing and scraping when I realized that a car pulled up outside. Erich Spickschen was still on the road and a driver brought him home. As far as I know he came from Berlin. An important meeting was held there with many senior party leaders, especially from rural districts. The meeting was probably under the direction of Hermann Goering. The kitchen door opened cautiously but without hesitation. Father Spickschen entered and encountered me in all of my black glory – my face was probably also black. My mouth was stuck open in amazement. As always, he looked great in his whole appearance – but now he wore an SS uniform.

"His driver drove him to Berlin in an SA uniform and now late at night he appeared as an SS officer. He knew that I had to work late in the kitchen and that I could keep a secret. He just said, 'Dodo, don't tell anyone! Got it?' I replied 'Yes'. He walked through the kitchen and quietly closed the door behind him. No one was supposed to know anything about this change but Ursel probably knew. For me it was an experience that impressed me deeply.

"The whole thing took place in 1936 or 1937. I graduated from high school in 1935 and came to Woydiethen after that. Why should no one – at least for a while - learn that Erich Spickschen had become a SS officer? I do not know. I told no one and never talked

Ursula and Maria Spickschen / 1934

to Mother Spickschen about it. Erich never wore the SA uniform after that day. In Berlin, the induction into the SS had been prepared and all Landesbauernfuehrer were inducted into the SS. And I, the little grimy apprentice, had the feeling that something very mysterious had happened."

In the interview with Dodo, Ingolf suspected that his father was made an honorary member of the SS, possibly with the rank of Obersturmbannführer. That Erich Spickschen was invited in January, 1942 to a personal interview with Heinrich Himmler will be discussed in the following section.

Ursula Spickschen remembered additional details about living in Woydiethen. Besides the daily work there were the social obligations and social pleasures. When Ursel and Erich came to Woydiethen it was proper to make official visits to the neighboring estates. Before the First World War, it was also common to hand out your business card when making the initial contact. In the 1920s, all manors and estates had telephones so that a meeting could be arranged via a phone call.

Ursel related:

"We would call a neighbor and say, "Mr. or Mrs. So-and-so, would it be all right if we came for a visit?" "Sure, come next Sunday for coffee". On getting this reply you knew that if they liked you they would ask you to stay for dinner. Our first visit was to the estate owners Wiegers. We did not enjoy our visit because the atmosphere was very stiff. Mrs. Wiegers was super hyper and therefore very assertive in her behavior which made us uncomfortable. After that we visited the Wichmanns. He was the administrator of Kirschappen at that time. The lady of the house was refined and delicate - and soon we were asked to call her "Aunt Greta". He was a solid, genuine, home-grown East Prussian so the two did not fit together very well. Both were immediately welcoming and open-minded. While we were there, to our surprise a distinguished-looking gentleman arrived with a dark-eyed beauty on his arm. As it turned out, it was a Herr von Nathusius, another neighbor, with his girlfriend.

"Immediately, a dramatic story ensued. In our presence, Herr von Nathusius, who was completely unknown to us, began to degrade his wife. Mrs. Wichmann tried to slow him down, but in vain. After he left we learned that he was about to divorce his wife. He ran away with his beauty a few days after we met him. We had also planned to visit the Nathusius but did not dare to do so after that encounter. Six weeks later, I finally phoned Mrs. Nathusius to ask if we could come. "I've waited a long time for you to call!" she said. Apparently she was not distressed about the trouble she had with her husband.

"We made our visits to other neighbors and some developed into closer relationships. We mainly made visits in the winter. In summer and autumn all were fully occupied with the harvest. On Sundays, you were invited for 6:00 in the evening. We were usually greeted with a glass of Likör or a Schnaps. Then at 7:30pm, we were served a three course dinner with wine. Wine was also served with dessert or the gentlemen were offered grog."

Even more important than the visits from neighbors were the visits from relatives who came to Woydiethen.

In an interview in July, 2009 siblings Helga and Karen remembered that their Grandmother Maria, Erich's mother, had a special place. During the thirties she came to Woydiethen each winter for several months. Later when she was older and it got too cold for her, she visited in the summer. Her greatest talent was knitting. She operated the needles without having to look at them. Instead, she had a book open on her lap and read it aloud to the children. She read a lot, which was greatly appreciated because there was often little time for reading.

Grandmother was also very popular with Ursel's apprentices. Every Christmas she gave them knitted woolen mittens as gifts. These gloves had raw twisted sheep's wool knitted into the inside so they were wonderfully warm. According to Helga, she knitted Baumwollhöschen (cotton underwear) for all the grandchildren and their friends. She also knitted braids, colorful ribbons that could be worn on top of buttons of shirts and dresses. Such accessories were her specialty and they were loved by all and have been kept by many as a keepsake. Helga's children grew up with those ribbons.

Whether Grandmother Maria was also loved by Ursel, who had great respect for her, remains unknown. Karen thinks that Grandmother was not directly feisty but she was very assertive and dominant. Maybe she seemed very strict because she was usually serious and did not seem particularly happy. In Vluyn everyone said that she ran the whole store, even during the lifetime of Grandfather Gerhard, who was a happy-go-lucky, cheerful man - unlike her. He maintained personal contact with customers while she ran the business. She was a strong, capable woman who probably found some fault in Ursel's household management style since Ursel was also a strong woman. When Ursel complained that her mother-in-law was constantly finding fault with something, Helga and Karen could not understand it. They felt that their mother was being unfair in her judgment of Grandmother because to them, as children, Grandmother was always so kind.

Ingolf with Grandmother Maria / 1935

Ingolf has particularly vivid memories of the grandmother. First, he confirmed that she was never idle and that as a dutiful Calvinist she was constantly knitting. Because she needed a lot of wool, he would often help her with unraveling skeins into round balls. She read “Peterchens Mondfahrt” (Little Peter’s Moon Ride) or "Struwwelpeter" and other children's books, during which she never forgot about knitting – not even for a moment. The tension between Grandmother and his mother was felt by Ingolf as a child when the children and adults were sitting together at dinner. Sometimes the grandmother would speak Dutch with Erich - and Ursel, who did not understand the language, showed clear displeasure. Ingolf watched this with a certain glee. Ursel spoke several languages, but not Dutch. On the other hand, she spoke Danish with Erich, especially about things that the children should not hear. However speaking Danish also excluded Grandmother from the conversation.

Ingolf believes that the relationship between Grandmother Maria and his mother was basically good but Ursel was always under some pressure when Grandmother was in Woydiethen. Maria was completely ladylike but she was also an assertive woman. Because Erich admired his mother, he considered her almost flawless and untouchable. Ursel was walking on a tight rope, so to speak, and did not feel free again until Grandmother had departed from Woydiethen.

Ingolf had a frightening experience one winter when the snow was deep and he, with his sister Bergild, rode in a sled that was pulled by a pony from Woydiethen through the neighboring school village (Weidehnen) almost to the estate Kirschappen. They were about 2 1/2 miles away from Woydiethen when for some reason the sled tipped over and the pony got lose and ran home. It was icy cold - maybe below -20 degrees C (-5 degrees F) - and the children were forced to walk back to Woydiethen. When they arrived, their faces, hands and feet were almost frozen. The parents were not there, but Grandmother had already missed both of them because the pony had returned to the farm without the sled. Grandmother took her grandchildren into the kitchen, stripped all their clothes off so they were naked and told them, "Now, out into the snow!" It was a shock that Ingolf never forgot. He and Bergild had to rub their face and body with snow. Then they were immediately sent to the bathroom where the bathtub was ready with hot water. The hot water hurt terribly and their skin tingled, but it was a success. Bergild had no damage and Ingolf had a wound on his left ear which later hardened into cartilage.

In the fall of 1935, a crucial event happened for which unfortunately there are no details in letters or in later stories. Only the valuable “Buch der Kindheit” (book of the childhood) exists. On January 20, 1935 the son Ingolf came into the world in Woydiethen. Considering that his father had already written in his letter of November 28, 1933, that Ursel and he will sooner or later have to think about an heir to the Estate it is obvious that the birth of the first son was of the greatest importance. There was an Ideological cult in the Third Reich that was driven by the production of sons, especially the firstborn. The "blood and soil" idea of an "Aryan Hoferben" (Estate Heir) was loaded with all sorts of high expectations, not only in view of his ability as a farmer but also in view of his soldierly qualities. However, whether Erich Spickschen's behavior toward his first son was influenced by the Nazi educational ideas such as indicated in the popular saying, "quick as greyhounds, tough as leather and hard as Krupp steel" is questionable considering his relationship with his children.

Ursel wrote about the early days of her first son in Buch der Kindheit.

"Ingolf was born on Sunday the 20th of January, 1935 in the morning at 4:48am in the clinic of Dr. Abernethy, Giesebrechtstr.7 Königsberg, Pr. Ingolf came down with chickenpox at the age of 14 days.

"He was infected by his big sisters. He came down with the flu at the end of May and has been pale since then. In the winter of 1935/1936 he constantly crawled and ran behind his mother crying, 'Mama, Mama'. The favorite toy is the typewriter. Since December 1935, he always awakes around 5:00 in the morning. He slept very little and was very sensitive to noise. He is orderly and does not like any open doors, cabinets or drawers.

"In the summer of 1936 Ingolf bathed for the first time in the Baltic Sea. He fearlessly jumps into the water and screams when he has to come out. In the summer of 1937, a large wave threw him down and he swallowed a lot of water until he was rescued but he immediately wanted to get back in the water."

The booklet entitled "Das Buch der Kindheit" was published by the Reich's Association of Registrars of Germany by the Berlin-based publisher of Standesamtswesen (registrar's office). In the categories "Additional entries for the 1st Year" and "Other records of the infant's time" Ursel hand wrote the above quote. Because the "guidelines" published with the book the personal notes gained a kind of official or semi-official character. Ursel's notations were not as freely and spontaneously composed as her letters.

There is also a childhood book for daughter Bergild, born on April 20, 1936, which probably originated around the same time as the notations in Ingolf's booklet. First, one can assume that the birth of Bergild was a special surprise for the family in Woydiethen, because she was born on Adolf Hitler's birthday, a date that had very high propaganda value. In the "Buch der Kindheit" Ursula Spickschen provided further information on the birth and early life of Bergild.

"Bergild was born in Königsberg PR, Giesebrechtstr.7, Clinic Dr. Abernethy, on a Monday at 1:30 am. Bergild almost never cried, was always happy (artig) and also healthy. After weaning from the breast she got tonsillitis and flu. In early January, 1937 she again got the flu with colic. Even during her illness, she was always patient and well-behaved. From very early on she looked intelligent, which is probably caused by the clever expression of the eyes. She has a very petite body and is therefore called “Pueppchen” (Little Doll). Ingolf calls her: “Pippi'. Bergild sleeps a lot and she does not seem nervous.

“From the moment that Bergild could walk, her exemplary good behavior was replaced by assertive energy and stubbornness. What Ingolf has, Bergild wants. If she does not get her way, she gets obstinate and screams like a banshee. - Otherwise she is a very cute and friendly child."

During the years between 1935 and 1943, after the births of the first two daughters in 1924 and 1925, Ursel gave birth to six more children. On February 6, 1938 son Udolf was born. What first was a source of great joy for the family soon reversed into growing concern and ended up in misery and pain. Udolf, who was no older than two months, died after a long illness on April 10, 1938. Erich wrote about the sad event five days later, on 15 April.

"My Dear Mother!

Alfred, who was so touching and loving to us these last few weeks that it cannot be expressed in words, just called us again. Such a brother you will not find again in this world. He said that they had visited you today and that you were very sad for us. Dearest Mother, as sad as we are, we have resigned ourselves to the inevitable. Thank God for our four healthy children and now they demand their right for life. The two little ones are a comfort in their ignorance. They were stroking their weeping mother and saying "eia" and Ingolf said, “Mutti, please don’t cry, little brother will come back from heaven!" "But that can’t happen!" "Then the stork will bring a new brother, and he will not die!" Another time he will cry heartbreakingly, “because little brother is dead." Of course he cannot quite understand the idea of it. The two big girls are already quite their mother’s confidants. Once they thought that it would have been better if one of them had died so that we could keep the boy. Then they secretly took a few 20.00 RM bills out of their savings books and put them in our wallets, ‘because we have so much in medical expenses’. They are really touching children of whom we are very proud. No, to lose one of the big children would have been even harder.

“We cremated our little guy yesterday. He looked so cute embedded in the little coffin with daisies, violets and primroses. He looked so peaceful, after the agonizing last days. He probably did not feel much of the pain himself, but it was terrible to watch. The small head was covered in punctures from all the syringes, which we always hoped would heal him. The ceremony yesterday was very nice. The small white coffin was covered with flowers and garlands. Our close associates from the Landesbauernschaft came to the crematorium. Later we had breakfast together at work. The father of one of our new apprentices held the service, a pastor Czygan (German Christian) who spoke about many very beautiful things. The organ played before and afterward. We sang "So nimm denn meine Haende” (Please take my hands) and "Naeher, mein Gott, zu Dir" (Nearer, My God,

At Udolf's Grave / March 1942
Ursel, Thorlef, Runhild, Bergild

to Thee). Today we have requested a burial place in our forest, which we selected a couple of days ago with Berg. Until then, the urn remains in Königsberg.

"Yes, you cannot believe how such a small creature can bind us in his spell, in particular us parents, and put his stamp onto us for the rest of our lives. He was a piece of us which, although he is gone now, is still there. He always draws us to him and can never be forgotten. We are looking forward to the time when we can get the urn. We will give him a nice resting place that will always give us peace in the bustle of the hard times.

"I will be in Berlin for the Fuehrer's birthday where we again will be able to deliver our congratulations to him. Berg is now also M.d.R. [Member of the Reichstag] which makes us very happy. Now, we wish you a very happy Easter.
With love, your Ursel and Erich, along with children.

"PS: Ursel's letter was so completely under the influence of the first great pain and sorrow, because she still firmly believed with an admirable confidence to the last day that there would be some improvement. In addition to this came the unpleasant behavior and the conditions of the "Old Man". Now she is calm and relaxed."

The early death of the second son again brought new suffering to the Spickschen family, especially for the parents. This misfortune was not the last one and the family had to suffer other severe distresses time and again. However, the person described as the "Old Man" (who was just mentioned above) offered some perspectives. In a typewritten letter with the salutation "Dear Children!" sent from Lauenburg / Pomerania on March 25, 1938, Ernst August Dietrich, Ursel's father, started the letter by asking about the well-being of the sick child. "I hope that little Udolf is feeling better." On March 25 there was obviously no indication that Udolf would not live much longer. Ernst August then wrote about himself and reported in great detail about his remarriage. Finally, he assessed the overall political situation and provided a glimpse into the future.

"The accomplishment of the Fuehrer is singular in the history of the world! The ability to defeat ones opponents by extraordinary strength of weapons and armor and without striking a blow has never before been accomplished by a world power. This is Hitler's achievement - victory without war. This principle will soon prevail over Czecho-Slovakia and all other nations that intend to harass the German people. Also, our colonies will be returned to us without a war. Now it is finally understood that we have not lost the (first) world war. The war was supposed to last - according to Barz – for 30 years. I believe that this war will be completed in 1944, if not before, and then the map will look even better for us than now, after the coalition with Austria."

To what extent the view described here by Ernst August Dietrich is typical of the time cannot be checked. In any case, the image presented is interesting because it clearly shows a virtually unlimited view and opinion about the overall political and historical situation of Central Europe. A year and a half before the Second World War, Ernst August believed in the slogan "Victory without War". Looking at this perspective from today's view, his opinion could not be more misguided. It is also revealing to see how Germany at the time is seen as the offended and persecuted innocent. The country did not lose the First World War. It was the wounded innocent country harassed by neighbors and it is again the persecuted innocence. After all, the assumptions after the war began in 1914 was that the war would last another thirty years. Looking back, it has some truth to it. The prediction of the "Old Man" that the war would last until 1944 is not far wrong. The argument that during the years of 1914 and 1945 there was one Great War now finds some advocates.

Articles from newspapers and press releases that were published in the summer of 1938 as well as Erich Spickschen's own writings chronical the sequence of events. It must be said that after five years of National Socialist rule Erich Spickschen as Landesbauernfuehrer and Gauamtsleiter undoubtedly had an impressive track record and not only from his own perspective. He wrote of the occasion of the district party day, which took place in Königsberg from June 16 to 19.

"It is a proud festival that the Nazi Party is holding in the provincial capital showcasing what has become of East Prussia in the five years of Nazi leadership! East Prussia was impoverished and desperate during the time of the badly managed Marxist government and it was by far the most miserable state in our tormented country. We are still poor today but everywhere you look there are flowers and everything grows. The will to build again rises from bold and joyful hearts."

Whether it was justified to speak of a "Marxist slovenly economy" before 1933 is unimportant. Erich Spickschen then gave concrete figures to demonstrate how East Prussian agriculture had improved.

"Since coming to power, the milk collection of 630 million kg was increased to over 1.1 billion kg. The total volume of pigs in East Prussia increased from 1.2 million units to 1.6 million units, even though we had a very bad year for potatoes in 1936. The slaughter of cattle increased from 250,000 to 331,000 units and the slaughter of calves from 182,000 to 254,000. Potato production increased from 2.1 million to 3.1 million tons and the sugar beet harvest from 90,000 tons from an area of 3200 hectares to 233,000 tons from a planted area of 7,000 hectares."

In other publications from the “Gauparteitag” the Landesbauernfuehrer delivered specific figures with which he showed the record growth from year to year. For example -egg collection- was shown as follows: in 1934 - 66,518,555 eggs; in 1935 - 77,628,495 eggs; in 1936 - 90,803,456 eggs and in 1937 - 95,761,976 eggs. The report concluded that

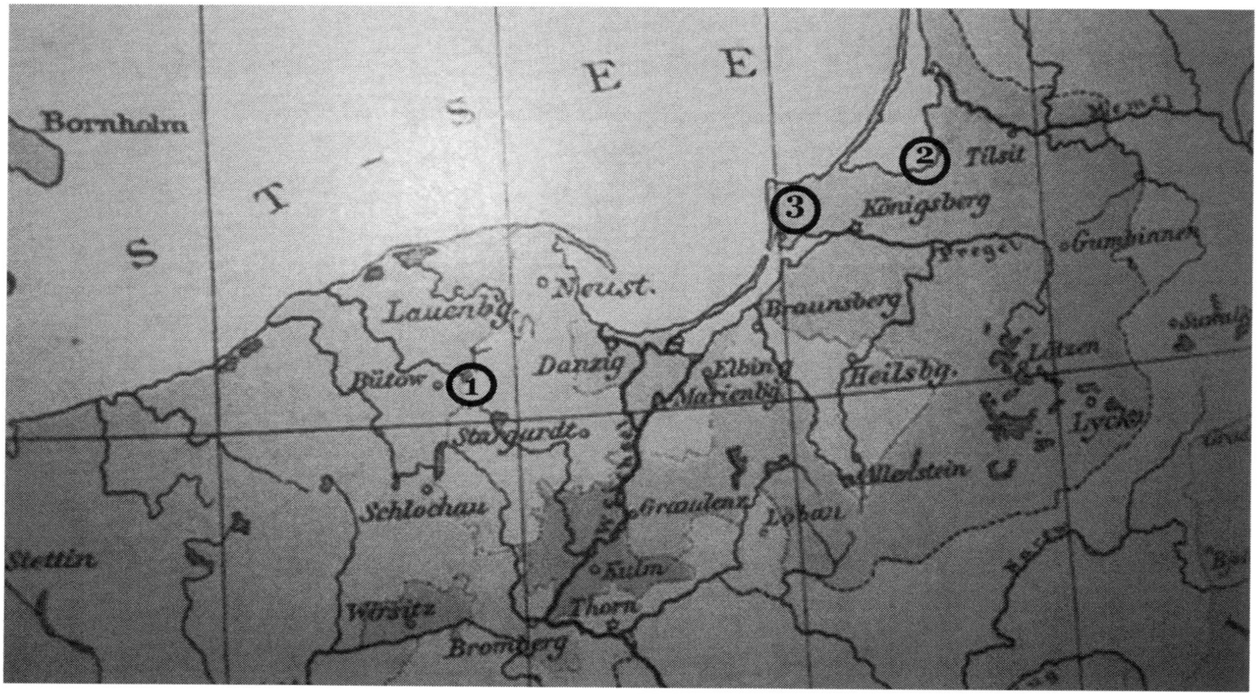

Residences of the Family
1. Bonkow
2. Schwesternhof
3. Woydiethen

"thanks to this constantly increasing egg collection ever greater surplus amounts could be made available to the other provinces."

In all these reports Erich Spickschen did not fail to point out the obstacles and constraints that impeded the progress in East Prussia. For local agriculture, the unfavorable climatic conditions created obstacles every year. In addition, the "remoteness from the market” had an adverse effect. Erich therefore began talking about "freight equalization aid" which Ursel previously mentioned in her 1979 interview.

"Today, the average market distance for the East Prussian products is 600 km and this results in a significant additional burden on East Prussian agriculture despite the government freight subsidy. This is especially true since East Prussia has little industry and the necessary requisite goods are burdened by higher freight rates."

However, according to Erich Spickschen’s reports, the agriculture of East Prussia as a whole made considerable progress since 1933. This was a positive point which the Landesbauernfuehrer could attribute in part to his own ability.

Reichsnährstand

Der Landesbauernführer
Ostpreußen

Blut und Boden

Königsberg Pr., 29. III. 39.
Haus der Landesbauernschaft
Beethovenstraße 24/26
Fernsprecher 24051, 24251
Postscheckkonto: Königsberg Pr. Nr. 3295

Gesch.-Z. ....
Bei Rückantwort stets angeben.

Meine liebe Mutter!

Vielleicht habe ich diese Viertelstunde Ruhe, um dir kurz für deinen lb. Bf. zu danken u. dir etwas zu erzählen. Seit gestern früh bin ich von Hause weg. Hoffentlich haben sie dir den Käse auch gleich zugeschickt. Gestern waren wir zum 2. Mal in Memel, wo ich vorgesehenen Bauernführer zusammenriefe, um ihnen Anweisungen über den Aufbau des Reichsnährstandes dort zu geben. Den armen Kerls rauchte richtig der Kopf, sie machten aber fast durchweg einen guten Eindruck. Für sie ist das ja alles Neuland. Einer meinte, die Sorgen, die sie hätten, wären weniger schlimm als die Angst, ob sie das Neue auch alles schaffen würden. Im Memelland sieht es teilweise trostlos verkommen aus. Seit 1914 also 25 Jahren haben die Leute kaum was aufwenden können in der Wirtschaft. Verfallene Gebäude sieht man überall, totes u. lebendes Inventar fehlt sehr, der Acker ist ausgesogen, weil kein Geld für Kunstdünger da war. Saat fehlt. So habe ich am Tage der

Erich Spickschen had long ago been promoted to a high position when he wrote this 1939 letter. The first line of the printed letter head is in big, bolded letters stating "Reichsnährstand". Below that there is an eagle emblem, swastika and the slogan "blood and soil". To the left is the name of the sender: "The Landesbauernfuehrer of East Prussia". On the right, among other things are the notations: "Königsberg, Pr. (Preussen), home of the Landesbauernschaft, Beethoven Street 24/26".

Erich wrote this handwritten letter on March 29, 1939 in his office in Königsberg, not in Woydiethen. For historical context, the letter was written after an agreement with Lithuania on March 23, 1939 by which German troops entered the Memel region. About a week earlier, on March 15, the Wehrmacht marched into Czechoslovakia.

"My Dear Mother!

Hopefully I will have this quarter of an hour alone in peace to thank you for your dear letter and to tell you something. I have been away from home since yesterday morning. Yesterday we were in Memel for the second time where I met with several Bauernfuehrer (farmers' leaders) to give them instructions about the structure of the Reichsnährstand. The poor guys were overwhelmed (their heads were almost smoking) but almost all of them made a good impression. For them, this is all new territory. One of them said that the concerns that they have now are not as bad as the fear that they would not be able to manage all the new instructions.

"Many areas in the Memel land look bleak and partially decayed. Since 1914, so for 25 years, the people had hardly anything to spend on the economy. Dilapidated buildings can be seen everywhere, machinery and livestock are lacking. The fields are exhausted because they had no money for fertilizer. Seed is not available. So on the "day of liberation" I donated 10,000 zentner (1,100,000 pounds) of crop seed which they gratefully accepted. At 10:00 am in the morning we made the decision; by 1:00pm we had contacted the various agricultural institutes, cooperatives, trade associations and breeders and collected over 100,000 RM; and by 2:00pm the news was broadcasted over the radio. So we were the first to arrive with practical assistance to the Lithuanians on March 22.

"In the afternoon the Gauleiter (Governor) called me. He told me to be in Tilsit the next morning around 7:00am and accompany him to the reception for the Fuehrer. In the evening I celebrated with Dr. Peters of the herd book society until midnight. We got up at 3:30am because we feared that the road to Tilsit would be clogged with military vehicles. Luckily the military vehicles were already at their destination. So we arrived in Tilsit before 6:00am, a drive of 120km. At 7:00am, Frick, Bouhler and Koch arrived by plane where party and labor services were already deployed for their reception. After that we drove with many cars over the Luisen Bridge (about 92 km over very diverse roads) back to Memel where we found out that our car had broken shocks. The enthusiasm of the rural population assembled on side of the road was indescribable. Most people were in worn and tattered clothes and old former infantry soldiers could be seen with their EK (Iron Cross) on their coats. Many of them were weeping with joy. SA, SS and youths, many already in uniform without insignia were there and thousands of swastika flags were waving in the air. The girls just threw flowers into the cars while the SS equestrians were standing guard.

"In Memel there was still some confusion because no one knew exactly when the Fuehrer was to arrive. The meager platform where the Fuehrer was schedule to give his speech was still getting additional preparations. The city was swarmed with people drunk with joy. After a nice breakfast we all rode with Frick, Koch, etc. on a small steam boat through the harbor, past the jetty and into the sea. Many destroyers were already anchored at the port - decent, sleek ships and also minelayers. In line with our keel we met a mine sweeper flotilla, those black devils.

"Out where we anchored a magnificent picture could be seen, including a large fleet of torpedo boat destroyers, cruisers and battleships laying at anchor in a calm sea. I shall never forget this image of mighty power and strength. Fighter, hunter and dive bomber squadrons roared and thundered in the air. Here Germany spoke from its newest north-east pillar, the last ice-free port before Petersburg. On the next day the press release was given that Memel would be developed into a strong naval port. (They are already working on it today.)

"After returning from the sea we strolled a bit through the city and stumbled onto a Lithuanian hotel whose owners had fled. Everything had a warlike appearance. Tables and chairs were partially covered with uniforms. There were half eaten plates, no waiter in sight, garrison and SS personal sat and left. Suddenly a young lieutenant from Adolf Hitler's personal guard in a gray uniform came to us and asked if we wanted to dine with the Reichsführer SS Himmler who already started his meal on the floor above. I had Schumacher, Berg, Adam and Grossman with me. Himmler, as always, was very gracious and friendly and welcomed me and invited us to eat with him. On that occasion I learned that he had landed in Tilsit the previously evening with Daluege who also ate with us. They were at the head of the column and got lost until suddenly they were halted by a Lithuanian guardsman with a drawn rifle while three other Lithuanians ran away and hid under a bridge. He accidentally got to Tauroggen which is almost 3 km inside Lithuania.

"After dinner we went to the harbor where we waited for the Fuehrer. Many boats, all properly aligned, had moored and the navy-blue guys were in parade formation. The Fuehrer arrived at the scheduled minute and he was smart and neatly attired. After the parade walk-by we left for the theater. The masses were raging with excitement; a lot of wet eyes were visible. Many experienced the Fuehrer for the first time. After his speech he gazed for a long time seriously at his beloved and his loving people. Finally a smile spread across his face as he waved several times as if to say – 'we have again accomplished something great and I was again able to make about 100,000 people happy, the world notwithstanding. Our path is sacred and therefore legal and proper!'

"After that we went into one of the rooms of the theater. Most of the people were standing to drink tea and brandy and eat sandwiches while the Fuehrer sat at a table with the Memel "convicts". So we were able to watch him for about one hour. At 4:00pm in the evening the Fuehrer drove through the crowd to the ship and we went home. Many people were standing all along the road with their horses from early morning on, and tens of thousands more in Tilsit, waiting for the Fuehrer. However, it was all in vain and we were very sorry for them. At first it was said that the Fuehrer was going to drive to Tilsit and fly from there. It was probably his intention all along to go back with his fleet.

"So, now you also have a run-down of the day, albeit belatedly. Tonight Ursel will come back at 9:34pm from Franzensbad. Tomorrow I may have to go again to Memel with the Gauleiter, who is expected back from Italy today."

Erich who was clear and relatively sober told his mother about the important historical event of the incorporation of the Memel land into the German Reich. It should be noted that Britain and France regarded this act as an annexation and did not agree with it. It is obvious that Erich was particular fixated on the stature of the "Fuehrer". What he observed and learned from Hitler is in many ways the object of his descriptions. Erich's commitment to the Nazi cause appeared to be due in part to his belief in the person of Adolf Hitler. This man was rumored to have a compelling charisma which is something that today seems to be incomprehensible. Hitler's overwhelming rhetorical skills are not readily understood today but they have been preserved on newsreels for history. Erich's inclination to almost raise Hitler to a kind of God status appears in the letter he wrote his mother on May 5, 1939 from Arys near Konigsberg.

"My Dear Mother!

I have not written to you for a long time even though you must have been eagerly expecting a report about the 20th [of April]. I can only say it was wonderful, a memorable, unforgettable experience. The great thing was the fantastic humor of the Fuehrer. The meeting began with sustained laughter, as the Fuehrer gazed with a smile at the thickness and entire weight of the manuscript in his hand that Schaub had given him. Then his speech was given in all its sharpness, irony and ridicule followed by the more serious issues so that we were all completely caught up in it. Sometimes you felt transported back to ancient times when the Duke rode before his men to challenge the opponent to a duel in order to bring the issue to a decision. He will stand alone in front of his people to spare his people a war. They are all embarrassed that one man dictates the actions of the whole world even though it is they who supposedly have all the money and power. Is it not a great wonder how the mind in this one man triumphs over all physical powers? Where are the priests and rectors who refer to this greatest and most glorious proof of the omnipotence of our Lord God, this greatest miracle of all times? Instead, they bury themselves in phrases and dead dogmas and trinkets. As life pulses and boils and gives birth around them to a grandiose extent which makes us tremble with awe they see nothing and hear nothing and understand nothing and therefore call it sin. Poor wretches!

"I just remembered that I have not told you about the birthday of the Fuehrer. He was in great humor and looked quite well and it seemed that he was more happy than usual about the colorful youth. Not one gray hair can you find on the man's head. He looked like forty also in the Reichstag. It is hard to believe that the Fuehrer to a degree determines the fate of two billion inhabitants of this globe that, when you see him in his great naturalness, such faith and clarity you will never find again. He expressed to the party leaders that in his assessment the political situation is as good as it could be. He is of the opinion that he can give the German people the living space and all that our people need without having to sacrifice a single soldier, 'and that at one hundred percent!'

"Shortly before then, I took the two girls (Helga and Karen) to Heiligengrabe (near Hamburg). The boarding school made a very good impression on me, especially the abbess, a widow in her late forties who is very smart and down-to-earth. I've talked extensively with her."

Runhild Spickschen

The final sentences talk about the education of Erich's daughters Helga and Karen who, then almost fifteen and almost fourteen years old, who were taken to the boarding school at the historic Monastery of Heiligengrabe. In 1939, Armgard v. Alvensleben (1893 - 1970) held the office of abbess. It is interesting that both Armgard v. Alvensleben and her predecessor Elisabeth of Saldern were able to prevent a complete integration of the collegiate school into the National Socialist state education system and knew how to at least partly keep a Christian education orientation in place.

To outsiders it may be particularly revealing what Erich wrote four months before the beginning of World War II about the greatness of Hitler, his guiding principles about habitat (living space) and his alleged desire for peace. Erich's adulations demonstrated his blind faith and total delusions. Such judgments are easy to make today after historical events unfolded. However, it is probably more reasonable to consider the events at the time – before history clarified the picture. In May of 1939, Erich Spickschen could not imagine what would develop in the future of the next five years.

At the end of May, 1939, Runhild, the fourth daughter of the Spickschens, came into the world. As in the case of Bergild, Ursel's notes from the Book of Childhood provide important information.

"Runhild Yrsa was born around 5:35am in the morning on May 31 (a Wednesday) at Dr. Abernethy's clinic in Königsberg Pr, Giesebrechtstr.7. Dr. Abernethy recognized before the actual birth that it was a girl again because of the curly black hair. Runhild was a very friendly, quiet child who ate well, slept a lot and never cried until December 15. From then on she was pretty stubborn, emphatic and often grumbled and seemed to be highly self-willed. She always wants to have company, especially that of the two young siblings who loved her dearly. When she gets her will, she is very amiable and cheerful."

Erich's letters have a special value for the present but not through their objectivity and reasonableness. The extent to which his judgment can be trusted should be critically questioned based on his letter dated May 5, 1939. In the following letter Erich uses the pathos which was typical of the time but hardly acceptable given today's perspective. This time it is not Hitler and his determined world domination but his own father who is in his thoughts. On July 10, 1939 Erich wrote from Woydiethen.

"My Dear Mother!

Tomorrow it will be 50 years since you and Father exchanged wedding rings in order to give us life later on. God's blessing has really rested on your marriage, even if it was not as long as all of us would have liked. Especially today when our nation stands proud and free again after the years of shame and of feared demise we would love to have our dear father still with us. Certainly, we feel as if life rushes by but is not the abundance of our very powerful memories. Does our existence not draw us ever stronger under its spell? The more we are willing to promote teamwork and performance, the greater will be our success and the more we appreciate our own existence. And so the Fuehrer gives every individual part of his strong character and we stand grateful in front of God who gave him to us. Thus we have an irrepressible faith in Germany and our great future.

"So now let us once again turn to the present. Four members of the Danish Government Commission were here and they met with the German Commission in East Prussia. The leader, a kind undersecretary name of Vassard, a Secretary of the Ministry of Agriculture, the agricultural attaché at the Danish embassy in Berlin, whom I have known since 1935, and the director of the Danish National Bank (Reichsbank). All are very nice people who were very surprised to come here to a home where they could speak Danish. Tomorrow is the farewell dinner in the (Blutgericht?). Thursday, about 40 people including us were at the dinner reception at the house of the governor.

“We just got back from Palmnicken where we bathed with the four "big kids" in the glorious sea and it was wonderful. Soon we will drink tea in the garden under the large umbrella and in the evening we will drive briefly to Grubers with the two girls. By the way, our big apple tree here in the front garden was recently uprooted by a storm - too bad. A terrible storm raged 14 days ago in the counties of Lyck and Johannisburg. I visited the area recently with Gruber. In Lyck alone over 100 barns were destroyed by the storm, large areas of woodland were ruined and crops smashed by hail. It looked really bad. But there will be help coming.

“The two big girls arrived home pretty healthy and fresh and feeling comfortable now in Heiligengrabe. You clearly feel the good influence - especially with Hase. It feels so good to have all your little sheep safely home again. Ingolf and Bergild have made great mental and physical progress in recent times. And our “little creature” is already fully human and always tries to smile with its dark blue eyes. The two big girls are quite infatuated with her which earlier prompted Hase to remark “we have to have a shock of seven (children)”. She is a real clown at times, full of funny things and dumb ideas that make us laugh a lot.

Bergild’s Baptism / Woydiethen 1936

"The general situation strongly needs speedy clarification. In September, we will drive only through German territory to Berlin - despite England. Those people disgrace themselves every day as best they can. But later they will not help Poland even a little and the same goes for the Soviets. The stronger right to the future is ours for now; there is nothing that can change it. In today's time of speeds of 500 kilometers or more per hour, only large, strong nations have possibilities of life. The smaller countries fall behind first economically and then their national behavior takes over until they give up. The last unallocated and unused space on the globe happens to be on both sides of the Ural Mountains. So we are still early in our development.

"Given the current situation we now have a lot to do. My appointment to the Advisory Board of the Reichsbank is more an honorary position - not paid. The Gauleiter had suggested me. Work is not connected with it."

It is striking how Erich changes the tone of the letter after the first paragraph with the sentence "So now let us once again turn to the present". It appears that he wrote the first paragraph (regarding his father) as a kind of a chore and that he at least considered it his duty to adequately deal with the anniversary of the death of his father in some form. Then he turns his comments to diverse topics. Next he discusses the idyllic beach and garden of Woydiethen and that it appears that the storm did great damage. The positive development of the children and the clowning around of the second oldest child stand together with the remarks about a friendly meeting with a delegation from Denmark. It should be noted that the "Blutgericht" is a restaurant in Königsberg. Later in the letter Erich definitely reckoned with the possibility of an impending war less than two months before the war actually began and perhaps even knew what lay ahead.

2. The Second World War

Ursel's report to her grandson Erich Hart in 1979 provides a quick, very condensed overview of what happened to the Spickschen family in the period between the beginning of September, 1939 until the end of January, 1945. Please note that Gaga, who is spoken of repeatedly in the report, is Gerda Haase who was the nanny.

"During the peace time of the thirties we were naturally hoping that our situation would continue to get better and better. But then the war started in 1939. Opaps, who was a reserve officer, immediately reported to the army and fought in the Poland campaign. He was with the Riding Insterburg Field Artillery, a type of command that was still active at that time. They had lightweight guns that were pulled by horses. Otherwise, riders and horses, such as the cavalry, were no longer used at the front lines. When the Poland campaign came to an end, Opaps was recalled by the Ministry of Agriculture. East Prussia was considered a province which was very important for its agriculture, and therefore for the general food production of the nation. The Landesbauernfuehrer could not remain an officer of the army since it was his duty to concentrate on and be available to fulfil his civilian job.

"Naturally, I was very relieved that Erich came back from the war unwounded and that he did not have to go back again to the front. But for him, the next few years were not good years - especially with the party organization. He had great difficulties with Gauleiter (governor) Erich Koch, who repeatedly put obstacles in his way. Opaps frequently had to defend people who were not Nazis and who Koch wanted out of the way or who he treated badly because he did not like them. This concerned not only officials at the Landesbauernschaft but also the landowners. It would take too long if I wanted to get into details.

"Initially we hardly felt anything of the war; we were largely spared. No enemy aircraft came our way so we did not have to suffer bombing raids. From 1940 on, the war played out mainly in the western part of Germany. Then however, with the beginning of the war with Russia (in June of 1941), we were getting scared. But when the German armies were advancing rapidly in the east and far away from the East Prussian border, the fear passed. However, fear returned with the terrible winter of 1941/42 when our soldiers froze to death in large numbers. In the spring of 1942, the tide turned again in our favor and we were relieved.

"Of course one wondered why we attacked Russia. It was said that Hitler wanted to provide more living space for the German people. We asked why do we need more space for the Germans? But that was not for us to answer. One reassured oneself by saying that the leaders of our country would know more about the reasons and what sense the whole thing made than we little people.

"Then a year later - in late January or early February of 1943 - there was the terrible setback at Stalingrad. I still remember that I was expecting Astrid at that time. Opaps and I were in Berlin for meetings for a short time. I heard the terrible news on the radio while we stayed with Uncle Hans Spickschen (Opaps younger brother). At that time I had the terrible feeling that the war would now be lost. But apparently there were only a few of us who believed that. When the Germans finally had to completely withdraw from Russia in the summer of 1944, everyone knew that the war would come to a bad end.

"At that time Erich had a lot of trouble with Gauleiter Koch because he had worked out a plan of escape for the East Prussian population. He wanted to announce this plan to the Kreisbauernfuehrern (district farm-leaders), so that they would know exactly which roads the people had to take if they ever had to flee from their villages. Koch did not want the distribution of the plan under any circumstances. He said, "What are you thinking; are you crazy? We shall win this war! If you publish this plan, I'll put you in jail!" But Erich went ahead and gave the plan to Herbert Backe, the Minister "fuer Ernaehrung and Landwirtschaft" (for Food and Agriculture). But he also was not able to prevail in the fight between the government and the party. There were constant battles between these two factions and Herbert Backe did not dare support the plan. When Backe did nothing, we were all stunned. Why would a minister of the country not prevail against a mere Gauleiter (governor)?

"Around Christmas time in 1944, an offensive began in the West. Many hoped that now the tide would turn. I remained skeptical and more than that, I saw completely black. And I was correct. I still remember how we celebrated New Year's Eve with the feeling that it would be our last time in Woydiethen. To celebrate the day, a very large, beautiful salmon was served for dinner. We received it from a gentleman who worked in the fishing cooperative in the harbor of Pillau. We (all apprentices, the children, we parents and Gaga) all sat together and felt a little wistful. As was the custom every New Year's Eve we watched as the Christmas tree candles burned down to the last stubble. Everyone was thoughtful and pensive. Soon after that the bad news came that the Russians had advanced into East Prussia. "

Erich Spickschen / 1939

A large number of letters have been preserved for the years during the Second World War. Since letters and diaries very often show the writer's thoughts and feelings at a particular time, the letters that Erich and Ursel wrote are significant and will in turn be quoted at length. Erich's letter written on September 6, 1939 from Marienburg in West Prussia where he served as a duty officer, discusses the early days of the war with Poland.

"My Dears!

I quickly want to try to send you a short greeting this morning. I am currently on an inspection tour of the occupied territory and yesterday was with the Gauleiter in the town of Graudenz which we had just taken. In the border area almost nothing is destroyed. Even all the fields of rye are still standing. Only in the Ossatal, eastward of Graudenz, many farms and houses are destroyed and are still smoking. All the bridges were blown up, but already replaced by wooden ones. The fortress of Courbiere near Graudenz did not fall until the night before last. Except for the suburbs, Graudenz is not destroyed. The whole population is in the street with dark and frowning faces. The ethnic German population was mostly deported and only approximately 3,000 out of a total 60,000 are still here. In the city, many of the soldiers were in civilian clothes but they gradually came forward because of the threat of being shot to death (there were about 1,000 soldiers in the Graudenz fortress). The population is fanatical. Shortly before our arrival a German soldier got a serious head injury when he was shot through the steel helmet. Women and children kept on shooting from the fortress after the soldiers fled. Everywhere the Pollacks are hiding in the woods and venture out at night. The day before yesterday they cut the throat of three German soldiers. The bitterness is great. The Poles, however, are incredibly brave and dogged. They let the tanks advance, jump on top, lift the slits with their bayonets and start shooting. They are lying dead in swaths like mowed grass. Our losses here in Graudenz are low, but very heavy in Mlawa. Today I will probably get to Soldau [Działdowo].

"Over 1,000 prisoners were taken in Graudenz. Strange figures! On the other bank of the Vistula there are about three divisions still in the corridor that are cut off. Gdingen (Gdynia) is also still holding out, as well as the Westerplatte in Danzig (Gdansk). Our planes are continuously flying over the areas. No, I would not want to be a Pollack. An acquaintance of mine was shot from behind by a wounded Pollack. In my department a battery chief was killed. It is certainly not a military cake walk.

"On Saturday I was with Koch in the districts of Johannesburg and Lyck which still have little or no military protection. But no one fled the area, except for the few Polish occupied border villages. What a fabulous attitude of the population. Hopefully the English will always remain in their rut. It will all be okay. If Japan and Russia will finally come to an agreement, then good night, Britannia. We're all doing well. The poor Africans (O. Guste and T. Martha) are to be pitied. To you all the best. Yours always, Erich."

Erich's short, precise language is that of a soldier to whom the hardships of war were already familiar from the First World War. He reported on only a small section of events that told the story of the overall development that have resulted in the defeat for Poland in a very short time. Although Erich used the derogatory term "Pollack" (in a letter from Ursel dated July 8, 1931 she used the word "pollaksch") the questionable choice of this word might be outweighed by the statement "but the Poles are incredibly brave and dogged". In general the tone of the letter, which narrates the often cruel events and issues of war, is comparatively factual. However, Erich related something which is not entirely clear - resentment among the Germans for the conquered Poles. He also notes that the fighting women did not surrender immediately. All this is written largely without bitterness from the position of the winner who feels himself to be in the right. Subliminally one can certainly feel a great tension.

Nearly two weeks later, on September 18, 1939, Erich wrote a letter from Duczki, a town north-east of Warsaw.

Considering that the distance between Graudenz (Grudziadz) and Warsaw is about 400 km, one gets an idea of the rapidity of the German advance.

"On Thursday I happily got back to my troops just when they were ordered to go to Warsaw that night. You probably have gotten the detailed description from the big girls who I asked to forward the letter to you. Two days ago we moved to a new firing position and shelled the suburbs of Praga where we routed the Poles from various positions. By 15:00pm we set off a barrage aimed at the forts and suburbs of Warsaw in response to the Polish rejection of our surrender request. My observation stand was on top of the water tower of the asylum of Denica [Drewnica?] from where I could see Warsaw. On top of that a thunder storm soon moved over Warsaw. There was one lightning strike followed by another. Soon there was one fire next to the other with black smoke everywhere – a real inferno. An unforgettable gruesome spectacle! During the night the Poles made several counter-attacks which triggered a murderous aircraft artillery, machine-gun fire and flares. But they did not give up. The front ran in zigzags; it was very confusing and you did not know what the situation was. I slept in the open air a few hours.

"In the morning the picture changed very little. Our front line was pushing forward a little and one could perfectly observe it with binoculars. At noon our cavalry brigade was withdrawn 10 km to rest. First we slept ten hours on straw and then for the first time in days were able to take our clothes off. Today we can shower and get fresh clothes - gorgeous. Then for hours we had to inspect our horses. The horses actually have survived the war quite well. On the whole, only the patrols have a hard time all along but the heavy infantry and cavalry only have trouble at river crossings and in forest attacks. Except in Warsaw, we did not face any significant artillery or aircraft. The Poles have fought fabulously in many areas. Fighting the counterinsurgents behind the front line in a kind of Franktireurkrieg (Franktireur war) was devastating because many of the soldiers wore civilian clothes. This cost a large number of villages total destruction and many innocent civilians their lives. You often see sad images of long lines of refugees, or repatriates, who find only ashes. To most of the folks that stayed at home, nothing happened.

The biggest part of what I have seen so far is desolate sand that is good only for forestation. But even farms with good soil look like hell because they have not been farmed correctly. Now the war with Poland will soon be at an end because the Russians marched into Poland yesterday. Now that it happened, my active army duty will be terminated. What will France and England do now? We learn nothing here. I believe that the Fuehrer cannot let England go unpunished. May it be so!"

In fact, the war with Poland ended on October 1, 1939 and the last Polish troops surrendered on October 6. The remark that "the Russians marched into Poland yesterday" meant the occupation of eastern Poland by the Soviets which was part of the secret protocol to the Soviet-German Non-Aggression Pact of August 24, 1939. Accordingly the invasion was carried out on September 17.

In this letter of September 6, Erich sounds somewhat harder, more militaristic and one can even find a certain brutality in Erich's expressions. He sees himself as a fighting soldier who through necessity has to be hard and who frowns upon softness. This is also his conviction as a National Socialist. However, he seems to differ in his style from the fanatical and/or ideologically incited Nazis even though there are no style comparisons here to support this assessment. It can be said that Erich ultimately differed only in nuances of his normal style objectivity and balance that otherwise almost always characterized him.

The following letter, which Erich wrote to his mother almost half a year later on March 12, 1940 from Konigsberg, contrasts drastically with the previous letter. Most of the pre-war letters deal with family or even the weather. The second part of the letter is very interesting.

"At the very beginning I have to prepare you for a big disappointment. The gloves you sent have not yet arrived either in Woydiethen or at the Landesbauernschaft. I am very, very sorry, and I thank you greatly for them. But we did receive that most adorable yellow jacket for Runhild that fits her perfectly and is worn all the time. Right now she caught the chickenpox from Bergild, but is quite cheerful anyway. Bergild was quite sick for a few days and now she looks as if she is covered with raisins. She is full of scabs that had previously been itching terribly. The day before yesterday Karen arrived home. She is seven pounds heavier with red cheeks and looks excellent. The food seems to be really excellent. The main joy is the promotion to sixth grade. Before she said hello to us she had traipsed through all of the stables.

"She traveled here during terrible weather. Yesterday for the first time the Thierenberger train went on strike at minus 10 degrees C (12 degrees F). We are sick and tired of snow. Yesterday on the way to Warnicken the road was impassable near Plinken in several places. We had to go out into the fields. It is said that in Zichenau [Ciechanów] the storm was so bad as if the world were coming to an end. The train from Zichenau, which was to arrive at 23 hrs. (11:00pm) the day before yesterday, still had not gotten there by noon the next day. Today it is thawing with rain coming down. There will be terrible floods, especially in the lower areas where the ice is 1.35m (4ft) to 1.50m (5ft) (meters) thick. It will be a while until that is melted! I have flown several times now because I was in Berlin every week since I came back from Landeck. The Baltic Sea is all pack-ice as far as one can see for miles and miles. We fear very much for the fate of the Dirschauer Vistula Bridge. The Vistula is constantly being kept open by icebreakers and explosions, but one does not know what onslaughts will come from up stream.

"Last Wednesday I had a very lively debate with Erich Koch that lasted about a half hour. When he was getting loud, I got even louder. He demanded three times that I resign, but I refused to do it because it made no sense and I told him what was on my mind. Finally, he quieted down and we were able to talk sensibly. Well, and then he wanted me to team up with him against Berlin. But I am more careful now. The following day I flew to a meeting in the Reichsernaehrungsministerium (National Ministry of Food and Agriculture) and spoke with Darré and Backe who will remain firm against Koch. You have to show him some teeth and then he will become reasonable again. The day before yesterday he drove back to his cold-water spa resort in Wörrishofen for three weeks. I am glad that the air is finally cleared up and he knows where he stands with me. I spoke my mind and gave him my opinion straight on. He will have to look elsewhere to find someone immature enough to be bossed around."

The town of Landeck which is mentioned in the letter is probably Bad Landeck in the county of Glatz (Silesia). Erich and Ursula spent some vacation days there. As to the subject of the dispute with Gauleiter Erich Koch nothing further is mentioned or explained. Nevertheless it is important to see that Erich Spickschen is not afraid to let it come to a vehement, controversial debate. When it was said after the war in the context of the denazification by some individuals that he was a blind follower of the Gauleiter, this letter of March 12, 1940 delivers authentic proof that this assertion cannot be maintained. Ursula had already made it clear in her narrative from 1979 that Erich continuously had trouble with the Gauleiter.

However one must remain aware of the fact that there was nothing special in dealing with Koch when it came to disputes. The ruthless, strong-willed manner of the Gauleiter constantly led to conflicts.

The subject of the letter that Ursel wrote to her mother-in-law on April 30, 1940 from Woydiethen relates to the precarious relationship with her brother-in-law Alfred. In other words, the dilemma between dependence and gratitude was an ongoing issue that came up again and again.

"It helped us a lot that Alfred sent us the 500RM. It was really a nice surprise when suddenly the money letter arrived. We are tremendously grateful to him for that. You can look far and wide to find such a brother. Dear God, when will the time finally come when we can make life easier for him! It is really depressing to always just take and take and God knows it is not for our personal pleasure."

During the war, Alfred Spickschen was able to extend his seed business profitably into Eastern Europe, especially to the Baltic States. So periodically in 1940 he obviously had enough profit to send his brother in East Prussia a sum of money. Again and again, even in later years, he helped out, which filled Ursel and Erich with gratitude, but also brought them embarrassment.

In the following letter which Erich wrote to his mother on August 19, 1940 from Woydiethen, it became clear that he traveled a lot and was often able to combine business with pleasure.

"Yesterday the four of us came back from Poland. Wednesday, Ursel and I drove to Niedersee (Rudczanny) after we had previously visited a "bio-dynamic" managed estate. Thursday we had some work to do in the district of Johannesburg and then swam in the Niedersee. After that we picked up the girls from an estate on the border of Lyck /

Johannesburg where they visited a friend from Heiligengrabe who had stayed with us for several days a few weeks ago. Her name is Rotraut v. Kannewurff and she is a nice, quiet girl. We drank coffee with her mother (widow), a real beauty at 46 years old with five children. Then we headed via Ortelsburg [Szczytno] and Zichenau to Opinogora, the estate where the local staff of the Landesbauernschaft resides. Friday we drove to Płock via Płońsk, where we were served great coffee by the local Kreisbauernfuehrer. We visited a few farms and estates and arrived back in Opinogora at 9:00pm in the evening after we had three flat tires. We bought some crawfish and brought them with us and had a pleasant evening. Gruber and Berg joined us, as well as some other gentlemen. Saturday we inspected the estate that E.K. (Erich Koch) confiscated for his foundation, about 30.000 Morgen (18,533 acres). He is building a huge castle here which is almost finished. The park and courtyard alone are many hundreds of acres. In the evening we played Skat in the light of a kerosene lamp. Yesterday (Sunday) we drove home; it took us five hours. For the two girls it was a great experience for the first time to be in the former Poland. Down south (Poland) they got the last grain in yesterday. Here we found the same old rainy weather as before. So far, we harvested only rye and barley. The green feed is mowed but is germinating with all the rain and the barometer is falling. But the sun has to come back sometime! We are grateful that our family and livestock are healthy.

"It was very interesting for me to visit Denmark once again. One is pleased again and again to see that nice clean little country with its clean looking people. From the air, a gorgeous picture, the whitewashed farmhouses like toys in the green countryside. Here life is still as in peacetime. One only needs stamps to buy coffee, tea and sugar. Cars are mothballed for the most part. The Danes expect a much stronger alignment with Germany. The farmers are already trying to make changes in their crops because they know that they will get no feed from abroad. I came across a lot of congeniality in the rural areas and only in the cities are the people friendlier toward England. But all are hoping that England will soon be defeated because only then will the economy recover quickly.

"Upon my return we immediately went into the bustle of the fair. I could only see part of it because we had to rush from one reception, conference, etc. to the next. The government was mostly represented by Frank. Wednesday and Thursday Darré will arrive with the Hungarian Agriculture Minister Count Teleki. We will drive via Tannenberg, Jaegerhoehe, Trakehnen and Königsberg to the closing ceremonies. You see, variety is guaranteed."

With the defeat of Poland, a territory of northern Mazovia which was situated south of East Prussia, was Germanized and declared "government district Zichenau". In this district the Gauleiter secured huge tracts of land for his Erich Koch Foundation, which encompassed over 30,000 hectares. To be able to do this, 38 villages were completely evacuated and 25 partially evacuated. One thousand families were displaced. The description of the castle that Koch built within this district on the Krasne estate is given in the commentary of a letter that Ursel wrote on August 4, 1941 (see below). The estate Opinogora will be discussed in detail later on.

Following the expansion of East Prussia by the district of Zichenau in October 1939, Erich Spickschen, as Landesbauernfuehrer, had to cope with additional responsibilities. His letter dated August 19, 1940 provides a good understanding of his inspection tour of the Polish territory to get familiar with the situation of the agriculture there. What detailed decisions he had to make in Zichenau and what he actually achieved is not known. However, it should be noted that actions were taken in Zichenau by high-ranking officials of the Nazi occupation regime that were harmful. In the territories that were conquered by the armed forces as was also the case in Zichenau, the property of Polish land owners were expropriated to make room for the settlement of German farmers in wake of the policy to regenerate German peasantry. It is not clear to what extend the Landesbauernschaft was involved in the expropriation measures. No details are known about if and how far the Landesbauernschaft was involved in the action that concerned the deportation and forced labor for agricultural use within Germany.

At the end of the "notes" that Erich Spickschen enclosed in his "Questionnaire for Political Review" dated February 15, 1949, appears this statement:

"As far as my assigned activities and influence in the occupied Polish territory are concerned, I have successfully done everything to raise agriculture output and to increase production. I was able to procure payment for the Polish farmers for their agricultural products according to German prices with the REM (Reich Ministry of Food). Large wetlands were drained, plowed with chain track plows (private companies) and sown with hemp which was followed by the grass seed. I imported several thousand bulls to the area not only from East Prussia but also some were purchased in Denmark. Likewise, rams, boars, sows and piglets were introduced to the territories from East Prussia. Premiums were given for good deliveries (at my request, the REM made 2,000 tons of sugar available, among other things). I was able to prevent the arbitrary expropriation of thousands of small-scale Polish farms which were meant to increase the landholding of Gauleiter Koch. The prevention of expropriation of Polish estates and large farms for German use was beyond my powers."

While the first part of the especially detailed letter that Erich wrote to his mother from Woydiethen on October 23, 1940 was about the children (Runhild at that time was the youngest at almost one and a half years). The second part of the letter pertains to a stay in Berlin where he again meets with Hitler.

"I just got done playing "slide in the bathtub" with Runhildchen which caused great excitement. Of course there were some tears when we had to stop. The little shrimp is too sweet. She does not talk yet but always lets us know what she wants and tries to get her will by other means. She flits through the whole house along walls and furniture, eats all day long and proudly wears her double chin like a matron.

"Bergild and Ingolf are always outside in their coveralls and rubber boots when the weather is not too bad. Today I went with them and the pony over the fields and in the woods. They took turns riding bare back. From time to time one of them would fall off but that did not matter. Both sit up quite well, even at a trot. Ingolf has to brush Minka Erika (their pony) every morning for half an hour - (they came up with that name by merging both proposals). The other day Ingolf was complaining to Nolting, "You know, I'm not going to be in the cavalry, I'll be a pilot". "Why is that?" "Yeah, you know, because I won't have to brush a horse!"

"We have no information from Karen yet as to how she is doing. Her report card was quite tolerable and hopefully this positive development will continue. She is supposed to transfer to the Augusta-Stift (Abbey) in Potsdam after Easter. She wants to get her abitur (high school graduation). She does not know what she wants to do in the future. She is still immature; therefore it is good that she remains at the school for the time being.

"Helga does quite well as an apprentice. According to Miss Greta, she works much faster and better than Karen. She is not very neat in her work but that's not surprising when I think of her father! Housework is quite exhausting for a 16 year old who had been sitting on a school bench for many years. Therefore it is very good that she can do her first practical year at home, although there are some considerations for sending her to a strange household. In November, she will attend the Riding and Driving School in Gotha for four weeks. She really wanted to get her abitur but I was able to dissuade her. To compensate, I promised to send her on various trips and different courses. We really don't want to let her go because we need her. So, that is as far as the youngsters are concerned.

"Ursel and I are doing quite well. Today, the seamstress finished her new dress which she tailored so it would stretch when necessary! Next week Ursel has to go to Berlin for a meeting and I'll be in Zichenau at that time. I was there (in Berlin) eight days ago. I want to tell you about that now. On Sunday the 13th, seven of us (including one woman) rode in a sleeper car. There was one Kreisbauernfuehrer (district) from Memel, two Ortsbauernfuehrer (local), one from Lyck and one from Treuburg who behaved exemplary when the war started. Their villages were evacuated and off and on invaded by the Polish at night. They remained in the villages while local leaders and mayors fled and they took care of the cattle, fed the pigs, etc.

"The sleeper cars were a big deal that no one had experienced so far. In Berlin, we were housed in the princely Fuerstenhof Hotel. After breakfast, a city tour in six buses (there were about 100 active military farmers from the Saarland, Pfalz and Rheinland), was followed by a tour of the Olympic sports field. After that a reception by Darré in the local restaurant was followed by lunch. The whole complex is really worth seeing. Most of all I liked the Dietrich-Eckardt open-air stage which is next to the stadium. From there we went for tea to the Propaganda Ministry where Goebbels spoke quite well. Then back into waiting buses to the German Opera House where "Undine" was playing. The decor was fabulous as well as the artistic performances but I did not care for the opera itself. One of my farmers said, "Well, it's amazing how some people can make a living!" At half past 9:00 in the evening we had dinner in the hotel and then went to the basement for dessert (beer?)! In total we had five and one-half hours of air-raid alerts.

"Tuesday morning was the presentation of the War Merit Cross to the active military farmers by Darré (to the three I mentioned earlier) in the Ernaehrungs-Ministerium (Ministry of Food and Agriculture). At noon we were guests of the city at City Hall. At that time there was a rumor that the Fuehrer would probably not be able to receive us because important military meetings were scheduled. But finally it became true that we all could have this great experience. At 4:00pm in the afternoon we stood in front of our Fuehrer in the Ambassador Room of the Reich Chancellery! He looked wonderful, fresh, with red cheeks and a cheerful, confident air. He radiated an incredible certainty of victory and confidence in the future, which captured us immediately. He spoke to us for about 25 minutes. He told us that since coming to power he has insisted that we make ourselves independent from all foreign countries and produce most raw materials ourselves."

Erich cited Hitler's speech in detail. Among other things Erich wrote,

"He was pleased to announce that the losses in the West are only 50 percent of those from 1870! (Isn't that wonderful?) For him, the war has already been won one hundred percent. One does not understand the English; they run blindly into destruction. A few weeks ago he communicated with them through a third power that he saw no reason for this senseless war and that we wanted nothing from England. But they rejected him again and now they must bear the consequences. We all experienced the air raid shelter during the night. It is good that we now know what city people have to deal with. That was not too bad when you consider that the number of British bombs only accounted for two percent of what German bombers dumped on England. After that he thanked the German farmers, especially the farmers' wives, and we left newly strengthened in the best mood. We went to the Ufa-Palast to see - Jud Suess- a strong, fabulous film."

The war against France, which began on May 10 in 1940, was over one and a half months later on June 25. With the winning by blitzkrieg Hitler reached the zenith of his power. Even though he was able for some time to amass huge territorial gains in the war against Russia, the attack on the Soviet Union, which in retrospect can be said with reasonable certainty, was for Hitler and his policies the beginning of the end. It is not surprising that in his speech in October, 1940 he declared that for him "the war is already won one hundred percent" because to many enemies abroad he seemed to be invincible. As can easily be seen today, most of Hitler's statements that Erich documented in his letters were based on illusions, misperceptions and were often misleading. However Erich continued to have devout admiration for the Fuehrer.

In the following letter, written in Königsberg on March 7, 1941, Erich focused exclusively on a special family event when six days earlier, on March 1, their third son Thorlef was born.

"My Dear Mother!

Tonight I finally find time to describe to you, even if briefly, the recent happy days. I was in Tilsit on Friday, February 28th, where I spoke at a large farmer's convention. I arrived here late in the evening at 23:00 (11:00 pm), changed and started for Woydiethen. The whole week long I tried to be at home at night, even though we did not expect the little one until March 8th. One can never know. Near Fuchsberg a truck was stuck in front of me and an Adler (car) was behind me. Since I knew that the road conditions were always the worst near Kumehnen, I turned around and called Ursel. She was glad to know that I was in Königsberg because Pressmar (the dairy owner) had already told her that all cars were stuck on the road. She called me early around 7:00am and was a little weepy. She said that she was feeling a little strange but it was probably a nervous feeling about being stuck and not being able to get out. Ironically, all the chauffeurs were gone and I did not want to drive alone. I was lucky that it took me only until 8:30am to find Unruh's apartment phone number and we got on the way and arrived in Woydiethen at 10:00am under our own power.

"Ursel was quite petrified and Helga, who had bravely comforted her, now began to cry with joy. I quickly had some breakfast, was unshaven, and almost had to force Ursel, who was rushing through the house to gather everything that could possibly be necessary and/or unnecessary, into the car.

"Then came the wild drive back on the road full of obstacles. Even I felt like I was giving birth soon. Helga also came along to run errands. We finally arrived at the hospital at 12:00 noon where everything was ready. Ursel was taken immediately to the examining room. Helga and I drank a cup of coffee at Abernethy's and waited for Ursel's appearance and the result of the examination. Instead, Abernethy appeared at 13:00 (1:00pm) with the wonderful news - it's a boy! You can hardly imagine the wonderful feeling of happiness that overwhelmed me. It is always a great feeling and one is so happy and grateful to the Creator when all goes well. The little guy weighed just over eight (pounds). Ursel has never lost so little blood so she feels quite well. Only today there was one visitor after the other so she is quite exhausted. One cannot tell people not to come and it's also well-meant. A forest of flowers is in her room and more arrive daily. I always visit Ursel in the evening and she really enjoys the peace, good treatment and food. In the beginning she kept thinking about the things at home, but not now, thank God.

“The little guy is really cute with his shock of bright blond hair and of course, again he is the most beautiful child in the hospital (according to his father)! He looks a lot like Ingolf but it looks like he is not getting enough food yet. It seems like it’s not all milk! Let's hope for improvement. Ingolf and Bergild have been studying the little guy with great enthusiasm. Karen is jumping with joy in her letters. The names Thorlef (heir of Thor), Odmar and Alfred were only finalized on the ride to the hospital! He will make his entrance in Woydiethen the day after tomorrow. It will be a beautiful Sunday afternoon and we’ll play our first game of Skat. We miss you here, dear Mother. One is now very strongly reminded of little Udolf. This little boy is not a substitute and should not be. Even if we don’t understand why his little life had to be wiped out so quickly, he will always remain in our memory. We are happy and grateful with hopefulness that the other six will remain with us. A healthy group of children is still the greatest happiness that the earth can give us.

With Love, your happy Erich."

Among the substantial quantities of documents available to the Spickschen family, this letter is somewhat unusual because only for the birth of Thorlef does an authentic contemporaneous description exists. The authenticity of what Ursel related about the births of Helga and Karen should not to be doubted even though they were described from memory, some of it after an interval of more than fifty years. The births of Bergild and Runhild are documented in each case in the "Book of Childhood".

Erich's letter is also something special in so far as he documented a complete narrative of only the event of the birth. What is written about his work (the farmers’ conference), the traffic situation involving the bogged down truck and no drivers available, is all indirectly related to what Ursel expected in the coming hours. The letter is therefore not the usual typical hodgepodge of topics about family, the weather, agriculture, the work in the Reichsnährstand, the overall political situation, etc. Thus it is timeless and could have been written long before 1933 or after 1945 – anytime when the child was born.

Erich’s usual writing form of constantly changing topics is found again in a letter written on May 16, 1941 in Woydiethen to his mother. The first paragraph is about a political incident which caused a great stir.

"The Hess tragedy seems gradually to fade. It is great that the Fuehrer and our people are resilient and strong enough to quickly get over such a blow. Of course the masses say, "The first one of the top leaders has saved himself". It is incomprehensible that the Fuehrer let this unworldly, idealistic dreamer remain by his side. During the Reichstag meeting Hess looked sick (before his action). His eyes were sunken into his skull and on my ride home I mentioned that he would probably not live much longer in my opinion. The Fuehrer in comparison looked very serious but healthy with red cheeks. It is hard to understand how such a man as Hess does not realize that by his action he does not only slap the

Fuehrer's hand but stab him in the back. He also may have put the lives of thousands of German soldiers at risk. One consolation is that those types of men often take themselves out of the picture.

"We are all quite well, thanks be to God, both personally and medically. Thorlef grows like a weed and weighs 13 pounds. Runhild is gradually talking more and more and is becoming a complete rascal. The "middle kids" are yearning for Omi to come to read stories aloud. All three of them enjoy romping around outside with the neighbor boys Butzer, Erich Fischer and Klaus. Runhild looks comical in her overalls and inherited rubber boots. The foals of Gerda and Marushka are the total joy of the three. If only it would get a little warmer so that we humans and animals could romp full of joy outdoors. So far it is bitterly cold with icy wind and little sun. The rye is dying more and more every day and the pasture has not sprouted yet. Nevertheless, many farmers have taken the livestock out to pasture to feed since there is none left in the barn because of the bad harvest. Everywhere the cattle look pathetic and are hunkered down against the wind. At least we were finished with the planting yesterday. The farms with the heaviest soils are the worst off because they could not sow the winter crops. They now have to plant double the area. But a lot can still change for the better if only a warm rain comes down. Trees and shrubs are also still dormant. This year the East Prussian farmer can rightfully say when asked, "we were shit on!"

On May 10, 1941, Rudolf Hess, -Deputy of the Fuehrer- flew to Scotland. He jumped by parachute from the plane near Glasgow, where he was supposed to pave the way for a German-British compromise. The attempt failed. Hess became an English prisoner of war and was declared insane by the Nazis. Erich's letter shows that this affair caused some excitement.

The three children, who romped around outside and played with their peers from the neighborhood, could only have been Ingolf, Bergild and Runhild. The older sisters, Helga and Karen, are separated from their younger siblings by almost a generation. Between Karen, who was born mid in 1925 and Ingolf who was born early in 1935 there is an age gap of almost ten years. The two older children often were not at home for months at a time, so in the everyday life in Woydiethen the parents had to deal mainly with their younger children.

Of the following three letters from the war year 1941, the first two are particularly rich in content. After that, a gap occurs in the sequence of letters, much like in 1932. No letters are preserved from the year 1942. To understand the following letter typed on a typewriter by Ursel in Woydiethen on August 4, 1941 and addressed to her mother-in-law, it is crucial to remember that on June 22, one and one-half months earlier, the war against the Soviet Union started. A huge German army, which included troops of foreign allies, attacked a country without warning – a country with which the Hitler government had signed a non-aggression pact on August 23-24, 1939. Following their "Blitzkrieg" strategy, the Germans were able to advance far into Russian territory during the first few months of the war. The fear that Ursel said she felt at the beginning of the Russian war - as told in retrospect in 1979 - cannot be noted in her letter.

"From us all the most intimate and best wishes on your birthday. And then I wish that we will already have peace next year. Then you have to get on a plane and come for Erich's birthday and stay until after August 7 so we can celebrate your birthday here. And one of the days the whole family has to come so we can have a family reunion. And if it can't be next year, I'm sure that the year after next we'll have peace again and our plan can be carried out.

"We write so little because there is so much to do. Erich was not here last Sunday and yesterday we were gone with Helga. We were in Krasne to see the Gauleiter with whom Erich had to discuss some business. Koch is being assigned governor of the Ukraine and has big plans. He is a brilliant guy who gets what he wants and is able. In his absence from East Prussia, Erich alone has to manage the whole agriculture organization and marketing. In addition there are new territories which increase the area of the Old Prussia by as much as three-fourth. This area includes Lomza, Bialystok and way down to Brest-Litovsk, Ostrow (formerly General Government), Mariampol up to almost Grodno and the whole curve of the Memel. With all that, the work is almost inhuman, especially because Schumacher and Berg are gone and Gruber is not a big help. He is a good thinker and gives good advice, but never does any work and is therefore inactive. Tomorrow Erich has to drive to Grodno. The head of the Land Commission, who previously managed the agricultural insurance in Zichenau, is also going to the Ukraine so that Erich now also has to bear full responsibility for the management of that whole big new area.

"There was another argument with Gaga, thankfully it is now resolved. It's not worth to get into all that nonsense and gossip here in the letter.

"Thorlef almost weighs 17 pounds now and is always cheerful and happy. He laughs all day and rarely cries. I hope he remains so nice.

"The trip to Opinogora will probably remain one of the most beautiful memories for them (the children). The new environment, the freedom, the large horses which they were allowed to ride - those were all great things. It was a lot of fun for all of us. Even Runhildchen said when we were leaving, "no driving, stay here!" It was wonderful for us to get away on a trip together with the little ones.

"We admired the new house of the Gauleiter in Krasne." (A detailed description of the opulent interiors followed). "It's like living with royalty! But the Koch's look suited to this environment. One does not have the feeling that they don't belong there. The house is the official residence of the president. Hermann (Goering), Himmler, Daluege – they were all guests there already. She (Koch's wife) is running the household fabulously - has only one German and all the other staff is Polish. We were there from 11:00am until 4:00pm.

“If only the war would end! In the district of Mariampol there are supposed be some beautiful estates. Perhaps there is something there for us.

“It must be terrifying indeed for the Russians. Mountains of corpses are piled up (Russians), so that the German soldiers are often unable to shoot at the storming Russians until they are all destroyed.

“It must be bad indeed for you with all the air raids. When the Russians are dealt with, the planes here will be freed up again. Then the British attacks will probably be stopped."

It might make sense to quote Ursel's description of the "castle", as her husband called Koch’s new house in his letter of August, 1940, but this is not the life story of Erich Koch. Instead, a quotation from a biography about the Gauleiter of East Prussia about the building he constructed in the Polish village of Krasne (then District Zichenau) is somewhat revealing. The historian Ralf Meindl writes:

"The property (on the estate Krasne) was renamed “Buchenhof”' (Beech-tree Estate) and was supposed to serve as the Gauleiter’s country estate to regale high-ranking guests to hunts and other amenities. The existing manor house was not very impressive so he had it demolished and then built a much larger castle in its place. He apparently did not have a lot of taste in the exterior design because, according to one guest, the structure, which was completed in October 1940, looked more like a hospital than a residence. Inside, according to the same guest, it was “baroque gorgeous” with too expensive furnishings and impersonal but not really pretentious."

Meindl confirmed that Himmler and Goering had been received there. However more revealing than the confirmation that Meindl provided of Ursel's letter is Ursel’s assessment that Koch is "a brilliant guy who is able and gets things done". Ursel's other remarks on the ability of Koch and his wife clearly conclude that she found nothing wrong with the Gauleiter in August 1941. On the contrary, she rather admired him. It may not be too surprising, however, that in retrospect in 1979 she only highlights that her husband had a lot of trouble with the Gauleiter. Ursel began to thoroughly rethink her position at the latest by the time of her escape from East Prussia in January of 1945 and immediately after that. The contradictions between her views in 1941 and those after the war ended are undeniable. They illustrate unsolvable entanglements but are not appropriate to make moral judgements today.

What role Koch played as Reich’s Commissioner of the conquered territories of Bialystok and Ukraine, is only briefly discussed. He "continued the occupation and racial policies of the Nazi leadership in responsible positions cool and determined, and can thus be characterized as one of the main people responsible for the murder of Jews" – (as written bei Thomas Koehler in 2007). This fact might make it difficult from today's perspective to impartially judge the relationship between Erich Spickschen and the Gauleiter of East Prussia. Ursula’s remark that hopefully a nice estate will be found for the Spickschens in the district of Mariampol seems awkward. However she only confirmed what many dreamed about back then, especially since in the summer 1941 it looked as if Hitler's habitat expansion phantasy was taking concrete shape.

Additional information is needed regarding the place Opinogora and who the nanny Gaga was during the "gap" between the letters of 1941 and 1943. However, it should not go unmentioned that the occupation practices in the district Bialystok must be described as extremely brutal and inhumane from all that is known about it. What has been suggestively told about the conditions in Zichenau was also true to a worse degree for Bialystok. It is important to note once again that nothing is known about the actual tasks of the Landesbauernschaft and the actual activities of the Spickschens. The answer Erich gives in the "Questionnaire about Political Examination" is that he was appointed as commissioner of the REM to elevate the local agriculture from July 1941 to the summer of 1944. His office remained in Königsberg.

The historical context of the next letter that Erich wrote to his mother on August 7, 1941 from Woydiethen is that after the German invasion of Russia, the Baltic States (Lithuania, Latvia and Estonia) that were previously annexed by the USSR, were now under German rule. On July 1, 1941 the Latvian capital of Riga was conquered by the I and XXVI Army Corps.

"The next morning (apparently the baptism of Thorlef and the birthday of Erich were celebrated on the same day) I drove with Horn and Dr.Schwarz to Riga where we quickly found Ortmann and Schumacher who are located there and are working as chiefs of the War Governing Body after a seven hour ride (from Konigsberg). In Lithuania we found the already familiar picture - mostly dilapidated wooden huts but acceptable fields. The country is virtually intact. Only two cities on this road are completely destroyed by the Reds, Tauroggen and Kelme while Schaulen and Mitau (Jelgava) have not suffered. One only sees a few Jews because the Lithuanians themselves got rid of them. The Bolsheviks were able to blow up only three bridges on their hasty flight but they are long passable again. Yeah, the whole road to Riga is already being put in top shape by the OT (Organisation Todt). We counted about around 15 steam rollers, many Russian tanks (two German), trucks, tractors, canons and indefinable iron debris which adorned the ditches along the entire route. German soldiers' graves were seen in greater numbers in only two focal points - before Tauroggen and outside Riga. Lithuania's landscape is very beautiful with lots of woods and groves, especially around the farms. This is in contrast to Poland where they are almost all completely without trees.

"At the Latvian border one has the feeling of arriving in an Old-German country. There are well maintained farms, gardens and walkways and the public buildings more beautiful and tasteful. Mitau has a purely German character. By the way, there are no villages in either country. On the 240 kilometer long road from the German border to Riga there are only seven towns and not one village. The suburb of Riga on this side of the Duena (Daugava) shows a lot of destruction in the vicinity of the bridges. Two decks and the middle arch were blown up on all three bridges. But today, even the trains cross over again. The first sight of the beautiful city Riga from the south shore made one a bit wistful. The beautiful typical German facade looked sad. The Reds burned everything down in the old German neighborhood including the Petri Church and the Schwarzhauperhaus, but not the castle. But anyway, this is only a very small part of Riga with its more than 400,000 inhabitants. The city itself is undamaged by the war except for a few bullet holes, fragment impacts and broken windows. The Reds fled very quickly. Riga is a beautiful city, has a lot of impressive buildings and many magnificent parks, like Dusseldorf. It is a beautiful area. Königsberg is a ridiculously small village in comparison. But the population here is quite downtrodden. The distinct German hatred of a few years ago has disappeared. All at once almost everyone can speak German. The GPU (KGB) was too radical here. From Riga alone they killed or abducted about 20,000 people. Parents were torn apart and separated from their children.

"We visited the GPU house. There are about 400 cells, each about one square meter in size. It's impossible to lie down and at most the room has only for a narrow board to sit on. One could see all kinds of tools with which tortures were performed. Different interrogation rooms, empty except for a desk and spot light. On every desk is a kind of icepick with which the victims were stabbed under the finger nails. I saw wooden helmets with nails on the inside. We found areas with equipment that we did not know how it was used. Then there were different rooms that looked like medical treatment rooms with many drugs and chemicals where the ones who were tortured to unconsciousness (and in a happy paradise of dreams) were brought back. And finally, the 'slaughter room'. In the first section, the victims had to strip naked, then go into the interrogation room one last time. From there a door led to the final stage. Here everything was thickly clad in wood behind which wood shavings were located. Large rubber sheets hung on the walls. The floor tiled with a drain. A mysterious box sits in the middle of the floor. Here the victims were shot in the back of the neck. The bodies were rolled into the rubber sheets and right onto the waiting trucks. Everything was very practical just like at a slaughterhouse. The citizens of Riga can sing a song about the horrors that happened every night between the hours of 11:30pm to 2:30am because only during this time were people picked up.

"No one in Latvia expects to have an independent state again. The economy is picking up more and more. Everything had been nationalized by the Russians. The Latvians had many state-run operations, but now all the businesses are also included. So, in this huge city, only a single department store was open. All others were still taking inventory. Only hairdressers, bakers, some groceries, flower shops and the like were open. Also only a few restaurants were open, mainly for the Germans. Everything was ridiculously cheap, because one ruble is only 10 Pfennigs. A meal costs only 30-40 pennies, a haircut = 20 pennies. Ten cigarettes = 6 pennies. Tram ride = 1 penny. But that must be changed soon, because everything would soon be depleted. Particularly the agriculture would be bled dry and production would quickly suffer. Businesses would no longer be able to replenish their stocks.

"In a lot of places the Reds established Sowchoses (several larger farms which are separated in area but are managed from one place) and Kolchoses (a collection of smaller farms to more than 1,000 acres being run together). Often they placed the more efficient farmers whose own farms were divided up into smaller parcels and giving to the farm workers as managers of such establishments. Thus many of the larger farms are often well managed according to the ability of the manager. I understand that this is often the case inside Russia itself.

"Here everything was still in development. Lithuania, Latvia and Estonia are supposed to become the German Gau Ostland (province of Ostland) under Gauleiter (Hinrich) Lohse of Schleswig-Holstein. The agricultural group will be under State Chairman Mathiesen, who is also from there. At first Koch was supposed to go to Riga and I was supposed to take over the agriculture slot with O[rtmann] and Schum[acher]. However Lohse wanted to have his own man. I would have liked it there, but now there is ample work here in this large area."

Viewed from today's perspective, one sentence of Erich's description of the situation in Lithuania cannot go unnoticed, "You only see a few Jews, because the Lithuanians got rid of them." Looking backward to the gruesome murders of the Lithuanian Jews that had happened shortly after June 22, 1941, there is the depressing question of what Erich Spickschen himself knew of these actions and what his thoughts were. This question cannot be definitely answered even after looking at all available documents and other material. There is no question that Erich was a devoted National Socialist and also a staunch anti-Semite. But how far he condoned and endorsed the persecution and extermination of Jews, about which he must have known a lot, is unclear. Even if there is no documented evidence that he "actively" participated in the murder of the Jews, it can be assumed that in many ways he had knowledge of the situation, given the high position he held. It should also be said that with the position that Erich achieved under the Nazis as Landesbauernfuehrer of East Prussia, it was absolutely impossible for him to lead a completely flawless life.

A report by the commander of Regiment A, Franz Walter Stahlecker (1900 - 1942), as it was reprinted in a documentary called - Schoene Zeiten - (Good Times), edited by Ernst Klee, Willi Dressen and Volker Riess and published in 1988 recounts that the Germans expectation was, "That they strove from the outset that the reliable (Lithuanian) people themselves will participate in the fight against the 'subversive rabble' in their land - in particular the Jews and Communists. Over and above controlling the first spontaneous self-cleansing action one had to make sure that reliable forces were employed to manage the cleanup work and to permanently assist the Security Police."

Furthermore, Stahlecker reported that the "reliable forces" were recruited from "activist national" Lithuanian partisans units. The existing first 300 men of the "auxiliary troop" were "used in appeasement work [sic] not only in Kauen itself, but in many locations throughout Lithuania. They always followed through with their assigned tasks, especially in the preparation and implementation of major "liquidation actions" under the constant supervision of EK [SWAT team] without significant objections."

In particular, the words "control" and "under constant supervision" make it clear that behind the Lithuanian murderers were the commandos of the German security police who pulled the strings. Whether and to what extent Erich Spickschen was aware of these circumstances is not clear. His son Thorlef found it highly unlikely that his father's expression "got rid of them" could have meant "murders" since he wrote this to his Calvinist influenced Dutch mother who would have strongly condemned such actions as murders due to her strict Christian morality. Thorlef said that it was impossible that his father would have mentioned the crimes of the German-Lithuanian side only in one short sentence if he had known about it when on the other hand he extensively discusses the crimes committed by the Russians.

It is remarkable how Erich described his visit to the GPU (KGB) prison in Riga in the letter dated August 7, 1941. It was a terror center and the place of execution for the Soviet Communist State Police. He almost completely refused to give way to his feelings of disgust which would have been understandable and legitimate while describing this criminal institution. Instead, he delivers a factual - documented report of what he saw with his own eyes. Again it is confirmed that he was without doubt, at least in 1941, not opposed to the Nazis, but he was certainly - at least in the letters to his mother – not a Nazi zealot or a fanatic.

Ursula Spickschen's last letter of 1941, written on a typewriter on August 14, discussed the exact description of goods (fabrics, yarn) which had become scarce, and the reflections on Churchill's speech. But this letter made very clear that speculations about the progress and outcome of the war were always a dominant theme.

"On Sunday, three submarine officers who are teachers at the Submarine School in Pillau, visited here. One of them, Schuhart, has the Knight's Cross. It was quite interesting. They told us a lot. They are expecting the war to last about another four years but feel that the air strikes would subside considerably in the West as soon as we are done with the regular troops in Russia. That would free up many of our pilots and anti-aircraft in the East. They are figuring: Russia this year, England next year, year after next the Mediterranean, or vice versa. After that, East Africa and about a year later, peace. But they certainly are not prophets! That would not be good."

In the typical format, forecasts made by these officers for the remainder of the war are not informative because of their obvious absurdity. After all, if the assumption of a four-year duration of the war was true it would only be true because of the rhetoric of their clear expressions of certain victory and an almost uninterrupted megalomania. Only Ursel's reservation, "They are not prophets", reveals that she does not put her implicit faith into the conjectures of the officers.

The following historical perspective relates to this period of the war. In one of the first days of 1942, insightful entries can be found in the service calendar of Heinrich Himmler. On Wednesday, January 21 at 14.00 o'clock (2:00pm) the Reichsführer-SS met with the Landesbauernfuehrer, SS-Oberführer Spickschen for dinner at Friedrichsruh. From 15.00 to 17.00 o'clock (3:00pm to 5:00pm), the two had a meeting. The fact that the meeting took place is already significant enough but it becomes even more remarkable when one considers – as Ingolf pointed out in August, 2009 - that the conversation of the two was interrupted at 15.30 o'clock (3:30pm) by a telephone call. As stated in Himmler's service calendar, SS-Obergruppenführer Reinhard Heydrich called Himmler from Berlin to inform him about the "meeting in Berlin about the Jewish situation". In a notation it is explained, "The day before, the Wannsee Conference, chaired by Heydrich, had taken place in Berlin." This infamous conference is of key importance to the so-called "Final Solution of the Jewish Question". A lot of research has been done about this. But the crucial question is what can be deduced from all this? Can it be that Erich Spickschen knew more about the crimes of the "Final Solution" than can be proven with written or oral documents?

While Thorlef considers it highly unlikely that Himmler discussed the content of Heydrich's call with his father, there is no clear answer possible. In this context it should be noted that Adolf Eichmann, who was in control of the recording clerk , made every effort to make sure "that the protocol had a different tone than the actual discussions in the meeting where words like "killing, elimination and destruction" were used. Again, historians depend on estimates and assumptions regarding this question because there is nothing definite available.

But it can certainly be stated that in 1942 not only Erich but also Ursel hardly had any doubts about the policies and beliefs of the Nazis. This can be recognized, for example, by an extensive article titled: "The Third Summer of the War!" that Gerda Ursula Spickschen published on January 25, 1942 in "Die deutsche Landfrau" (The German Country Woman). The first paragraph of the publication that is dedicated to the slogan 'Endurance' is quoted in full:

"For two and a half years now the German people have been in their most severe struggle for existence of life and death. Fate has already cut deep wounds into many families who have given their fathers, sons and brothers to the cause or those who lost their families through ruthless air attacks on open towns and farms. The restrictions imposed by the war have become increasingly more severe. It is therefore understandable that the end of the war is yearned for by all sections of the population. The German people especially see the fulfillment of their existence in the creation of values and peaceful construction to secure the livelihood for their children and grandchildren. But our enemies, under the leadership of the international Jewry, want to destroy this foundation. They want to kill the hated, industrious German people. This can clearly be seen. The longing for rest and orderly circumstances will not bring us closer to peace, only action will do this. The heroism of our soldiers who provide unlimited sacrifice and the example of our Fuehrer who guides the destiny of our people with a rock hard will and foresight, make it easy for us to see the right path and believe with confidence. All of us must help to achieve the final victory by continuously using our power, each in his own way."

While the following discussion is generally not political it is quite typical for the time, with events that concern, among other things, the nanny Gaga and the Polish estate Opinogora. . Ingolf, born in January 20, 1935 as the oldest son of Erich and Ursula Spickschen, was seven years old in 1942. In 2009, Ingolf reported that he distinctly remembered some of these incidents which occurred about this time (some sooner, some later).

After the war with Russia had begun, Ukrainian farm workers came to Woydiethen, and they taught the seven-or eight-year-old Ingolf how to smoke. They rolled their cigarettes from newspapers and Ingolf soon imitated them. His "crime" led to stern discussions among the adults, which was followed by severe penalties.

Ingolf also stole a bottle of arak and a bottle of cherry brandy from his father's wine cellar. The high-proof arak-brandy could be procured during the war because Indonesia belonged to the region of the war allied with Japan. With his buddies, three children from the village, Ingolf drank the entire bottle of arak and half of the cherry liqueur. After that he had alcohol poisoning, probably because he had smoked while drinking. Apparently he must have been lying in bed for hours raging out of control. His parents were not there (they arrived home the next morning) but his siblings and the household staff tried to calm him down. Even a doctor was called. (Actually, the "doctor" was Helga's friend, who was a medical student and knew how to treat Ingolf who could have died otherwise).

Ingolf had a lot of respect for his father, in fact he worshiped him like a god. Erich had a very serious talk with Ingolf when he found his son conscious after the binge-drinking. He did not punish Ingolf but made him promise never to steal and to smoke again.

A few weeks later, the wife of the milk man appeared before Erich and said, "Mr. Spickschen, my son Klaus" (a playmate of Ingolf's) "is at home and constantly vomiting. When I asked what was wrong he told me that Ingolf had gotten some cigarettes and that they had smoked them and now he is feeling ill." Erich got his son out of bed and interrogated him. Because Ingolf steadfastly denied it, his father got the riding crop. After he had given his son several blows on his rump, Ingolf finally stopped lying. It was the only time that his father hit Ingolf. He admitted that he had stolen several cigarettes (brand name "Stamboul") from the gun cabinet.

Ingolf's memories of his father are mixed. When his father was at home in the evening, which did not occur too often, he settled after dinner in an arm chair in the ladies' parlor. The children jumped on his lap and he told stories of Isegrim, the wolf, or Reineke, the fox. While his mother always told fairy tales his father entertained his kids with animal stories. He also took his oldest out to hunt. Sundays, his father sometimes went off alone with him - sometimes with and sometimes without a rifle.

Around the year 1943, Ingolf had now grown enough for them to go duck hunting. There was a pond in the forest. Once when Erich only nicked a duck and it fell into the pond Ingolf had to get it. When Ingolf had the duck in his hand his father told him how to kill it. "Hold the duck tightly by the neck, hurl it once through the air with a jolt, so that its neck breaks!" Ingolf's comment to this was, "Blessed be what makes us hard. I had a strong aversion to killing but I did not want to disappoint my father. So I did what he wanted and was a good boy. My father was basically soft-hearted but he could also be tough."

Little Ingolf was both passionately and at the same time helplessly fixated on his father, especially with regard to honoring a promise. Father Spickschen told his son, who attended elementary school in Weidehnen, one day, "Tomorrow I'm going to Königsberg, not in the morning at 7:00am, but in the late morning around 10:30am. You should ask your teacher if you can leave school early and be allowed to ride with me." In school, Ingolf immediately asked and received the permission. Recess was at half past ten. The long wait started. Every few minutes he asked his classmates, "Have you seen my father's car?" Nothing. He did not know if the car had already passed or if it would still come? And if it came, would it stop? Recess was over and finally he saw the car, a six-seater Horch, slowly rolling forward. "I stand there, I wave. No reaction. The car keeps rolling forward and then suddenly it stops. This moment is indescribable. For the first time in my life I felt a tremendous exhilaration. Because of me, my father had actually let the chauffer stop the car!"

The building of the Landesbauernschaft in Königsberg, the seat of the highest Board of Agriculture in East Prussia, made a tremendous impression on Ingolf. His father did not only have a large private office but also a regular little apartment with two rooms and a kitchen where meals were eaten. In the office was a gigantic, unique globe with relief on the surface. Ingolf has never seen anything like this since then. On the globe the front line was staked with flags and the clever son, of course, knew plenty about this. Russian city names as Rshev, Wjasma or Smolensk were familiar to him. When he could tell his father about the latest special reports, which he followed continuously, he was praised and complimented.

After the occupation of Poland, the Mazovia Region Zichenau was made part of the Gau East Prussia. In this district the estate Opinogora was made available to the East Prussian Landesbauernschaft. What happened to the original owner, a Polish count, Ursel might have known. But no details have been supplied to the existing Spickschen family members. Perhaps the count was able to go abroad with his family or maybe he was taken to a KZ (concentration camp) or was killed. After the estate was confiscated, it served the Landesbauernschaft as a meeting facility, a reception building and pleasant resort with lots of development opportunities.

Twice, in the summer vacations of 1942 and 1943, Ingolf remembers extended stays in Opinogora as pleasant experiences. As Ursel writes in a letter dated August 4, 1941, several of the Spickschen children had previously visited the estate. Ingolf connects a memory with the "big horses" that Ursel wrote about that in turn says something about his relationship with his father, and thus of himself.

The Polish manager who oversaw Opinogora was a good rider who rode a large, silver-gray stallion. Little Ingolf was allowed to be lifted into the saddle and the manager taught him a little about how to ride. Then once when his parents were present, Ingolf wanted to show off his riding skills. His parents were standing in front of the castle entrance and watched as he rode the proud horse around a round flower bed. Suddenly the horse reared and Ingolf fell out of the saddle but one of his feet was stuck in the stirrup so that he was hanging upside down while the horse continued to gallop around the flower bed dragging Ingolf. Ursel seemed almost to die of fright and Ingolf heard her screams. His head did not touch the ground or the stallion's hooves. Finally, the manager stopped the horse and Ingolf, the fallen rider, was both pitied and admired by everyone.

Ingolf remembered the unique feeling that came over him when everyone felt sorry for him and at the same time were proud of him. He had survived a terrible danger, had mastered it and proved himself in a way as a hero who greatly impressed the adults. Finally, Ingolf commented (in 2009), - "I always had the feeling that I did not quite live up to the expectations of my father."

However, there were less sensational experiences that impressed him. The children had Polish servants. The food was brought up from the kitchen, which was in the basement, to the dining hall on the ground floor using a dumbwaiter. In a special room old engravings hung on the walls. One of them, which depicted Prince Eugen, attracted the attention of the children because they recognized him from a picture in Woydiethen. They also knew the song, "Prince Eugen, the noble knight, hey, that sounded like a thunder storm far out into the Turkish camp ...". If Ingolf and Bergild were not able to play outside in the huge park in bad weather, they extensively contemplated the old engravings.

Ingolf was eight years old in 1943 and much that happened during this time has been firmly impressed on his mind. Ingolf recounted an experience that is not directly related to the biography of his parents but documents some essentials about the situation of the advanced war time. In all probability, Ingolf traveled in the summer of 1943, not 1944, for six to eight weeks to his godmother Martha (his father's sister) and her husband Gustaf, called Uncle Guste. The two no longer lived in East Africa and they came back to Germany during the war and Uncle Guste had taken over the leadership of a former candy factory in Tomaschow (Tomaszów Mazowiecki, a town 55 km southeast of Lodz). Probably on a Sunday Uncle Guste took his little guest with him and said, "Do you want to see the ghetto?" Ingolf did not know what a ghetto was. The uncle probably explained it to him. "Jews once lived here." The former ghetto consisted of a long, cobble-stone clad street. Ingolf can still vividly visualize it. The old houses right and left looked tidy but were deserted. The rooms were full of furniture as if the inhabitants had just left. Whether Ingolf asked, "Where are the people?" and whether Uncle Guste replied something, he does not remember. From then on Ingolf observed that theater scenes look like the streets of Tomaschow.

Later Ingolf learned further details about that ghetto.

Governess Gerda Haase - called Gaga / Bergild's Baptism 1936

"The German government established a ghetto in Tomaszów in December 1940. There, about 16,000 Jews from Tomaszów and surrounding area were crammed into 250 homes. On October 31, 1942 the first deportation of 8,000 Jews began and by November 2, 1942, the ghetto was liquidated. A total of 15,000 Jews were deported to Treblinka where many were shot."

Regarding Gaga, the nanny, for Ingolf certain problematic memories are surfacing in connection with her. The younger siblings, especially Thorlef, remember Gaga, called Gagi by them, quite differently and in a positive way. A disagreement and contradiction becomes evident. The elder (Ingolf) and the younger brother (Thorlef), six years apart, cannot agree on the assessment of Gaga or Gagi. Gaga, as per Ingolf, previously was a nanny for the infamous SS and Police Commander Erich von dem Bach-Zalewski (1899 - 1972). As commander of the SS-Upper-East section in Königsberg, he was transferred to Breslau (Wroclaw) in February 1936, following clashes with Erich Koch. Gaga, who remained in East Prussia, came to the Spickschens.

The relationship between her and Ingolf must have been very difficult over time. Ingolf was not only punished and beaten repeatedly but Gaga was sometimes downright sadistic. While Ingolf forgot some of the incidents, Bergild remembers them. In one such incident, which was almost criminal, Gaga tied Ingolf's feet firmly to the bedposts to beat him in a kind of bastinado.

Bergild actually remembers exactly what went on after Ingolf had done something wrong. She shared a bedroom with him in Woydiethen and their beds were on either side of a window. Gaga tied Ingolf's feet firmly to the posts of his bed and with a riding crop, which was hidden in a laundry basket in the nursery, she beat him on the soles of his feet. Bergild said, "Both of us got hit on the palms of our hands as punishment. If our parents were not home, we - sometimes Ingolf, sometimes I - had to kneel in the corner of a room on hard, dried peas because perhaps we had not told the truth. That was Gaga; she was really sadistic. Ingolf says that she favored me (Bergild), but I have bad memories of her myself. I was punished just as he was. But because he often talked back to her, he probably was punished more often than I was. She hit him on the head with a riding boot. The riding boots had metal guards on the heel. Ingolf's head began to bleed."

Clashes between Gaga and Ingolf also happened because she would at times force him, who was "considered a poor eater" to empty his plate down to the last bite. Ingolf explained that he would sit almost all day at the dinner table. At noon he was still choking on his breakfast and at supper he was trying to finish his noon meal that was not finished yet. To this day, he hears the pebbles rattling against the window when his comrades were calling him to finally come out to play. That there were conflicts with Gaga that demanded mediation efforts also revealed in Ursel's letter dated August 4, 1941.

From Thorlef's perspective, the parents were often faced with the question as to who was the source of tension: the too - naughty Ingolf or the overly strict Gaga.

According to Thorlef, the three youngest siblings loved Gagi very much. "We can only say good and nice things about her. In later years, 1953 and 1954, when she became head nurse at the Hamburg University Hospital, she invited first Runhild, then later me for a week, to take us to the opera and do all kinds of other interesting things with us. These were extraordinary experiences for us. But she must have actually beaten my brother Ingolf with a stick!"

It is not important here why these conflicts happened. While the problems with the "Opinogora complex" probably caused Ursel to dream of a large private estate in the East, Erich was against such dreams according to his children. On May 5, 1943 Ursel sent her mother-in-law a typewritten letter from Woydiethen.

"The pants you knitted for Ingolf made from the different yarn are perfect! During this hard time one cannot be too picky and we have to be glad when the kids have something warm to wear. The wool from the Ukraine which you finally received is also not bad and would be good for the sweater for Thorlef. One will just have to put up with the stiffness and scratchiness of it. It's really not bad. I saw the stockings here that you knitted from that wool. Did you get my letter in which I wrote that the wool that you still have there - if I understood you correctly - you can have spun in Druskieniki? You just have to write to them, "for knitting wool socks, gloves, etc., medium strong, not spun too tightly". The address is: Miss Ruchay, Staatsbad Druskieniki / county Grodno, Bialystok, Frigga house. Value package. To be twisted as loosely as possible!

"The Russians visit East Prussia from time to time. They created havoc in Tilsit. They now installed some flak. The town had no defense and the Russians swept down and shot at everything with machine guns while they were still trying to douse the fires. They no longer dared to attack Königsberg in recent weeks because there is now strong flak. But they have thrown bombs several times in the country and hit farms but so far almost no deaths, thank God. There were very many deaths in Tilsit. They still have not thrown any bombs here in the vicinity and the closest has fallen about 14 km away from us. Near Schlossberg, Gumbinnen and Insterburg they have bombed and shot at the farms. They are also constantly dropping soldiers by parachutes who are supposed to incite the Poles and others here to sabotage. A number have been caught. They carried radio transmitters, lingerie, maps etc., and a lot of money. In Bialystok there are live partisans and bandits; only Druskieniki is still quiet. We have too few soldiers and police. There, the Poles are already our allies and friends against the Belarusian peasants, who often are in cahoots with the partisans.

"The other day a group of 40 soldiers walked into machine gun fire from guerrillas in a meadow in an unsafe area near Bialystok. They were almost out of ammunition when help arrived. A soldier had crawled back to the next village where Polish auxiliary police was stationed. They came and rescued the soldiers and also incurred dead and wounded and battled like the devil against the partisans. Also the Polish village mayors are keeping together with the Germans and are therefore persecuted by the partisans. It's just too bad that we cannot protect the Poles against the vengeance of these partisans. This is why they lose confidence in us. The partisans have already killed many of the village mayors and burned their houses and farms. Now, after drafting so many men, it will hopefully be possible to better fight the partisans because the delivery of goods from the outlying districts gets less and less because partisans steal a lot. On top of that, the German land managers cannot go into some of the areas because they will be killed. In Bialystok it's not bad but in the district of Minsk, which does not belong to Erich's area, it is very bad. There, the partisan rule to 80 percent."

This letter clearly demonstrates in a drastic way that even if the "big" political events are not discussed the general war situation has changed for the worse. A change which commenced with the defeat at Stalingrad in winter 1942/43 and was perceived as such by much of the population. The supply conditions had deteriorated and East Prussia was now attacked by Soviet aircraft. The "partisan nuisance" developed which became a particular problem for the German occupying power in the East. Both in the civilian and the military supply routes, bottlenecks increasingly developed. At no point did Ursel's letter show that she was beginning to doubt her conviction in view of the reported threatening development.

As for the children of the Spickschen family, for the year 1943 there was one event to report, as Ursel already indicated in her 1979 interview. On June 8, 1943, the youngest daughter Astrid was born. Since their son Udolf who was born in 1938 had died at the age of two months, there were now seven children in the family.

More than three months after the birth of Astrid, on September 15, 1943 Erich wrote from Woydiethen:

"My Dear Mother!

Today I finally decided to write to you but you beat me to it. Your letter dated the 10th seems to be a little worrisome. In the meantime you probably heard the Fuehrer's speech and the liberation of Mussolini, which was just described in detail on the radio. You are probably just as excited as we are. I have to say that this development in Italy was to be expected. One finally has the feeling of being delivered from a bad nightmare and having a heavy load lifted. Last year the Italians have cost us both a lot of people and material as well as foreign policy problems, see Balkan Greece, Croatia, etc. Finally the conditions are now clear. The war materials like coal and food supplies that otherwise would have gone to them can now be used for ourselves. For the Anglo-Americans, the walk through Italy will probably not run quite as beautiful and easy as desired. Now this gang has shown itself in all its wretchedness from the king on down. How difficult it must have been for Mussolini. With few exceptions he stands out like a white raven among the black. His goal in life is gone because Italy has crossed itself off the list of great nations. No, for us a fresher and purer air is blowing again. From now on no one can disappoint us but ourselves and that is not even a question. We will keep our front lines steady and pretty soon the villains will pay dearly for any terrorist attacks. The retribution will be terrible but only by that will we be effective. Perhaps the rational minds of mankind will come to their senses in time and stop the insane self-laceration and mutilation of the white Nordic race, which has every reason to stand together for once. Only the Jews are enjoying this. We have to save the heritage gained in thousands of years by our ancestors through countless successes by our species and to secure a decent life for our descendants. Maybe that will happen overnight sometime. How brave, loyal and faithful our soldiers are fighting on all fronts! But overall, the mood at home is confident and attitude is good."

On July 25, 1943 the fascist regime in Italy collapsed "unceremoniously" with the arrest of Mussolini. Marshal Badoglio was appointed the new Prime Minister and stated that he would continue the war on the side of the Germans. However, on September 8 the allies, who had landed in Sicily on July 10 and had conquered the island by August 17, announced an armistice with Italy. Subsequently, German troops occupied Italy, the country they were just allied with and took over the fight with the Allies. On September 12, a German paratrooper unit freed the imprisoned Mussolini who was held in Abruzzi.

Erich's whole letter, especially the final section, makes it clear that the Landesbauernfuehrer, by describing the fight of the German soldiers as "brave, loyal and faithful on all fronts" is also identifying himself in the process. In an interview on December 18, 2009 Thorlef described his father as a man who was a "very idealistic type". Ursel described him repeatedly as an incorrigible optimist. This quality can be confirmed somewhat by his letters from February 1945 (cited below) when the situation in East Prussia was already desperate. It can be called tragic or even unrealistic. In addition, the recently cited letter reveals that Erich was still convinced about the righteousness of the Nazis' anti-Semitic ideas and the superiority of the Nordic race.

As regards his attitude towards Jews and Judaism, however, attention should be paid to the differentiations. Basically, one has to ask whether and to what extent the bias against Jews extends to potential aggressiveness and what is meant by "aggressiveness". Anti-Semitism can occur in many different forms and affect actions in a variety of ways. The many possible varieties of anti-Semitism - which appears to fluctuate with the times – can come in perilous or less hazardous forms. For example, the historian Eckart Conze distinguishes between a "nationalist-racist anti-Semitism" which was characteristic of the Nazis, and an apparently less dangerous anti-Semitism (or general anti-Semitism) practiced by national conservative groups. What does this exactly mean? Is the national-conservative anti-Semitism an abstract form of anti-Semitism? Should the nationalist-racist anti-Semitism be described as Daniel Jonah Goldhagen did as "eliminating" the Jews? Regardless of the wider considerations of anti-Semitism it is probably easier and more sensible to focus on the anti-Semitism of Erich Spickschen.

Erich shared the views of the Nazis as demonstrated by individual remarks in his letters and public statements as far as it concerned a "general" definition of anti-Semitism in the sense that he made "abstract" statements. During a meeting on October 22, 2010, Erich's second oldest daughter Karen explained the attitude and behavior of her father toward Jews as far as it related in particular to the Nazi era by saying that her father personally would never have done any harm to a Jew. The opposite is true. The fact is that Erich stood up decisively for the protection of several Jews, as Thorlef emphasized in another statement. But at the same time, he represented a belief in anti-Semitism which may have been "abstract" or perhaps "idealistic". The back and forth about to what extent he knew about the persecution and extermination of the Jews and possibly approved it cannot finally be solved. To what extent did he go above the "abstract-idealistic" anti-Semitism to an "elimination" anti-Semitism is speculation and cannot be proved.

The question of his father's relationship with the Jews drives his son Ingolf crazy every time he thinks about his own relationship with his father and his father's entanglement with the reality of the Nazi era. Ingolf knows that he will not find a clear answer. Nevertheless he is still looking for answers. Ultimately he probably has only vain hope of finally being able to absolve his father from all guilt. Again in the conversation on August 14, 2009 the problem of Erich's attitude towards the Jews arises. When Ingolf was asked if he had ever noticed as a child in Woydiethen that there was an anti-Semitic attitude by his parents, he explained that there was nothing at all to notice. (It should be noted here that both older sisters remember no anti-Semitic statements by their parents before or during the war.) Per Ingolf, to the contrary Erich was "sometimes very tolerant". The son did not remember an instance concerning a Jew but rather in regards to a declared communist. Despite continued Nazi propaganda against the "evil communists" Erich employed on his farm a communist tractor driver. The son of the tractor driver was Ingolf's constant playmate.

On the other hand, Ingolf came to the conclusion that his father had at least consciously closed his eyes and did not want to see what he needed to see. He had accepted what he could not change. Ursel, who for obvious reasons was anxious to unburden her husband, claimed after the war that he had made sure that not a single concentration camp was built in East Prussia. Ingolf questioned this statement since if this were true, it would prove that Erich knew about the existence of the camps. Thorlef explained that when he was grown up he talked to his mother again and again about the Nazi past of the parents. Never on any such occasions - and this is confirmed by his sisters - was there talk about their father "ensuring that no concentration camp was to be built in East Prussia." Regarding the extermination camps, until the very end Ursel, with all credibility assured everyone that she and Erich were not aware of the systematic killing of the Jews. - The problem remains; it cannot be solved. After his return from Russian captivity Erich Spickschen withdrew into silence and into a sadness that appeared again and again.

According to his sons Ingolf and Thorlef, in 1943 or in the first half of 1944, Erich had to be in contact with representatives of the resistance against Hitler. However, statements to that effect remain indeterminate, contradictory and perhaps also not free from the tendency to subsequently construct connections that on closer look are not very meaningful. Considering the attitude that Erich took in his letters until the end of the war, he remained a devout Nazi. On the other hand all evidence suggests that Christian moral standards always remained valid to him. The principle of justice was never subordinated in a reckless or fanatical way to harm any target of the Nazi party. He never dishonestly procured personal benefits and he remained very much in line with the term later officially used in the denazification process "decent".

If he was approached by middlemen of the resistance, it was clearly linked to his integrity. Ingolf recalls, probably in October 1943 during a visit to Rudczanny (Erich mentioned the place in the letter of August 19, 1940) that his mother said to him that there would be very important visitors coming that day. Later he saw tall figures in uniforms standing in the vestibule. He was introduced to the military men and then he was allowed to go out to play. The men conferred with his father for several hours. After that, Ingolf was done with the subject. After the war, Ingolf asked his mother what the meeting was all about and she replied that the men wanted get an idea if Erich would be willing to get involved in the resistance against Hitler. They were very careful in their discussions because they were not sure of Erich's reactions. After the conversation, they probably came to the conclusion that Erich was still too much a member of the Nazi party. In addition, the middlemen must have realized that it was too risky to draw Erich closer into their confidence since he had to consider the welfare of his large family.

Thorlef's memories are also based on stories from his mother. He brings a different protagonist from Ingolf's into play - Fritz-Dietlof Graf von der Schulenburg (1902 - 1944). That Count Schulenburg and Erich Spickschen knew each other well is confirmed by the letter of January 30, 1948 authored by his wife, Countess Charlotte von der Schulenburg. She wrote that her husband was District Administrator of Fischhausen from 1934-1937. The fact is that from November 20, 1934, Count Schulenburg was the active district administrator in the Office of Fischhausen - a place not far from Woydiethen - as deputy until he was made full administrator in August 1935. In July 1937 he was appointed Vice-President of the Berlin Police.

It is important to briefly list the biography of Count Schulenburg because much of his development and his views have certain parallels to Erich Spickschen's. Though five years older, Erich belonged to the same generation as Schulenburg. The Count became a member of the Nazi Party on February 1, 1932 "with membership number 948,412 in the NSDAP." He remained, to be somewhat simplistic, a convinced National Socialist until the turn of the battle at Stalingrad, that is until the winter of 1942/43. However, per his biographer Ulrich Heinemann, in the summer of 1941 "he seemed to come a good deal closer to the Nazi regime. The attack on the Soviet Union had his full approval." As he wrote in his war diary on August 28, 1941, Schulenburg wanted the "extinction of Bolshevism" and the creation of a "large economic European area with eastern construction areas."

Some years earlier, in March 1938, Schulenburg had "argued for the elimination of Jews from government and civil service". Whether he changed his mind later is beyond our knowledge." As far as Schulenburg being a "militant anti-Semite" said Heinemann, there is "no evidence". These few indications suggest that a sufficient number of points of contact or agreements between Schulenburg and Spickschen any time allowed for a free exchange of ideas. Per Thorlef, after he was no longer in Fischhausen, Schulenburg was in contact with Erich to inquire about any particular situation in East Prussia.

Schulenburg became a resolute opponent of Hitler in the winter of 1942/43. He was a staunch resistance fighter who was involved in the coup plots until July 20, 1944. Above all, he was the crucial main contact among the various resistance groups who used numerous contacts or created them. In "some cases, Schulenburg only refreshed old acquaintanceships". Thorlef remembers that his mother told him that in May or June 1944 Schulenburg made an appointment with his father for a meeting. However, the meeting was canceled. His mother believed that Schulenburg probably decided not to question Erich about a possible willingness to join the resistance because he would then bring Erich into serious conflicts of conscience. The biography of Heinemann makes it apparent that Schulenburg was in East Prussia in May 1944 where he talked with Marion Graefin Dönhoff, Heinrich Graf Lehndorff and Heinrich Graf zu Dohna.

Fritz-Dietlof Graf von der Schulenburg and Erich Spickschen could have been very close to each other in many ways over many years and yet in the end there was a deep trench that divided the way-of-life of the two. Albeit in very different ways, both had to pay with their lives for their beliefs. Count Schulenburg was executed after the failed assassination attempt on Hitler on August 10, 1944. Erich Spickschen, because of a sense of duty, actively defended East Prussia to the final defeat and fell into Russian captivity and afterwards was a sick man who had only a few years left to live.

As already mentioned, there are no private letters available from Ursula and Erich for the year 1944. A nightmarish event that Bergild remembers probably dates to the last year of the war. Eight years old, Bergild was admitted to a hospital in Konigsberg because she had dislocated her right elbow. After she had been there a day she definitely did not want to stay longer. She cried so long and so hard that her father finally got the permission from a senior doctor to take her home. During the night, a few hours after she left, there was a bomb attack on Königsberg and the hospital in which she stayed was severely damaged. A bomb went through the room that Bergild had been in. To this day, she cannot forget the three children who were staying there with her: a quiet girl, a boy with a broken leg and a second boy who happily hopped on his bed because he was waiting for his father to come pick him up. For some reason, the date when his father was to pick him up was postponed.

This micro-history of the Spickschen family provides a contrast of sadness and joy, terror and serenity in the middle of war. This is especially true for kids. Thus, the disaster about which Bergild spoke can go along with the stories told by Ingolf in discussions on October 20 and 29, 2010 about the Christian way of life in Woydiethen. He cannot remember if his parents were regular or irregular churchgoers. Only at family celebrations, such as baptisms, did a pastor appear at the house. But the parents were very adamant that Ingolf and Bergild should go to Sunday school every week to Tante Mielchen, as she was called. Tante Mielchen was the widow of a former worker who lived in one of the houses in Woydiethen. The Spickschens had given her a picture Bible and she owned a song book. She told the biblical stories based on the Bible. In between stories, hymns were sung and all of the verses of these hymns had to be learned by heart by the children. Ingolf remembered that he always looked forward to the hour in Sunday school. The parents made sure that they regularly attended every Sunday at 11:00am. Besides Bergild and Ingolf, three or four workers' children appeared at Tante Mielchen's house.

Every night the parents prayed extensively with their children. There were various prayers in which they prayed for everyone who was important to the parents. It started with "our beloved Fuehrer" and continued with Hermann Goering and then naming all the relatives. Every single member of the large Spickschen family was mentioned. "In all honesty," said Ingolf, "can I state that we received a Christian education in Woydiethen."

The Christmas celebrations every year were for Ingolf something special and exciting. In some details they may have resembled the Vluyner Christmas parties which Tante Martha previously described. But they were celebrated differently in some important aspects.

Ingolf explained that "the Christmas season began with the Sundays of Advent when songs were sung in the afternoon while our mother played the piano in the Damenzimmer (parlor). Candles were burning on the Advent wreath and we were allowed to eat cookies. It was cozy. But I waited with great anticipation for St. Nicholas' Day. That is when Knecht Ruprecht (Santa's helper) appeared, which most of the time was Gaga dressed as him. In the afternoon we children gathered in the hallway in front of the coal furnace. I don't remember if the older sisters or our parents were there. Knecht Ruprecht told me each time what evil deeds I had done in the course of the year and then I got struck with a rod vigorously on my behind.

"But on Christmas Eve, St. Nicholas came. He was a dear friend who did nothing to harm me. Each December 24 morning Bergild and I were sent out into the snow. The Herrenzimmer (my father's office) was being prepared for the fest so we had no access at all and the house was closed for us. We were bored and we tried to spy on what was going on without success. Then the noon meal was served. This was something exciting! There was rice pudding in which an almond was hidden. This was actually not for us children since it was said that whoever found the almond in his or her rice would get engaged the following year. The apprentices, the older sisters and the inspector looked forward to this every year with great enthusiasm.

"Afterward we kids had to go to bed for an afternoon nap just as we had to do very often throughout the year. When we were done with our nap we were allowed to dress in our festive clothes. Christmas Eve started with a big meal. A large wooded chandelier full of gleaming candles hung above the table. For the main course there was blue carp and a specially prepared plum pudding for dessert. The flambé was provided by the lighting of rum or arrack which was poured into half of a goose egg. It was then lowered into the center of the pudding. In addition, wine cream sauce was served.

"After the meal, Christmas songs were sung again in the parlor for a while. At the end, we always sang the song "Silent Night, Holy Night" and thereafter my father read the Christmas story aloud from the Bible. Suddenly there was a tingle of delicate bells from outside. My father slipped silently out of the room and we were told, "The Christ Child is coming. Father is opening the door for Him." But he actually lit the candles on the Christmas tree in the Herrenzimmer. After a few minutes he came back into the Damenzimmer. Mother finished playing the piano, the double door was opened and with shining eyes we saw the Christmas tree. The gifts were placed around the tree. However, I was mostly disappointed because I often received a gift such as a building set which I could not do much with. In 1944, on the last Christmas Eve, I received a small metal gun into which you could push a cork made of rubber and then shoot it. I loved this toy very much. I took it with me on our flight. Unfortunately, it got lost somewhere."

[THE FOLLOWING IS NOT IN THE GERMAN VERSION.]

Bergild has slightly different memories of the Christmas season:

"St. Nicolaus' Day is the night of December 5-6. We wrote our Christmas wish list during the prior week, placed one of our shoes in front of the bedroom door and placed the list in the shoe. St. Nicolaus came over night on his winged white stallion to pick up the list. If we were good during the year, he would leave us cookies and maybe an apple in the shoe. If we were bad we got coal and a switch made from brush. This was Ingolf's lot most of the time. I don't remember Knecht Ruprecht, the one who Ingolf said spanked him.

"After our nap on Christmas Eve, when it was already dark (around 4:00pm), the Weihnachtsmann (Santa Claus) came to our playroom carrying a big burlap sack on his back. We had to learn a new poem each year and recite it to the Weihnachtsmann, who would then give us a small gift out of the sack. If you forgot your poem, you might get a little swat from him with his switch.

"The festively decorated dining table not only had the large chandelier but each person also had his or her own little candle holder in front of the plate, so that the whole room was in a festive glow.

"When the large double door from the Damenzimmer to the Herrenzimmer was opened you looked directly at the Christmas tree ablaze with candles. It stood at the end of the room which was at least 20 feet if not 30 feet long. I still swear that I saw the Christkind (the Christ child), who lit the candles, float once around the tree and then out of the door which was on the left side of the tree. As far as I remember, the gifts were not stacked around the tree. There were tables set up on either side of the tree and we each had a space separated with greens. Everyone had a Christmas plate on his space that was filled with cookies, nuts and one orange - the only one we would get each year."

Some historical perspective to the three letters that Erich wrote in February 1945 that evidenced the radically changed circumstances of the time. It is appropriate to consider some accusatory statements that show how the competing government appointees in East Prussia under the Nazis inevitably were associated with conflicts and problems. Egbert Otto, who was the Landesbauernfuehrer of East Prussian until the end of August 1934, took a hostile attitude toward Erich Spickschen after the war. As confirmed by several previous letters Erich Spickschen, according to the historian Ralf Meindl, might be considered to be a "follower" of Otto well into the year 1934. What the relationship of the two was during the following years remains unclear. Around 1950, during the denazification process, Otto tried very hard to discredit his successor as Landesbauernfuehrer and his comments were specifically directed toward Erich Spickschen and his past. To show the alleged compliance of Spickschen against Gauleiter

Spickschen Family 1941
Front Row: Ursula, Thorlef, Bergild, Runhild, Erich
Back Row: Karen, Ingolf, Helga

Koch, he inferred that the phrase "dumb like Spickschen" was in general circulation in East Prussia.

Ingolf also speaks of this phrase, but in a different context. When long after the war Ingolf heard from an acquaintance, a former Kreisbauernfuehrer named Henry Luke, that his father had been called in Nazi circles, "the stupid Spickschen" he was angry. He questioned why? Luke replied, "Yes, your father was a bloody idealist who always saw the good and nothing else." Ingolf later discovered confirmation of these characteristics in the denazification documents. Like his brother Thorlef, he concluded that his father must have really been an idealist but in his 2009 conversation, he added that this idealism remains baffling. Erich Spickschen was a prudent thinker. His humanist education that characterized him since his high school days was extremely important to him. He had a strong sense of justice, was sensitive, felt pity for others, but he could also be strict when it was necessary. Therefore a final judgment cannot be made. At least in the end if he was designated by the Nazis as "the stupid Spickschen" it should ultimately be considered an honor.

In her retrospective interview in 1979, Ursel previously reported that her husband was hit with harsh rejections by Gauleiter Koch in the second half of 1944 when he submitted the evacuation plans he had worked out for the East Prussian population because of their close proximity to the Russian front. Ingolf reported (in 2009) that the attempt by Gauleiter Koch to depose his father as Landesbauernfuehrer was only partially successful. However, the backing that his father received from the Minister of Agriculture Herbert Backe was weak. Erich Spickschen's scope of activity remained limited and in the late fall of 1944 he felt compelled to get more involved with the organization of the National Guard. In the meantime, the Russians had advanced into the Memel-land and East Prussia.

The following letters were written by Erich in February, 1945 against the backdrop of a war situation, which was becoming dramatically worse for the Germans. The war was lost. At the end of January, Ursel had to flee to the West with the children and house staff. However, Erich remained in Königsberg because he saw it as his duty to continue to defend the city. He did not, like most other government and party leaders, take off to save his own skin. This steadfastness, that is somehow desperate and tragic in itself, did not break Erich immediately. But becoming a Russian prisoner of war for over 3 years greatly contributed to his ultimate death a short decade later. Erich's crucial decision to separate himself from his family - a decision of life and death that Erich made in support of the common good as he understood it - makes it hard for an outsider to judge him in any sense.

On February 8, 1945, Ursel received a Feldpostbrief (military field post letter) from Erich that did not indicate a location. It was her birthday and she was affectionately called "Muschchen". The letter contained many abbreviations and some passages are in the Danish language. It cannot be determined if Erich used these subterfuges, which perhaps

O.U. 8.II.45.

Mein lieber Munsch'chen!

Heute ist nun Dein Geburtstag, der 2. seit unserer Verlobung, den wir nicht zusammen feiern. Aber dennoch bin ich bei Dir auf Schritt und Tritt. So oft ich nachts wach werde, mein 1. Gedanke gilt Dir mein lieber, guter Tier. Ich wünsche Dir so von Herzen alles Gute u. Beste, das sich garnicht auf Papier bringen lässt. Vor allem bleibt Ihr 8 schön gesund, dass wir uns zusammen recht bald eine neue Zukunft bauen können. Unsere wirklich grosse Liebe macht mich so stark, froh u. glücklich trotz allem. Ich glaube fest an ein gutes Ende, wenn Du vielleicht auch auf den „nicht dazugelernten" Optimisten schimpfst. Vor mir steht die Erwartungsfreude des einmal kommenden Wiedersehens. Wir beide sind noch rüstig genug, um weiter gemeinsam das schwere Schicksal zu meistern, Du auch. Ich habe Dich bewundert gerade in der letzten harten Zeit und bin Dir so dankbar dafür. Bei solcher Mutter werden auch die Kinder rechtes leben können.

Nun wirst Du böse sein auf Deinen ungehorsamen Urops ob ~~Deines~~ Werdegangs. Sonntag ging's im Nachtflug nach K. aufgesetzt auf gewöhnlichem Gelände ohne Beleuchtung. Hier wurde mir am nächsten Tage vom 4a. im Auftr. K's ein 45 Bttr. übertragen, das ich gestern übernahm. Vi ligger hos Gartner prof. der kved nok, i anden Linie, det er temlig rolig her! Driften løber forløbig videre, Kun og flere Flygtn. er her; Bar paa den anden Side Kanalen er stadig væk Trommelild og Kamp. Det gaar der om Tilgang til Romanowski's Kreds. En gang er det aaben, engang lukket. Her er stærk Forsvar i Byen og Fødevarer nok. Frontendløber mest foran Ringchaussé. Kun i Østen gaar det til Massows Fædres Gods (dengang) + vor Kreds er Fjenden tvungen tilbage i tin. Hegdek.-Gang. Die Bevölkerung klagt. Hält sich fabelhaft. Die Kinder laufen vergnügt in den Strassen umher. Ab u. zu kommt mal ein Tiefflieger, dann fallen Bomben auch mal einz. Art. Feuer. Auf jeden Fall sind meine Männer lieber hier als in der Stadt. Jeg haaber stærkt at

Ich bin ganz bei und in Dir, mein Lieb. Bald schreib ich wieder. Also nochmals guten Wind im neuen Lebensjahr, der uns bessern Zeiten zutreibt. Innige Küsse Dein Erich.
Schreibt mal an Mutter und Alfred. Ist Martha nun bei Euch? Dann grüsst sie schön.

only his wife understood, due to censorship or whether he just wanted to correspond with Ursel in a very personal manner.

"The people of Königsberg are fabulous. The children are happily hopping around in the streets. From time to time a low-flying aircraft comes along, drops bombs, and sometimes we get a single artillery shot. In any case, my men like it better here than in the city. Now we are anxiously waiting for the big attack from our side that must come sometime. You know, my good Muschchen, I am actually glad and thankful that I have a task again. The last few months have been terrible for me. My men seem to be very capable and are very eager. My battalion stenographer is a lawyer named Strauss who volunteered at age 62. The people that are here from the Military make a good impression. I believe the cooperation will be very good. Tactically, there are two battalions under my company, one of which is led by our state forest master Neumann who I visited for lunch. A while ago I was at M's for tea and listened to the military news about the annihilation of the Combat Team at Thierenberg. I wonder how our farm is doing.

"Now, good night, my sweet little ones, you who are my most precious possession even if you are sometimes a little naughty. Has Ingolf had his hunting lessons yet? Does Bergild still holler "gaar nicht" (not at all)? Little mother Runhild will hopefully not be bullied too much by rowdy little Thorlef. How many stories do you have to tell every day? The fewest demands will be made by Astridchen, but she will be the one who will be the greatest knowledge seeker of them all. Does she miss her "Wati"? Now to the big two. Does Helga help with the household and Hase with the garden and other outside chores? The tears of those two dear ones were coming too quickly in P (illau). But your eyes remained so clear and sea green, my darling, so beautiful. I will never forget the way you looked at me. "

Erich was 47 ½ years old in February 1945. The reference to a 62 years old fellow soldier makes it clear that the National Guard at that time was actually made up of makeshift military-trained, ill-equipped civilians between (regular) the ages of 16 and 60 years whose fighting strength was more than doubtful. Erich tried hard in his letter to give himself courage. The sentence "Now we are waiting anxiously for the big attack from our side that must come sometime" - with some certainty, the deployment of the "wonder weapon" which is constantly invoked by the propaganda, proves that he is an incorrigible optimist. But especially in the last paragraph of the letter one can feel something like restrained pain, a sadness or grief that would be too simple to be called sentimentality.

Two days later, on February 10, 1945, Erich wrote to his mother from Königsberg.

"If and when this greeting will reach you is very questionable, but I'll try anyway. I have often thought about you, that you must be very concerned about us as you are watching these tragic developments that have now directly affected us as well. Thank God that it is not necessary because even though we had to leave the farm, we are doing well personally. By now you should have heard that my gang has arrival safely (i.e. of the successful escape of the family), at least I hope so. For the time being, I cannot receive any messages. I was so relieved when I finally had my loved ones on board the torpedo boat. Soon afterward, I flew by plane to my old place of work and got a National Guard battalion handed over to me. I am glad to have some active work again. My men are quite old, but they do a great job. My lodgings are at an estate of an acquaintance of ours. It is a relatively quiet place. Life in the city has almost normalized. The children play innocently and carefree with the thunder of cannons firing all around them until a low-flying plane scatters them for a moment. We are all confident that we will be able to hold our position until the big counter attack happens. Upon my arrival here, I visited Miss Frantz, who did not want to leave her father and siblings. She is now working with some of my people who are concerned with the food distribution.

"A few weeks ago we would have never dreamed that Thierenberg would again be made famous by the W-Report (Wehrmachtsbericht = military report). I do not know where the rest of my people are. On Friday the 19th (January) I sent a couple of my workers with refugee women and children with the tractor and farm wagon (that was converted to a camper equipped with a stove) to Pillau. After that my own family was supposed to be one their way. But on the way back the tractor driver got stuck in a snowstorm. So then we had to take the sleds drawn by horses. The DKW (car) with the children in it was hooked up to one of the sleds and that is how we got to Grubers where we stayed one night and from there on Sunday to Pillau. We tried in vain for three days to get on a ship. All nineteen of us shared one room but luckily we had taken food with us. For the little ones it was exciting. In Pillau one saw sad sights and it is especially bad for mothers with more than one child. In the freezing cold, some children just froze to death. But every day 10,000 to 15,000 people are loaded onto ships and that helps. The able-bodied men remained here.

"Despite all the suffering that has fallen over us here in the East, we are convinced that in the end everything will be fine. A good special-forces army will throw the Reds into disarray. The main thing is that we stay healthy because after that we can start again from scratch. What seemed important and meaningful weeks ago has become so unimportant today.

"Now let me take you firmly in my arms, dear Mother. Do not worry and believe in God and the future. Many kisses from your Erich."

Again, Erich swore with firm conviction that "everything will be fine". Whether and to what extent he actually believed this, nobody knows. The determination to begin again "from scratch" reminds us of the twenties and thirties, when he and Ursel did not lose heart despite constant setbacks.

On February 14, 1945 Erich wrote a last letter to his wife before his capture by the Russians. This was his third letter and it was marked on the front in the upper right-hand corner with a "3". Of the three letters sent to Ursel from the besieged city of Königsberg, one was lost - at least it is not preserved.

"If only I could find out whether you received the last two letters from Pillau and the one from here. I am numbering them now (see top right). We still do not have a F.P.Nr. [Fieldpostnumber]. Perhaps you could try to address it to "Kr L Kbg."(Königsberg) and inserting the letter for "Btl.F.Sp." (Battalion commander Spickschen). It is pretty quiet here in the district in the last few days. Ivan is quite openly moving around at the front until he gets knocked on the head. Then he becomes cautious again. This afternoon we have a battalion leaders meeting with Wa (?). I want to take the Bf.(Bauernfuehrer?) with me.

"It really is a very strange situation here. Saturday I took a bath like royalty only a few hundred meters away from the enemy. From time to time being invited by Munier (?), a nice room, sleeping on the sofa, off and on you hear an explosion, only 30 kilometers away from our own farm. I wonder what the situation there is? Thierenberg was again in the news.

"Yesterday I had a great pleasure. Close to here an activated infantry captain, a nice guy who is stationed with his men in the middle of the marshland, still without a protective bunker. I had gotten a pound of coffee from the "higher ups" and invited him and Munier and also a count who was still in the LB (Landesbauernschaft). After that we were invited to Munier's for a roasted hare dinner. Per my request they drew a bath for the captain. You can't imagine the gratitude and joy he showed. And then I had to lend him a shirt and hope to see it again in the future.

"I made quite a bit of progress with my men regarding their training and getting them uniforms to wear as well as building fortifications. They are very willing and eager. I have to replace the Lt. Company commander. I have requested Koenig-Ganthen, hopefully he'll be assigned. My aide is a nice, decent (?) vocational school director. Strauss is a bit nervous but a great guy and interesting. We often have long conversations about history, religion, etc. His outlook is similar to ours. Now I agree with you. One should have had contact earlier with people of different professions. Almost all physicians have remained here. Many were ousted from the party, High Court President Drieger (?), Attorney General Gelinsky, Pres. Gau Wi Ka Rodenstr. (?) Kr.L Mötsch, G.AL Hartung (technology), some from the governor's office."

This mainly objective letter conceals the fact that Erich was staying in an area where it was only a matter of weeks before it would fall into the hands of the Soviet troops. On April 9, the commander of Königsberg had to surrender with his troops. What Erich perceived as very strange - "a royal bath, a few hundred meters away from the enemy" -

corresponds to a typical everyday life of war where terrible conflict and peaceful serenity repeatedly merge almost inextricably. In any case, that is what is found in countless accounts of war. From the remark "One should have had contact earlier with people of different professions" Erich seems to give the impression that he realized that people in other professions may have different ideas and views that maybe even contrast to his own. This might have given rise to his first doubts.

With Erich's separation from his family, the connection that was between him and Ursel since1921 was broken for several years. Erich, the husband and father was no longer present as an active participant in life's decisions. But in Ursel's mind he always remained present, as her diary of the escape clearly shows.

3. The Spickschen Family Escape from East Prussia

In this section mainly Ursula Spickschen reported the events. The story of the escape is recited as she told it in 1979 in a conversation with her grandson Erich Hart. This story of the escape is a balance between summarizing the events for clarity and descriptive detail. The diary itself with its many details is a small maze into which one could lose oneself again and again because it is so captivating and revealing.

First, a short prologue. In 2005 Ingolf Spickschen published a diary-like account of the end of the war in 1945, in which he wrote the following.

"January 20: My 10th birthday. As every year, we celebrate with several friends into the evening and take them home in a horse-drawn sleigh. After we bathed and said our prayers our mother told me and my four younger siblings that the war front was close and the Russians were not far off. We have to flee. All wept bitterly."

Ursel's narrative:

"On January 20, 1945 Ingolf was ten years old and we celebrated his birthday still in Woydiethen. A few days later we were told that we would have to leave the farm. I said, "We will send Gaga with the children to friends of Opaps in the Mark Brandenburg". - Helga was probably supposed to go, too. – "I did not know the people. The whole gang went on their way, waited for hours in a train that did not move. Then they had to return back home. It was said that the Russians had broken through the front near Elbing and had moved up to the Vistula Bay. There would be no more trains to the Reich. They returned home again.

"Opaps had to go to the province since he had finally received the permission to take charge of the escape of the farmers. On January 25 or 26, I don't exactly remember, soldiers of the signal corps appeared suddenly at our farm and said that the Russians were only 12 kilometers (around 7 ½ miles) away. If I remember correctly, they were already near St. Lorenz. I was terribly frightened and thought that now the only thing that may help is to pray that the Russians will not attack and kill us all. That is what they had done in many villages, especially to those who were part of the Nazi regime. But then the Russians apparently thought that strong German commandos were in our close vicinity. They therefore did not move forward, and that was our good fortune.

"Opaps finally came home on the evening of January 26. He brought with him two Kreisbauernfuehrer from Masuria who had stayed there until the last moment to arrange the escape of their countrymen. It was said that tomorrow we all would have to leave. I had already sent away the refugees who were staying with us the day before. These people from the Memel region were staying in our house because that area was threatened much earlier than our region. These refugees were quartered in East Prussia instead of sending them into the western provinces of the Reich, which would have been more reasonable. I sent these families to Pillau because I had heard that ships that accepted refugees were sailing from there. There were two farmers' families who Mr. Naumann, the successor of our efficient inspector Nolting, drove with a tractor and wagon to Pillau. Mr. Naumann had been wounded in the war and he limped.

"Sometime before that, Tante Gudrun had come to us with her daughter Pinchen. Her apartment in Dusseldorf had been bombed. At first she found accommodation with relatives on another estate in East Prussia. She then moved on to Tapiau, where she was able to move into the house of the son of this family. The son had left the apartment because he joined the army. Tante Gudrun came to us with Pinchen after the Russians bombed Tapiau into a heap of rubble. Besides these two, Gaga's sister and her child were also in our house. So we were 17 people all together.

"On January 26 I tried to persuade our farm workers to escape but unfortunately I was quite unsuccessful. I could only convince the family Eggert. Mrs. Eggert was very smart and she explained that "we'll do what we can to get away." The family of the man who was in charge of milking the cows refused to be separated from their good furniture; they later died miserably. The Fischer Family said. "No, we stay here, we are Communists. The Russians don't hurt laborers." Our finance man Hinz and his wife said, "We are too old; we do not want to move away." And finally Frau Düppetell, whose husband was drafted into the National Guard, did not want to flee without her husband. I tried to persuade her and said to her, "Your husband will come later. It will be much easier for him to make it to the West by himself than if he has you and the kids with him." But no, I could not change her mind. The whole thing was awful. Her husband returned and both of them died of typhus. The children were sent to a Russian orphanage and later deported to East Germany. I am still in touch with them."

Ingolf Spickschen made a correction to his mother's report about Mr. Düppetell. From their daughter he learned that her father did not die of typhus but was picked up shortly before the end of the war by the German military police. As with many others on countless occasions during the last few months of the war, Herr Düppetell was summarily executed for alleged desertion.

Back to Ursel. "January 27 was the day when we had to flee ourselves. But we only got going in the evening because something was wrong with the tractor. Whether someone played a bad trick on us by putting a foreign substance into the tank, we don't know. Anyway, the oil had to be drained and replaced and fresh fuel had to be added. We then drove off, and stayed the night with friends, the Grubers.

"A large wagon was hooked to the tractor in which Helga, Ingolf, Hase and the apprentices sat." However, again Ingolf remembers it somehow differently when talking on January 25, 2010. He said that the tractor was no longer usable. Horses were harnessed in front of the rubber wheeled wagon. Ursel continued: "In addition, we had two cars - one, a big car, was driven by one of the Kreisbauernfuehrer and in the other one I believe that I along with Opaps and the two little ones, Astrid and Thorlef, sat. Whether Runhild was with us in the car, I cannot say for sure. Perhaps it was that Astrid, Thorlef and Runhild were in the wagon with Helga and Hase. And the other Kreisbauernfuehrer? – I don't remember how we were divided; it's been too long.

"We started out taking several crates which contained many valuable things with us. However, Grubers stated that it would not serve any purpose to take the crates with us because we would never be able to get them on a boat. So we left all the crates at the Grubers and never saw them again."

Here Ingolf in the presence of his sister Karen remembered an important addition to the story. Several stops were made on the road. On one such stop at night in bright moonlight he got down from the wagon. There he saw dead people lying in the ditch. He had never seen anything like that and he was shocked. On the jacket of one of them, he saw a star. He asked his sisters what it meant. He was told that the dead are Jews. Karen said that there were Jews from Königsberg on the road. She had heard that from her father who had seen the death march of Jews that afternoon when he came back from Königsberg. They must have come from a forced labor camp in Königsberg.

Back again to Ursel. "On the next day, on Sunday January 28, we continued on to Pillau. For a long time we were unable to find a place to stay until we finally got a single room for all of us. The next day we discovered the abandoned home of a Navy family. Only one bed and a sofa were available so that many of us had to make do with the floor.

"In Pillau there was an incident with Ingolf. He was in the car with us when we drove to the port and we noticed a plane in the air. We thought that it was a German plane and didn't worry about it. As the car came to a stop, Ingolf jumped out to check on the plane that approached at low altitude. Suddenly we heard a "tack-tack- tack-tack". It was a Russian plane! We had a terrible scare. Ingolf just watched and did not realize that is was machine gun fire as we pulled him back into the car. Thank God nothing happened to him.

[THE FOLOWING IS NOT IN THE GERMAN VERSION.]

Bergild remembers: "I must have been in the car on the pier with Ingolf and my parents because I distinctly remember seeing the airplane flying toward us, fire coming out of its nose and people falling down on the dock in front of us."

Ursel: "At this point I want to add that about two weeks before our escape, Erich was fired as Landesbauernfuehrer by Gauleiter Koch and replaced by a Mr. Adam. Adam, a farmer's son from Hanover and former employee of Erich, always acted toward Erich as if he were very loyal and reliable. Erich had been fired because he did not do what Koch wanted. The details are not important.

"Erich was determined not to leave East Prussia when we were in Pillau. He was an officer and did not intend to just leave. For the rest of us, no ship was scheduled to leave. Russian submarines were in the Baltic Sea and, as we later learned, had sunk the "Wilhelm Gustloff" a short time before. It was a large ship and several thousand people drowned. We were very worried because we were not able to leave. Tante Gudrun was very worried that we could not get away. She was also very sad because she had lost her son just before Christmas. He was a naval officer who had gone down with his submarine off the Norwegian coast. From the news casts we learned that most of the Samland was already occupied by the Russians and Königsberg was besieged.

"One evening a boat was finally supposed to leave but I have forgotten its name. We waited the whole night to board, until half past two in the morning. But suddenly someone yelled, "The ship is full." One hundred or two hundred people had waited in vain just as we had. But it was our good fortune that we had to stay on land, because this ship sunk after it had hit a mine or was torpedoed. Only a few people were saved. God protected us!

"When I look back on that night, I see little Thorlef before me, who was not yet four years old. Hour after hour he stood there with his backpack on his back. His feet were freezing since it was icy cold. At times the temperature dropped to -20 degrees Celsius (-2 F). When I think of what we saw on that pier in Pillau - babies frozen stiff in their prams - I shudder even today."

In Ursel's diary of the escape she wrote on January 30, 1945, a Tuesday:

"We stood in a snowstorm again for almost five hours. The crowding of people around the ship is catastrophic. The children are almost squeezed to death. They cry and wail. Thorlef and Runhild can no longer carry their little backpacks. But none of us has a free hand to help because we are groaning under the burden of our own baggage. Suddenly we are told that the ship is full – no more will be let on. Mothers with children cry and beg - but it's impossible. The ship is too full already."

In her 1979 interview Ursel continued with the story of the escape.

"Tante Gudrun once again walked around everywhere and by chance met a lieutenant commander, the captain of a torpedo boat. She asked him if there is room on his boat and he answered, "Yes". She then quickly walked back to the apartment in which we stayed and all 17 of us followed her. This was February 1st. We had waited from January 28 until the evening of February 1 to get on a ship.

"When we left the harbor on February 2, Opaps stayed behind. Those were terrible hours for me. I did not know if I would ever see him again. We first sailed to Gotenhafen, which is called Gdynia today. As we left the torpedo boat, we realized that one of the suitcases had been stolen. It was the one with all the silver and jewelry that had been given to the children for their baptism in it. Our other bags had to be stored in a warehouse. At the housing office we asked where we could stay. They told us that there was an abandoned apartment at such and such address. We found the place and moved in during a change of weather. Suddenly it became a bit warmer."

Ursel also wrote about the loss of the suitcase in her flight diary.

"February 2nd. A Friday. In the morning we finally arrived in Gotenhafen. What will happen next with us? No one can give us information. Our luggage is unloaded. When we finally are allowed to disembark and want to sort out our luggage, the suitcase with all the children's things has disappeared. We searched. Two of us are going into the city to ask at the refugee camp if someone accidentally took the suitcase. They return without it. All clothes and all of the children's jewelry - can everything be lost? I'm desperate. The ship is searched again. The suitcase is not to be found. "

[THE FOLLOWING IS NOT IN THE GERMAN VERSION.]

Bergild vaguely remembers that she saw the suitcase fall off the gangway and disappear into the water. But no one believed her at the time.

Ursel's interview in 1979.

"We found a place to stay in an empty apartment in a large apartment building. The heating did not work; it was bitterly cold. No food was there. We had taken a lot of provisions but most of it had already been eaten in Pillau. Against the advice of friends, we had packed our silver instead of taking a slab of bacon. Helga carried all of the silver in her backpack. I had sewn a bag from sheep fur for myself in all haste that I could wear around my neck. Astrid, who was still very young, sat in this bag.

"But then we received food stamps so that we did not have to go hungry. A doctor Schweitzer, who was the principal chief of staff in Gotenhafen (today he lives in Ladenburg) got the stamps for us. In the basement of the apartment building we also discovered a large amount of onions. I can still see it today how we cooked those onions. We also found feather duvets there, no sheets, but they protected us from the cold. And fortunately, the water pipes were not frozen so we could use the sink and toilet.

"But now the question arose again: how do we get away from Gotenhafen? Again we heard that no ships were leaving. "It is quite hopeless," they said, "You have to wait." Incidentally, I forgot to name one of the 17 people who were with us. She was the younger of Opaps' two secretaries, who we called Spatz (sparrow). Spatz, Helga and Hase were sent to the port to ask every ship whether they had space available. They came back and said that they had found only a single ship, a small survey vessel named "Boergen" whose sailors told them that they had some free space. But the sailors were not the ones who could decide who to take. We should go to the master at the naval station, a Doctor Fabricius.

"I immediately went to the naval station and asked around and was told that he usually held office in such and such a room. When I entered, the room was already full of people. Dr. Fabricius sat alone at his desk and wrote; he never once looked up. After waiting a few minutes, I approached the desk and said, "I want to talk to Dr. Fabricius." "Yes," he replied, "I am he." Then I explained that I had heard that there is still some space available on the "Boergen" to be awarded to refugees. I told him that we were 17 people. I asked, "Would it be possible that we can go?" And Mr. Fabricius said, "Yes." Behind me stood a farm woman from West Prussia, who also asked if there was room for her family. After a third person asked, the ship was full. We had some un-heard-of luck.

"The "Boergen" had been purchased by the Germans from the Norwegians, therefore the Norwegian name. The ship had probably been on the way to sweep mines in the Skagerrak. But the captain was an old civilian. Before we were able to leave with the boat, we had a scare. I had promised Uncle Alfred that I would call him to tell him the exact time of the departure of our ship. When I returned to the apartment building, there was a small wagon, a small horse-drawn cart, parked in front of the house, and the children received me very excitedly. They said, "Mutti, for God's sake, where have you been? The ship is leaving earlier than expected; we have to go to the port immediately, or we will be left behind!" But fortunately we made it to the ship in time.

"Some of us had to go forward to the bow, some of us to the stern. I remained back in the stern with Tante Gudrun, Pinchen, Thorlef, Astrid and perhaps Runhild. The big girls, the apprentices and the others were camped in the bow. During the day we were able to move around, but for sleeping we had to stay in the front or rear space. So we left Gotenhafen but the ship made a sudden stop at the Hela Peninsula and we were wondering why. It was said that we had to wait for a convoy from Libau in the Baltics. We would join it. Late that night the convoy finally arrived and we started moving and very slowly we sailed toward the West. We intentionally kept close to the shore in shallow water so we could not be attacked by submarines. The only danger that still existed was mines. But we were close to the coast line, which was in sight, so apparently we did not have to fear them.

"The "Boergen" was supposed to take us to Swinemuende. When we were approximately at the level of the city, we saw a huge aircraft squadron approaching. It was a British air fleet which was planning to bomb Swinemuende. The "Boergen" was a civilian ship but there were a few Navy anti-aircraft soldiers aboard and a small antiaircraft gun had been installed on deck. One of the soldiers, a mate or NCO among the three or four men, misunderstood a command and began to shoot. That was most unwise. The aircraft, which did not even notice us before, started dropping several water bombs. We could hear the muffled strikes, could hear an echo from the water and did not know if the ship had been damaged. There was great excitement. At that time I was praying that nothing would happen to us. And then I thought that if we sink now, I'll take the two little ones in my arms and then nothing will help if we perish in the icy water. But God protected us again and nothing happened to us. But it was clear that we could not land in Swinemuende; the city was burning.

[THE FOLLOWING IS NOT IN THE GERMAN VERSION.]

Bergild remembers the attack on the minesweeper. She and a couple of her siblings were lying in bunk beds given up by the sailors for the children. During the attack of the water bombs, the ship violently rocked back and forth and she fell out of the upper bunk and started to cry. Her mother came and one of the sailors carried her into the captain's room which had a table and a build-in bench that was deep wine-red in color. The captain gave her a can of sweetened condensed milk as a prize, which was the best treat that she ever had.

Ursel: "We heard from the sailors that the captain had decided to chug around the island of Rügen. I say "chug" because we had to go around the island very slowly because of the danger of mines in order to land in Stralsund. This created new excitement because on board there were also wounded soldiers for whom the long journey was difficult. However, the wounded themselves did not really care what happened. They must have been seriously wounded because they lay there rather indifferently and apathetic. The only thing they wanted was water to drink and we brought it to them. At one point one of them said, "We were on the ship to search for mines and our Old Man, the captain, can smell the mines. You don't have to fear that we will hit a mine." We actually landed safely in Stralsund.

"By the way, both on the torpedo boat and on the "Boergen" we were well looked after. The sailors from the torpedo boat gave us several small cans of condensed milk and on the second vessel we received several canned goods. That was very great for us.

"In Stralsund we reported to the NSA and were assigned two rooms in a hotel where we could stay. We all had to sleep on the floor because there were no beds for 17 people, as you can imagine. We could not stay in the hotel long and it was almost impossible to find new accommodations. At the NSA they told us that the situation was quite bad because the city was flooded with refugees. Finally I had the idea to go to the Kreisbauernfuehrer, the district farmers' representative. He was a very nice German-Russian. His parents had farmed a portion of a huge landed estate, which a German company, either Krupp or BASF, had once leased from the Russian or Bolshevik government. This Kreisbauernfuehrer could only name a single place, a large country palace, where we would find some room. However, there were already 75 refugees who came from the local area and had lost their homes through bombings, quartered there.

"I drove there and met very nice people. I think their name was Wette or Wetting. As I heard later, they did not flee and the man was arrested by the Russians. They told me, "Yes, two rooms are still available, but we have no more firewood. There is no forest on our domain and the next forest is far away and we did not get any coal deliveries. You need to realize and understand this." I told them that we have no choice; we have to stay somewhere. We are unable to stay in the hotel where we are living at the moment because the NSA needs the space for new refugees. So we took quarters in the castle.

"Most of the over 70 refugees with whom we came in contact were pretty "red" in their views. So we just greeted them with a friendly "good day" and went our own way. The more educated people stayed away from them. Mrs. Wette was particularly friendly. Late at night, when everyone else was asleep, she came and brought us a small basket of wood so we could at least cook. She also brought us potatoes, vegetables and a piece of bacon. But we knew that we could not stay there permanently.

"In addition, I had every intention to cross the river Elbe. While we waited in Gotenhafen for a ship, I met a teacher or the Director of the School of Agriculture of Liebenfelde, also a very nice man; he is dead now. He told me that he had often secretly listened to the English radio channel and thereby learned about the conference in Yalta. We knew nothing about it; we had no idea. He told me, "Make sure that you get across the Elbe. The whole area east of the Elbe will be given to Russia; the Russians will control it." This information was firmly ingrained in my mind and I decided to leave the castle and go further West.

"In Berlin, there was a Mr. Meinberg. He was formerly chairman of the Reichsnaehrstandes, the country's Human Services Department. He had a falling out with the then Reichsbauernfuehrer Darré and subsequently became a director of the Hermann-Göring-Werke, the iron ore factories in Salzgitter. He was always very kind to us and we knew him quite well. For a while, when Opaps was the Bauernfuehrer, he substituted for the Landesbauernfuehrer. Around February or March I tried to contact this gentleman. Since he had his main office in Berlin, I went there twice. Each time the train came under heavy shelling from aircraft weapons but nothing happened to me. Unfortunately, I did not reach Meinberg the first time. I finally met him and he gave me two options where we could get housing. One was an empty apartment in Steterburg, a small town; the other option was on an estate where an unmarried inspector lived in a big house. But Meinberg made me aware of the fact that these places were in bomb threat zone number 1 because of their proximity to the Hermann-Göring-Werke. A bomb could easily be dropped on our head there. I told him that a bomb could fall on us anywhere; it lies in the hands of God. "When I hear there is room, that is most important to me. I would like to go to the estate; I have a better chance of getting food there than in the city." It was therefore agreed that I could go to the estate Bleckenstedt.

"But how to get there? To get a ride to Braunschweig, was extremely difficult because the railroads were barely running and they were certainly not on the track that we had to take. I went to an SS officer in Stralsund, a former general. He was a very decent man and I could explain my situation to him. He told me that he could have us taken to Rostock. He said, "Something has to be picked up from there and the truck, which will be empty when it leaves here, can take you." I was very happy but how we would get from Rostock to Bleckenstedt I did not know. Finally it occurred to me that when I was in Berlin the second time, I met the union boss from the Reichsnährstand in the subway. He was no longer a farm worker and he had married a wealthy nurse and bought a farm in Mecklenburg. If we wanted to get from Rostock to Braunschweig, we had to cross Mecklenburg. I called this man; fortunately the phone still worked. Yes, there would always be someone on his farm who could pick us up in Rostock.

"So we got to Rostock and from there we went to the farm of this union boss. But I wanted to get away from there as quickly as possible because that man was after me. He had a lovely wife but he himself, although helpful, was a nasty guy. It was very unpleasant. However, he then told me, "In Wismar there is a butcher who has to pick up aluminum canning supplies from a company in Seesen. He can take you to Braunschweig." That again was very lucky. I then telephoned Mr. Meinberg, who was already in Salzgitter, and told him when we would arrive in Braunschweig.

"The butcher had an empty trailer and we were able to climb in. Even though it was a bumpy ride and shook terribly, we did not care. When we crossed the river Elbe near Dannenberg, a big millstone was removed from my heart. Now we are saved!"

In her flight diary the crossing of the Elbe which happened on March 20, 1945 was described differently:

"We were driving through the small town of Dannenberg. Here also, the war has put its mark. Many of the cozy, small, half-timbered houses are laid in ruins. I'm thinking about it. We drove across the Elbe. It seems to me as if I had burned the bridges to the past. It seems to me as if I had somehow broken the bridges to the past. It is choking me."

Ursel continues with the story in 1979.

"West of the Elbe, the driver took a break in the forest. The bushes everywhere were covered in tinfoil that had been dropped by enemy planes to disrupt the German radar. The children rushed around and shouted, "Oh, chocolate wrappers, chocolate wrappers." Meanwhile, the 20th March had arrived; it was warmer. The flight from East Prussia lasted nearly two months, from January 27 to March 20.

"The moment we arrived at the agreed meeting point in Braunschweig, there was an air-raid alarm. We waited in a basement until the attack was over. Sometime before that, a few important things were lost somewhere. I think that toys disappeared and the children were crying bitterly. And in Braunschweig, Thorlef's small backpack that contained some things that were especially dear to him was stolen. I consoled him and said, "The main thing we are still alive; losing things is not the worst. Come, let's go to Bleckenstedt now." Mr. Meinberg had organized a bus for us to take us there.

[THE FOLLOWING IS NOT IN THE GERMAN BOOK VERSION.]

Bergild remembers the air-raid. "It was terrifying. It was evening when the sirens started to wail. All of us had to drop our backpacks and other luggage on the ground in the plaza where the truck had stopped and run to a bunker (or basement) where many other people were already hiding. The noise of the screaming bombs and the explosions was terrible and very scary. When it was over, we emerged from the cellar and came into a nightmare. Fire and smoke was everywhere. When we got to our pile of luggage a few things were gone, among them my backpack with my new doll that I just had received for Christmas and my hair brush. I was very sad!"

Ursel: "During the whole flight I had some money with me, but not much. Again it was fortunate that I was able to get about 4,000 marks while in Bleckenstedt. I had deposited the money into a bank in Berlin. I wrote to the bank and received the money on the last day that the post office delivered mail for a while. I do not know how I would have coped without that money. I even think that it was 4,500 marks which were paid me. When we left East Prussia, I wanted to take all the cash we had, but Opaps was against it. It was not an excessively high amount but still about twenty to thirty thousand marks."

VI

Erich Spickschen as a Russian Prisoner of War

Erich Spickschen's last letter to his wife from Königsberg was written on February 14, 1945. Not quite two months later, on April 9, Königsberg fell into the hands of the Soviet Army. What happened to Erich between February 14 and April 9 is known only in sketches with very little details. However, Erich wrote the following CV on February 15, 1948:

"In February, 1945 I took over the Volkssturm (National Guard) battalion 82/25 in Metgethen near Königsberg. I was wounded in a counter-attack on April 7, 1945 and became a Russian prisoner of war while in the military hospital in Königsberg."

There is also a typewritten letter from Ursel of March 5, 1945 to her childhood friend Karl Warnecke about the final weeks and months of the war. From few subdued hints can be seen how much she was worried about her husband. But much more forceful are the quotes from her diary entries of the flight to the West that convey her feelings of anxiety about Erich and the longing for him that were constantly present in Ursel's mind.

In the letter she says:

"I received word about Erich from a gentleman from the REM (Reich Ministry of Food) who is a soldier in Königsberg and is able to call Berlin often on the military phone line. So I know that he was still alive yesterday. I think I wrote you already that he is a commander in the Volkssturm. That is not a comforting thought considering the situation Königsberg is in. What should we do if he cannot come back to us! But I still hope that God will look out for our good. I still have hope politically, in spite of everything. Otherwise one could just hope to die and be buried. Perhaps a miracle will happen because that is what it would take.

"The fact that East Prussia was not evacuated was partly due to the fact that they apparently did not regard the situation as bad. This is partly because it was thought that East Prussia would exist as an island if the Russians were to come up the Vistula. Erich was an advocate for evacuation but did not get anywhere with that plan. Afterwards the evacuation was supposed to go speedily but of course there were not enough trains available. It was precisely because of his evacuation plan that Erich had serious differences with his superiors since last summer. Our part of the country was still fully inhabited!"

Ursel's hope for the much promised "final victory" was not quite abandoned in this letter but she now sounded a lot more fatigued or desperate than Erich did in his letters of February 1945. But basically one doesn't know how much Erich actually believed in his overall confidence. Ursel made it clear that her husband was a supporter of the evacuation plan but she left open what he actually did or possibly could have done to put that plan into effect.

Ursel disclosed the efforts she undertook to extract Erich from East Prussia in a typewritten letter she wrote on March 5, 1945 to one of her husband's former coworkers who was already mentioned several times. Ursel's family found refuge during their escape at the home of a Mr. Wette and her letter was posted in Lassentin (Post Niepars via Stralsund), the town where the home is located.

"Dear Mr. Gruber!

Thank you for your letter. I also spoke with Backe. It now appears to him to be quite impossible to let my husband come to Berlin to give a lecture as long as Königsberg and the Samland are still a bridgehead. That may be correct. I drove with Zschirnt from Guestrow to Rostock. After talking with him I saw that he agreed with me. I was already of the opinion earlier that my husband should not have had to resign but that Berlin should have given him another special assignment at the moment they realized that nothing could be done in the matter and that they had to give in. My husband did not want to resign because to him it seemed like a cowardly way out. He feared for the collapse of the entire Reichsnährstandsorder (Food Distribution Order) in East Prussia. It was easy to understand but Berlin should have ordered him to go ahead and do it instead of constantly saying "hold on!" Now we are in a situation that seems unsolvable and we can only leave everything to God to do the best for us. Nevertheless it looks desperate. Backe told me that "he could have released him to the Wehrmacht (Military) but then he would have just been doing so and so a favor". When I mentioned that he could have given him a special order, for example to go to Denmark as he did two years ago, he did not know what to say.

"Meinberg strongly advised me to move further west. There I can get hold of some weaving equipment and hopefully get people to weave something for our women. A weaving teacher named Miss Lindenau is already there. I met her in Güstrow. I have already taken steps to take care of the registration for the apprentices and helpers. RO [?] Behrendt has approved that I can continue in this function. My work is done quietly and no other bureau will even notice. Since I can work from home, I will have the time for my children and that I have desired for so long. The typing will be done by Miss Neubauer. I want to add that my husband specifically told me in Pillau that I should continue with my work. The person who disappears into oblivion is quickly forgotten he said and he is right. I also benefit personally from it because only by working will I get travel authorizations. Because of the trip to Berlin I will now get the quarters for us further West with the help of Meinberg. All that would not have happened if I stopped working. In addition, it also distracts me from all the concerns and problems that would otherwise get me down in the monotony of the daily drudges. In addition to worrying about my husband inevitably comes the concern for the whole situation. The news about the military is never good and I'm sitting here alone with my young children. My husband is far away and not even accessible through letters."

The conversation that Ursel had with Backe to obtain a transfer for Erich that would have freed him from the encircled Königsberg was disappointing. Backe obviously did not possess the influence to achieve a transfer. So Ursel's initiatives ended in desperate speculations about what else could be done as long as there was still time left to do so.

However, Ursel's efforts were successful in finding living quarters that offered safety for an extended period of time. Wilhelm Meinberg implored her to move further west to an area that the Soviet army would be unlikely to reach. Although there were bomb attacks to fear this risk did not deter Ursel.

Moreover, it is clear that Ursel remained an active, dedicated farm woman. The hardships created by the flight west did not prevent her from continuing to work for the benefited of other rural women. And it helped her to temporarily break free from oppressive worries. Ursel's main concern was first and foremost for her husband. But Ursel was also concerned about the political- and military developments in Germany. Even after the total surrender on May 9, 1945, her day to day concerns were mostly for the difficulties of her family's refugee existence as they survived through all the months since January 26, 1945. In a typewritten postcard dated August 4, 1945 sent from "Bleckenstedt via Wolfenbüttel" to Erich's mother Maria, Ursel confided that because of the miserable circumstances the family was experiencing she felt "that her worry about Erich had doubled".

Ursel's postcard from August 4 effectively ended the dual storytelling – at least for a while. Correspondence initiated by Ursel stopped for a long period and it was not until June 1948 that there are letters from her that contain important information about the progress of the life of the Spickschens. For the period from October, 1946 to January, 1948, with few exceptions, only letters from Erich are exclusively documented. Since only a few of these letters have been preserved compared with earlier times of more intense correspondence, most of these letters are reproduced in full.

Very little is known about Erich's time of captivity. He talked reluctantly or not at all about this stage of his life. Sometimes he told about small, harmless events that hardly allowed any glimpse into the hardships and horrors he had to go through during his captivity. However, the sparseness and meagerness of what Erich was able to tell in his few cards and letters written between October, 1946 and January, 1948, give his written word their own intensity.

Erich's first letter which arrived in West Germany bears the date of October 14, 1946. According to that letter it had been more than one and a half years since he had any contact with his family. That means that for one and a half years Ursel lived in agonizing uncertainty about her husband's fate. A letter from a man named Ludwig Kreuzer gave the family at least a rough idea of what life was like for Erich after his capture and his hospital stay. The typewritten copy of the letter was written on January 15, 1948 in Bad Salzschlirf and addressed to "Herrn Lühl". Lühl had to be a close relative of Maria Spickschen (Erich's mother) whose mother's maiden name was Lühl and therefore she was Erich's maternal grandmother.

"Dear Mr. Lühl!

Your dear letter is a disappointment for me in so far as it convinced me that your nephew Erich Speckersen has not yet returned from captivity. At his age he would have deserved it. I met your nephew Erich in the winter of 1945/46. We were in Königsberg together. Later we were sent to a village called Weynothen where we built a camp in the forest and got the job of cutting down trees - which everyone preferred. We were always put into groups of three and had to cut three and one-half cubic meters of wood per day but that amount later was somewhat increased. By itself it was a very healthy activity and during the brisk, icy cold winter we did not suffer much from the cold. We had plenty of smaller branches available from the tops of the trees and were able to build large fires so we were able to take turns warming ourselves. When we met our assigned target quantities we received leave passes on off-duty Sundays to visit German civilians in Schoneckemoor and Hohenbruch (Laukehnen). Here we had a chance to feast with peat potatoes and fish dishes. Erich came down with rheumatic fever and had to go to the infirmary. This meant that he did not have to go back to the forest and found employment in the kitchen for the Russian soldiers. It was a pretty good time for him because there were always some left-overs. The work in the forest came to an end on January 31, 1947 and we had to march on foot back to Tilsit. From there we were taken by train to Insterburg. There we received a medical examination and Erich, who looked good and was strong, was sent to Georgenburg, while I was denied the transfer. I was told that I was sick and belonged in a hospital. I could see and feel a noticeable loss of weight and my strength was quite diminished. I stayed in the hospital until March and was soon in a much better overall condition. From there I was sent to work at the railroad as a loader and did not work again with Erich. Erich was always a sincere and loyal friend - far beyond a simple camaraderie."

What is immediately striking about the letter is the fact that Erich Spickschen now appears as "Erich Speckersen". According to his children, the name change occurred in connection with a remarkable and quite dramatic event. After his capture, Erich succeeded in changing his last name. If the Soviet guards would have heard his actual name and associated it with the title "battalion commander" or even "Landesbauernfuehrer," he most likely would have been immediately executed as a high-ranking Nazi. The children remember being told that during a roll-call, the names of the German prisoners were called out. At the mention of the name "Erich Speckersen" there was no reply. At that moment Erich had the presence of mind to call out. Maybe his name had been misspelled or misread. Anyway, from then on he went under the name of Erich Speckersen. And not one among his many fellow prisoners who recognized him betrayed him.

Ursel's letter dated May 15, 1961 to forest master a.D. (retired) Loeffke differs from the memory of the children regarding Erich's name change.

"My husband fought as a battalion commander of the National Guard near Königsberg, was shot in the leg and was then captured by the Russians in a military hospital in Königsberg. With the help of a chauffeur of the Ministry of Agriculture who had an arm wound and was in the same hospital Erich removed his epaulettes from his uniform and changed his signature on the military ID. This way he became a prisoner of war as an ordinary soldier and was not identified by the Russians as a Nazi official. During his three years in captivity many people from East Prussia recognized him. However, no one betrayed him."

As is shown here Erich did not need to have presence of mind at the roll-call; he previously was smart enough to change his name on the military ID. –

Ludwig Kreuzer's letter written in January, 1948 revealed that at first Erich was imprisoned for many months in East Prussia and that he lived in a forest camp and had to perform work as a lumberjack. In the cold of a "brisk winter" he did not suffer. It is important to note that because of illness he temporarily could work in the "Russian kitchen" of the camp. Erich also made reference to this circumstance in two of his letters. Erich sent the first of these surviving prisoner-of-war letters on October 14, 1946 from Tilsit. All letters are written in mostly easy to read Latin letters with pencil. Individual letters, like the "d", appears in Sütterlin font.

"My Dears!

In short intervals I am sending letters to you in the hopes that at least one may reach you. I'm still doing pretty well. Today we are being sent to another camp, allegedly for forestry work. The hope for an early release of us "old ones" is still quite large. Day and night I think with worry and love about my loved ones but the good Lord will take care of you. Thank God, I still have the strength for a second life that we have to start now. To a happy, healthy reunion in Herford.

Your Erich Sp."

Obviously, other letters preceded this first letter but these letters did not receive a response - or so Erich suggested with his first sentence. The connections were highly uncertain and any sign of life received was a cause for great joy. From today's perspective and looking at it from a historical perspective, it is unclear how far to trust the statements of Erich's well-being. Every letter contained information about health and welfare but the Russians did not allow such letters to be openly critical or negative. The letters sent by the prisoners of war were censored. Erich's statement that he was doing "quite well" was almost meaningless. Maybe at times he was actually reasonably well as the letter from Ludwig Kreuzer suggests. However, at other times he was in extremely poor health - he was then given kitchen duty.

A letter from November 8, 1946 (sent from an unspecified "Forest Camp") showed that Erich finally received a response from his relatives.

"My Dears!

I am so happy and grateful for the receipt of the first message from you with good news about Ursel and the children. Even though I would also have liked to hear how they are doing, I absolutely understand that the letters have to be kept short. I am also very glad to hear about Mother and my siblings and hope that Gerhard and Marianne (the children of his brother Alfred) are well. We are still sitting here full of hope on the Wartburg (castle of waiting). My health is quite well except for my yearning for you all.

"I am quite concerned about your return address! Is your house destroyed? Remain healthy and thank you so much. Maybe I'll get another message soon. I am now a helper in the Russian kitchen!

Cordially, your Erich."

The two keywords "Wartburg" and "yearning" should be read together. In addition to his concerns about his physical survival (health, nutrition) these words mark a central concern that weighs heavy on Erich's psyche. While enduring the agony of waiting for his release from imprisonment he joked about sitting on the Wart-Burg and the longing for his family. These are both directly linked to the agony of waiting. "The imprisonment was a continuous state of waiting." Without doubt, Erich heard the soothing Russian phrase "skoro domoj" (home soon) again and again. What gave him concern about the return address of the letter from Germany cannot to be clarified.

A few days later, on November 13, 1946, Erich Speckersen, still a prisoners of war, wrote a longer letter to the relatives at home - again from a forest camp.

"My Dears!

How happy you have made me today with the very detailed letter of September 15. It arrived after Uncle Arthur's letter that came exactly a week ago. I wish you a continued strong recovery, dear Mother, so that you can survive my big hug when I come home. How grateful I am to fate that you are all doing well and that I am able to keep all my loved ones.

I was so very worried, especially about Gerhard after he was wounded. But then again, he is already an old professional soldier. Congratulations! How long was he in captivity? We are still waiting for word as to when the next group will leave here. Since I am the third oldest I have a good chance to be in that group. All the men above 50 years old were let go at the end of July. I still have not given up hope to be able to celebrate Christmas with my loved ones. But after receiving your letter, everything is a lot easier to take. But now the longing for my wife and children is stronger because now I know where they are located. I am so looking forward to the first greeting from Ursel after such a long time! How wonderful that you were able to give me the news about all of them. I am mostly concerned about Ingolf's school situation. So little is known here of the conditions in your area. All thoughts about the design of the future must be completely abandoned and sent back to their original source because such thoughts are nothing but futile and nerve wracking. And one has to toughen the soul and keep it healthy exactly like the body because both will be needed and are important to help structure our "second life". The dear Lord has made life quite well for me despite all the troubles. Because of working almost always outdoors and getting mostly adequate food I'm doing well and am quite strong. I currently have the very envied job of handyman to our guards where often I am able to get kitchen scraps to eat. Now farewell my dear ones. Should I not be with you for Christmas, try to have a merry one anyway and be thankful for all we have. Now one can be happy with very little and have totally new and different values from before. Somewhere we might even find a new track of land that we can work together. I wonder if my little ones will recognize me. Little Astrid probably not, my little sweet one. Again I thank you from my heart. God bless you.

With love, your Erich."

For the second time – (the first was in his letter of October 14, 1946) Erich talked about the "construction of the second life" and the "strength for the second life". This expression confirmed Erich's incorrigible, even indestructible optimism and perhaps it even became a motto during his captivity. But of course one does not know the source of Erich's optimism. Maybe it was an inner voice Erich heard that told him that he and others should be courageous and never to let go.

Otherwise the pleasure he gained from having direct contact with his relatives dominated the letter. But the joy is inseparably connected with the concerns he perceived as "nerve wracking", and as incessantly concerning. Like his previous letter, Erich's whole letter expressed his longing and waiting for the end of his captivity.

The following is the detailed final portion of a particularly long letter dated November 22, 1946 that Erich wrote to Ursel from a forest camp. He addressed Ursel with "My dear, good Fee".

"We know so little about the situation there [in West Germany], so one can make no firm plans for the future. Do the agricultural bonds still have value? I sometimes think about purchasing or leasing a small farm. We'll have only the best breed of cattle and possibly also some sheep. We'll grow mainly vegetables in the fields. Perhaps you might want to open a wool-spinning business with the big girls and gradually expand it to dyeing and weaving. There should be no problem getting wool. Just imagine, I met the sheep farmer Alfred Sanden from Sandenfelde in our camp in Tilsit. We became good friends. Unfortunately, we have been separated for a good five weeks now since I came here to the forest camp (the lumber commando near Heinrichswalde). Sanden and I hope to be released together. He is only a little younger than I and a quiet and likeable guy. Maybe you can ask Pflaumbaum for advice on our behalf. You can get his address from Rhedn. He is a clear-headed, practical man. He would probably be able to get top quality cattle for me. But maybe my plans make no sense. I don't know the situation there.

"There is not much news to report from me. The main thing is to stay healthy and strong. I was in the military hospital in Insterburg until September of 1945. Then in Königsberg until March where we worked mainly in and for the mill. After that we were in the forest camp near Tilsit. In August and September I was in the city and now I am here in the outskirts where most of the land is flooded. For the last four weeks I have worked as the kitchen helper for the guards. I chop wood, wash the dishes etc. There are always some leftovers in the kitchen. Everybody envies me. Otherwise I did not meet any one we know. The only person I met was the chauffeur Brown when I spent time in the military hospital. He was very nice to me as I lay helplessly in the bunk. Thank God, my leg is as good as new again. God will continue to help us. Yes, we must trust in Him and do our best to help ourselves. When I pray at night I always take you in my arms in my thoughts. I want to write about so many things to you but will have to wait until later when I can do it orally.

"We just ate a delicious fish soup that was made with pepper, bay leaf and a little flour. A buddy of mine got the ingredients and made it. Yes, we have become culinary artists. For several Sundays, together with Sanden, we even had real bean coffee and rye flour pancakes (just flour and water and sugar on top).

"I wonder how so many of our friends are doing? Where are Gruber, Heister and Soppa? Is Gaga still with you? Her mother and also Miss Frantz are probably no longer alive. Now good night, all my dear ones. I am writing this by the light of a sooty, small flame from a can filled with gasoline. Should I not be with you Christmas, spend the festival full of grateful joy that we are all still alive. Hopefully we will be able to start our second life together in 1947. With warm regards and kisses your Erich Speckersen."

This section of the letter revealed two aspects of Erich's life and Psyche. First, it showed how Erich planed for the future with great determination even though he was afraid that it was all make-believe. Maybe he actually was a real optimist - one who has had one set-back after another in his life but pulls himself together again and again to start over. Following the same pattern of shaping his life as he had done already in the 1920s, Erich wanted to start a new life after his release from captivity. Second, Erich relayed even if only in outline form, about his initial time as a prisoner of war. After his leg injury and then his capture, Erich was in a military hospital in Insterburg until September, 1945. Until March, 1946 he worked in Königsberg for an unspecified mill, followed by alternating stays in a forest camp and in the city of Tilsit. From these and other explanations a somewhat clearer picture emerges of the circumstances of Erich's life during the first eighteen months of his captivity.

Ingolf recalled from memory (in an interview on August 14, 2009) a story told by his father (a rare event). Shortly before his capture Erich was wounded by shrapnel from a grenade which hit him in the thigh. Fortunately, he had with him some drugs that came from the medicine cabinet in Woydiethen and those drugs enabled him to prevent a dangerous infection. When the hospital was taken over by the Soviets, he was treated by a female Russian doctor who was "pretty tough" but efficient. She treated all of the wounded the same, whether they were German or Russian. When his leg became inflamed after all and his condition worsened, Erich did not dare to continue taking the antibiotics in front of the Russians. However, after the doctor decided that his leg had to be amputated, Erich confided in her about his stash of medicine and gave her his bag containing them. Erich repeatedly witnessed that fellow soldiers did not survive a leg amputation. The doctor used the medicines on him but also on others who needed them. At the end, the treatment was successful.

Per Ingolf, following his stay in Königsberg, Erich was transferred to Tilsit where he was lodged in either a former grain warehouse or in the stables of a former barrack. He had to sleep on straw on the ground. During the day the men had to load grain from silos into railroad cars that went off to Russia. Ingolf does not remember the exact sequence of the other places where Erich stayed. However, he knows that his father was sent to Siberia in 1946 or 1947, and he was imprisoned near a great city which is located on the same longitude as Calcutta. The prisoners had to cut down trees into lumber. But during the three short summer months they occasionally were allowed to spend time with cattle farmers and during these times they were well fed.

Later Erich wrote a letter to Gaga about the time when he was located "on the Mongolian border in Siberia". Bergild remembered that a postcard from Erich arrived in Bleckenstedt on which the following letters were dotted: N O V O S I B I R S K. This was a widely used practice of providing a single letter with a dot as a way to smuggle a secret message past the censorship. Novosibirsk is at about the 84th degree longitude and Calcutta is at the 88th degree longitude. This gives you an idea where Erich Spickschen ended up.

Ingolf continued his story. It was unspeakably cold during the winter months but since the work in the forest produced enough wood for fuel, the men did not freeze in their barracks. However, there were terrible storms and sometimes comrades who were in charge of bringing the food from the kitchen to the barracks in boilers never reached their destination. They literally were swept away by the storm, never to return. When that happened, Erich and his fellow prisoners got nothing to eat.

The food was horrible. Grits were mixed with sawdust and the bread was so soggy that water gushed out when you squeezed it. But the Russians themselves did not have anything better to eat.

Even if one was constantly busy with basic survival, what free time remained was spent in a meaningful way. The prisoners formed cultural groups. One of these groups provided training and the rejuvenation of ancient Greek literature. Somehow someone had been able to get a copy of the "Iliad" by Homer. In tiny penciled writing, the Greek text was copied and then memorized in long passages. The humanistic education which Erich had acquired in high school in Moers remained very important to him as long as he lived. It influenced him in his whole behavior even later after his return from captivity as the younger children, like Thorlef, became aware of when they consciously began to notice him.

Unfortunately very little about these details were provided in the letters. A handwritten letter dated January 19, 1947 from an Ella Beyer from Tilsit was preserved. Is this name fake? To a large extent, the handwriting of Ms. Beyer is very similar to that of Erich. Hardly anything important was communicated in this letter.

"Erich also sends his regards and good wishes with his whole heart. After three weeks of rest after a hard case of lumbago he is back in the old barracks and in good spirits. We hope that the upcoming negotiations in London and Moscow will finally bring the end of captivity for him. All rumors of freedom are silent at this time. Let only the good Lord rule! Erich is in pretty good spirits and confident. After four weeks of extreme cold that reached as low as -24° C (-11.2F), the weather is milder again."

At the end the letter says:

"Only this short note today. I'm afraid that the longer letters are more difficult to get through the system. I have heard nothing from you since November. All the best and warm regards to all in Gemen and Vluyn.

With love, your Ella"

Correspondence remained highly unpredictable. The next preserved letter from Erich is dated July 11, 1947, sent from Riga. That means that the letter writer at times resided in Latvia.

"My Dears!

I just got through a terrible disappointment! Together with many others I was at the old Barrings Wirkungsstaette (Barring's place of activity, namely Insterburg) to be processed for discharge. Then I got diarrhea because of a cold or flu and was shipped back to the field hospital in Insterburg either by mistake or on purpose to make room for others. They told me that they suspected dysentery because allegedly there had been blood in the stool but that was not the case. Now, after five days of transport, today we arrived here in Kaunas – Vilnius. But tonight we are going back to Duenaburg (Daugavpils). However, in the meantime the transport home from Insterburg left. I already dreamed about being able to celebrate my birthday with you. It was not meant to be! Keep your head up! Who knows why it had to be. Let's keep on hoping. At least I am well. Lean but healthy. The food is good here and the work not difficult. I have heard nothing from you since February! So one worries about what could have happened to you by now. Hopefully unnecessarily. Every month I have sent you the approved RK card (Red Cross card) with the allowed 25 words. Did they arrive?"

Apart from the "terrible disappointment" the letter includes in almost litany like repetition the matters that Erich could write about and which determined his daily routine. Erich's life consisted of staying healthy and adequately nourished while maintaining hope on the one hand and being plagued by worries on the other hand. The monotony of prison life was reflected in dismal messages that had to be brief, especially when they had to be kept to only 25 words.

A letter mailed on July 18, 1947 by Erich from Duenaburg (Daugavpils), Latvia reported about the makeshift accommodations with which he had to be satisfied at the time.

"We have already spent six days trying to move a paramedic camp. After spending a few nights in a tent, we built ourselves a few permanent octagonal tents from Ensoplatten (a type of hardboard panels) which are very spacious and pleasant. The food is excellent and we even have real butter. One can work with that kind of nutrition. Everything should be completed in September and I therefore strongly hope that the promised return home will happen. I do want you to know that my health is excellent."

Perhaps Erich's letter should be read with due skepticism since he twice used the word "excellent". One can assume that Erich was temporarily doing well in the summer of 1947. However, a month later on August 17, 1947, he again used the undefined expression of "pretty good" to describe his health. This time, the hand written and highly legible letter provided an accurate return address: Erich Speckersen, Duenaburg (Dvinsk), Kaunas St.169.

"My Dears!

I will try again to reach you this way to tell you that my health is quite good. We cannot complain about the food. We receive wonderful new potatoes and cucumbers from some people here. I have had no news from you or Ursel since February. Of course I'm very concerned. Hopefully my fears are unfounded! I have thought of Mother on her birthday and wished her all blessings; the wish for a healthy and speedy reunion was at the forefront. For our 24th wedding anniversary (on August 12) we had fried potatoes and cucumber salad with sour milk dressing, then some apples and papyrossen (??). Today we even fixed some fried potatoes with meat and cucumber-tomato salad.

"My only hope now is that our current work detail comes to an end in a few weeks and we will then be released. The transport on July 8 on which I was scheduled to depart, left without me because I came down with a mild case of diarrhea and had to go to hospital even though it lasted only a few days. That is fate against which one cannot fight.

"Today is a beautiful Sunday, no labor. In the morning everything was laundered and mended and we are planning to go on a scavenger hunt again. What may the future bring us? According to the news from the West the food situation looks so devastating and I am greatly concerned about you. It seems very doubtful to me that the purchase or lease of a small farm will be possible in these circumstances. But we do not want to give up hope. The dear Lord God will continue to help us! If only I could come home at the latest in the early Fall so that I could still have time to visit some prospective farms to buy. But at least I am now trained to be a jack-of-all-trades."

This letter contains hardly anything new. Erich confirmed the dreariness of prison life. However he provided a clear message about the obviously exceptionally good nutrition. The fact that the letter had an accurate return address caused an unpleasant consequence - but the letter survived. Erich wrote on September 3, 1947.

"Unfortunately, the letter was returned because of improper address procedure. I continue to feel excellent. Sorry, there is nothing definite yet about our release. Greetings to all my loved ones who I hope to see again soon. I wonder how you are doing at the age of 79 years, my dear Mother.

With love, your Erich."

On the same date, September 3, 1947 a typewritten letter was sent by Alfred Spickschen and his wife Lotte, to Ursel.

"Thorleff [sic] (here called Josef or Jupp) has now unhappily infected his dear Aunt Lotte with the mumps. We wanted to drive to Wickrath today to go to Mieze's birthday party in conjunction with a meeting that I had scheduled in Neuss. But that is now blown to the wind.

"The children are giving us a lot of joy. They eat and sleep a lot, are obedient and Bergild is very helpful so that there is little scolding to be done. By the way, Bergild is the one taking care of that. She could become a real "governess" à la Tante Martha, if you are not careful. She spanks Jupp - sometimes well-deserved - at least in Bergild's eyes. I disagree.

"The news of Erich is in itself good. He is still physically well. If it will work out with the transport home, I would be more than satisfied. But to be honest I do not believe it and I am not sad about it. Our domestic political situation is not yet ready enough to be looking forward to a return.

"We are still in a drought here and you can honestly speak of a catastrophic food situation for vegetables and most likely also for potatoes. I do not know how we will get through the winter."

The letter throws a light on the situation in which Erich's relatives lived in the western sectors of Germany for about two and a half years. The children Thorlef and Bergild, six and eleven years old, spent some time with their aunt and uncle in Vluyn as guests and this probably was to relieve their mother Ursel in Bleckenstedt for a while. As the letter showed, in the autumn of 1947 the West Germans suffered from a major food shortage and this shortage was not just for the Russian prisoners of war. Alfred and Lotte were free to write about it while Erich is not allowed to speak so openly.

Two pieces of correspondence from Erich, adhering to the "25-words-default" were likely postcards. Only typewritten copies were saved. The first card bears the date of October 6; the second one is dated October 25, 1947.

"Doing excellently, hope you too. The best birthday wishes to Martha. Still waiting to be released. Longing for our reunion, especially with Mother. No news from you since February. Erich."

"Still here, future unknown! Still hoping to spend Christmas with you. Greetings to Kleinmentig-Oeding and Barten-Odenkirchen. Stay healthy. I am well. To a happy reunion. Cordially, Erich."

On the first card can be found, in a shortened form, everything that occupied Erich's thoughts incessantly in his bleak situation. Again, a big question mark should be located after the word "excellently".

On the second card, it was important to Erich for him to send greetings to individuals from his former private life with the few words that are allowed him. Otherwise the cards had no room for long-winded communications. While they supply a proof of life for Erich of course they are immensely important not only for Erich but also for his family and friends.

A final letter from Erich is dated January 20, 1948 and is the same as the two previous cards -without a location and available only as a handwritten copy.

"My Beloved!

Finally more words. We continue to wait patiently for the hour of our release which hopefully will not be delayed until the end of 1948.

“If only I would have received some mail from you since February of last year (it was probably prevented by the frequent changes of our prison camps) everything would be easier to bear.

“I'm so worried about you! Every day and every hour I'm with you in my thoughts. In my thoughts and with my warmest wishes I will soon celebrate Ingolf's, Mother’s, Thorlef's and Alfred's birthdays with you. The later ones hopefully in person. Great desire to see Mother! I wish her good health for a long time! What progress will the children have made? Maybe I'll be a grandfather soon. Concerns about the future are useless, I will have to wait! Will we ever be able to own our own place again? Stay well as I do and may your table always be richly laden. I dream of you almost every night!

“The most heartfelt wishes to you all. With love, your E."

As in the letter of November 13, 1946 where Erich said that he "must ban all thoughts about the design of the future back to their place of origin again and again, because they are futile and nerve wracking". Erich admonished himself to recognize the futility of worrying about the future. Yet he could not help but being constantly ruled by these concerns and to speak of them. His mind told him that his daydreams were useless but the feelings of worry and hope were stronger.

It was not until the beginning of June 1948 that Erich returned to West Germany. The exact details as to the date of his release from captivity, the circumstances of his journey from Russia and his arrival in Germany are not known. But from the remarks of a fellow prisoner it appears that Erich first arrived in the Soviet Occupied Zone before he traveled to West Germany. A close relationship had developed between Erich and this fellow prisoner during the captivity. This man was Robert Keil (1905 - 1989), a native of the Rhineland who later lived in Vienna and became a well-known painter. Keil wrote about more details in a letter of condolence from Vienna to Ursula Spickschen on October 14, 1957 two weeks after Erich's death:

"Until my death I will always think of him with my deepest feelings. He was a good friend, a candid, open-minded, honorable man who had a very deep and clear love for his family. During the most severe, most difficult hours, we spoke about everything that we had to leave at home. This gave us our strength to withstand the adversaries. Our surroundings and having to be in the company of completely demoralized inmates were the hardest tests for us except for hunger and inhumanely hard labor. And I have to tell you and your children this! We remained unbroken and even though seriously ill, we believed in the eternal and indestructible goodness of humanity and we endured. We said good bye in some desolate railway station in the East Zone (Soviet) with a quiet but determined attitude to give life what we can still give."

VII

Time in Bleckenstedt / Salzgitter

1. March 1945 to June 1948

Previously Ursula Spickschen told us about how she finally arrived with her children and several companions in Bleckenstedt, a village that belonged to the Salzgitter complex, at the end of their flight from East Prussia. Her pocket calendar and the diary from 1945 indicated that she arrived in Bleckenstedt with her flock on March 20, 1945. In a 1979 interview with her grandson Erich Hart she related how the refugees fared after they crossed the Elbe River.

"The reception in Bleckenstedt was not very friendly. Mr. Klemp, the grumpy inspector, and his housekeeper were apparently not pleased that they had to accept other people to be sheltered with them. But this could not be changed; they had to put up with it. We experienced several bomb attacks there in the time before the war ended. The inspector had built a small bunker right behind the house in the basement were the oil heater was located and it was pretty safe. We sat there almost every night during the air raids. We were also joined there by the nice owners of the local brewery, people by the name of Borg.

"Those who stayed with us and came along to Bleckenstedt, namely Helga, Hase, Pinchen and some others, had to work in the local nursery. We received ration cards from the government so that our food supply was reasonably assured. We were able to make cottage cheese from the skimmed milk which was allotted to us. In comparison to the cities, we had it relatively good. Of course we had very little to eat and one can even say that we were hungry at times.

"One day we heard that the Americans were very close. Soon they would conquer Bleckenstedt. We sat in the bunker and heard a lot of bombs and shells exploding. All of a sudden the door of the cellar was thrown open and two sinister-looking American soldiers rushed in and searched every nook and cranny. They told us that they heard that a German officer was hiding in the bunker. Then we remembered our nephew Gerhard Spickschen. He was an officer and he had been wounded. He had been convalescing in a hospital in Westphalia. He visited us for a few days in Bleckenstedt because the hospital he was in was closing. But when I heard that the Americans were not far off, I sent him to the hospital in Wolfenbüttel, a neighboring town. One of us was able to communicate to the two soldiers that he was no longer with us. They accepted that answer.

“The next morning we moved into the big room which was previously used as the dining room when guests came to visit. Today it is the grand parlor of the Traube family home (more detail will be given about them. later). All the windows were broken in the room. When we were in the middle of sweeping up the broken pieces, two more American soldiers appeared. One was obviously of mixed blood and we were afraid of him. But he was quite nice. With the little bit of German he knew, he said: "Oh, cleaning, cleaning" and "sweeping, sweeping!" He did not hurt us.

“Later an unpleasant incident occurred. More Americans arrived and moved into the house. They threw us out of the rooms where we slept and used our beds for themselves. When the water suddenly stopped running, the sergeant who was in charge of the platoon claimed that we had turned it off. He screamed and hollered and made a huge scene. I slowly remembered some of my school English and with Helga’s and Hase’s firm support we were able to explain to the man that we had not turned off the water. Because he was still angry he cleaned out Mr. Klemp’s wine cellar to get even. I also had a couple of bottles stored there.

“The war had ended, at least for us. After some time had passed, Mr. Klemp declared rather maliciously, ‘Ha, you will have to vacate the house. Mr. Traube’s farm in Engelnstedt was expropriated and he is here now to take over the farm house and probably also the farm itself. He will probably throw all of you out.’ But Mr. Traube did not kick us out. On the contrary, I became friends with Gerd – that was his given name.

“Our friendship happened like this: I had some coffee available which I had gotten by trading with Poles who lived in the area. Everything was so incredibly scarce. In the evening I asked Gerd if he would come for a cup of coffee so that we could get to know each other. He was probably curious to find out what kind of person I was because he knew that I was a committed National Socialist. He came over to see me and we got along very well. Obviously we ended up liking each other a lot. During the next few months he often visited me and we talked a lot.

“Hase did not want to stay in Bleckenstedt anymore. One of her friends, a Miss Salz from Romehnen in the Samland, told her that she was employed as a horse trainer by the British occupation forces in Herford. Before our flight from East Prussia, Hase had started her training as a livestock breeder assistant in Silesia. After that she worked at the horse breeding estate of the Wiegers, our neighbors in Weidehnen. She was also accepted at the University of Rostock training school in Mecklenburg. She could not go there after the war because the Russians occupied Mecklenburg. Despite my protests, Hase went to Herford and reluctantly I finally gave my consent. After she left I told Mr. Traube of this incident and he was quite indignant. He said, ‘You allowed your daughter to leave?! I would not have done that in your place.’ Fortunately Hase soon came back because she had not been accepted by the British.

"Meanwhile, Inspector Klemp had another house renovated for himself. The house had also belonged to the Reichswerke and was property of the State. We had to leave our living quarters because Tante Grete, Jutta and Inge Traube moved to Bleckenstedt from their temporary living quarters in Hallendorf. Klemp would have liked to send us to an apartment in Hallendorf, a neighboring village, but under no circumstances did I want that. I wanted to stay in Bleckenstedt.

"At this time Hase and Gerd Traube were not involved since he had another girlfriend. I wanted to stay in Bleckenstedt because of the Borgs, the very friendly brewery owners, and also because of the many other people who had helped me. I was aware that there was a vacant apartment on a farm that also belonged to the Reichswerke. Only a few minor repairs were necessary on the ceiling of the large family room. A mason would be able to do that in a few hours. However, Klemp said he had no one to do the repair. I went to Mr. Borg who had quite a lot of pull in the village and he said to Klemp, 'Well, look here my man. I'm sure you can find someone to get this small job done!' Klemp got the ceiling repaired and we were able to remain in Bleckenstedt. We moved into the house on the so-called pig farm.

"Our apartment was on the second floor. In the large room there was a furnace which unfortunately gave out no heat. We were cold all the time - actually froze - like so many others at the time. After all, we should have been satisfied because we also had two small bedrooms, a kitchen and a tiny pantry available. The toilet was outside the apartment. To get to the toilet, we had to go down a flight of stairs and through a long corridor in another apartment. The house was divided into four apartments and each family had to take turns to clean the toilet. The big waste box had to be emptied with a large scoop and the contents had to be dumped onto the manure pile. I did not mind doing this job; it did not bother me and Spatz (Opaps' secretary) helped me. When you know something has to be done, you do it.

"In the meantime, Hase and Helga started to work on the farm. I was able to secure an apprenticeship contract for them so that they could work as farm apprentices and not just as farm workers. The apprenticeship was completed by an exam.

"As for the food, we ate very poorly. Potatoes were extremely scarce. The main food was vegetables which we could buy at the nursery shop. Mostly we ate red beets, cabbage and sometimes celery. Every now and then we got turnips which I liked very much. Since Helga and Hase worked on the farm, we had the right to one free pig a year. But Mr. Klemp cheated us one time by giving us a sick pig, an animal with encapsulated tubercles (a type of tuberculosis). Only by the intervention of Opaps' acquaintance Mr. Welge, who was still considered the local farmers' representative, could I get a certificate to get a new healthy pig allocated. Without the pork we would have hungered much worse than we actually did. The children hardly remember today how often we had to go hungry. They know that there was little to eat but they were not really aware of how great the need was. It is good that they do not remember the bad times.

"From time to time I baked a cake with sweetener and dark flour. We could not always utilize everything available that was grown in the garden. For example, we had more berries than we could use because we had no sugar for canning or cooking jam. We used syrup that we made ourselves from sugar beets as a substitute for jam. The berries I could trade for other things, as I already indicated, sometimes with the Poles in exchange for coffee beans. The Poles were people who had previously worked in the Reichswerke and who still lived in the area. We added a few coffee beans to the malt coffee which we usually drank so that it had a more pleasant aroma.

"There were always people who visited us and we played a lot of Doppelkopf (a card game) with them. We also invited the Traube family and after a while a strong bond developed between us. I cannot explain in detail how Hase and Gerd gradually got to know each other more intimately. Anyway, those two fell in love and then got married.

"I always made sure that the two of them did not do anything stupid before the marriage. At one point I noticed that Hase was not in the house and Tante Grete, Gerd's mother, realized that Gerd also was missing. Both of us probably thought the worst. Tante Grete and I were not close at that time so that we could not openly talk about the situation. Later I learned that she thoroughly questioned Gerd as I had questioned Hase. Both of them swore that nothing happened that was forbidden, they only talked and discussed several issues. They had a long discussion with each other. To get some privacy, they talked the whole night in a barn that belonged to Gerd. I do believe that they told us the truth. Those two were still far from being engaged at the time. It was a long time before that happened.

"The fact that I heard nothing about Opaps for many months was far worse than all of our problems about the scarcity of food and inadequate housing. I did not know if he was still alive. My concern for him often made me despair. I was constantly on the lookout for someone who could possibly give me some information. A nice Agriculture Director from Liebenfelde, who I happened to meet once in Braunschweig (Brunswick), said to me, 'Well, I've heard that your husband was wounded in the leg.' He did not know any details. Later I learned that what he told me was true. Opaps was in the hospital in Insterburg with a leg wound. One year and nine months had passed after our flight from East Prussia before I actually heard from Opaps for the first time.

"When we parted in Pillau, Opaps and I agreed that he would write Uncle Arthur in Herford when he was dismissed from the service and was looking for us. He would find out from Uncle Arthur where we landed. After one year and nine months, when I was visiting Tante Gudrun in Garmisch, I finally received my first post card from Opaps. Tante Gudrun worked for American officers as a housekeeper in the home where they were staying. I was greatly relieved and hoped that he would come home very soon. I had no idea that he would not come back from captivity until the summer of 1948. Thank God I did not know that I would have to wait so long because the wait was terrible. We were so close all those years. We always tackled everything together and always talked everything through so that one could rightly say that we were of one heart and one soul. The separation from him caused by our flight and the long wait afterwards was the worst for me.

"When Opaps came back in June 1948, he was yellow like a quince. He had hepatitis, an infectious jaundice. This jaundice, which had severely damaged his liver, in the end was the cause of his early death. Unfortunately at that time, medical science was not yet advanced enough to adequately assess the impact of such a disease and treat it. On the contrary, the social security office would not recognize that Opaps was ill. His heart had also been damaged by malnutrition during his captivity. This damage was treated by injections of Strophanthin to the extent that his health appeared to be largely restored. The severity of the liver damage was not detected until shortly before his death.

"Hase and Gerd and also Helga and Hubertus were already engaged when he returned. I think it was in May 1949 when the two couples got married on the same day. Opaps had gotten a small job with his older brother Alfred who ran the seed company. He sold and bought seeds from the neighboring farmers. In addition, he sometimes earned small fees as an agricultural expert to help out."

This ends the detailed conversation about the time up to 1948 that Ursel had with Erich Hart in 1979. Ursel's memories are enhanced in part through stories by Bergild, Thorlef and also Helga. Bergild remembers very accurately the air attacks she experienced during the last few weeks of war in Bleckenstedt. The noise of the approaching bombers filled her with terror because she knew that a little later she would hear the whistle of the bombs as they dropped down from the airplanes and then the great crash of the explosions.

They all spent the night in great fear before the arrival of the Americans. Throughout the prior day the thunder of cannons could be heard. Around 10:00 to 11:00pm the children, who were half asleep, were taken to the air raid shelter that had been built under and behind the house. There they huddled together with the adults while outside the shooting continued and the bunker trembled. Everyone thought the house was totally destroyed. When someone finally opened the iron door of the bunker and looked out they all saw with relief that the house was still standing. However, the stairs and the hallway were covered with broken window panes. An American soldier came through the door and asked, "Up so early?" They were stunned! Three tanks were sitting in the garden behind the house and had been shooting all night into the village. Several houses in Bleckenstedt had been destroyed by the shells. Later, the ruins served as the children's playground. They practiced gymnastics on the broken and burnt roof beams and played hide and seek among the ruins.

Double Wedding – Bleckenstedt June 1949
Karen with Gerhard Traube and Helga with Hubertus Von Eller-Eberstein
Back Row: Betty von Eller-Eberstein, Erich Spickschen, Margaret Traube, Karen, Gerd, Helga, Hubertus, Ursula Spickschen, Balduin von Eller-Eberstein
Front Row: Bergild, Thorlef, Ingolf, Astrid, Runhild

remembers that on some days in the winter of 1945-46 the hunger was agonizing. Once he sneaked into the kitchen where a jute sack that they all knew about hung on the wall. It contained dried bread for extreme emergencies only. With a terribly bad conscience (which he still thinks about today), he stole a piece of bread out of the bag. Not because he just wanted it but because his stomach really hurt from hunger.

Another time, in the summer of 1945 or 1946, Thorlef broke into the family garden with three friends. The four little rascals had located a loose slat in the fence and through this gap they sneaked onto the prohibited grounds. But they were discovered while they were feasting on the ripe raspberries. It was the only time that Thorlef received a spanking from his mother, not only because he had stolen raspberries but also because he was stupid enough to steal from his own garden and getting caught doing it.

In the ruins of Bleckenstedt numerous sparrows made their homes. The small eggs were taken out of the nests and used. Eggs that were already fertilized had to be discarded.

But 14 to 17 fresh sparrow eggs were enough for a small meal. They could be fried as scrambled eggs in the pan.

Obtaining tobacco was very important to Ursel since she had always been a smoker. She knew how to help herself by beginning to grow tobacco in her own garden. After harvesting the tobacco leaves they were wrapped in oilcloth and put under sheep dung to ferment. She got the sheep dung in the neighborhood where there were stables with a herd of sheep. The fermented tobacco was then cut into thin strips and cigarettes were rolled. The children all helped with picking the tobacco leaves and all the other jobs that followed.

Not only food but also leftovers, waste products and any other valuable materials were used in the most economical manner. Every day the large family accumulated a whole milk can full of urine which was not discarded but used as fertilizer for the garden. The rhubarb, for example, flourished well with such care.

Despite all efforts to provide adequate nutrition, it could not be prevented that Bergild contracted tuberculosis. In April 1948, she entered high school in Salzgitter-Lebenstedt. Since there was no other transportation she had to ride her bike daily about seven kilometers to the school and again seven kilometers back. After a few weeks she could only manage the way home by stopping at the roadside near Hallendorf to lie down and nap for a while. During the summer holidays she was diagnosed with TB. She had to leave school and was sent for rehab to the Sauerland Mountains to Onkel Guste and Tante Martha. Thorlef was also in danger of contracting tuberculosis. To strengthen his immune system he was given an extra ration of butter. Thorlef was very frugal and often saved the butter in his box so long that it was almost rancid. Helga recalls that the butter was such a precious commodity that Bergild often secretly nibbled on it during that dire time of need.

But there were also bright spots. Before Christmas, the family received packages of food from Danish and Swedish friends who formerly had been agricultural students in Woydiethen. In addition to basic foodstuffs a Swede named Davberger, who later became director of an agricultural school, also sent jam and spices that Ursel could use for baking. Uncle Niels Bangen from Copenhagen also proved to be a benefactor. Besides edibles, he also sent clothes. An old tuxedo arrived from Sweden and was saved for Erich. In early June 1949, he wore it for the wedding of his two eldest daughters.

But for Thorlef, the post-war period that he experienced in Bleckenstedt at the ages from four to nine years could not be perceived as a time of continued gloom. The difficult life that the adults had with all the hardships was always very exciting to him. However there were often unpleasant things to endure when it came to clothes. From his grandmother he received woolen stockings that she knitted for him and they scratched him terribly. They were secured with elastic bands that had button holes in them that were attached to a knitted camisole, also knitted by the grandmother. To get rid of the ghastly stockings, Thorlef once cut a hole into one of them. He hoped he would be believed when he told everyone that the hole was caused by a fall. Of course, the fibbing was discovered and he was punished. In addition to stockings and camisoles the grandmother also knitted undershirts and underpants from cotton. Even the children of Helga and Karen wore garments knitted by the grandmother. Thorlef recalled that she knitted day and night and it was said that she died while knitting. In 1948 she was walking across the street to try on a newly knitted article for a neighbor's child and she was hit by a car and was fatally injured.

In Bleckenstedt there were get-togethers at the Spickschen place with local dignitaries or members of the Traube family. The "little ones" were allowed to join the festivities until the early evening. During these occasions when there was an opportunity to celebrate an event, a rare drink appeared on the table. Liquor! Ursel traded on the black market for some of the alcohol but mainly she produced it herself and even knew how to refine it. Somehow she discovered how to set up a distillery in the kitchen with boilers, glass tubes and carbon filters and she proceeded to burn liquor. The alcohol was infused with pieces of orange peel so that it took on a special flavor. The adults played the card game Doppelkopf and they became more and more relaxed and funny as they drank Ursel's concoction. The children had fun watching everything.

On holidays the good china and the silverware were brought out which Ursel had saved from Woydiethen. Thorlef thinks that he remembers that two crates filled with these valuable items were sent to Vluyn in late 1944 or early 1945 and arrived undamaged. It was an experience, especially for the children. To them it was an assurance that a piece of unspoiled family tradition was maintained when such treasures were brought out and used.

The name "Traube" had been mentioned off and on and Ursel explained that Karen, always called Hase, had married Gerd Traube in May 1949. In an interview held in Bleckenstedt on July 20, 2009, Karen related details about the Traubes. She gave details about her parents-in-law and her husband although she was not related to them during the time about which she talked.

"When we came to Bleckenstedt shortly before the war ended, the farm was managed by the inspector Klemp. Unfortunately, he soon started to make trouble. The farm owned by my father-in-law, Walter Traube, was four kilometers away in the village of Engelnstedt. This farm had been taken away from him by the Nazis. My mother-in-law was able to find another place to stay, a rectory which was also nearby.

"My husband Gerhard Traube, born in 1919, was a soldier in the war. When he was supposed to be promoted it became known that he was a half-Jew. Thereupon he was dismissed from the military. That was in 1942. Looking back one can say, "Thank God". As a rider in the Signal Corps he had to lay down new cable to the front lines again and again. The cable was carried along in a drum, which was carried by another horse that was led by a lead. Two days after Gerhard was dismissed – we always called him Gerd - his successor was killed. The stakes were quite high.

"There were some half-Jews who survived the Nazi era. My mother-in-law's brother had a special place as a high-ranking SS officer. He was a dentist in Berlin. My mother-in-law, who was an 'Aryan' under the Nazi classification, always hoped that her brother could prevent the deportation of my father-in-law. But the local political district representative named Deinert did not like my father-in-law. The two did not know each other but my father-in-law was probably the last remaining Jew in his district. Deinert was a disgusting and callous man. For example, he told people that whoever would drown my father-in-law in the canal would be given a reward.

"Anyway, Deinert succeeded in having my father-in-law interred in the terrible "Camp 21". In this area there were very many sub-camps of Neuengamme. "Camp 21" was a prison camp. One of my sisters- in-law was the last one to see her father. He had to work in the slag heap where the hot glowing slag was dumped. A truck driver who took the prisoners to the work site noticed that my father-in-law was no longer able to manage the job. He sometimes dropped him off at a private house where he could get some rest. It was there that my sister-in-law visited him for the last time and was able to give him some food or clothing. I do not know why my mother-in-law did not visit him or why she felt that she could not go. Perhaps it was because people might see her and report the incident. Indeed, someone was watching everywhere they went. They had to be careful.

"Then all of a sudden my father-in-law was gone. Incidentally, he was a diabetic. My mother-in-law did not know where he was. She tried to inquire and of course she received no information. He was probably brought to Braunschweig (Brunswick) to the Gestapo and they made sure that he was deported to Auschwitz. The uncertainty was made worse for my mother-in-law because people emerged who claimed that they could get her husband released if she would pay them so and so many thousands of marks. That was all fraud. Later the news arrived that my father-in-law had died of diabetes. The camp administration always thought of some other way so explain a death. It never said: Gassed.

"Before he was taken prisoner, my father-in-law had transferred the title to the farm in Engelnstedt to his son Gerhard. He hoped that perhaps the estate would thus be saved for the family. But it was given to another farmer who had originally received a farm in Hallendorf but then decided that he did not want to stay there. He was actually a very decent man who did not really want to take the farm away from the Traube family. However, he was more or less forced to do so. When my mother-in-law did not know where to store all their furniture he offered that she could leave the furniture in two rooms of the farm house and that he would lock them and keep it safe for her. The man never used or sold even one piece of the furniture, contrary to what so many others did who took over properties and possessions of Jewish families.

“Gerd came home for a short time after his discharge from the military. Since he had to fear that the Nazis would continue to persecute him, he accepted a position as an inspector on an estate near Torgau on the Elbe in order to hide. My mother-in-law was in daily fear that he would be interred. I think it was in 1943. He learned a lot there because some crops were grown on the estate that were not grown in the Engelnstedt region. For example, after the war we benefited from the knowledge he acquired in radish cultivation. In the immediate postwar period when no one had enough to eat, we were able to offer consumers mountains of radishes and earned good money.

“But finally Gerd was discovered by the Nazis on the estate near Torgau and he was interred in a labor camp. When the Nazis closed this camp shortly before the arrival of the Russians, the inmates were told that they would have to leave. No one knew where they were going. So Gerd stayed behind under the pretext that he had to take care of a team of horses. He probably ripped off a horseshoe before the command for departure came. If someone questioned him, he could explain that the horse had to be shod before he could follow the other inmates. However, instead of following the other inmates, he hid in a barn until the Russians arrived. Someone he knew was able to tell the Russian soldiers that he, Gerd, was a prisoner at the labor camp and not a Nazi. He remained unmolested and was able to cross the Elbe River and return home.

“A little later he went to Lebenstedt, the seat of the British military administration that was the governing entity of the area at that time. There he described his case and declared that he wanted to claim ownership of a farm. However, he did not want to return to Engelnstedt because the memories associated with that town were unbearable. In addition, Gerd mentioned that the current owner of the former Traube farm would have to be evicted although he was not guilty of any crime.

“And here in Bleckenstedt, Mr. Klemp was only the inspector - not the owner. With the establishment of the Hermann-Göring-Werke program in the 1930s many farms were purchased by the government. Those who sold their land were hoping either to receive much larger estates in the East after the beginning of the war with Russia, or to be given a farm located within 30 miles which was 20% to 25% larger than their own farm as a substitute.

“In 1947 Gerd was able to lease the farm in Bleckenstedt. Gerd came there in the spring and had to drill (sow seeds). The estate manager Dr. Koetting, who was in charge at the time, smiled and said, "Mr. Traube, he’ll never amount to much!” Previously, when the farm in Engelnstedt was expropriated, Gerd and his mother only received a small amount of money and that money was in a frozen account so that they had no access to it. In view of the actual value of the farm, the amount of compensation was extremely poor. Also the compensation amount had been reduced by the "Judenbuße" (atonement of the Jews) and a few other deductions. The result was that they barely had anything left.

"The only thing Gerd initially was able to buy was a Hanomag tractor and a farm wagon with rubber wheels. He had to borrow all of the other equipment from farmers in the neighborhood. A few individuals actually gave him some old machinery. As I remember, Gerd came to Bleckenstedt with someone from Engelnstedt, the son of a blacksmith, I believe. The two performed all the necessary work. Inspector Klemp renovated another small farm for himself a little further along the road. Our Spickschen family had to move to the Schweinehof. It was also one of the farms that the Hermann-Göring-Werke project bought. The Schweinehof was where the pigs were kept. We lived upstairs in the house with two other families. In the late autumn of 1947, my mother-in-law arrived with her furniture and moved into the farm house in Bleckenstedt.

"To explain how Gerd and I first met, I have to go back in time a bit. In 1945, I was twenty years old and an avid horsewoman. I could ride well. A friend of mine from East Prussia had been present when a herd of Trakehner horses was brought to West Germany. Originally I wanted to join this horse herd but this was forbidden by my parents. Today I can understand but at the time I was very angry. After the war, one of my girlfriends was hired by the British as a horse trainer. The occupying forces established a great training center for cavalry horses in the city of Herford. We had relatives in Herford - the parents of Tante Lotte - and I thought it might be nice for me to stay with them and become a professional rider. I really had no desire to stay in Bleckenstedt any longer because Helga and I had to work like men in the fields. Although I was interested in agriculture and successfully ended my agricultural apprenticeship, I was just too tired of the hard work and boredom. Therefore I traveled to Herford. However, when I got there the British cavalry was reduced or disbanded, so the opportunity to work there as a professional rider was gone.

"My mother told 'Mr. Traube' that I was in Herford and he said, 'Now listen to me, I would have never allowed her to become a trainer for the English!' I was very annoyed when I heard that. However, when I first met Gerd on the stairs in our house I thought, oh, he looks quite nice. But I also had the impression that he hardly noticed me. I always thought that men didn't really find me attractive. Usually all the men immediately fell for Helga. At the same time, I always had the feeling that if I find the man who really likes me, he will be the right one. That sounds funny but for me it was a kind of certainty. But sometimes I was really sad when someone I liked showed absolutely no interest for me.

"Everyone thought that Gerd was more interested in Helga than in me. We both found that quite funny. In addition, it was a little strange that our mother always seemed to fall a little bit in love with her potential sons-in-law. Another quirk of hers that I did not appreciate became evident, namely she asked a lot of questions and kept digging into everything. In her diary there is the notation where she wondered 'Did he finally declare himself? It cannot go on this way. You go out every night!' At night she stayed awake until I returned. That also annoyed me. I never told her anything. In any case, Gerd and I got married and had a very happy marriage.

"In later years, our relatives always liked to come visit us. We were generous and the brothers and sisters, nephews and nieces who spent their vacations and holidays with us probably found something like a haven here. We never seemed to worry a lot about time so it sometimes happened that a train was missed. A couple of times we did not reach the station on time because the train had already arrived and the barriers were down. Then the children arrived one day late for school. Helga always called our lives 'somewhat bohemian'.

"We did not have an easy beginning, but I found it wonderful that no one ever whined. If something was missing we just had to do without it. Gerd was almost thirty years old when we started our lives here. We married in June, 1949 when he was thirty. He was a very good farmer who not only soon proved that he had mastered his profession but also that he was very popular with the local farmers. However, it took a while until we had the operation under control."

In the chapter "Erich Spickschen in Russian captivity", only the last part from a letter dated November 22, 1946 was quoted. What Erich wrote about in the first part of the letter discloses a dilemma he was tackling. It was obvious that Erich was having issues with his anti-Semitic attitude when he learned of his possible son-in-law Traube. Ursel in her own way soon questioned her anti-Semitism and overcame it. The following is the beginning of Erich's letter written in a forest camp.

He addresses Ursel as his "Dear good Fee".

"My heart began to beat excitedly with joy last night when your dear letter of October 9 arrived as well as Heta's from October 1. And yet a deep sadness has taken hold of me when I read them. My poor Muschchen (Ursel) is sitting alone entangled in her concerns that threaten to completely envelope her. She so desperately needs assistance and I, who is physically in very good condition, have to spend one dull day after the other and still cannot leave (even though we have not yet given up hope for an early release). If I could only hold your hand and be able to discuss everything with you in peace; writing is so difficult. I purposely waited to write so I could sleep on it overnight. I only know one side of the story (perhaps fortunately).

"I believe that all the events and troubled times may have initiated the feelings of love [between Gerd Traube and Karen]. I am not a great genetic theorist or even a fanatic but you and I both are familiar with the laws of genetics and should realize the danger that an atavistic[?] jump can represent. I don't want to say that my daughter might produce a little Genghis Khan but just imagine our good Hase with a little "Itziglein" (Jew boy). That's why I think we need to slow her down and advise her against this marriage with all our strength. If their love and therefor fate proves to be strong I would be the last one to stand in the way of my dear child who is of age. We see again and again that opportunity creates love and so I hope that she will find a new opportunity which to me seems quite likely to happen in Gudrun's sphere of activity, particularly at Marg.[?]. Why should she not be able to find a man who is more suitable in age? Although exceptions confirm the rules, it is certain that most marriages break up when the woman is older. And God help her if she is possibly told, 'Just be glad that I married you!' Again, one can only warn and otherwise let destiny work. You might even think that this is "convenient diplomacy" speaking but in the last two years I've largely become a "doubter of man" who knows well that the really decent guys (even among women) are very, very few and far between. So it may be better to have a spiffy younger man than a paltry or even popular older one. Should

Polterabend (Night before the Wedding) / June 1949
Karen, Hubertus von Eller-Eberstein, Gerd Traube, Helga
Background: Thorlef, Ingolf

a decision on your part be necessary before my return, if it meets your criteria, I will not blame you. Just remember that to be hard is sometimes a blessing."

It should be noted that these statements come from someone who was cut off from the world and who knew nothing about what increasingly has become known to the general public about the crimes of the Nazis. Erich Spickschen remained stuck in what he thought were his abstract, principled and self-conscious anti-Semitism. At the same time it is clear that he is anything but hard-headed. The absurd statement of "great danger of an atavistic jump" that "is horrifying" is the semi-true nonsense that was spread by the Nazis in blind insistence which had settled in the minds of the blind believers. Although nothing is known about when and to what extent Erich began to rethink his believes, his closing sentences of this letter precisely reveal that he did not make his views a dogma.

Gerhard Traube had a formative effect on the whole family with his generosity, his exemplary tolerance, his obvious balance and independence. He was undoubtedly most important to Karen, his wife. But he was also something like a second father for all the children, especially for Ingolf and his younger brother Thorlef. He was the counselor and role model who would often provide crucial guidance and assistance to the children after Erich's death.

Gerd Traube's special effect and radiation can be found in a dinner speech which he delivered on the occasion of his 85th birthday in November, 2004 in front of a great gathering of the Spickschen and Traube families about half a year before his death. The speech can be seen as a kind of legacy. Gerd first talked about his father and his father's assassination and then about his own dismissal from the armed forces and the death of the soldier who had taken his place as a dispatch rider. After he spoke of taking over the farm in Bleckenstedt he continued with words of healing:

"Both my parents-in-law Spickschen had been dedicated and loyal Nazis. But we children did not worry about that and held it against them. They both realized after the war how inhumane and criminal the Nazi regime was. And so we all got along well together and we had a great time.

"One should never condemn something or someone at the beginning as being totally bad. One can always find something good by looking back in time. I want to tell you to not ever give up when things are not going well. One should look ahead and trust the Lord God that he will take care of you and make things right in the end."

Thorlef added, "Gerd Traube had wisdom and tolerance, as distinguished by Lessing's Nathan. He judged people not by their status or their club memberships but always looked at the individual personality. He did not dwell on the past but looked forward with deep trust in God. He was a living example for all of us. In spite of the hard times that he had to go through he had a full and happy life with his large family."

The following were written during the first few weeks and months after Erich Spickschen's return from captivity. Most of the sometimes extensive letters were written in the short period between June 6 and September 20, 1948. The question of how the parents should handle the situation of their daughter Karen and Gerhard Traube is one issue among many others.

2. The Correspondence between Ursula and Erich Spickschen in the Summer of 1948

The youngest Spickschen daughter Astrid, who was born on June 8, 1943, preserved in her memory a picture that addresses the circumstances of how Erich arrival in West Germany after his release. In an interview on October 15, 2009, she explained:

"The most dramatic experience for me was when the letter came, announcing the return of my father from captivity. I was five years old. My mother stood with the letter in hand and we small children pushed chairs around her to be able to look over her shoulder. I just have this image in my mind. I cannot remember the moment when I saw my father again. Maybe he was surrounded by so many people and there was such a commotion that I could hardly see him."

Unlike Astrid, her then twelve year old sister Bergild clearly remembers the moment when she saw her father for the first time after he returned from captivity. "The heavy front door from the Schweinehof house where we lived was only partially open and I looked through the gap to the outside. My father was talking to someone so he did not see me. When I saw him, I thought, oh my God, this is not my father! He had on a quilted jacket, wore straw boots and his face was bloated, yellow and pale. He had lost almost all his teeth. Then I went outside and hugged him. I felt so sorry for him!"

In the previous section Ursel already pointed out that Erich returned from captivity as a sick man who was "quince yellow" as a result of jaundice which had severely damaged his liver. Karen, the second oldest daughter who was born in 1925 lovingly called her father "Vaterchen". She explained in more detail in an interview from July 20, 2009 how Erich was doing in June, 1948.

"He really came home a very sick man without teeth and water edema all over his body. He looked terrible. His mother Maria insisted that Erich come to her in Gemen (which is very close to Vluyn) because his brother Alfred knew some very good doctors there. There he would be able to get a thorough check-up and all of his issues could be dealt with. But ultimately the doctors realized too late what was wrong with him. His severe liver damage was not discovered until it was too late. He did not drink - not even later on. Maybe he drank an occasional glass of wine, but he was absolutely not a drinker. He had a malignant form of jaundice." (Hepatitis).

Ingolf illustrated with an example that Erich did not like nor tolerated alcohol. A rather funny incident in this regard was related to him by an acquaintance, the previously mentioned Lukas. He told Ingolf what had probably repeatedly occurred during the Nazi time. At official receptions given by the SS and other agencies drinking of alcohol and toasting was customary so drinking was inevitable. At these functions, Erich would take an employee with him, an adjutant, who would discretely stand behind him and quietly take the glass from Erich after he had taken the customary first sip.

Bleckenstedt 1948
Bergild, Thorlef, Karen, Runhild, Ingolf, Astrid, Helga

Karen explained further what happened during the summer of 1948.

"It was very difficult for my mother to deal with the fact that Erich went to stay with his mother. Presumably she thought that when her husband returned, life would go on as before. Her dream did not come true! In the years since the beginning of 1945 she probably always imagined that her husband would be the same man as when she had last seen him. And now he came home completely changed. This was a very tough disillusionment for her. When he came back, Vaterchen was not only a sick, but also a broken man. Deep in his heart he probably thought, 'If my life ends now that would be all right with me!' He had no strength or will to live left."

In retrospect, this interpretation of the awareness and emotional state of Karen's parents is convincing in its overall assessment. However, the way that her parents seemed to find each other, then lose each other again during the months of June to September 1948, may have happened somewhat differently in view of the parents themselves. The intensive exchange of letters from this time provides a different picture. Sometimes the facts coincide with Karen's views but at other times they differ. The letters indicate that there was a brief reunion between Ursel and Erich in early June, before he traveled to his mother in Gemen. In a long letter that Ursel wrote on the typewriter on June 6, 1948 she mentioned Erich's brother Alfred, then talked about various refugees. Following that she discussed the relationship between Karen and Gerd Traube. Only after that did she discuss her own relationship with Erich.

"My Darling!

Alfred has cared for us so touchingly. I got as much money from him as I needed and he also helped us a lot with other things.

"Mr. Berg has had a difficult time, his daughter died after returning from Siberia. He is an economist and lives near Hameln with his family. Gruber has leased some land and owns two horses and also works for other farmers." (Ursel then updated him on several of their mutual acquaintances.)

"And Hase's issue has not yet been finalized so you can give your input. Alfred has no concerns. Gerd is not a bad person just because he has a little Jewish blood in him for God's sake. Aryans are not any better as we have now seen! The anti-Jewish propaganda was more than exaggerated. I have finally met "the good Aryans". The Jews have lived 2000 years under burdens, but we Aryans are ten times worse than the Jews. Well, we'll talk about it and you can observe Gerd when you get here.

Erich's Return / Bleckenstedt 1948

In her story of the escape Ursel mentioned that Erich had been "deposed as the Landesbauernfuehrer by Gauleiter Koch and was replaced by a Mr. Adam". The original good relationship between Erich Spickschen and Mr. Adam had deteriorated both before and after Erich's replacement. Ursel's report in the letter about other refugees, including Berg, Gruber and Schumacher indicates that the old relationship network continued.

Ursel's casual but quite clear comments about the connection between her second oldest daughter Karen and Gerd Traube indicate that she is definitely on the side of the son-in-law-to-be and she seems to have no doubt that she can convince Erich to see it her way. It is unclear whether anti-Semitism was ever a very serious concern to her.

Ursel also wrote a very extensive typed letter to Erich on June 30, 1948. He is affectionately called "Mops'chen".

"My dear Sweetheart!

If the enlargement of the heart can be cured, what I am hoping for, it will mean that you will not qualify for disability. But I got a shock when I read about the strict instructions the doctor gave you. That means that the enlargement of the heart must be very serious.

"[I often use] the 'rose-colored glasses' when I can possibly do it and look through them at the people and events. Had I not done that, I certainly would not have made it through these three years and four months as well as I have. That explains why you recently said that I was sometimes inconsistent regarding my evaluation of different people that we talked about. Sometimes I had those glasses on and saw only their good sides, sometimes not. But it is much nicer when you are wearing the rose-colored glasses. Then you yourself are a much more lenient and better person and are joyful and happy. But you also have to have inner harmony and be in a good mood to be able to put on those eyeglasses. I cannot do it in the controlled, sober and uninspired atmosphere of Gemen and usually Vluyn. Here at home – despite the unrest, primitive conditions and eternal small problems that come up – it works much better because our own atmosphere prevails here. But now don't get mad again, my dear Mops'chen. I don't want to offend you. I just want to explain how I feel. We just cannot pick up where we left off in 1945. We both have experienced much too much in the meantime. Experienced different things, evolved quite differently. We are not the same people that we were before. And between 1933 and 1945 we actually were only a weekend-couple. Our real life was over in the fall of 1933 when you went to the Landesbauernschaft. At the time that was life-altering although we were together most evenings and dined together at noon. But there always seemed to be strangers around us at the Landesbauernschaft. But the way it was before 1933 - that neither of us made the slightest decision without consulting the other; that one was hourly and daily exposed to the same influences and involved with the same people and knew exactly what the other one was thinking - all changed in 1933. And now we want to restore the old situation. We want to be together again, to live and work together again in our own home."

Ursel continued writing about her memories of happy hours and intensive discussions which always accompanied her through the years of separation.

"Yes, I definitely say that one needs words to achieve intimate understanding of each other. Only words can deepen feelings. Perhaps you are of a different opinion. But that is how I feel now. And I would also like to say that if I had not always insisted that you tell me your thoughts and feelings and made you clarify your thoughts and feelings in your mind and then put them into words we would not have been as happy as we were.

"And now I want to tell you that I am very worried about your ability to travel home to us by July 12 because I miss you very much." [At this time Erich was still too ill to travel.]

"Hopefully by that time your front teeth will be taken care of so that you can look human again. Ingolf described the current condition of your teeth as abysmal."

Ursel also wrote about Ingolf, who was staying with Erich's sister, Tante Martha and her husband Onkel Guste. Ingolf was not very happy there.

"They never let him (Ingolf) get a word in as I myself experienced during my visit. As soon as he expresses the slightest opinion he gets told to be quiet. When asking a question they tell him. 'Just worry about your homework!' And he doesn't have much time to read books. So this boy, who thinks a lot about everything and has tormented me forever with questions about God and the world, has created a novel-like inner life for himself. I can imagine such a thing if you have a very lively mind and are not allowed to speak or ask questions, never being able to express your opinion about something, never getting an answer to your questions. That is what is happening to him there. Hopefully it will work out and he will be accepted in Gütersloh (a boarding school)! I have had grave concerns about that boy for a long time but now even more so because of what you noticed. He did not show this tendency at Pentecost. It could be that he will go crazy! We know that he is very unhappy there and if he has inherited only 50 percent of my sensitive disposition, then under the right conditions he could really be ripe for the crazy house if he stays there much longer.

"I probably already wrote that Karen is coming back on Monday. Her vacation starts on the first. Hopefully you expressed to her in your letter that you only want her to give the matter a lot of thought. I hope that you told her that it is not that you are against it, but you want to make sure that she believes that she is so deeply in love with him that she does not care what you gave her to consider. At least that is how I have always understood you. If you did not express this very clearly, she may be in a terrible conflict between love for her family and her love of Gerd Traube. Anyway, she knows Gerd Traube now over two years and they know each other very thoroughly and surprises in the marriage are not to be expected. He has something very harmonious about him that suits us very well. And he has a fabulous way of dealing with her, to be respected by her, all in a calming way. You cannot force her to do anything because she and I are too similar.

"And since we are talking about 'force' Mops'chen, please do not torment me with trying to stop me from smoking. I have smoked ten years longer than you have seen and certainly more than you would have liked because we were not together much during the daytime since 1933. It was good for me and I just want to tell you that my nerves would definitely be worse off if I had nothing to smoke in the last three years. I just don't have such a laid-back nature as you. This is in some ways my weakness, I know, but it is also in some ways my strength. If it would seriously be harmful for me, then I would try to limit myself. But that is not a fact. And so therefore I have to take your constant harping as an attempt to make me succumb to your will without there being a good reason for it. And my love of freedom does not tolerate that. A comparison with you unfortunately is not possible because you have such a moderate nature. But just imagine that you were like Schumacher who has to consume several shots of liquor and a few glasses of beer daily to feel comfortable and happy. What would you say if I would constantly nag you that you should have enough with five drinks but you would like to have seven drinks? It certainly would be different if the money situation would not allow it or cigarettes were being bought at the expense of the children. But so far, because of growing the tobacco ourselves and being able to trade with it, the cost issue is still bearable. And if you have a defective heart

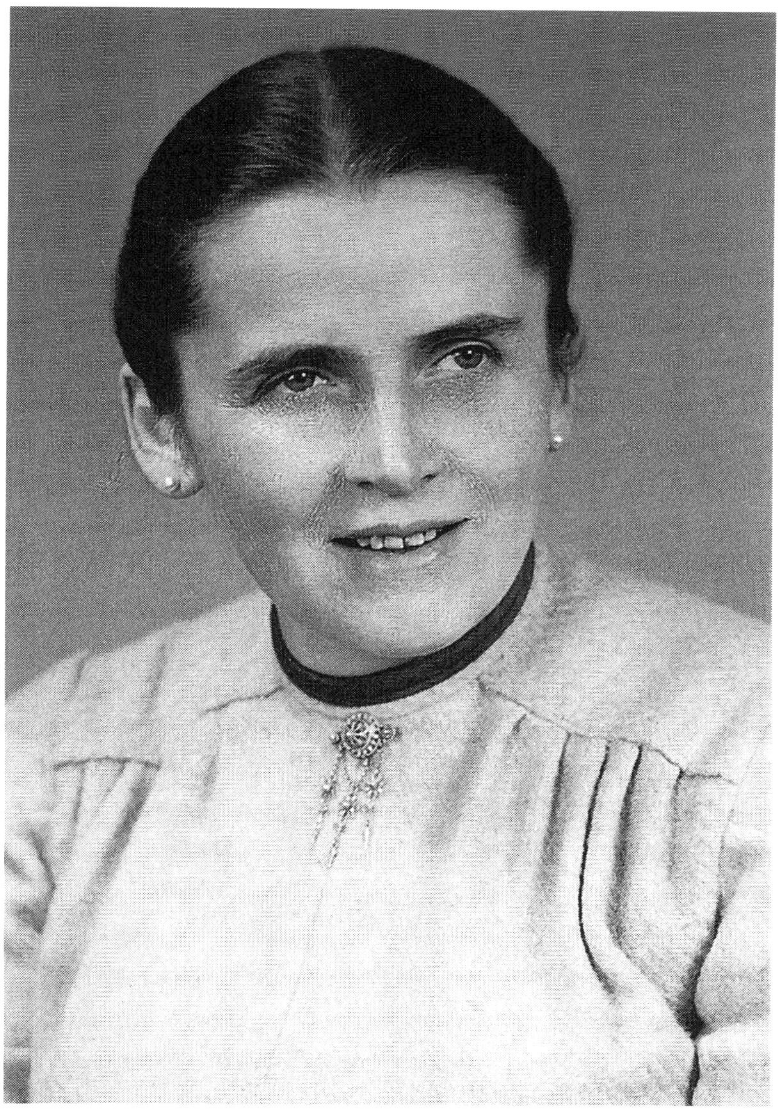

Ursula Spickschen, 1948

and know that you greatly shortened or endanger your life, then it is also something else. All this is not a problem for me because half a year ago I had my heart examined and I am fine. I am by nature very emotional and my nerves are naturally not very good! And what they had to go through during the last few years!"

In Gemen, Erich's mother was constantly worried about her son.

"If one concern about you is resolved, a new one arises. This way one is never glad and happy and the whole home atmosphere reflects this. This is not a sign of old age. That was already the situation 27 years ago, often with much less important things. One never really laughed out loud in Vluyn or could be happy. There was always something that stopped cheerfulness, always some concerns about something. Your father was probably quite different. Onkel Arthur once told me about how happy he was, but also about how many times he was berated for something."

Ursel also wrote in detail about shortage of money and money worries. The Reichsmark was being converted and devalued into D-Mark at this time at a 10% value. 100.00 Reichsmark therefore became 10.00 D-Mark. Ursel was dependent on Alfred, who has long supported her.

"As far as I could find out all the other girls got paid their 40.00 D-Marks head money (per person) and also one-third of their June salary. The remaining two-thirds will be paid out at 10% value in D-Mark. I withheld the money of Fee and Spatz, only gave them 10.00 D-Marks each and no salary. Clothes are given away in Braunschweig. All girls can get something there but they [Fee and Spatz] are not allowed to even though their salary has always been less than is usual here. That is not right! One can buy large zinc tubs here for the laundry. So far I have always just borrowed clothes but in the long run it is embarrassing. It was excusable because there was just nothing to buy. Rent, health insurance and the supplementary insurance are due to be paid - how will I be able to do pay it? I have no idea if I can count on getting money or how much and especially when I can expect it. I would really like to buy some fresh berries for canning but of course I cannot. Then in the winter we will miss it! I'm pretty despondent about this uncertainty with which I have to live. And it is particularly embarrassing for me that I cannot give anything to the girls. Since Alfred sent Omi 200.-marks via Lotte [Alfred's wife] it must be possible in some way that I can get something, too. But I really can't ask him again because you are there and you are his brother! I just cannot suddenly buy fruit for canning or give the girls some money and after that I sit here without a penny. I am living here without direction. And if you talk to him about it I need to know how long the possible hand-out would be expected to last before I would get more. I have to know that so I can decide what I can buy and what has to wait. If it is just a little, I cannot buy fruit, the laundry tubs, etc., but I must pay the rent, insurance, and pay the girls. So please clarify it because I am almost at the end of my wits when you think that there are nine people daily sitting at the table that have to be fed and all I have is 210.00 marks in ready cash. Alfred probably never even thinks about it. Yes, the dependency is quite hideous but it happened through no fault of ours and it cannot be changed. I always feel comforted by these thick-skinned thoughts because I've become very thick-skinned. Unfortunately not towards you though! How nice it would be if you were sitting next to me now and were able to take me into your arms like you always did in the past! But I'm sitting here all alone and worry about the vexing money. A lot of worry!! The 210.00 marks (actually only 160.- because I am not supposed to get your 50.00 marks until the end of the week) don't even cover my debts:

35.00 Rent
60.00 Rest of the money owed to Spatz and Feechen
28.00 Health insurance
65.00 Supplementary health insurance - Deutscher Ring
10.00 Potatoes for two weeks (200 lbs. incl. feed for our pigs)
28.00 Wages for both girls for June (⅓ in D-Mark, ⅔: at 10% in D-Mark, they received 35.-marks)

———
223.00 [sic]

"I have never felt so miserable, not even in the worst of times in Woydiethen. At first I did not want to write you about my problems but Helga said that it would be better that you get some inkling about my worries, despite your illness of an enlarged heart. And possibly you may be able to help me with Alfred. You have to get accustomed again to the role of the father in the family and this is now the most pressing concern, apart from many little worries that occur on a daily basis. I could write to Alfred myself - but I am sick and tired of having to ask him for money and help for the last three and a half years.

"I am sending to you in Gemen my diary about the last 3 ½ years. You have to somehow experience what we went through. But you have to read it objectively, not subjectively and you cannot suddenly dislike some people because of what you read in the diary. I very often had to outwardly act differently than I thought and had to be very diplomatic and self-controlled against the outside world. But since I have always had a need to vent and have often been intemperate I wrote everything down just as I felt it at the moment, depending on whether I was wearing rose-colored glasses or not. So it is written entirely subjectively and you cannot take it the way it is written. It's not all as bad as it looks. But that is exactly the way I felt at the time when I wrote it. Maybe you will realize what kind of stress my nerves and body and brain have gone through. And now that I am writing this down you will quite rightly think - and I ??? I have been living here under pressure all these years, completely without happiness and seeing only gray, being hungry and in danger, overworked, unfree, just a number, a nothing. I know that what I went through is nothing compared with what you had to suffer. Whenever a reassuring letter came from Vluyn saying how well you were doing, I knew that it was not so."

This letter does not need to be commented on because it speaks for itself. It gives us a comprehensive description of the current situation and also a recap of life's daily problems. Ursula Spickschen has won a new self-awareness during the three and a half years she was separated from her husband. Without doubt she already gained considerable self-confidence in the 1930s. She indirectly confirmed this by referring to the changing roles in their marriage since 1933. But only since 1945 was she completely on her own. On the one hand she is aware of the fact that her relationship with Erich has to be placed on a new level. On the other hand she is still yearning, perhaps sentimentally, for the maybe glorified memories of harmony that existed in the past. In all this she puts her claims to Erich, justifying her needs more decisively than before, being self-assured while remaining at the same time considered to Erich's side. In the section about smoking, which is not a minor issue, she clearly states that she will not be influenced by her husband's nagging.

Every single paragraph in the long letter provides an in-depth insight into a specific problem. Be it the relationship to Alfred or to Erich's mother, the general issue of Gemen and Vluyn. The question of further issues with Karen and Ingolf. Ingolf's parents worry about his strong fantasy and imagination. The worry about their own future marriage or, more urgently, about the constant shortages of money and financial difficulties in the daily life of the refugees. Again and again Ursel brings up her shattered nerves. Of course she does not realize that she must be a very strong woman in all this.

Erich wrote a response letter on July 2, 1948. He used a symbol that is near to a farmer to describe his own inner state.

"My best Muschchen, my Dearest one!

My inner soul seems to remind me of our poor East Prussian fields - full of weeds, looking like a tundra - but the core of my soul must still be the same. Now we have to plow and harrow it and tend it to get ready again for the delicate plants and crops that want to be continuously maintained with hoeing and weeding by hand and to be fertilized again and again with new compost. My soul had to grow a thick skin, had to be transformed into defensive armor during the years of my imprisonment, to remain uninjured, healthy and fresh in order to preserve the core for our future together. The current short separation may be beneficial for both of us to get the needed clarity about the essentials and to give our tender sprouting tendrils of love the needed warmth, rain and especially the sun. You will see, my Love, we will soon feel at home with each other again, reverberating together in perfect harmony. So far you have mastered all things alone, therefore together we should have no problems making it."

Compared to the openness and directness that Ursel shows in her letter of June 30, Erich's letter is flowery and idealized. He obvious believes that the marriage can continue like in old times "in perfect harmony" - a hope that Ursel clearly, though not harshly, marks as an illusion.

Ursel's response is a letter dated July 5, 1948, again typed and quite detailed. The subject is again the children and her relationship with her husband. The eldest daughter Helga had met Hubertus Freiherr von Eller-Eberstein, so there was now reason enough to think about two possible sons-in-law.

"My dear Treasure!

I am continuously thinking about when you will come home. It is all so strange that you are here, but not here!

"I naturally always compare him [Hubertus] with Traube who seems to win when comparison is made. But Traube is indeed a man for himself - and matured because of all the difficult experiences he had to go through and he is well educated. Have you already written to Karen since your dissuasive letter to Witzenhausen? Everyone seems to have something negative - one has Jewish blood, the other is married, the third one has peculiar traits. Anyway, Traube is particularly objective, clear and honest in his thoughts and loves to discuss his feelings and thoughts. He recognizes his mistakes and tries to overcome them. Hubertus has to be shown his errors because he believes that he is quite fabulous. But that is Helga's concern now.

"I have written again to Gütersloh. Hopefully it will work out with the boarding school for Ingolf. He cannot remain there [at Tante Martha's house]. Hopefully he will get along at school and catch up. If we were not so short of money he could get some hours of Latin tutoring from the teacher who had prepared him so well, when comes home for vacation.

Karen and Gerd Traube / June 1949

"Thorlef just did something cute. Fee took Thorlef and his friend in the little wagon to the coal merchant. On the way a little girl wanted to climb into the wagon with them. The friend said, 'No way, no women allowed in our wagon!' And Thorlef chimed in, 'Nah, we do not want any women on our wagon.' That 'woman' was around five or six years old. Last night I told a made-up story that the kids particularly liked. Astrid said this morning in bed, 'That was the best story you ever told. You have to write it down so that I can always read it when I go to school. Otherwise you will forget it. All of them always ask when you are coming home. They can't really believe yet that you are here. Their brains have not accepted the fact because you were here only one and a half days [when they first saw you again], too short a time. - My nerves – well, don't worry about them. Once you can fly again, I will follow you. If I have happiness and feel comfortable then I will always be happy and get things done. I will not be able to work as hard as I did before 1933 because I am fifteen years older, had six children and yet accomplished a lot and lived through a lot. During the three and a half years [since the escape] all has been seen a bit in a romantic light. It seems like we were always in agreement, that one always treated the other 100% correctly and with total understanding. That was probably true about 90% of the time. On the other hand that was perhaps true because we were not always together. And on top of that, both of us have changed somewhat. And you know what, Mops'chen, you have to let me have my freedom. Already during the years in Woydiethen have I been able to make decisions on small things and could do what I wanted. And now when I realize that I am being forced to do something I don't want to, like with the cigarettes and going to bed early, my opposition rears up. I feel like I am being treated as if I was fifteen years old and then I get angry. You do have to understand that! On the one hand, I had to be my own man for years. So now, on the other hand I can't be obedient and dependent and always do what you want me to do. If you leave me in peace and give me freedom I will probably do out of love most things you want me to do. That will happen on its own."

Helga and Hubertus von Eller-Eberstein / June 1949

With these letters it was apparent that both Ursel and Erich were in a dilemma when it came to the realignment of their relationship. In the search for a new balance it was not simply enough that Ursel was aware of her own independence. The experience of the past worked powerfully in both of them so that difficulties in the future life together were almost inevitable. The letters between Ursel and Erich reveal an intense effort to speak in theoretical terms prior to the entry into practice, to come clean about the expected difficulties and or disappointments.

On July 6, 1948, Erich wrote from Gemen that his return to Ursel was delayed because of some complicated dental treatments.

"My Dearheart!

My teeth will not be ready before Monday. I want to leave no later than Wednesday. Naturally, Mother tries to keep me here with all her might by saying that I was not healthy enough, etc. By the way, Mother has been very nice lately. The day before yesterday she even went so far as to say that she had enjoyed a rare good life, had a happy childhood, a happy marriage and a beautiful 'evening of life', like rarely anyone has had because she had never been dissatisfied!!"

Ursel responded in a typewritten letter on July 9, 1948.

"If only we could lease some land again so that we would not feel the stupid dependency on money so directly. We would be able to work in a positive way again. But I fear that nothing can happen before spring. We have to keep a stiff upper lip for at least three quarters of a year. We are in the middle of hard work. Everything in the garden is ripe. Cleaning and laundry is due, a lot of things need to be darned and three of the children, except Astrid and Ingolf, are lying in bed. Bergild and Thorlef have German measles, a very harmless illness. Runhild has swollen tonsils with a temperature of about 38 degrees (100 degrees F). Naturally they are quite chipper, try to get out of bed, are terribly noisy and constantly have wishes. But better that than if they were seriously ill."

Later in the letter, Ursel talked about Gerhard Traube. She said that he was worried and felt uncomfortable about having to talk to Erich about his upcoming engagement and subsequent marriage to Karen. While quite pale with excitement, Gerd spoke with Ursel and told her that he has "not the slightest feeling of inferiority". He would not try to justify himself to Erich on the grounds of his birth. According to her letter, Ursel replied to him, "My husband knows that Karen would never choose a man who is inferior to her and therefore my husband himself does not see you as inferior, because he will look at the person."

After this letter there was a break of several weeks in the correspondence. The previous letters between June 6 and July 9 were very closely spaced. It was mid-July when Erich was able to leave his mother in Gemen and return to Ursel in Bleckenstedt. In a letter to Gaga on July 28, 1948, Erich wrote an overview that summarized and described how he fared during the recent years and weeks. First he talked about the house of Gaga's mother in Königsberg which he was able to visit in 1946.

"Dear Gaga!

As a prisoner of war I passed by the house in the back of a truck in February, 1946, and saw that it was still intact. Not much else was still standing since the Russians burned most of the houses down after their conquest because they were signs of capitalism.

"I am happy and grateful that the hard times - that now seem not to have been very long - are behind me like a bad dream. I was pretty close to being released four times. But something always went wrong until in the fall we were sent in the wrong direction and ended up in Siberia on the Mongolian border. However, I was mostly in the hospital there and did not have to work outside during the coldest times at -50 degrees Celsius (-58F), thank God.

"During the first few days of my happily regained freedom I was quite alert and ate like two starved lions. This was soon followed by major weakness of my greatly enlarged heart that was caused by the inhospitable change of nutrition and climate. At the slightest movement or intake of food I felt completely drained. I then recovered nicely in my mother's quiet house and am now here a fortnight. Every day I have to get a syringe full of medicine in the heart and then plenty of rest. I'm a lot stronger now even though these dog days are hard on my system. Monday we will go to Gemen and then Vluyn where we will celebrate my mother's 80th birthday. Helga and Karen will join us there. Then back to Bleckenstedt where we have to celebrate our silver wedding anniversary. On August 26, I will take Ingolf to the new boarding school in Gütersloh. To my great joy he brought home a great report card on the 22nd, my best birthday gift. Then it's back to Gemen, where my last defective teeth will be replaced. Well, all the best to you! We hope to be able to lease some land later on, but first I need to get healthy, which hopefully will happen by October from what the doctors tell me."

Erich went back to his mother in Gemen several times. This led to a renewed letter exchange with Ursel. In a letter to him from August 12, 1948, Ursel mentioned that she would visit a "woman auxiliary meeting" on August 19. On September 5, she made a list of what Erich should take care of. Additional notes made it clear that Erich's health was still not particularly good. Among other things, he was being treated by a Dr. Mensing. In a typed letter shortly thereafter, on September 7, Ursel once more raised the question on the prospects to lease land.

"One agent wrote to me that people are reluctant to make any changes until after the Lastenausgleich [load distribution], then there would be enough farms to be leased. When I think that we may never again be completely independent and never be able to bequeath a farm to one of the boys, I get very sad and feel that it would be much better to emigrate, even if it might be quite primitive there. It is not nice when we have to completely let go of our life's dream that we built together for ourselves. As a merchant, it's quite normal to be an employee of a company. But as a farmer, you have to be your own boss. But what's the use - we need to be thankful that we do not have to be farm workers. But perhaps somehow you may be able to change your position by trading for a better one."

In the following days, letters were again exchanged almost daily. Some issues entail practical matters but then again and again the subject returned to the strengthening of their relationship and to come to something like a marital self-assurance. In a letter that Erich sent to Ursel from Gemen on September 7 he spoke about this effort of "enlightenment letters".

"My sweet Musch'chen!

"Yes, yes, business letters - my head is spinning and I have meticulously noted everything. I'm wondering what all is still falling through the cracks. No, the delicate enlightenment letters were more beautiful and interesting.

"I miss you, too, very much. Is it right that we are getting used to being so comfortable with each other again? Yes and yes again! The pain is part of the joy and the high in the purest sense. Sometimes I want to burst with happiness that I have you again."

The day following that intensive exchange of letters with Ursel, Erich's mother in Gemen was prompted to remark that he and Ursel behaved like bride and groom.

Further on Erich wrote that his cousin Emma "finds that love letters are magnificent". By the way, she says that men are much more selfish than women. I say, that on the other hand women are just more clever and diplomatic, which she then confirmed. Actually it's a sad sign for humanity that we stand out with our happiness! But we want to be grateful that we are able to live it and enjoy it. I'm so glad and grateful that Dr. Mensing was amazed at how well I have recovered. But I have to tell him that my lung is still quite congested and I still can't do a lot of digging in the garden. (By the way the walking with the suitcase went pretty well)."

Considering the opinion that Karen expressed retrospectively in 2009 regarding her parents' relationship after Erich's return from captivity, it seems that the experience of disillusionment that Ursel undoubtedly had to go through may have been what Karen saw but was not the entire story of what was going on between Ursel and her husband in the summer of 1948. Between alienation on the one hand and mutual rediscovery on the other hand, their emotions must have been swinging on the pendulum, as the letters reveal - a strong back and forth between euphoria and disillusionment. Even though she was emotional, Ursel looked at all the changes in her marriage in obvious realism; she has no delusions. Erich on the other hand looks into the future with emphasis on the positive and perhaps with forced optimism.

The letters which Ursel wrote on September 10 and Erich on September 13 can be ignored. Erich's letter dated September 12 states that "a quarter of a year has passed since I came to Bleckenstedt". That means that Erich returned to his family permanently on June 12, 1948. In one of his letters Erich added, "How wonderful it was to be able to take my children one after the other in my arms." He also commented on Karen's upcoming engagement party in remarkably succinct form stating, "I'm ok with the engagement." Erich's process of rethinking the marriage had perhaps come to a temporary end.

In a letter typed by Ursel on September 14, she went into detail again about the question of a safe existence. Ursel apparently thought that a detailed list of all of the expenses that must be dealt with in Bleckenstedt should serve as a tool to convey to brother Alfred in reasonable clarity the cost pressures placed on the family in Bleckenstedt. Moreover, Ursel tackled Erich's intentions for the future.

"Now to your other plans. Getting together with the Eschs to build cold storage facilities etc. is quite impossible I believe. You are not an expert nor are you a salesman - so what possibly could you do there? No one is going to build refrigeration facilities here in the country until they have completely restored their buildings and upgraded their farm equipment. They say, 'improving the conditions for the farm household'. But you are not an engineer! You don't have enough knowledge for that! You could go into any small business and work your way up to a good position, be it a shoe factory or a cider mill or whatever. But first you would still need money from Alfred. And then you might be cheated by a partner or possibly get into a fight with him. First of all you will have to decide what type of business you would be fit for. Then you could offer to work as a volunteer in that operation until you believe that it would suit you. After that you could open your own shop. That is how it should be done. But in the end it would be just as easy and probably better if you asked Alfred to let you work as a volunteer during the winter. Either in Vluyn or Bueren or in any other company that he deals with if he does not want you in Vluyn or Buren. You need training in the seed business so that you can get familiar with it. That really makes a lot of sense. Especially since we could combine a seed business with a small farm at a later date. We would not be able to handle it in our present condition because we are completely clueless in business matters and we would be just limping along. In any case, I would firmly tell Alfred that this sitting around doing nothing is impossible for you. You would have to drive around the district and visit people we knew from East Prussia who are already settled - and that costs money! And maybe you can find out from them if they know of a farm that is for rent. We can't sit around and wait until something is offered to us. I am convinced that we will still be sitting here a year from now if that happened and all I can say to that is, 'no thank you!'

"I am looking forward with horror to the winter when the back room where the girls sleep will probably become uninhabitable again. At about -5 degrees C (22 degrees F.)

moisture builds up on the walls and then freezes because the tiles on the outside are gone and the wall is unprotected. Where would all of us sleep then?? We cannot live like that on a permanent basis. After a while we might just give up and start to live at the expense of other people! One just goes crazy here in all this confusion and lack of space. It is now the fourth year that we are stuck here and soon the fifth will start! Is Alfred really convinced that we will be able to lease a farm this coming spring? Or what else causes him always advise you to wait and see and do nothing? [I mean that] we have to talk about all this in detail because you have been home now for three months and nothing has changed.

"Maybe Alfred is afraid that you cannot really run a business. First, we had one failure after another until 1933, the causes of which Alfred cannot explain to himself, because he is not a farmer and not familiar with the agricultural conditions in East Prussia at the time. Second, I can imagine that Ortmann has told him in round about ways that you are not a good farmer, that you are a theorist, not a good practitioner, etc. And third it may be that he thinks that you are no longer a good farmer since you were the "Landesbauernfuehrer" for so many years. It was very important that you told Alfred that you do want to try to obtain a farm mainly for the children. You have to overcome your inhibitions in this regard because I can imagine that Alfred sees you unfit to fight for your existence if you don't dare to speak frankly with him about these things that are so very important. You don't have to have inhibitions because we are in this situation through neither stupidity nor laziness.

"If all else fails, we will lease an inn or a grocery store in the country with some land attached to it. "What Alfred now believes about the coming of the Russians is very vague. Those years ago he had no idea that the Russians would be in Woydiethen two months later! "The best practice is: Cobbler, stick to thy last! You learned farming and agriculture so we definitely have to lease some land.

"If only you could be here so that we could talk! I'm only half a person when you're gone and we cannot share our thoughts. And that's why I am longing for a real home that we can establish and work on together. And I want some inner peace because in this temporary situation and all the worries about the future one can have no peace."

Erich obviously undertook almost desperate efforts to free himself and his family from a permanently difficult position. All sorts of considerations were made and all sorts of plans were forged so that a way would finally be found for a life that is less tense and free. Ursel's letter showed that she needed to talk to free her soul from worry because of what appeared to her to be absurd appearing undertakings of Erich's. To a certain extent she reserved the right to criticize and complain. She voiced her regrets in a letter dated September 19, 1948 that Erich was rarely at home for years in Woydiethen. The younger children had never had a regulated, stable family life.

"I once figured out that during the war years you were gone a quarter of the year, day and night, and the other half year you came home so late that the children were already in bed. You were actually only a "Sunday Father" for the little ones. Then you were gone altogether for three and a half years! Ingolf is the only one [of the younger children] who has experienced you as a proper father, at least somewhat, since he was already four years old when the war broke out. Hopefully we will soon have a proper family life and working life together again!"

The list which Ursel enclosed with her letter on September 14, 1948 showed in detail what expenses had accumulated between August 5 and September 5. This list was supposed to inform Erich but it was to be shown to Alfred specifically to give him an accurate insight into their expenses. In the letter from Vluyn that Erich sent on September 18, 1948, Erich explained that he could not sleep at night because of the list. "Your monthly expense statement just killed me". - Then he continued.

"I must confess that I cannot see how or where we could cut expenditures, except on little things. I knew immediately that it was also meant for Alfred but he refused to look at it with the remark that he need not always be convinced that no unnecessary expenditures have been made. But I insisted that he read through it this time because otherwise even I would not have believed it. Later I asked him what he had to say since I didn't know what to do. His comment was, 'Well, nothing can be done; life is just very expensive these days'."

Ursel responded on September 20.

"It certainly is awfully nice that Alfred understands what necessary expenses we have! Luckily he is in a position to help us. The fact that you got heart palpitations when reading it is a bad sign that you still have problems with your heart and nerves! It seems that you are still far from being in good health! It was exciting but not shocking. It would only be shocking if I did not know that Alfred can and wants to help us. That sounds quite cynical but it is only meant to be flippant. But you will have to get used to quite a few and different problems in this refugee life. One has to develop a hard outer skin, otherwise one will perish. All this is horribly embarrassing to me, too, but I don't get heart palpitations anymore from something like that, thank God, despite nervous circulatory disorders and smoker nerves (!!!)"

For decades the Spickschens who lived in East Prussia and then had to flee from there remained connected to the Vluyner Spickschens in a partly friendly, partly conflictual manner. Unfortunately, money problems again and again played a burdensome role. On one hand, Ursel and Erich were thankful that they received help from Vluyn; on the other hand this gratitude left a bitter taste in their mouths. It always meant dependency on Vluyn and because Erich was co-heir of his father's possessions, perhaps he had the right to assistance from his brother. The letters provided a vivid picture of the tensions within this particular family group.

During the period of 1949 to 1955 only three letters were available which selectively give further insight. Parts of these letters are quoted in the following section.

3. Incidents between 1948 and 1950. Denazification

With the help of the memories that Erich and Ursula Spickschen's children relayed in the years 2009 and 2010, the refugee life that their parents lived or were forced to live in Bleckenstedt were supplemented in some areas. Ingolf still clearly remembered the first meeting with his father after he returned from captivity. His father got out of the train - he was on his way to Gemen to his mother – and Ingolf recognized him immediately although his father was changed, with yellow skin color. The unhealthy, bloated appearance mistakenly indicated to Ingolf (then thirteen years old) that he was well-

Ingolf, Ursel, Erich, Helga, Bergild, Runhild and Astrid / Bleckenstedt 1948

nourished. The first thing his father said to him when he greeted him was, "You have not grown!"

This spontaneous remark after three and a half years of separation was probably meant to be harmless and kind and yet it betrayed something of the expectations that Erich had of his first-born son from the very beginning, since 1935. A son always wants to live up to the high expectations of his father with all his might. Yet now the first signal from his father was that he did not satisfactorily meet his expectations. The feeling of inadequacy brought up a memory for Ingolf of an event that occurred back in Woydiethen around 1938-39. The Reichsbauernfuehrer Darré came to visit and as he left, he made a somewhat off-colored and also recognizably brown colored (Nazi) remark to Erich. The remark, which he made with the children Ingolf and Bergild present, was probably supposed to be a praise as well as characterization; "Well, Spickschen, your breed of heifers is of the highest quality, but you still have some work to do with your bulls!" As a young boy, Ingolf showed a rebuffing, uptight nature to strangers. While his sister Bergild was funny and outgoing, he could not speak.

Because Ingolf loved and admired his father more than anything, he wanted to do everything to please him. An incident that must have taken place shortly after Erich first arrived, disclosed how much he admired him. During the time when Ingolf lived with Tante Martha and Onkel Guste - a difficult time for him as previously stated in Ursel's letter dated June 30, 1948 - Erich came to visit. At the dinner table, Erich could not do enough to effusively praise the food. "Oh, this tastes wonderful! How I enjoy that!" Ingolf enjoyed it with him. Then Tante Martha got up and brought the dessert for everyone, a bowl of vanilla pudding with a fresh raspberry sauce. When Erich saw this, he began to cry and said, "That I may live to see this!" Ingolf had the same inexpressible sensations at this moment. He felt completely at one with his father, suffered and rejoiced with him, so that he also was overwhelmed by emotion.

How much Ingolf himself and his extremely right-thinking father could get into trouble, was already shown in Woydiethen. An event in 1949 was firmly imprinted in him. The harvest festival was to be celebrated in Bleckenstedt. Just before all of the Spickschens were to meet in a large granary, Ingolf went into the parents' bedroom where he found his father lying quietly on the bed. The son did not want to disturb him so he left the room without saying a word. He went to his mother and asked, "Tell me, Mutti, is Vati still asleep? Doesn't he want to come with us?" "No," she replied, "Vati does not want to come." "Why not?" His mother said, "He is sad. He is thinking about all the beautiful harvest festivals we celebrated in Woydiethen." Ingolf also had many fond memories of those festivals. At that time video tapes were shown that Erich had taken during the course of the year. Everyone always loved those films.

The son felt terribly sorry for his father in Bleckenstedt. In the granary, where the large party had assembled, Ingolf was asked by his future brother-in-law Gerhard Traube to supply all guests who wanted them with cigarettes and cigars on a regular basis. Ingolf constantly thought about his father. He knew how much he liked smoking a cigar. He especially loved Villiger cigars made in Virginia. This brand had a straw as a mouthpiece and a blade of hay to light it. Ingolf had to pass around a similar variety of cigarillos at the harvest festival. He put aside about five cigarillos to give them later to his father as a gift.

When Ingolf came home late that evening, his father was still on the bed in the bedroom. Ingolf woke him and said, "I brought you something". As soon as Erich saw the cigarillos he asked with an expression of horror, "Where did you get these?" Ingolf responded, "I brought them for you from the fest". His father asked, "Did you just take them?" "Yes", Ingolf replied. "Did you ask Gerhard Traube?" Ingolf admitted, "No." The father sank back on the bed, tears running down his face and he said, "For God's sake! Now this has to happen to me. My son is a thief!"

Ingolf said that his father was never self-pitying but at that moment he felt sorry for himself. Ingolf was petrified! He wanted to make everything right, to please his father in every way. He was totally dependent on him for his self-esteem. The paternal influence had a much stronger impact on him than that of his mother, although Ingolf's relationship with her was much more personal and intimate. The harvest festival was over but his father said, "You have to go immediately back to Mr. Traube, return the cigarillos and apologizing to him!" It was late so Ingolf waited until the next morning. Gerhard Traube smiled expectantly and asked what he wanted. "I am supposed to bring back the cigarillos and apologize to you." "Apologize? Everything is ok, everything is good." Gerhard Traube reacted calmly to the incident; it was no big deal to him.

Later Ingolf often wished that his father would have treated him as liberally as Gerhard Traube did. He was able to develop an unlimited trust with Gerd Traube, someone with whom he could speak about his worries and problems, while there often remained a distance between him and his father. But Ingolf remembers that when he was little, he sometimes crawled onto his father's knees or would lie down beside him on the bed and his father would tell him a story. It also often happened that his father lifted him onto his shoulders in Woydiethen, went with him through the woods and told him the names of the trees. On the next walk, the son had to remember the names of the trees. The relationship with his father remained ambiguous. Gerhard Traube later took over the role of a father, just the way Ingolf had always wished the father to be. Ingolf remembers Gerd with feelings of unconditional love and devotion until the present time.

For Thorlef, who is six years younger than Ingolf, Gerhard Traube was a kind of mixture between big brother and father figure, perhaps even more directly than for Ingolf. The younger brother met his biological father at the age of seven and was only able to experience his father until his death in 1957. For Thorlef, Erich was a loving father who he did not want to hurt as young as he was. With his strong sense of justice his father was always an example for him. He was always very proud when someone compared him with his idol. He emphasized both his love for his father and his loving relationship with Gerd. When he was asked if he had also experienced his father as a disciplinarian, Thorlef explained in an interview of December 18, 2009.

"In raising us, my father was more distant, unlike my mother who reacted spontaneously and impulsively, like with a speedy little, ultimately harmless slap. My father however always took us children seriously. Only once in my life did he slap me. Before he did so, he asked me to come into another room because he did not want to humiliate me in front of the others. I think I was thirteen or fourteen years old. Vati gave me a gentle slap on the cheek and almost apologized for it. And it was immediately clear that I deserved the punishment.

“I clearly remember the reason. We had herring for dinner and I did not like herring. We usually had to eat at least half or even a whole herring. I said, 'If I have to eat one more piece, I have to throw up'. Vati said, 'Well, come outside with me, please'. He was absolutely right. Because he had to suffer hunger so terribly during his captivity he was particularly sensitive in everything that concerned food."

Astrid also knew of an incident that could have created a conflict. She had just turned five years old when she sat in an armchair and scratched around on the armrest. Her father said, "Stop that!" Astrid replied, "You have nothing to say around here." Erich knew how to handle this rebelliousness and was not angry. His youngest child said that she probably was already very direct as a small child. She might even have added, "Mutti took care of everything here; I only have to obey her." When Thorlef was asked at that time about how he felt about things, he hemmed and hawed and said in his even then diplomatic way, "Well, maybe you can see it the way Astrid sees it." Erich wrote about this little altercation in a letter. Astrid is not sure now if she actually remembers the incident or if her memory has been renewed by later reading the letter.

The incident of "insubordination" that Astrid describes in 2009 can be found in a letter that the Erich wrote to his mother on September 28, 1949. Astrid was already six years old. Erich wrote:

"I could laugh my head off at the thought that Ursel and I could be walking around as respectable grandparents in about half a year. But we will have to live up to the new dignity and hopefully will be able to stay young with the grandchildren for quite a long time. It's also about time that our people have children again. Even little Astrid seems to think about her role in a marriage. When I asked her about it she expressed her willingness to get married. When I tried to persuade her to stay with us instead of going off with some guy who might not treat her right and abuse her, she said laconically, 'Well, he wouldn’t dare to do that more than once; I would show him who is boss'. One should really write down all these little treasures. Recently I failed to grant her a wish. She said, ‘Well then I have to ask Mutti’. I replied, ‘She has no more authority than I'. Astrid responded, ‘That’s not true, she has more.’ 'Why?' I asked. ’When you were in captivity, Mutti had to take care of everything.' When Thorlef was asked his opinion he said diplomatically: 'Yes, Vati, you have to admit that this was really true.’ Hats off! Ursel is giving the children a worm treatment with enemas, etc. Thorlef just exploded in front of the bucket. Oh well. That's it for today. Ingolf is arriving tomorrow. The students got an early vacation because there is a kind of fair in Gütersloh for which the school building is needed. Bergild is ok again. She had a mild case of jaundice."

In 2009 Astrid said that only on one occasion did she feel very unfairly treated by her father. The Spickschens had a female Dachshund which was in heat at the time. A door was left open so that the dog snuck out and had some fun. Erich was convinced that Astrid had failed to keep the door closed. A tendon on Erich’s right hand was slightly shortened so that his little finger was crooked. When he gave his daughter a slap on the buttocks, the crooked finger came down first so that she felt a sharp pain. She resented that a lot because she knew that she was not to blame for the open door.

It is not surprising when the children remember events in which they had come into conflict with their parents. On the other hand, this might give a distorted picture of Erich Spickschen if one saw him as an especially strict or even punitive father. Punishing behavior was the exception; that is why the children remember it. Astrid explained in retrospect that she knew her father only since 1948. She had no memory of him from before his captivity. She always experienced him as someone who stood up for others. She knew that her mother once told her father, "I wish you would do as much for our family as you do for others!" As in the years as the Landesbauernfuehrer, or even before, Erich thought of himself and was also viewed by other as someone who cared for his fellow man.

The willingness to actively take care of the needs of others was a prominent characteristic and an essential quality of Erich Spickschen. All his children concur that he was very popular with everyone. He was particularly appreciated by the ladies because he was not only helpful but also genuine, clever and a charming conversationalist. He was a gentleman of whom one could say that it came naturally to him. During the silver wedding anniversary which was celebrated in Bleckenstedt in 1948, numerous ladies presented him a flower - so many that a bunch of 25 flowers came together.

Erich's skillfulness and friendliness might have been partly a reason why he tried to work for some months in 1949 in a profession that soon became troublesome to him. The difficulties to obtain financial security were still very oppressive. To earn some money Erich became a representative for a liquor distillery in Wolfenbüttel. After a short time it was clear that he could not handle it. He could not invite his customers to drink with him because of his liver problems. But the children were all very busily helping him as much as possible by cleaning and labeling bottles.

Erich's good qualities could not give him dispensation from a process which countless Germans had to undergo soon after the war. In hopes of largely eliminating Nazi influences the victorious powers adopted the Law for Liberation from National Socialism and Militarism that classified possible Nazis into five groups: Group I - main culprits (war criminals). Group II - full offenders (activists, militants, beneficiaries-of-war crimes). Group III - lesser offenders, Group IV- followers, and Group V – Not guilty. All potential criminals had to fill out the extensive Questionnaire for Political Review. A committee then reviewed the questionnaires and ordered the respondents into one of the five groups. Erich Spickschen also had to go through this procedure after his release from captivity, probably in 1948, or at the latest in1949. A letter Erich and Ursel sent to friends and family in May, 1951 discussed some of the vexations, worries and problems the denazification procedure gave Erich.

Erich was initially classified in Group IV: a follower. Then he wrote:

"I received a message from the denazification authority in Braunschweig that my classification into Group IV was canceled because important new information had been received to have me classified into Group III. I then saw in the files that were sent to me that Mr. Egbert Otto (Landesbauernfuehrer of East Prussia in 1933) filed an appeal and was the chief witness against me. This matter brought a lot of work and wear and tear on our nerves. The court's decision on 28 March [1951] was to keep me in Group IV."

Unfortunately, Erich's happiness when he wrote this letter was premature. On July 2, 1951 he received a notice from the Appeals Board for the Denazification in Braunschweig with the decision to re-classify him again because of renewed extensive grounds against him. Before discussing this fact, the individual steps of the entire previous process that led to the decision of July 2, 1951 will be briefly detailed. A detailed discussion of the denazification procedure, which includes extensive correspondence, cannot be outlined here. Denazification, as it was carried out in the years after 1945, has been criticized. The renowned historian Lutz Niethammer, who in 1972 presented a voluminous study on the problems associated with denazification, gave Bavaria as an example and called attention to a central problem in his re-launched study in 1982. This study concluded that: - The large scale denazification conducted by the victorious powers that in theory was supposed to bring about the liberation of the German population from the views of the Nazis, actually created in practice a "mass of followers". That is to say, an army of innocent people who supposedly were all just followers. Around 1950, a lot of people could not and did not want to know too much about what had happened between 1933 and 1945. The evidence for the procedures that were performed after the end of the war was therefore accordingly fractured.

Affidavits again and again played an important role in the denazification process which was supposed to help those who had to face charges. The accused would contact close and not-so-close friends and acquaintances and petition them for testimonies that would absolve him or her from the taint of Nazi perpetrators and complicity as much as possible. These letters which were in a way the usual "form letter certificates" should in turn be fundamentally evaluated in a critical manner since they clearly and deliberately served the purpose of giving credit to a person and therefore were unilaterally positive. However, these were sworn statements and even though they always gave only positive images they were not wrong; they were one-sided.

Ursel requested favorable testimonies already by the end of 1947 or the beginning of 1948, at a time when Erich was still in captivity. For example, the officially certified opinion of the professor of agriculture Emil Lang who taught at the University of Königsberg before the war ended in 1945, carries the date of January 10, 1948. Erich Spickschen's initial classification into Group IV, a follower, did not happen until June 11, 1949 after he had completed the Questionnaire for Policy Review, (undated) to which were added "notes" and a "resume" dated February 15, 1949. The cover letter to the questionnaire which was completed by Ursula bears the date of June 27, 1949. Two days later she received the decision from the denazification main committee of the district of Watenstedt-Salzgitter that she had been classified in Group IV. She had to pay the court costs in the amount of 50 marks.

It would be easy to dwell on the questionnaires and explanations of Erich and Ursula, as all are important sources of evidence, but that would take too long and go into too much detail. It should only be noted that with the decision of June 11, 1949, Erich Spickschen was given a bill for the payment of legal costs in the amount of 200 marks. This was a painfully high amount at that time and not only for him. The retrial was ordered on July 5, 1950 by resolution of the denazification main committee in Braunschweig. For reasons that were not known to Erich at the time, the decision of June 11, 1949 was invalidated.

It soon turned out that Erich's classification into the comparatively harmless Group IV had been challenged by the former East Prussian Landesbauernfuehrer Egbert Otto and also Rudolf Adam. One of the main objections raised by both concerned the allegation, that Erich Spickschen had been a more than obedient follower of Gauleiter Erich Koch. For this purpose, a previous detailed letter from Ursel could be used to show the unpleasant history that they had experienced with Otto. Another reason given by Otto that led to the re-classification of Erich Spickschen concerned his membership in the Reichstag. In a letter dated May 15, 1961, Ursel remarked that in the questionnaire the status of Erich's capacity as a member of the Reichstag had not been asked. "It is surely obvious that one would not volunteer possible incriminating facts" in completing the sheet. Erich receive 500.00 RM monthly as a member of the Reichstag - a purely "passive role" - as stated later in the papers of the appeals committee, because the deputies under Hitler were merely figure heads, had nothing to report, and Erich Spickschen had only participated in a single session in the years from 1936 to early 1945.

As a result of the opposition of Otto and Adam in the first half of November 1950, a meeting of the denazification committee did not come to any decision. In a letter of November 16, 1950, Erich wrote to his lawyer from Bleckenstedt, "I missed by a hair being classified at the meeting into Group III." He was granted a deferment; he was given the opportunity to procure exculpatory evidence that would allow a classification into Group IV. Accordingly Erich's letter continued, "I now have asked a large circle of my former colleagues to stand up for me and be available as witnesses or to testify in the form of affidavits for me." Erich's efforts were crowned with success, as the excerpt from the above letter of May 1951 shows. It was decided on March 28, 1951 in Braunschweig to classify him again into Group IV.

However, on May 9, 1951 opposition again was raised, now by the public prosecutor who demanded that because of Erich's membership in the Reichstag his classification should be Group III. Erich had to face a new hearing in Braunschweig. Meanwhile he lived in Dannenfels / Pfalz where he had urgent work to do. A trip to Braunschweig would have been costly for him. Gerhard Traube again provided proof of his generosity and impartiality under these circumstances by declaring himself ready to represent his father-in-law in Braunschweig. However, in the end a date was agreed upon that allowed Erich to appear personally before the committee.

However, all his attempts to avoid the classification into Group III were in vain. On July 2, 1951 he was informed by the appeals committee for the denazification in Braunschweig that he was "classified as a major contributor to and beneficiary of National Socialism into Group III". The demotion held sanctions that Erich had to accept and it injured him to the core. These sanctions not only affected and hurt his honor, but also led to practical and political constraints. The effective measures were awkwardly listed in the decision letter of July 2, 1951:

"He is forbidden to work as a teacher, youth worker, journalist, writer etc." He also "is forbidden to serve as an official or employee of a public service in communities or to hold an office in other public bodies."

Erich was likely particularly hurt by a fifth bullet point:

"He loses the right to vote and the eligibility for election to political offices and should not be politically active, not function as an employee of political organizations."

The judgment of July 2, 1951 was accompanied by a detailed justification, which states, inter alia:

"Opinions differ about Erich Spickschen's attitude toward Koch. It is clear that he did not enter in Otto's footsteps. Instead, he tried to get along with Koch and thereby had been occasionally willing to make concessions. On the other hand, there is much evidence that he was not a pliant tool of Koch's and internally always stood in opposition to him. It is not proven that the person concerned (Erich Spickschen) channeled goods to Koch or that he accepted presents or gifts from him. Or that he otherwise used his position as the Landesbauernfuehrer to obtain special benefits for himself. Until the end he owned and managed only his small farm."

The memorandum also stated that "the subject always decently managed his office and had kept away from the evil machinations and methods of Nazism."

Considering these statements, which speak far more for Erich than against him, the reasons given for his classification into Group III seem fairly subtle and peculiar. The only "tangible" reason given to consider him as a "promoter and beneficiary of National Socialism" was the fact that he was a member of the Reichstag and as such received a monthly allowance of 500 RM. Although it was also emphasized that the Reichstag was "nothing but a farce". As already mentioned, in the eyes of the appeals committee Erich Spickschen was guilty of being a "figure head". His attempt of July 30, 1951 by writing a detailed reply to once again bring about a revision because he found himself demoted "to the 2nd class citizen" failed.

In a brief flashback it should at least be made clear how individuals - there were very many of them - tried to support Erich in his effort not to stand there as a "promoter and beneficiary of National Socialism". The variety of exculpatory evidence that he received testifies not only that the East Prussian network, in which Erich was embedded, continued to work, they also witnessed the sympathy and "positive bias" of the very many people who knew him. Charlotte Countess von der Schulenburg, wife of Fritz-Dietlof Graf von der Schulenburg who was executed after the failed assassination attempt of Hitler on July 20, 1944 stated in a certified letter of January 30, 1948:

"That Mr. Spickschen regarded his post as Landesbauernfuehrer purely technical and that his decisions were made according to these aspects in cases of debt relief, personnel issues, etc. Its 'objectivity' was resented by Gauleiter Koch. He accused Herr Spickschen of not being a good political activist. Only because of a sense of responsibility did he hold on to his position until the end, hoping to weaken the policy of madness in East Prussia through the organization of a timely evacuation. He was thus viewed as a defeatist and was replaced in the fall of 1944. My husband stayed in contact with Mr. Spickschen even after his departure from East Prussia and was happy that he kept him up to date about the situation in East Prussia."

Countess Schulenburg emphasized in her letter of October 14, 1947 regarding the denazification process of Ursel that her connection to the Spickschens did not break off. It had quality, even in later years. This stability in maintaining the relationship on the part of a woman whose husband had become a determined opponent of the Nazis until his death has always been an indication, especially for Erich's son Thorlef that his father who was dedicated to National Socialism, ultimately remained a solid character.

Similar to Countess Schulenburg, Adelheid von Kannewurff wrote on January 26, 1948 in a hand-written, certified statement three years after her escape from East Prussia:

"I declare under penalty of perjury that Mr. Erich Spickschen became Landesbauernfuehrer of East Prussia only because of his expertise. He is not to be counted among the so-called activists. I've known him for many years since I myself am from East Prussia and owned an estate of 3000 morgen (1,853 acres) in the district of Lyck. I have often asked for his advice and help and both were always granted me although I was neither a party member nor a party contender. He was an idealist. This showed itself in all of his good governance and therefore he often came into conflict with the district administration and in the end he was removed from office by Gauleiter Koch."

Carl Hüttenbach wrote on December 19, 1950 a long handwritten letter from Bonn, to which was attached a typed, sworn and notarized statement, carrying the same date, which states:

"I was the owner of the estate Waldheim in the district of Preussisch Eylau, East Prussia. I fell fully under the Nuremberg Laws of the Third Reich so that my estate was to be aryanized, meaning that I was to be dispossessed. Apparently, the Gauleiter himself wanted to take possession of my estate. Anyway, everything was initiated to drive me from the land.

"Then Mr. Erich Spickschen heard about it. Although Mr. Spickschen did not know me personally, he did everything he could to fight for my cause against the party establishment. As head of the East Prussian Food and Health administration Mr. Spickschen contradicted the expropriation and prevailed with Darré that the estate was transferred to my oldest son. He worked very courageously and selflessly, risking his own position against the will and intentions of the party.

"It was reported to me several times that Mr. Spickschen often went against the wishes of the Gauleiter if they were not in the interest of the common people. It is therefore incomprehensible to me that he was not given dispensation but instead was classified into Group IV."

Despite all efforts and all intercession Erich Spickschen did not succeed in obtaining the re-classification from Group III back to Group IV. He remained a borderline case between the two groups. One cannot readily contradict the statements of the expert who founded the classification in Group III, although looking at them from today's perspective they are by no means convincing. Erich Spickschen received a letter dated September 3, 1951 from the Lower Saxony Ministry of the Interior in Hannover that detailed why the decision of the assignment into Group III was not revised. How much this final decision hurt and possibly tortured him, nobody knows.

In addition to the dispute over the denazification Erich also had to deal with other concerns towards the middle and end of 1950. Ursel highlighted some of these issues in a typed letter dated July 7, 1950 to a couple of her children who were vacationing in Vluyn at the time, but especially to Bergild.

[**NOT IN GERMAN BOOK**] (After her illness, Bergild had been transferred to the Gymnasium Stift Keppel, a boarding school for girls in the Rothaar Mountains near Siegen in January 1949):

"My dear Sweethearts!

Yesterday I was with Vater in Hachum. This is a village near Elm behind Wolfenbüttel. We were offered a farm for lease there. The farm is located at the edge of the village. The farms are not as close together there as in Bleckenstedt. In front of the house are two old trees. They look quite nice. Tomorrow, Vater is driving to Braunschweig to negotiate about the lease with the representative of the refugee settlement department. The farm is 60 morgen (37 acres) in size, but now only 17 acres are available to lease. The rest will be released after the harvest. There are only a few buildings and those are somewhat dilapidated but they are already being repaired. Vater says that he would prefer to go further to the West. But if we find nothing there during the next month and if he gets good conditions here, he wants to lease the farm. Otherwise we might have to remain here in Bleckenstedt for another winter. The soil in Hachum is very good, almost better than here in Bleckenstedt. So Vater has to decide in about three weeks."

Adelheid von Kannewurff with Ursula and Erich Spickschen

So in July 1950 Erich and Ursula Spickschen were still looking for a farm to lease. The fear that Ursel mentioned in the letter of July 9, 1948, that the lease of a farm before the spring of 1949 would be difficult that at the time seemed to be very pessimistic, was actually a far too optimistic assessment. Not until mid-November 1950, were the Spickschens able to leave Bleckenstedt with some of their children and some of the other individuals that had lived with them for over five years and find a new home in the Palatinate.

VIII

The Years in Dannenfels (Pfalz)

Helga, Erich Spickschen's eldest daughter, married the Forest Assessor Hubertus Freiherr von Eller-Eberstein on June 2, 1949. In a newsletter to family and friends dated May 1951, sent from Dannenfels (Rhineland-Palatinate), Erich Spickschen wrote that "he (Helga's husband) died in "a tragic accident on July 23, 1950". Erich gave no further details. In the second paragraph of the newsletter Erich stated:

"The mother of our late son-in-law Eller-Eberstein, who had acquired a little inn around here a year ago with the remainder of her assets, made us aware of the possibilities in the Palatinate. We came here twice last year to search for a suitable lease. But we soon realized that the lease of a solely agricultural site was not an option for us. Small enterprises up to 35 acres are prevalent here and the small refugee credit granted by the State of Rhineland-Palatinate would not be enough for a larger lease. So when the opportunity arose we grabbed the chance to lease an inn with 10 acres of agriculture land here – mostly small parcels - in the health resort Dannenfels. The township is adding 26 acres of newly deforested land that is in one piece to the deal."

Erich then described the scenic surroundings where he partly cited from a publication, perhaps a brochure.

"The area is very beautiful. Dannenfels, an ancient town of 1,100 inhabitants, is situated on the slope of the Donnersberg about 400 meters above sea level. Glorious woodlands stretch for miles behind the village. The whole Donnersberg area, with its many viewpoints, ruins and its healthy, dust-free air, is well known here in Southwestern Germany. We have a wide panoramic view from our house and on a clear day you can see across the Rhine River to the Odenwald and the Bergstrasse."

In an interview on April 7, 2010 Thorlef remembered that nearly 60 years ago on a clear day from the guest house that was called Dannenfelser Hof, his father showed him and his siblings the Melibokus Mountain of the Odenwald. With its 517 meters height, it is the highest mountain on the South Hessian Bergstrasse.

Thorlef provided a more detailed characterization of Dannenfels in a second interview which took place about half a year later, on October 27.

"Dannenfels, with a little more than a thousand inhabitants, was an interesting microcosm with a large number of active clubs, choirs and a theater group. There were many small farms run by farmers who were lumberjacks in the winter. There were craftsmen who worked after hours on their small fields or fruit orchards and generally had one or two cows that were used as draft animals. The biggest farm, which in Northern

Germany would be called a small-farm, was owned by the family Gümbel. These were educated people who had an ancestor who was a professor of geology and who had a street named for him in Munich. At the same time there were two young mongoloid men in Dannenfels - Hänschen and Hermännchen. They were taught at the local school according to their abilities and they performed light work in the fields and on the farms of their parents. The entire village helped to integrate those two. Only the children sometimes teased them, but rarely maliciously. On the other hand, there were young gifted children who were selected by the head teacher to go to secondary school in preparation for university. For example, one was Hans Siebecker, the son of a small farmer and brother of Hermännchen. Hans later became a physics professor who attained an international reputation.

"A group of older Dannenfelser men met regularly in the Dannenfelser Hof to play Skat with my father. This always included Herr Hess, a farmer who was a self-trained amateur archaeologist. He provided very stimulating conversation. His late father had been the Landesbauernfuehrer of the Palatinate. The village doctor, Dr. Wilke, was also one of the local contacts. He was a man with broad interests who was very skilled in fine arts and deeply involved in an effort to promote Dannenfels as a health resort. The medical practice was mainly run by his wife, also a doctor. She took care of the practice and her four children and was an excellent internist."

Thorlef, born in 1941, and his sister Astrid, born two years later - the youngest in the family - still recall very well the big move from Bleckenstedt to the distant Palatinate. Astrid was always up for a change, she said. She was thrilled to learn that her parents had finally found a place to rent and that a move was soon coming. With Thorlef, who was her confidant, she soon found out that one of their neighbors in Dannenfels was called Siebecker and that the land-lord (from whom the inn was leased) was called Merz. While Astrid and Thorlef were still in Bleckenstedt, they would lay in bed in the evening and take turns playing the roles of the Siebecker woman and Merz woman. "Do you know, Mrs. Siebecker, new people arrived here. What do you think of that?" "Oh, they seem to be quite friendly." And so on. Their slightly older sister Runhild, who slept in the same room with the two youngest Spickschens, wanted to sleep. The order "Be still!" was given. While Thorlef and Astrid would crawl under their blankets, they continued to talk. "I can still hear you," Runhild complained, "just be quiet!" Astrid as a child often thought that her next older sister was bitchy.

During the years in Bleckenstedt before the currency reform, it was the industrious and enterprising mother Ursel who successfully traded seeds on the black market for second-hand furniture and sometimes for actual antiques. She received the seeds from her brother-in-law in Vluyn. For example, Ursel bought chairs that are still in use today at Astrid's and Ingolf's houses. So the household consisted not only of furniture but also clothes, stores and many other things, all of which were loaded onto a moving truck that went on to Dannenfels. Astrid recalled, "We children sat in the back of the moving truck, which I found very exciting."

Erich wrote in a newsletter to family and friends that the "operation" the Spickschens took over in the Palatinate on November 15, 1950 was "extremely run down in every way and neglected." In a more drastic way, Thorlef explained that the inn that was leased by his parents was located in the middle of the village and was the "most run-down" of the several inns in Dannenfels. In all there were eight inns and the majorities were well-managed but they all had a sideline for income. The owner of the "Dannenfelser Hof" was an alcoholic. His father had been the mayor of the town. His second wife was also a drunk. Thorlef reaffirmed that the inn "was completely run down, no one went there anymore".

Like Astrid and Thorlef, sister Bergild, who was born in 1936, also had a lot to report about the time in Dannenfels. In addition, Feechen (Felicitas Penger, born in 1928) remembered. She came to Woydiethen in 1943 as a home economics apprentice and stayed with the Spickschen family until 1958. She married and moved to the United States. In Dannenfels she was an indispensable aid in managing the inn and kitchen. Feechen especially remembered the transformation Ursel made soon after their arrival in Dannenfels. In the dreary dining room white table cloths were placed on the simple, bare tables and an embroidered doily was placed in the middle. The table cloths were not necessarily new. They were hand-me-downs from relatives or were donated by a refugee organization. These table clothes instantly changed not only the appearance of the room but the entire atmosphere. The locals who were curious and wanted to see what was going on with the Dannenfelser Hof soon let it be known that this change to a new, neat style was important and should be retained.

Bergild stayed only temporarily in Dannenfels during the early 1950s. She lived in a boarding school called Stift Keppel from 1949 until 1953 and then became an exchange student for a year in the United States. The first time she came to the Dannenfelser Hof she felt like she was transferred back deep into the nineteenth century. The inn was completely outmoded. For example, the old kitchen was even more primitive than the one in Bleckenstedt. The entire property, which included the inn, was U shaped. On one side was the inn itself. Attached to that at a right angle was the house where the landlord lived with his wife. Opposite the inn were the barn and stables under one roof. Often to their chagrin the guests had to walk by the manure pile that was next to the stables, before they reached the inn.

The Dannenfelser Hof consisted of the ground floor, a second and third floor and above that an attic where the laundry could be hung to dry. The rooms on the third floor where the bedrooms were located had sloping walls. In the winter it was often so cold that in the morning the water in the wash bowls was frozen. There was only a single stove in a corner of the hallway on the third floor and the fire usually went out overnight. In the morning, the ashes had to be removed from it. Although wood had been piled on before bedtime the fire did not last long.

Feechen remembered a special experience regarding the accommodation in one of the third floor bedrooms. She shared the room with Runhild and it was located under the eaves. The little window looked out at the wall of the house next door where the landlord lived. One day some rats apparently slipped through the window from the pigsty into the room. "We did not notice the critters immediately - not until they ran across my face in the dark while we slept. It was a terrible shock when I woke up. We had left the small window open for fresh air. I think I grabbed one of the rats and screamed. Runhild awoke and was very brave. She turned on the light, took a stick and tried to shoo the critter away. But it did not find the way out of the window and at some point it landed on Runhild's chest. She grabbed the beast by the throat and threw it out of the window. Yes, she was very courageous. There's hardly anything more disgusting than a rat."

Guest rooms were located on the second floor of the house. At first there were four; later there were only three. As time went on it turned out that only a few overnight guests stayed at the inn and three guest rooms were adequate. The fourth room was transformed into a private living room for the Spickschen family. One room on that floor was inhabited by Frau Merz, the mother of the lessor. She belonged to one of the more respectable families in the village. As mentioned before, her husband had been mayor of the town. She was a quiet, reserved woman who never complained when the patrons of the inn became very loud, which seemed to happen quite often. She received 70.00 DM of the monthly 160.00 DM the Spickschens had to pay for rent. The rest went to the family of the son.

Regarding the financing for the urgently needed renovation at the inn, it is important to know that Helga, the oldest daughter, gave her parents 12,900.00 DM as a low-interest loan. She received the money from a life insurance policy after the death of her husband. Thorlef reported that this money was vital to help the parents in operating the guest house. The business was constantly facing bankruptcy. Money problems were a constant trauma. The money that Helga provided averted the risk of bankruptcy at least for a little while.

Ursula Spickschen wrote a novel about the time in Dannenfels. Thorlef said that most of the occurrences are authentic but some may seem strange and somewhat pointed. Ursel began the novel with a kind of gallows humor - a mixture of sarcasm, bitterness and wit - about what they found when they arrived in Dannenfels:

"And then we were offered a [lease]. Though tiny - it basically was just an inn with some land – it was exquisite! 'Auserlesen' (prime choice) is the word in German - and it was really the most primly chosen neglected guest house I had ever seen. It was especially suitable for a penniless refugee who wanted to establish himself. Rain came through the ceiling in the bedrooms. The terrace invited one to commit suicide because one step on the decrepit floor boards and you would inevitably fall into the garden below to the gleeful grin of the numerous generations of carpenter ants. The unspeakable 'out house' in the court yard almost became my husband's mausoleum. The partition between the men's space and the women's space slowly but surely fell on him when he sat there one day. On the other hand, the gap in the wall on the third floor seemed almost harmless. It was, after all, a ventilation which was quite welcome in light of the odor coming from gradually decaying mice who died in the cavity between the ceiling and floorboards. These creatures were cruelly killed by us with powerful poisons."

In fact, the wooden terrace was initially closed due to disrepair. As part of the renovation a new large terrace of concrete could be built. This renovation was made possible by the loan from Helga. This terrace became a popular meeting place for guests in the summer because it offered an amazing view over the Rhine Valley across to the Odenwald. The Spickschens were able to renovate and modernize the business but the inn retained something romantic and unusual through the years until the lease was terminated in 1957 due to the death of Erich Spickschen. It is not surprising that this environment gave the Spickschen children, especially Thorlef and certainly Astrid, an adventurous childhood world which offered material for unforgettable memories.

In the dining room on the ground floor of the Dannenfelser Hof, which might have measured sixty square meters, a bar was installed which was made from beautiful wood. After a contract had been signed with the Park Brewery, the bar was supplied and installed in addition to the normal furniture such as new tables and chairs. The brewery not only supplied the beer that could not be obtained from any other brewery, they also defined the procurement of other beverages. The contract was not very advantageous to the customer because it had some limitations.

In addition to the dining room there was a separate room of about thirty square meters in size which could be used for group meetings or private parties. Feechen recalled that before the Spickschens took over the inn it was apparently common practice for the locals to cross the main room, which perhaps was perceived as being unfriendly, and immediately go into the side room where they sat to play cards. A normal guest house operation slowly developed only after Ursel undertook her transformation. A pantry was part of the kitchen. There was also a cellar where supplies, particularly beverages, could be stored to keep cold.

Ursel's original intent, or rather her desire, was to establish an operation in Dannenfels which would be clearly distinguishable from the other guest houses in the town due to its high standards. But this could only be realized in stages. As the epitome of fine dining, Ursel designed the text for a lavishly printed brochure that offered, for example, a 'queen's pastry' as an appetizer. She also invited an editor of the Kaiserslautern "Rheinpfalz" newspaper who wrote a short article recommending the dining experience. But all the efforts to attract guests from Kaiserslautern, which was 30 KM away, were largely unsuccessful. While it was often very difficult for her, Ursel had to come to terms with the fact that she rarely was able to realize her dreams.

Feechen was, as she described herself, "a general factotum". She served the guests, cooked for the family and she also often cooked for the guests. In addition, she made sure that the guest rooms as well as the Spickschen family rooms, were cleaned and kept in order. Guests could appear at any time and if they ordered something to eat, it was immediately prepared. Very often and especially when a guest had a special request Ursel, who was an excellent, imaginative cook, stood in the kitchen to prepare a dish.

In addition, other help was always on hand. Whenever any of the Spickschen daughters were staying in Dannenfels, they automatically did any job that needed to be done. When Gaga was in between jobs for three months, she came to work as a nanny for Helga's little son, Christian. Tante Annchen, a distant relative of the Traubes, came for months at a time to take care of the guest room during the day. She was a widow who lived on a small social security income. When she stayed with the Spickschens she worked more or less for room and board by washing the glasses from the previous evening, taking orders from customers during the morning hours and helping with preliminary work in the kitchen. At times, Adelheid von Kannewurff, who also had fled from East Prussia, came to help out in Dannenfels. She made an enormous impression on the Spickschen children (who called her Tante Adelheid) by how naturally she served the guests. Not for a moment did she act as if she was too good to take on the role of a waitress. The guests seemed to enjoy getting food and drinks served by a royal highness, a countess. It was the same with Frau von Schmitzek (Tante Vera) a daughter of the Countess Arnim. She was a distant relative of the Eller-Ebersteins and also had no difficulty to perform waitress services.

Again and again it was shown that it was of vital importance that on top of the Donnersberg, on whose slopes Dannenfels was located, there was a radio station manned by American soldiers. As Bergild and Thorlef explained that two different units of the Air Force had living quarters in the village and worked at the radio station on top of the mountain. The Americans soon made the discovery that the woman of the house in the Dannenfelser Hof understood how to fry excellent, made-to-order steaks. Not only that but it was a very welcomed surprise that Frau Spickschen and several of her daughters also spoke English - a skill that no other guest houses in the surrounding area possessed. And finally, Frau Spickschen possessed several unusual qualities. She was open-minded and curious, interested in the needs of each American guest and for many, over a period of time, she almost became a surrogate mother to them. Life in the garrison was very boring for the American soldiers. Movies were shown no more than twice in the week. Otherwise the GIs and officers had to find a way to spend the day. Therefore the "Dannenfelser Hof" offered a welcome change.

The new Home in Dannenfels / 1951

As far as Thorlef remembered, in the early 1950s a steak with french-fries and salad cost 2.80 DM. But that might have been the wholesale cost. Guests paid maybe a little more. "But above all they drank beer and other things and that is what brought money into the till. The Dannenfelser Hof survived only because of the Americans." An agreement was made with the local butcher who provided the meat and sausages that he would supply only the very best meat for steaks. Not only tendons and cartilage but skin scraps and every bit of fat was carefully removed. Feechen explained, "Frau Spickschen always said that Americans do not like fat. We were famous for the fact that we served only prime steaks. The American guests were served meals that they were used to from home. Any left-over fatty parts were put through the meat grinder and used for a casserole combined with cabbage that tasted very good. Frau Spickschen was very skilled in the kitchen."

Of particular interest to the Americans was the fact that when Bergild returned from her stay in the United States, she brought back not only her language skills but also a flair for their American home-land. Moreover, she was a young woman. She met her American husband in Dannenfels. Bergild was not the only one who married an American. Helga, the eldest Spickschen daughter whose first marriage ended in such a tragic and abrupt way, married a soldier named Frank Carl Hart in March, 1952. He was the chief of the US station on the Donnersberg. Also Feechen tied the knot with a man who was stationed in Dannenfels.

How much the life in Dannenfels became unforgettable and how many lifelong memories some U.S. soldiers retained in regards to the relationship with Ursula Spickschen was disclosed by a letter that Mike Henderson wrote on March 27, 1993 to his former fellow soldier Frank Hart.

"Frau Spickschen was one of my favorite persons. She was a strong and positive influence on me when I was a young GI and I shall never forget her. I can see her now in the guest house with those children around table doing their homework. Back then, in 1952-53, times were hard but she and Herr Spickschen had the right stuff when it came to dealing with life. She referred to me as the "Prussian soldier". I did not know what a compliment that was until later in life.

"As I told you on the phone, I went back to Dannenfels in 1989. I was excited but saddened when I found the guest house closed and learned of Frau Spickschen's death. Unlike many of us, she left a legacy and certainly influenced the lives of many young GI's in a positive direction."

The American soldiers were among the most important customers who visited the Dannenfelser Hof and their payments significantly helped so that the business was spared from bankruptcy. Ursel also had historical links to Scandinavia. Probably since 1953, the aforementioned Davberger, director of a Swedish agricultural school, arrived in Dannenfels once a year with his senior class on a bus. From there they visited individual wine producers located on the Pfaelzer Weinstrasse (Palatine wine road) to study their operations. Probably other people from Sweden stayed at the inn - at least Feechen remembered some Scandinavian guests who overly enjoyed drinking too much alcohol and then they went into the village. Some were so drunk that they no longer knew where they were staying. In the village all the houses looked the same and they did not know the town.

One day a woman called Mischka appeared and brought excitement to the village. She turned out to be a double agent who had probably been spying for the Russians and was then "flipped" by the Americans. What she intended to accomplish remained unknown. She became friendly with several young Americans and also had an affair with a young Dannenfelser man who was regarded as extremely intelligent. Mischka was a worldly woman and she was liked by the children. She was a colorful person who impressed everyone with whom she came in contact. Later on she opened a small pub somewhere in the Ruhr area.

Around the mid-1950s another lady arrived who introduced herself as Frau Putat. She was accompanied by an American officer who rented one of the beautiful newly renovated guest rooms for his bride. The man explained that he had to attend a two-week training course and that his fiancée should be taken care of in the Dannenfelser Hof during that time. Thirteen-year-old Thorlef thought that Frau Putat was nice. A fortnight went by and the soldier did not return. However the room rent was paid only for two weeks. Frau Putat did not know what she should do or where she should live. Soon afterward, Ursel was approached by a young American soldier. "Frau Spickschen, do you know what's going on here?" "What?" "Well," replied the American, "upstairs on the second floor there is a long line of young men in front of the door waiting for the services of love from Frau Putat." Ursel was horrified. If there was even a hint of suspicion that a guest did not behave in a civilized manner she would not tolerate even an overnight stay. Frau Putat was told to stop her "trade" immediately but she did not have to leave the room. Ursel spoke severity and decisiveness to the woman's conscience and pleading with her to return to the path of virtue and righteousness. Frau Putat was Catholic and therefore she could be taken in by nuns of the Dannenfels convent. One morning, after a few weeks Thorlef was on the way to school in Kirchheimbolanden when a second floor window of a house suddenly opened and Frau Putat waved cheerfully, "Hey Thorlef, Hello Astrid, how are you doing?" She must have found a new location where she could pursue her chosen profession.

Only a few local guests came to the inn regularly. The area was poor and most people could not afford to frequently stop into a restaurant or bar. Throughout the day not much happened in the Dannenfelser Hof. One of the few regulars was a man who was called the "gravedigger". His job was to walk around in the village with a bell which he rang to notify the inhabitants of any new proclamations and also to let people know when someone had died. Despite his nickname, the "gravedigger" was a funny man. Apart from him, another regular was an old man who was considered the wisest man in the village. And finally, farmer Hauenstein came every morning from next door. He suffered from malaria in the war. As soon as the key turned in the front door, farmer Hauenstein appeared in the bar and ordered "a piffche", (1/8 liter) of wine. What he had to pay was noted with chalk lines on the raw wood of a cabinet that stood in the bar. Farmer Hauenstein kept his tab open for many years. In the end, to get rid of his debts, he gave the Spickschens a piece of land.

Feechen recalls that in general both the Americans and the locals were very quiet. Only sometimes, when someone got drunk, did they become loud. Ursula Spickschen was then very strict and knew how to solve the problem. There was always someone available who would grab the rowdy person by the collar and transport him resolutely to the door. The young girls thought of these noisy incidents as funny and an interesting change of pace. During these precarious situations, Frau Spickschen remained the prestigious, fine lady who was respected by all. On one hand, she was somehow able to accommodate the concerns of the local peasants and she was able to talk to them as an equal. On the other hand, she maintained a natural distance that was not offensive to anyone. For Feechen, Ursel was a mother under whose care she felt right at home.

When one considers the period between 1950 and 1957 as a whole, the fact that often "nothing was going on" in the guest rooms was very boring but in only one aspect. Especially for Thorlef, who was nine years old at the beginning of this period and sixteen years in the end, many incredibly exciting impressions were formed with many turbulent highs and lows. Regarding the low points, a bitter disappointment came in the first year - about 1951. A summer festival was prepared with great enthusiasm. Ursel designed a leaflet which was distributed throughout the village. A lot of meat and other food was bought - and then it rained cats and dogs. Not a soul appeared. The expensive meat was placed in the basement on top of ice to keep cold. But even the old house recipes that Ursel used to prepare the food could not prevent the inevitable outcome – in the end the meat got older and finally inedible. After such a failure the possibility of bankruptcy inevitably appeared more likely.

In 1954 or 1955, when Thorlef was old enough to stay up a little longer, he was allowed to attend some of the village festivals. He witnessed some dramatic confrontations during these festivals. The majority of residents in Dannenfels were Protestant. In the neighboring village Bennhausen, the majority was Catholic. The slightly more distant village of Weitersweiler was also predominately Catholic. The closer village of Jakobsweiler was Protestant. The villages had competing religions. So when some of the young boys from Bennhausen or Weitersweiler tried to pick up young girls from Dannenfels, the boys from Dannenfels quickly started to fight the "foreigners". Often these boys acted like gaming cocks in the manner that they went at each other with chains which they took from the nearest farm. The wounds these boys suffered during those altercations were regarded as a kind of mark of honor and they were casually disregarded.

Ursula Spickschen with Thomas Neary / Dannenfelserhof 1956

It also happened that the young Palatine boys picked fights with the American soldiers. The local boys had virtually no money to spend - since cash was scarce in Dannenfels - while the soldiers had plenty of money to throw around. That generated envy and created conflicts. Unpleasant situations sometimes arose for the Spickschens when the American guests decided at times, for no apparent reason, to make another guest house their favorite hangout. Fortunately for the Dannenfelser Hof, they would come back again just in time to avert a disaster for the Spickschens.

In addition to events that sometimes literally or figuratively went down the drain, Thorlef remembers festivals where everyone enjoyed themselves. The inauguration celebration that probably took place in late November, 1950 was a great success. The Dannenfelser people were curious to know what changes were made to the dilapidated inn by the refugees from the Salzgitter area (the Spickschens). Ursel impressed the village butcher with new recipes for making his sausages. She showed him how to make delicious liverwurst and blood sausage by using different spices. Everyone in the village knew that the improvements were due to the influence of Frau Spickschen. So not only were the rooms nicely decorated for the first slaughter festival (a pig) but also the available food tasted better than before.

Later on, wonderful Mardi-Gras festivals were celebrated. Two of the guest bedrooms were transformed into dimly lit bars and in the basement another bar was installed. Colorful garlands were hung anywhere and a three-man band played in a back corner of the dining room. The daughters of Tante Adelheid, who had specially come for the festival, together with the various Spickschen daughters, were dressed as barmaids and offered cocktails to the celebrants. Soon everyone was in high spirits and had a great time. There was a lot of dancing and the dull lighting created an electrifying atmosphere. A few GIs appeared with their "Ami-darlings"(prostitutes) on their arms. For this reason some of the good old Dannenfels citizens disdained the commotion as something almost wicked. However, for the twelve or fifteen years old Thorlef it was all very exciting.

The Basement Bar / Dannenfelserhof 1955

For both the parents and the children the daily guest house operation was quite often dreary and monotonous. So it was always a special, if rare, event when a dignitary came to visit. Hans von der Groeben, the son of an East Prussian landowner and an extremely prominent figure belonged to the far-flung network of acquaintances that Erich and Ursula Spickschen had since their time in East Prussian. Groeben had connections to the active resistance against Hitler through Fritz-Dietlof Graf von der Schulenburg but he remained untouched by the Gestapo after the July 20, 1944 attempt to assassinate Hitler. Later he became one of the fathers of the European Economic Community (EEC). With a personality like Groeben in attendance, the Dannenfelser Hof suddenly won a different and more positive reputation after being lovingly or ironically called by some a "Bumslokal" (down-trodden inn). The establishment was raised to a more sophisticated level. At least that is what young Thorlef felt. Other prominent guests who always felt very comfortable in the warm atmosphere which was created mainly by Ursel, were Johann Oskar Walter Bern von Baer, a man who started his career as an officer in East Prussia and who in 1939 married a woman from the Nathusius family from the Samland and then advanced to major general in the Bundeswehr (German Army) in 1963. Another prominent guest was Hans Graf Dohna (born 1925), a member of an old East Prussian family. The fact that such connections could endure long after the Second World War was a sure sign, especially for the younger Spickschen children, that their parents were not really guilty of any wrongdoing during the Nazi era.

In addition to the daily operations or occasional special events in the restaurant, the children of Ursel and Erich were always given full attention. As far as their funds allowed, the parents did everything they could to give their offspring a good education. It was not just about the education in the school. At home, a family culture was maintained. For example in addition to learning polite social behavior and good table manners, a ritual was maintained that Thorlef remembers particularly well. Rituals are important for children and Ursel performed this routine in an unusual way. Every night before going to sleep she told the younger children a fairy tale for half an hour or longer. Only on Saturday nights, when the restaurant was extremely busy, storytime was not observed. Ursel always told fairy tales that she created as she talked since she was particularly gifted in devising exciting tales. She used her talent to write a series of tales that were published in Denmark in Danish but they were not published in Germany.

Astrid especially loved the story of the knight with the folding castle. When danger approached he only needed to press a button and his whole castle vanished under a flap. Another tale was about Liselotte and the puppet; those two had exciting adventures every night. If someone told Astrid a story in an unambiguous way, she saw what happened before her like in a movie.

It is noteworthy that Ursel could captivate the younger children with her stories even when they were fourteen and fifteen years old. These cherished traditions might have played a role when the wish for an imaginary wonderland was still strong. Ursel obviously knew how to adapt to the age appropriate expectations of her children. Still existing is a whole basket full of audio tapes on which Ursel's numerous tales are stored.

Christmas Eve was the only day of the year when the inn was closed. For Christmas, not only did the whole Spickschen family gather together but also orphaned children from the former East Prussian neighborhood were invited along with individual friends and acquaintances. A large crowd came together and the whole thing was reminiscent of the Christmas parties that were celebrated in Woydiethen prior to 1945. Similarly, the Easter holidays were a special event unlike ordinary Sundays that simply interrupted the daily routine with an especially good dinner.

By now it should be clear that Ursel was unusually versatile. She cared in every respect for stability and continuity. However, she always had new ideas when it came time to overcome difficulties - especially financial constraints. Repeatedly the Park–Brewery cancelled its deliveries because the Dannenfelser Hof lacked the money to pay the outstanding bills. Ursel was able to sell some of her fairy tales to a Danish newspaper for which she was paid at least 900 gold kroners. She was able to pay the brewery the past due bills and the delivery cancellation was lifted. In 1949, Ursel wisely subscribed to purchase two copies of all newly issued postal stamps of the Federal Republic of Germany. In the mid-1950s she had gathered a collection that she could sell for good money. In 1956, she succeeded in putting together a book of self-tested tea recipes which she sold to a large tea company in Bremen for a fee of DM 900.00. Another time she tried to sell parts of her beautiful old porcelain from the Royal Berlin Porcelain Factory to an antique dealer but he offered such a low price that she kept the porcelain. Finally, she did not hesitate to take small loans from her children in the face of impending new delivery stoppages by the brewery. Thorlef and Astrid emptied their piggy banks containing a total of twenty marks that together sufficed as down payment to the brewery for future deliveries.

The large loan that Helga provided could be repaid at a low interest rate as the Spickschens received money from the Lastenausgleich (burden sharing). Of course, if Helga had invested the money in a fund with good interest rates she would have been much better off.

It may be that Thorlef inherited some of the business acumen of his mother. Astrid

Von mir allein 1956 geschrieben, Rezepte ausprobiert und aufgeschrieben.
Mutti.

Über 900.– DM Honorar, – damals fast unsere Rettung.

recognized early on that he was a skillful merchant. She recalled that the inn also had chocolates and sweets for sale because some of the guests wanted to buy them. According to Astrid, "Thorlef had the idea that we children should buy a bar of chocolate, divide into 24 pieces and sell each piece individually to Feechen, Tante Annchen and various others. With the money we made from the sale we were able to buy a box of chocolates. In turn, we sold the chocolates piece by piece and in the end, we made a profit of DM 32.00. For Mother's Day we were able to give our mother a purse as a present. Besides, I knew that Thorlef desperately wanted to buy a pocket watch from the catalogue house Quelle. He was able to buy it with the rest of the money. That there was nothing left for me did not bother me because Thorlef was so very happy and I thought that he was the one that had the idea to earn the money.

"He also found out a special trick. In the restaurant we had a slot machine. You could use a 10 penny piece and when it got stuck you could get it out again by pushing a button in the back. Thorlef discovered that the machine would spit out a ten penny piece even if you put only a two-penny piece through the return opening using a very specific, skillful finger wiggle. This happened only now and then, but sometimes it succeeded. He only told me about such tricks. He always made sure that no one was in the guest room during his maneuvers. But I tried it after him and was a bit bolder. I fiddled around with the machine even if someone was sitting in the back corner. When Thorlef noticed what I was doing he laid into me. He himself operated with the greatest caution. How my father found out who was responsible for this fraud I do not know to this day. Every few weeks a man came to empty the money reservoir in the machine. When he found the two-penny pieces, my father just said to Thorlef and me, 'I do not want to see this again'. He knew exactly who was behind our shenanigans."

Erich understood how to gain respect from his children in a quiet, confident manner. As Astrid says, for her, he was the ultimate. There was nothing about him to criticize and she never wanted to criticize him. But at times she wanted to criticize her mother a bit. Erich was loud only in exceptional cases, if at all. His older daughters did not ask to have their hair cut short, not because they were afraid that their father would scold them, but because they knew that he would be disappointed. Astrid said, "All of us children wanted only the best for him. At dinner he was not the one that claimed the biggest piece. No, my mother took the biggest piece of meat from the platter and I thought that was fine. She was the housewife! Nevertheless, I never thought that my father had thus shown any weakness. I always had the feeling that my parents were equal and considered each other as equals. Over all, my father could be extremely charming. Older ladies who appeared in the restaurant often made eyes at him and flirted with him. All in all, he made a formidable appearance without having an authoritarian demeanor."

Thorlef confirmed Astrid's memories and added that, for example, Tante Adelheid almost worshiped his father, whom she probably met in 1939. For Thorlef and his siblings, their father was the legitimate moral and educational authority in the house - as distinguished from simple authoritarian behavior. Also Bergild declared bluntly that she adored her father. With him she could discuss her concerns much better than with her mother. Bergild said, "I was scared of my mother. If I wanted to do something, my mother's response was always, 'No'. In retrospect I understand that because during the flight from East Prussia everything was on her shoulders. There was no room for extra wishes. But with my father I could ask anything. It impressed me especially that he knew the answers to everything. Whether the question was about nature or history or literature, he knew the answer. He was educated and had a great memory."

The following excerpts are from a June 3, 1955 letter that Erich wrote to Gaga from Dannenfels clarifying that the welfare of the family and the children's development are currently of vital concern to him the same as it was during all the past years. He wrote at a time when Astrid, who was just visiting Gaga, was going to celebrate her 12th birthday in the next few days.

"Thorlef is a happy adolescent and an avid Boy Scout. What do you say about Astrid? Puppe [Bergild] cleans the bedrooms in the mornings, helps with the laundry, etc. and then she serves in the guestroom in the evenings. But I am sure that Astrid has certainly told you everything. To finance his university studies, Ingolf has worked hard in the BASF factory in Ludwigshafen and then in the election campaign for the CDU. I was very pleased that he worked very hard and was consistently recognized as a good comrade by the other employees."

There is a typewritten addition by Ursel to that letter in which she suggested that the situation in Dannenfels does not make her happy. The Spickschens continued to look for a property that offered better opportunities than the Dannenfelser Hof.

Erich continued: "Well, come visit us next year. Hopefully by then we will have found something nicer. But we will definitely remain in the Palatinate if only for the fact that we now finally have some acquaintances and have built a few relationships over the years that could help us a little, but not much. To move again to a new and strange area, has no purpose."

As for Erich Spickschen's life of in Dannenfels, it was probably soon clear that the lease of the restaurant was a kind of desperate act for him. He felt that he was not right for a guesthouse owner; the work did not suit him. Also the small farm which he took over could not bring him happiness because he no longer had his former strength. In addition to the 24.7 acres of deforested land, the 9.3 acres which he wanted to farm consisted of probably 15 plots in hilly areas with poor soil, some of which was accessible only by indirect means. In the Palatinate, land was inherited by the principle of equal division, so that in time the parcel of land that belonged to the individual owner or tenant always became smaller and smaller and at the end it was quite tiny. More and more farmers could only hold onto their farm by getting a second job.

Much fruit was grown on the parcels of land in Dannenfels. The Spickschen children worked in the restaurant and on the farm land whenever time allowed. They picked cherries - a Dannenfels specialty – as well as gooseberries, currants and apples. They brought in the grain at harvest time, collected stones from the fields and helped with the potato harvest. Ingolf, who was rarely in Dannenfels since he was away in a boarding school, earned money during the summer holidays mostly at the Traube farm in Bleckenstedt. He recalled that he had to harrow the poor soil in Dannenfels when he came home for the Easter holidays in 1951. It was a culture shock for him and it must have been no less of a shock for his father. The harrow was pulled by cows, a farming operation that could not have been any more antiquated to someone who was accustomed to the modern ways of farming in East Prussia. The cows used as draft animals behaved completely different from horses. They were often, as Ingolf said, "stubborn and stupid and did nothing. For me, it was horrible."

Another time, as Ingolf visited his parents in the winter, half the potatoes were frozen in the cellar. For days, Ingolf and his father had to sort the rotten potatoes from among the good ones. Ingolf reported that, "It was an incredibly lousy kind of job. My father did not complain, but I grumbled and was moody as a 16 or 17 year old boy could be. At Traubes I could move around quite differently. I could drive a Jeep and did not have to slave away in the cellar."

The approximately 34 acres of farm land that Erich leased consisted not only of the small plots but also about 25 acres of newly deforested land. That land was quite inferior. With tree roots everywhere throughout the soil it was difficult to plow. The little tractor that Erich had in addition to the cows could not be used on the land because its 11 PS was so weak that it barely made it up the hills in the field. However, there were other, flatter parcels where the tractor was used. Even with the children and other helpers working the farm, soon it became obvious that working the land was too much for Erich and there was nothing left for him to do but transfer the rough field work to a neighbor. This in turn cost money.

The grain was harvested in late summer with the help of a leased thrashing machine. Two cows also belonged to the small farm for one and a half years. They were milked in the morning before school by Runhild. When she was on vacation in Dannenfels, the 15 year old Bergild also took care of the cows after her parents taught her how to milk. Thorlef's job when he was 12 or 13 years old was to take care of two pigs. One of the animals was slaughtered for the family's consumption and the other one was sold. There were also chickens and geese for the family's own use. But the whole agricultural project brought in nothing. On the contrary, one was lucky if it did not result in losses.

A severe crop failure in 1954 led to additional difficulties. Persistent rain meant that the grain started to grow out and was hardly worth anything. Ursel succeeded in getting a loan of a few thousand DM after filling out numerous and complicated applications with the large bureaucracy. In the mid-1960s she was able to settle with the lender and the balance of the loan did not have to be repaid.

A newspaper article that Ursel published in the "Deutschen Landwirtschaflichen Presse" (German Agricultural Press) on September 22, 1956 illustrated how the

Spickschens, after running the Dannenfelser Hof and leasing the farm for five and a half years always found themselves in a troubled, if not desperate situation. In the article titled "Mehr Gemeinschaftssinn" (More sense of community) Ursel related her thoughts about how severely the refugee farmers from the East, who have lost all their possessions, are disadvantaged compared to long-established farmers in the West. The various arguments that she brought to the fore-front showed that the refugees and displaced persons face a gloomy future. At the end, she could only appeal to the farmers of the West to forego purchases of newly available properties and let the farmers from the East have first claim in such transactions. She encouraged a "code of honor" where "the sense of community and decency prohibits the tradition where long established and well-off farmers multiply their wealth by buying or leasing a second farm thus taking away the possibility and chance from the displaced farmer who was once in the same position as they are now and who only want a chance to create a new life and home."

Unfortunately, this appeal, as obvious as it was, proved to be futile in view of the common business practices of that time and which were also true in the agricultural field.

Astrid thinks that her father was at a loss with the management of the small parcels of land in the Dannenfels area. Bergild believes that the hard work in the fields also ruined his health. "When he came home from the fields in the evening he was totally exhausted. He was pale and all the blood had drained from his face. He often looked drained and was weak but he never complained." He was very different from Ursel in his self-control. Ursel's responses were emotional and direct and she kept nothing in. Erich participated in the work in the restaurant by keeping the books.

After 1954, Erich was again politically active on a modest scale for the Arbeitsgemeinschaft Demokratischer Kreise (ADK) (Consortium of Democratic Circles). He was elected county chairman of the Refugee Association for the district Kirchheimbolanden. He gave short lectures at the membership meetings for which he was able to use materials provided by the ADK. Thorlef often accompanied him. Erich Spickschen was mainly committed to the security policies of the ADK which were implemented by the CDU federal government. It was a special experience for Erich when he was invited to a meeting at the NATO headquarters in Paris and where he could listen to lectures about military and political issues.

In this context Ingolf related that he learned from his mother that one day three gentlemen appeared in Dannenfels who were from the executive committee of the Deutschen Reichspartei (DRP) (German National Party). They spoke with Erich Spickschen for a total of five hours. One of the three men was Adolf von Thadden, who was one of the founders of the National Democratic Party of Germany (NPD). Later, in 1967, he became the Federal Chairman of that party. In addition, Wilhelm Meinberg was one of the three men. He was the man to whom the whole Spickschen family owed a lot because he paved the way for them to get to Bleckenstedt. Ingolf did not remember who the third man was. The three politicians tried to persuade Erich to join the extreme right-wing DRP which was founded in 1950. However, Erich said, "Gentlemen, that chapter is closed to me." By "that chapter" Erich meant that he did not want to be affiliated or associated with the policies of the National Socialist. According to Ursel, Erich did not quite "kick the gentlemen out" but he clearly explained to them that he now held other views. There were no further attempts to engage him for a far-right party.

As for Erich's health, he was probably ailing the rest of the years until his death. The family was very aware of Erich's condition as illustrated by an experience Bergild remembered. This occurrence also fits into the same type of similar incidents that were related by Ingolf and Thorlef. All of the children knew how sensitive their father was and how he reacted when there were complaints about the food on the table. Even though nutritious, the food was not always of the best quality because of economic reasons. Bergild related that, a "black pudding" was often part of the diet. This was made with pigs' blood mixed with grits, which was then preserved in cans. For the meal, the pudding was heated in a hot iron skillet. At one noon time meal served sometime between 1954 and 1956 the black pudding was again served. Bergild sat with the others at the dinner table and said, "What? This stuff again?" At that same moment she saw her father losing his temper. Of course she knew that he had been starving during his time in Russia and he often had to eat garbage left by the Russian soldiers or chew on green weeds to get some vitamins. She jumped up from the table and ran up the stairs with her father behind her. Suddenly she stopped on the third floor and turned terrified with a guilty conscience as she suddenly remembered that her father had a weak heart. "Oh God", she thought, "what if he dies now!" She hugged her father and he only reprimanded her by saying, "Don't ever say something like that again!"

In the novel that Ursel wrote about life in Dannenfels, she basically disregarded the fact that Erich was a broken man. The fictitious energetic and robust husband that she wrote about was probably wishful thinking. The novel was supposed to be funny and all the difficulties that had to be overcome were written in a comic sense. Perhaps the will to illustrate everything as a comedy sprang from wishful thinking because in practice, in daily life, the grief that tormented her often broke out in the open. After the loss of Woydiethen, after the escape from East Prussia, in the wake of the subsequent eternal drudgery and the impossibility of going back to her old form of life, Ursel quarreled with her life. She found herself being constantly, if not always, bitterly disappointed. Unlike Erich who never complained, Ursel could not hide her feelings. She was an emotional person whose moods visibly alternated. She showed her enthusiasm and joy as openly as her disappointment and sorrow.

Karen remembered that as a young woman in Bleckenstedt, she often could not muster patience for her mother when she wailed. She still remembered that sometimes she thought, “I cannot stand to hear that lament any longer”. Karen was at an age when she was particularly critical of her mother. Astrid, 18 years younger than Karen, expressed similar feelings by stating that the many complaints about the lack of money had been very stressful. Ursel felt badly treated by fate which, as Astrid said, was very evident and understandable. She added, “But nothing will change, no matter how much you whine." For a while the youngest daughter slept with her mother in the same room. Ursel cried again and again during the night and Astrid finally could feel no pity for her. She covered her ears so she would not hear the sobbing. Ursel could be theatrical. She was a strong woman, but in moments of weakness she was full of self-pity.

Ingolf also had similar experiences like his second eldest and his youngest sister. In January 1951, when he became 16 years old, he came home only during school holidays. The rest of the time he lived in boarding schools. As much as he loved to help his brother-in-law Gerhard Traube in Bleckenstedt with the harvest on his properly run farm during the summer holidays in 1951 and the following years, his feelings were ambivalent when he traveled to Dannenfels. There he repeatedly experienced that in the evening he would sit alone with his parents at the table, his father with a glass of white wine, his mother with red wine. It was not long before his mother would break out into bitter complaints. Ursel's lamentations were hard to bear for Ingolf, who by then was maybe 17 or 18 years old. His mother could not cope with his father’s loss of all enterprising spirit and love of life and his father always remained silent.

Erich Spickschen only reached the age of 60 years. In the summer of 1957, Helga, who was married and living in the United States, came for a visit to Germany. Her daughter Karen (called "Schwesti") was baptized on the 60th birthday of her grandfather Erich, on July 23. Two days later, Erich was taken to the district hospital in Kirchheimbolanden. His liver was giving him difficulties but the doctors concentrated mainly on his gall bladder. A liver function test was taken, but in 1957 it took a long time until the results were known. The doctors did not want to wait so they operated on Erich’s gall bladder. After the surgery, he could leave the hospital only for a day or two but he never came back to Dannenfels.

Astrid related what happened when she visited her father a few days before his death. "I went to the hospital directly from school and his condition was bad. He himself said, 'I am not doing well at all. You all think I'm a hypochondriac’. I said, ‘but why would we think such a thing?’ Her father responded, ‘Actually I should be feeling much better already.’ Two days later he was in a coma! We all came to the hospital and sat up all night with him. On the first of October 1957, he died.

Astrid continued, “The day after his death the surgeon who had treated him, came to Dannenfels and asked for permission to take a liver sample from my father. The result was that he actually died of cirrhosis of the liver. This finding was important for us because it provided the evidence that the jaundice which my father contracted when he was in captivity had to be regarded as the cause of death. He died from an illness that he contracted during the war and therefore my mother was entitled to receive a pension. The doctors had made a mistake in the beginning. They should have never operated my father on the gall bladder; the liver was much too damaged. Quite a lot went wrong!"

IX

Ursula Spickschen in the period 1957-1981

In Thorlef's words, the previous letters made it clear that over the course of their 34-year marriage, a relationship developed between Erich and Ursula Spickschen that was characterized by a "deep and great love". However, given the difficulties, upheavals and disasters that they had to endure during the 34 years, it was inevitable that the marriage was also burdened by tensions and stress. Ursel often found it especially difficult to come to terms with her lot in life. After suffering from the end of January, 1945 until June, 1948 under circumstances brought about by their forced separation, Ursel had to live in the years thereafter under stressful and often degrading conditions with a man (Erich) who was changed and physically weakened. Erich's early death forced Ursel to quickly overcome her new pain by reminding herself that she could be self-reliant given what she had learned during the years after the flight from East Prussia. So she resolutely tackled the problems that arose. She had to ask herself, "What has to be done to survive?" It was necessary to find solutions.

In the spring of 1957, shortly before Erich's death, the Spickschens tried to lease a freeway service station near Kaiserslautern because the situation with the guest house in Dannenfels was untenable in the long run. The application was in vain since someone else was awarded the contract. In the fall of 1957, now a widow, Ursel tried to sublease the Dannenfelser Hof guest house together with the associated farm land of 16 morgens (10 acres). She found a man who had returned from the Foreign Legion to West Germany. The man had DM 3,000 - a sum that was sufficient for him to be able to take over the assets and the inventory of the house. However he managed the inn for only half a year and then left one day under cover of darkness and was not heard of again. He was not able to run the restaurant so no guests frequented the inn.

Later on, a man from the village was found to sublease and run the inn. This new lessee was intelligent but somewhat weak and unprincipled. But never the less he and his wife operated the restaurant for several years.

Ursel had to prepare for the future in order to regain a solid base for her future life. She took advantage of the connections she previously established and used the diverse knowledge she possessed, especially in dealing with financial transactions and administrative matters. Huge amounts of paperwork and extensive correspondence had to be dealt with and these tasks took all of her strength and energy to complete. She was able to get an early termination of the lease with the township for the 42 morgens (26 acres) of farmland and recover a sum of several thousand marks.

It was also very crucial for her to convince the authorities that she was entitled to a pension. As Astrid previously reported, it was established that her husband Erich

Spickschen had died from the effects of hepatitis which he contracted during his captivity by the Russians and therefore his death was a consequence of his war effort. At first the authorities refused Ursel's pension application. But after objecting and citing the medical report from Göttingen, she was successful. Ursel half ironically and half seriously described the monthly amount that was granted her as a "Captain's" pension that was neither enough to live nor die on. After Erich's missions in World War I, then in 1939 in Poland and finally in the Volkssturm, he attained the rank of captain in the reserve.

It proved to be very difficult for Ursel to decide what to do professionally and where to find a place to live. To solve this problem, shortly after Erich's death (which was long before she received a pension) Ursel turned to the Ministerialdirigenten (minister of housing) Hans von der Gröben, a man who had been a frequent guest in the Dannenfelser Hof. Ursel seriously considered building a house in a Nebenerwerbssiedlung (sideline settlement housing development) in Kirchheim-bolanden or later in Dannenfels. Inexpensive loans were available to new settlers for the construction. However she considered taking a senior position in a group home. Gröben strongly advised her to apply for such a position. In a letter dated November 14, 1957, Gröben referred to the position as "best available option at a 'mothers convalescent home of the Red Cross' in Kirchheimbolanden". He believed this because all other plans would be "extraordinarily difficult" to realize. He went on to say that "the conditions for a grant for a 'sideline settlement loan' hardly exist."

In a letter dated November 1, 1957 from Dannenfels (a letter before Groeben's letter) Ursel justified why she did not like her advisor's proposal:

"You (Gröben) highly dissuaded me the other day from purchasing a sideline settlement and advised me that the best solution would be for me to take a job as director of a group home. At the time I did not say much because this proposal came as a surprise. I had not considered this option before.

"I now have had some time to think about it and have talked to some people who, just like you have my well-being in mind. During many sleepless nights of brooding I have come to the conclusion that it is my first and foremost duty to preserve a home for my four unmarried children, especially the three youngest ones of 14, 16 and 18 years. They were not allowed to grow up in a solid home and therefore they not only need me very much but they also must be able to feel safe and that they are not being constantly uprooted, but that they have a home. Despite what they had to go through, or perhaps because of it, they would be deeply affected when suddenly there would be no nucleus for the family and no place to call home. It would also oppress me! In this case, my existence would be only for the preservation of my own self. Having already lost something very important that had meaning in my life, namely the rebuilding of Woydiethen through hard work and many deprivations and sacrifices, to say nothing of Dannenfels, I cannot and will not volunteer to give up the most important job that still remains to be done and that is to rebuild a modest foundation for the family and to participate in the inner forming of my children. My inner voice certainly does not deceive me, which tells me that God has given me this obligation and I must take it to heart.

"It would certainly be very difficult to find a job as director of the home where the two youngest could live with me. And one more thing! I know from personal experience the daily routine and the responsibilities and duties of a matron. That's why I also know that I would be totally stressed by having to split my attention between this task to serve as a matron and the one I have to be a mother to my children. If I take a job, I give it one hundred percent. To me, it is not in me to do a job half way."

Additionally, Ursel noted that being older she now no longer possesses the drive and power to accomplish multiple tasks simultaneously when each requires her full commitment. Ursel's arguments were guided by emotions and a sense of responsibility that she used to justify why she did not want to take the position of a matron. The question of which other financial opportunities would be available to her completely fell into the background.

Ursel made it clear, and not merely in a general way, what further efforts she undertook to bring a sense of security and stability into the lives of her family in two other letters. On January 28, 1958, she wrote from Dannenfels to Armgard von Alvensleben, a lady she knew as the abbess of Heiligengrabe, who was then working in the Evangelical Mission Station in West Germany.

"Karen wrote me that you graciously contacted Countess Leuthrum at the Landfrauenverband in order to find a possible income opportunity for me. I have to tell you that there may be a possible problem. I receive a monthly grant from the load balancing fund of 410.00 DM for the three children. Ingolf is studying at the University and the other two go to high school. When I give up the lease here, which hopefully will happen soon, every penny I earn over the sum of about 200.00 DM (116.00 DM plus rent) will be deducted from the aid! Therefore, it is pointless for me to accept any full-time job.

"Karen has probably told you that I would like to build a house in the sideline settlement in the county town of Kirchheimbolanden. I will probably have to pay 3 percent amortization a year for the necessary credit but no interest. That means that what I would otherwise spend on housing rent will be used as down payment for the loan. This is reasonable. I also want to raise chickens in order to have an extra income that cannot accurately be calculated by the tax office. Also, I received assurances from three agricultural weekly magazines that they would publish a monthly article of mine. Since this revenue will not be enough to support us, I'm still looking for other work which will be paid on a case by case basis. For example, I could give lectures and do other literary work or work that I can do from my desk. This could be compensated as an allowance which would not counted as income.

"It's impossible for me to live on DM 116.00 a month and also pay electricity, water, newspapers and other general expenses for the household. But rules are rules! Therefor I have to find a way to receive income over and above the 200.00 DM that does not appear directly as standard income but as compensation.

"I am officially a *ländliche Haushaltspflegerin, a rural home-economics teacher* and I have been writing professional articles for many years, especially on nutrition and healthy contemporary cooking. I have also written fairy tales, short stories, etc., and often gave lectures, not only about domestic issues, but also other subjects.

"I am in contact to a certain degree with the Landfrauenverband via Miss Frankenfeld, the managing director of Countess Leuthrum. Miss Frankenfeld, who knows me from the Reichsnährstand times, was able to put me in contact with the Land und Frau, (or Land and Woman newspaper), for which I now regularly write articles.

"I believe that I have now been able to clarify the somewhat difficult situation in which I find myself and also define the possibilities and questions that I face."

Whether Ursel had a somewhat difficult or a very difficult situation is a judgement call. Frau von Alvensleben previously wrote a letter of condolence so it was unnecessary for Ursel to explain what triggered her to dwell on her acute dilemma. Ursel's letter revealed how she was forced to count every penny, to literally turn every dime over twice before spending it. At the same time it showed that she was absolutely committed to doing things legally: rules are rules. In the end, Ursel had to rely on her ability to find a narrow interpretation of the law to create income opportunities beyond what was allowed by the strict interpretation of the law by officials.

Two weeks later, on February 12, 1958, Ursel wrote a letter from Dannenfels to Herr Abraham in which she discussed the conditions under which a house could be built in a sideline settlement. - It should be noted that Ursel used the expressions 'sideline settlement' even though she meant the construction of a single house. It was also true that a home for people who possessed a sideline authorization did not have to be built within a closed sideline settlement. - Abraham worked as an executive in office of Lastenausgleich (or load-balancing) in Kirchheimbolanden.

"My son-in-law [Gerhard Traube] also considers it more proper to establish an agricultural sideline settlement because then I only have to pay amortization. I could immediately buy from Mr. Hauenstein a building site in Dannenfels located on the road to Bennhausen at the corner between the road to the Rodeland and the house of Fruit Heckmann. The lot is 1,620 square meters in size and will cost 3.00 DM per square meter, so that is 4,860.00 DM. Electricity and water connections are available. This would have the advantage that I could save approximately 1,000.00 DM since Mr. Hauenstein owes me for the land lease and his bar tab which I would otherwise lose. Confidentially, Hauenstein's situation is now so bad that the Raiffeisen farm coop has given his account over to a trust. Raiffeisen entered into a mortgage with Hauenstein on the building site of over 3,000.00 DM and Hauenstein has not paid interest for years. This issue would be covered by the purchase price and Raiffeisen would probably agree to this solution. The remaining 1,860.00 DM would cover what Mr. Hauenstein owes me (approx. 1,000.00DM) and the money could be used as a small personal contribution to the sideline settlement.

"I have to decide before March 1 (and that means in the last days of February) if I want to buy the Hauenstein building site. Otherwise, either Raiffeisen will grab the lot and everything becomes more difficult or he must decide to look for another buyer. Except for very small building lots in the village there is nothing else available in Dannenfels.

The Newly Built House in Dannenfels/ 1958

"So we came to the conclusion that if nothing more suitable becomes available in Kirchheimbolanden in the next twelve to fifteen days where construction could start this spring I want to buy Hauenstein's lot so I can move into the house in late autumn."

Astrid previously indicated that farmer Hauenstein, who enjoyed the daily one-eighth liter (or Piffche) of wine, ran a tab at the Dannenfelser Hof over the years. In the end, he paid off his debt by leaving Ursula Spickschen a 1,620 square meter building site.

The acquisition of the building site on the eastern outskirts of Dannenfels was thus established. As for the financing of the planned house, Ursel had to take a loan of 39,000.00 DM for which she did not have to pay any interest over the years, only the amortized principal. Regarding the building site, Ursel wrote a letter to Herr von Massow on December 7, 1960, in which she reported that the construction site had several old sweet cherry trees growing on it, "but they do not yield much because they are too old." In that same letter Ursel said that she had to commit to service the loan from funds that were granted to her by the Lastenausgleich (or load balancing) for the loss of the Woydiethen estate. She was able to contribute only 2,000.00 DM in cash as a down payment for the building of the house and an additional 1,000.00 DM was paid in the form of an "owner-labor contribution" by her son Thorlef.

The "owner-labor contribution" that Ursel referred to was a program whereby Thorlef, who was a junior in high school in 1958, together with his friend Erwin Müller, moved and distributed thirty truckloads of earth around the newly built house. It was an extremely difficult job. With shovels and wheelbarrows and hard labor they had to landscape the area to create a sensible design for the surrounding terrain. A small outbuilding located on the grounds was used as a chicken coop. For a while, Ursel was able to sell the eggs to the surrounding inns and guest houses. Astrid, who was fifteen years old in June, 1958, often dreamt about putting a huge window in the chicken coop and transforming it into a cozy studio.

During all this, the financial situation remained tense for years. Ursel always had to depend on her children who were living in Germany to send her monthly sums of money. The children helped her while they were still studying and not only after they had an income from a job. Gerhard Traube gave Ursel regular support during the family's time in the Dannenfelser Hof.

Astrid explained that the location of the new house was on the edge of the sideline settlement, not in the center. In Dannenfels there was an Upper Street, Middle Street and Lower Street. Those streets joined at one point and the so-called sideline settlement was located beyond that point. The new house stood on a corner at the end of the Untergasse (the Lower Street). Behind the plot was the farm of a bio (organic) farmer who had a beautiful garden. Astrid said that she would not have liked to live in the sideline settlement itself because she would be cut off from the village center.

Thorlef described in detail the house which was located on a hillside. The garage was entered from the street. The roof of the garage was level with the ground floor of the house and could be used as a terrace. The front door was located past the garage and across the terrace. It opened into a small entrance with a hall behind it. From the hall, a staircase led to the upper floor which had sloping walls that followed the roof line. On the ground floor there was the kitchen and a 32 square meter living room with an open, fully functional fireplace. Upstairs there were two large bedrooms and one small one, a bathroom and toilet. Thorlef slept in the small bedroom so long as he went to school in Kirchheimbolanden. Ursel and Astrid slept in one of the two large bedrooms and the second bedroom was reserved for guests.

In December, 1958 the construction work was so close to completion that Ursel was able to move in with her two youngest children. The stairs to the upper floor were not yet installed so it could only be reached by a ladder. But the Spickschens did not want to wait any longer. They also wanted to put pressure on the craftsmen to finish the job.

In order to supplement her meager pension and help pay off the loan for the house Ursel always had to find a way to earn extra money. Over the following years, she exhibited astonishing ingenuity. Her many talents, including her great practical experience, her engaging personality in dealing with others and her skill and confidence in writing, enabled her to work in various fields. She more or less regularly published articles in agricultural journals. Then in 1958, she began giving cooking classes every winter throughout Rheinhessen. An agricultural teacher friend from East Prussia, who was then in charge of the Rheinhessen rural women's clubs, helped her to organize the courses.

Thorlef was able to get his driver's license (with a special permit) at the age of 16. He drove his mother to different villages where Ursel had prior arrangements with certain inns to let her use their kitchen and dining room for her cooking courses. She usually started the course with a short talk about nutrition and healthy eating or how to manage a meaningful and economical household. After that she cooked different recipes with the course participants. The recipes that she used for specific courses were sent to the chairman of the relevant country women's association several days prior to the course date so that she could buy the necessary ingredients and have them ready the afternoon of the meeting.

During these events, which took place two to three times per week in mostly the villages where wine was grown, Thorlef sat in the dining room and did his homework. After the two or three different dishes were prepared and ready to be served, the 15 to 30 participating ladies ate the meal and Thorlef also received a plate. These courses were an important social event, not only for Thorlef but also for local ladies and the country women's associations. The meetings were a formative experience for everyone since all learned and ate well.

These cooking classes were held in the winter until the mid-1970s. The money Ursel earned was considered an expense, not a fee, and therefore it was not taxed nor deducted from the aid she received for the younger children.

Thorlef completed high school and graduated in March, 1960 and then he entered an apprenticeship. He was therefore no longer available as a chauffeur. A young man from Dannenfels took over the job. Ursel did not want to drive for longer trips because once she almost caused an accident on an icy road. Moreover, she did not like to drive a car.

The cooking classes and articles for agricultural magazines were by far not the only things that occupied Ursel's time. For a while she got together with the local husband and wife doctors (named Wilke), who also had built a new house located at the edge of Dannenfels. He was more of an artist, a musician and art connoisseur and a smart, pleasant conversationalist than a doctor. His wife was the better health care professional. Since Dannenfels was a spa and resort and the Wilke's new house was cute and located in the forest, the three of them got the idea of creating a place for spa guests where they could be served freshly squeezed juices, for example. Ursel also intended to take in boarders once her children left home. However it soon became apparent that the plans were not plausible in the long run. Dr. Wilke (the wife) was forced to leave her practice and move into the house whenever guests came. This situation proved to be untenable.

Cooking Class / Rural Women's Club
Aspisheim, Pfalz / 1964

In the spring of 1961, Astrid graduated from high school. She received an internship as a future pharmacist near Bleckenstedt. All of the children had now left the house in Dannenfels. Ursel had to cope with drastic changes during the years beginning in October, 1957 (the death of Erich) and the spring of 1961 (departure of Astrid). It was therefore not a big surprise that she began to write poems in the period 1960-1962. Ursel probably had many reasons for writing poems but certainly not the least of which was to give herself some comfort. Ursel's first poem writing began with a very melancholy poem she wrote in 1946 when she was separated from Erich and she did not even know if he was still alive. The foreword to the collection of her poems that appeared in print in 2009 said that they were written "during difficult times" beginning in "1946 during the uncertainty about the fate of her husband and in 1960-62 on the threshold of living alone, as the youngest child left the house."

Ursel left 80 poems that were written in the period from 1960 to 1962. It should be said that it was more than a passing mood that caused her to try her hand at a form of expression that turned out not to be written in an everyday, traditional way. Two arbitrarily selected poems that she wrote follow.

Jazz in New Orleans

Black bodies swaying, tones emitting from throat and Saxophone.
Longing whimpers. Greed whispers and screams like the jungle of the Amazon.
Swamp, lianas, mosquitoes and snakes, crocodiles with cruel jaw,
Orchids with sweet smelling flowers, masters and slaves,
Rice fields and tobacco - Uncle Tom's Cabin - mind and meanness -
A confusion of life, death and decay.

Visions in the afternoon

I am unhappy, sad, desperate,
Dark clouds race by like shadows at the window,
and the wind howls relentlessly around the house.
The room looks as viewed through dark lenses -
Distorted figures on walls; scorpions, where flowers bloomed.
Houseplants stretch deadly claws out to me.
I'm leaving, lost - and the huge spider on the ceiling there
Slowly descends and wets me with her sticky threads.

The outburst of despair in the second poem is easy to understand because of the very difficult time Ursula Spickschen was going through in 1961. However, she was always able to openly explore her emotions. But the context of the first poem may be a surprise. Ursel's love of music presents a vast range and widely diversified repertoire. The contrast between the first and second poem demonstrates the thematic range of poetry in which Ursula Spickschen moves.

In "Visions in the afternoon" Ursel clearly stated that in some moments of agony she felt alone or even abandoned - in spite all the contacts she had, in spite of her children who visited her again and again and despite the many trips she took. In 1960, Thorlef, who had started his apprenticeship in Ingelheim (which is not far from Dannenfels), came home three out of four weekends a month. Apart from numerous other visits and visitors, Astrid came home as often as she could. Thorlef often brought friends with him to the house.

For example, Thorlef's classmate, a man named Manfred Witte, kept in contact with Ursel and the Spickschens for decades. Ursel and the visitors frequently played the card game Doppelkopf or someone would tell stories and hold lively discussions. Ursel, who was a born storyteller, always moved quickly into the center of the activity. She knew how to captivate her listeners and she knew how to deal with them so that everyone was interested; she knew how to make everyone feel like they were taken seriously and were included. These conversations were often enough to create an event that all remembered.

Both Astrid and Thorlef particularly remember the intense discussions about the Nazi era with their mother. Again and again the now grown-up children asked probing questions like "Why were both of you convinced Nazis?" and "Did you not know about the terrible crimes of the Nazis?" Astrid realized that she and her brother often became offensive in their mother's opinion during these violent clashes and Thorlef said that these discussions sometimes became downright brutal. Thorlef recalled that several times he and Astrid demanded that their mother tell them about her "knowledge of the Holocaust". Again and again Ursel made it clear, and ultimately was believable even in very emotional situations, that she and Erich were well aware of deportations and labor camps, but did not know of the systematic extermination of the Jews.

Following one of those discussions, Ursel obviously felt distressed and cornered and she responded in a pathetic and theatrical way that was her nature. After the conversation ended she left the house unnoticed and without leaving a trace. She left a partially written letter in her typewriter as if she had been called away in the middle of it. She stayed overnight at an unknown location and returned to Dannenfels the next day.

Astrid, who told this experience on October 15, 2009, commented on this story in her own, refreshing way. "My mother left in the car without explanation and stayed in some hotel on the Weinstrasse. What did it mean? Maybe Thorlef and I were supposed to worry about her. She suddenly ran away and left us in the dark on purpose. I was slowly growing up at the age of 14 years (1957). Gradually I realized that it could not go on like this. I know that one day I said to Thorlef - Now listen up and let Mutti in peace! After that I had my own debates with my mother which I would not necessarily call friendly. These were very tough discussions between mother and child."

As Astrid reports, those two made their mother's life difficult also on other occasions. "Sometimes we were bad tempered and complained. For example, Mutti once cooked noodles with dried fruit for dinner. 'This is not a meal', we scolded. She was hurt. On the other hand, she could be tough and down to earth, for example when it came to animal husbandry. The number of chickens became less and less over time. I asked her, 'why are there only three chickens left?' She said, 'Well, one of the chickens was in mourning, it walked around with its comb hanging down.' So Mutti took an ax and transported the animal from life to death. Then we had a wonderful foie gras. My mouth still waters when I think about it today."

As for the relationship between Astrid and her mother, Astrid remembered that Bergild was always her mother's favorite. Her mother would say, "Bergild, oh, she is so nice, she never back talks or is sassy." To this I said, 'Mutti, it would not be good for you if you were never contradicted'. If you ask Bergild today, she will tell you that she actually was always a little afraid of Mutti. I myself was never afraid of my mother. I always had a quick retort. For example, when my sister, who was three years older than me was sick, I wanted to eat something from the fridge. But my mother cried, 'No, you cannot have it, that's for Runhildchen'. I answered, 'Do you know what, I will eat that now and we'll buy more for Runhild later!"

Ursel the poet was once a spontaneous painter. Inspired by a competition announced by the local newspaper "Rheinpfalz", she bought a box of paints and painted an abstract image in lush bright colors with a lot of feeling and she won the first prize. After this she never touched the paints again. For her the matter was closed.

Given the versatility of her intellectual and especially her emotional openness to all things, it should not be surprising that Ursel was also interested in the art of card reading and other types of fortune telling and telekinesis (moving of furniture with the mind). She probably wished that she had been able to look into the future while she lived in Bleckenstedt in order to learn more about the fate of Erich, whose return from captivity was uncertain for so long. Ingolf and Bergild both remember that their mother read cards until the end of her life.

Until 1975, Ursel was consistently busy in the winters with lectures and cooking classes in the Landfrauenvereinen, the Rural Women's Clubs. In addition, she had an idea to advantageously use the summer months. For example, during an intensive one-week course she offered to advise and train young women who were planning to get married in the near future in cooking and skillful financial management. She soon found interested people that came from the "Old Country" near Hamburg. These were daughters of wealthy farmers in contrast to the poor people of the Palatinate. The young ladies lived with her in the house as boarders and were thoroughly trained with a personal approach and guidance. Astrid's comments to these actions are amusing.

"The women traveled to my mother to learn culinary arts and fine dining. They were rich in the Old Country. No one would have spent the money on this in the Pfalz (Palatinate). My mother was able to put up two ladies at a time in the house. I thought that was great because when I came home there was always good food on the table. On the weekends, the ladies went to the nearby pubs of the village and had some fun with the local youth. My mother had no inhibitions in organizing these courses. I would have been embarrassed about our dilapidated kitchen where there was not a single decent cabinet. Our only kitchen cabinet was an old locker, partly organized with cardboard boxes instead of drawers. I envied my mother for not being held back by our lack of amenities."

In addition to all these activities, in addition to the teaching, the many visitors she welcomed and the abundant correspondence she kept, Ursel traveled extensively. First, she repeatedly visited her daughters Helga and Bergild in the United States. When Thorlef received a scholarship from the University of California, Berkeley in 1968, she stopped there to visit him. She usually combined these visits with extensive tours so that she came to know that huge country quite well. Helga, who was a resident of Wisconsin at the time, said that her mother probably travelled through the United States three times. With an inexpensive Greyhound bus round-trip ticket she was able to interrupt the journey at any time to see a city or just take a break for a day or two. Some of the cities she visited were San Francisco and probably also New Orleans. (Maybe the poem "Jazz in New Orleans" is evidence that she actually was in that city, which is also called the "Cradle of Jazz"?) Ursel was quite taken in by the United States. She travelled to the West Coast and from the South to the North then she turned to the east and traveled from Wyoming and Nebraska to Wisconsin. She could travel one hundred miles through the United States without seeing a single man. She told her daughter Helga that in Wyoming a man got off the bus with only a saddle under his arm. There was nothing around, not a village or even a house. She only saw the Rocky Mountains.

Ursel took many photos during her travels and she organized slide shows with her impressive pictures for the Landfrauenvereinen, the Rural Women's Associations. She had the opportunity to talk extensively about her experiences and impressions of the USA.

She also undertook other journeys, especially to the Scandinavian countries. Her love of northern Europe and everything Nordic gave an almost life-determining significance to her. She traveled with a mail ship owned by the Hurtigruten Voyage Company to the Norwegian fjords and she visited Copenhagen. After she visited Iceland she told her oldest daughter Helga that she would love to live alone in the Icelandic wilderness. That was wishful thinking! Per her daughter Karen, Ursel always had a lot of imagination. However, to her sorrow, her plan to visit the Faroe Islands was never realized. But she did not always travel to northern Europe or the United States; she also managed to visit Mallorca and Italy.

Ursel was always quick to connect with other people during her travels, especially with women in rural areas. She was not simply a tourist during her travels since she visited a few farms in North America and contacted the local chairman of the Rural Women's Association in Iceland. She used the knowledge she gained for her lectures and corresponded with the people she met. Ursula Spickschen was a woman of many, sometimes conflicting talents. She sought and needed activity and she outright demanded that her children visit her as frequently as possible. But at other times she was happy to be alone and often longed for peace and quiet.

In Dannenfels she had a constant companion who had been with the family since Bleckenstedt. It was a wire-haired dachshund who answered to the name Kroete, which means “toad” - or rather she did not answer because she was a cheeky little toad. In 1948 or 1949, Ursel’s son-in-law Hubertus von Eller-Eberstein smuggled the little dog from the occupied Soviet zone across the Harz Mountains. Kroete accompanied Ursel until around 1963 or later. If Ursel was away, the dachshund was boarded with the cleaning lady in Dannenfels. Thorlef always took care of the house, including the extended periods of time when his mother was away. Whenever he came to Dannenfels on Friday nights, Kroete would be sitting on the doorstep waiting for him. Likewise, the dachshund knew exactly when she had to go back to the sitter on Monday mornings.

Bergild remembered that during the flight from East Prussia in 1945, Karen carried her dachshund named Purzel from East Prussia to Bleckenstedt in a sheepskin lined bag. Unfortunately, the dog was killed a few years later when it was run over by a harvest wagon.

Overall, the years 1958-1981 were a period of relative calm for Ursel after decades of dramatic ups and downs and turbulent changes between many setbacks and few upturns. This reflected the overall development of the Federal Republic during those decades. The "tumultuous" story of Ursula and Erich Spickschen’s life, bouncing back and forth between the years 1914-1957 finally settled down into a clear and peaceful existence in the late 1950s. Erich never really found peace until his death. However, Ursel was not through with living life to the fullest. Yet there was very little to report for the long period between 1958 and1981.

What occurred in Ursel’s life during the years of 1963 to 1975 is not precisely documented. But Ingolf summarized and described a few of his scattered memories in an interview on October 31, 2010.

"Since 1964, I and my whole family consisting of my wife Inga and daughters Anja, Britta and Caroline regularly stayed for several weeks at a time in Dannenfels whenever we were able to drive our car from Hamburg. In 1967, when my four-year-old daughter Caroline broke her leg after she fell off a balcony, she stayed with my mother (Ursel), who was called Omusch by her grandchildren. My children learned to swim in nearby Weiherhof and acquired their swimming certificates. We caught crawfish in a stream and cooked them under the expert guidance of Omusch. Five years later, in 1972, my two youngest daughters stayed three months with Omusch in Dannenfels and were enrolled in the local primary school after my wife Inga had a serious horse riding accident.

“In my opinion, my mother’s political stance remained constant. I can still clearly see before me as I saw in 1947, with tears in her eyes my mother bitterly reproaches my sisters Helga and Karen after the first free parliamentary elections in Lower Saxony. 'How can you vote for the FDP (Freie Demokratische Partei [Free Democratic Party])? If only Vati knew!' In the following years she decided to vote in all elections - first for the BHE (Bund der Heimatvertriebenen und Entrechteten [Federation of the Refugees and Disowned] active during the time of 1950 until 1961) and later for the CDU (Christlich

Demokratische Union [Christian Democratic Union]), who – with only one exception – she supported to the end. Only in the fall of 1972 did she vote for the SPD (Sozialdemokratische Partei Deutschlands [Social Democratic Party of Germany]). She was probably persuaded by the discussions she had with me about the new Germany and Willy Brandt's Ostpolitik (Eastern politics). She therefore helped Willy Brandt to ensure the successful continuation of his policy of reconciliation and rapprochement of the systems."

During the years from 1975 until shortly before her death in 1981, Ursel sent yearly annual recap letters to relatives and friends and it is from these letters that clues are provided for accurately dating certain events. In these newsletters, which always came in December or towards the end of the year, she described in detail the wellbeing and/or sometimes problems of her children and her growing band of grandchildren. Each and every individual was mentioned and briefly characterized with the state of their development. Only at the end of the letter did she talk about herself. In one such newsletter dated 1975, Ursel spoke about herself.

"This has been a very restless but also very good year for me. I am thankful that I am by and large healthy and the small, age-related problems one can endure. In the winter I gave a few cooking courses with one leg in a cast because I broke a bone in my foot. But in March, I said good-bye to the Landfrauenverband, the Rural Women's Association. I always appreciated the work but now I am glad that it is over even though the extra income was appreciated. Your strength diminishes when you are over 70; it's time to slow down."

At Easter time Ursel took a car trip together with Ingolf and Runhild through Jutland and reported about the trip.

"In mostly sunny weather we drove up the west coast to Skagen, then to the island of Læsø - my dream for 55 years! It was beautiful. You felt as if transported back by several decades - old half-timbered farmhouses with reed covered roofs. We hardly saw any cars, only high dunes and such wonderful peace and quiet. Then we went along the east coast to the island of Alsen where I spent many happy years of my youth. I was even able to reunite with an old friend. But the visit to our old farm in Lambjerg was a disappointment. The thatched timber-framed buildings had burned down and were replaced by new structures. The formerly large, pretty garden was much smaller and pretty wild."

The newsletter dated December 1976 contains evidence of a visit to the North Sea island of Baltrum and a bus tour of the area around Garmisch-Partenkirchen. In 1938, Ursel and Erich had visited the Riessersee, Eibsee and Badersee in that same area. She then commented on a 40-day stay in the USA. In Wisconsin she took some "wonderful rides through the forests that were in full fall colors, past isolated lakes, picturesque old farm homesteads and sleepy little towns" with Helga and her son-in-law Frank Carl Hart.

Here the world seemed to be in good shape. Then she visited Feechen and Jack Seifert who took her for long rides to show her Maryland. In Philadelphia, she and Bergild visited the newly renovated old distinguished center city districts, the Liberty Bell, and the famous maritime museum.

In a section from her newsletter of December, 1977 Ursel wrote about her travel to Norway.

"In the fall I went on a trip by myself. I travelled from Kiel by boat to Oslo, then by train to Bergen, through a landscape varying from lovely valleys and large forest to barren, rocky highlands. From there we took a postal boat around the northern tip of Norway to Kirkenes on the Russian border. The ship sailed along the coast-line which displayed an ever changing spectrum. Every day we stopped at many small ports and surprisingly even at the most northern tip one saw small potato fields, vegetable gardens and even fruit trees thanks to the Gulf Stream that flows along the coast. We made several shore excursions and saw the landscape behind the coastal mountains - valleys with stately farms, rocky plateaus, small industrial cities. And in Hammerfest it happened! I stumbled on the street, fell and broke my left wrist. But doctors at the local hospital quickly and efficiently took care of me so that I could continue the trip to the end. Thanks to them and a lovely East Prussia lady on the ship who helped me manage."

In the same letter Ursel wrote that she had not felt particularly well in January and February of 1977 and longed "for the cold, dry and sunny East Prussian winters". Other than the accident in Norway and some "age-related small ailments like decreasing stamina and faster fatigue" she was doing well. The newsletter of 1978 contained nothing remarkable about Ursel's health.

Two years later, she stated that the year 1980 brought her a lot of unrest and problems relating to her health. That was the reason she gave for not answering a lot of correspondence from the previous year. That is probably also the reason why there is no newsletter for the year 1979.

Ursel continued. “In the late summer of 1980 my legs gave me more and more trouble. Walking became increasingly difficult and the pain continued to grow." The result of x-rays “was not very encouraging. Both hip joints had to be replaced." In addition, it also became necessary to operate on her gall bladder after a strong attack. “A large walnut-sized gallstone was extracted.”

Ursel reported in her final letter, written a few days before her death, that in the spring of 1981 the hip surgery began, first one and then the other hip followed in quick succession. However, the pain in her back got progressively worse.

"So the summer continued. At times I was at Thorlef's house and he lovingly spoiled me and sometimes I was in Dannenfels where Hellie and Has'chen [Helga and Karen] took great care of me. Finally I was x-rayed again and it was discovered that I had severe osteoporosis (bone loss). One vertebra was already extremely disintegrated. I first spent a few days in the hospital and then the treatment for osteoporosis began. I am now on pills and have to go to the hospital in Offenbach every few weeks. I am told that it will take a year to a year and a half to cure this disease. Hopefully that is true!"

Ursula Spickschen, Erik, Brigitte and Thorlef Spickschen in Glashuetten 1977-78?

In the course of two meetings held on May 27 and October 17, 2010, Thorlef and his wife Brigitte recounted some occurrences during Ursel's last few months. The two did not say anything about osteoporosis but they spoke of a much worse diagnosis - kidney cancer was detected. Thorlef believed that because of the quick succession of the two hip operations and the gall bladder operation, Ursel's immune system was severely weakened. Her body could not fight and prevent the very rapid growth of the kidney cancer and it metastasized. She received radiation therapy which at least somewhat reduced the pain. However her condition deteriorated from week to week and she died on December 4, 1981.

Brigitte recalled that her mother-in-law who, for all of her life was always curious and wanted to know everything, never sought an explanation or wanted to know about her last illness. She wanted to live. But probably she guessed that she did not have much time left. Only once did she say, "It surely cannot be cancer!" But she really did not want a response to this rather vague question.

Thorlef recalled his mother's last days with help of notes that he scribble on slips of paper.

"On the week-end before her death, her grandson Walter Traube came to visit. She felt relatively good on that Sunday evening. She was supposed to go to the hospital for a few days on Monday per the doctor's recommendation because of breathing difficulties, so she suggested that they should all listen to some of her favorite old records. Walter and

I carried her in the old large wicker chair into the living room. We talked, Mutti drank some red wine and even smoked a cigarette and then she enjoyed her favorite songs. Hans Albers sang "Einmal noch nach Bombay" (One more time to Bombay) and Zarah Leander sang "Ich weiss es wird einmal ein Wunder geschehn" (I know a miracle will happen) and "Kennst du das kleine Haus am Michigansee?" (Do you know the little house on Lake Michigan?). While listening to the music she closed her eyes, swayed to the rhythm of the music and sank into deep thoughts. In hindsight, we know that she had begun to say goodbye.

On Monday she had a severe attack of shortness of breath in the hospital in Bad Soden which could hardly have been manageable at home. Brigitte and my niece Britta, a daughter of Ingolf, visited her regularly during the week. I went to the hospital in the evenings after work. On Thursday night I took the 65 copies of her Christmas letter for Mutti to sign. But she looked very tired and was not in the mood to talk. On that night to Friday, she unexpectedly went to sleep forever."

Gerda Ursula Spickschen was transferred to Bleckenstedt, where the funeral service was held. She was buried next to her husband in the plot which had been established for the Spickschen family in 1957. Karen and Gerhard Traube's farm had grown into a new place of refuge for the Spickschens after fleeing from East Prussia - a kind of second home.

The memory of Gerda Ursula Spickschen was not extinguished with her death. On the contrary. How much she stayed alive was revealed by the stories of Manfred Witte who, being born in 1940 was around Thorlef and Astrid's age and who attended the high school in Kirchheimbolanden with the two of them. Witte, later an officer in the German Army and also a successful children's book author, came to Dannenfels as a teenager in the late 1950s. He probably visited the Dannenfelser Hof only once and he knew Erich Spickschen only slightly. For him, the acquaintance with the Spickschens began in the newly built house in the Sideline settlement.

When Witte saw Ursel for the first time she did not seem very imposing to him since her appearance was inconspicuous. She was a fairly short, slightly stocky woman with a round face and cheeks that were always a little reddish. Soon he realized that she put very little emphasis on her outward appearance. Fashion passed her by and she was indifferent and couldn't care less. Witte recalled, "We often laughed if she wore something that could have come from a donation pile of clothes." The important thing about her was something else. She personified "interest" in everyone and everything.

Witte went on to explain, "For teenagers, it is extremely important that you take them seriously. And Ursel took me entirely seriously from the beginning. For many years I called her "Madame" until she requested that I call her "you". However, after that I called her Tante (Aunt) Ursel. She would listen and respond to the other person. But especially in my talks with her she had an astonishing openness. For me, everything was different at the Spickschens than in my home. Everything that was never talked about in my home - like about sexuality - was a normal, innocuous subject of discussion for them.

"She knew, as we always say "Fox and Flint". If we mentioned a name, she immediately knew what we were talking about. 'Oh, that was - and then it started. She could go on and on! She was an extraordinary woman. Certainly she also had her peculiarities. For example, she could stay up forever. For young people, it's important that the older ones go to bed or leave the room after a while. Tante Ursel often sat with us until 2 or 3 o'clock in the morning and she liked to refill her glass of red wine. Her endurance did not bother me because I liked her, but her children rolled their eyes.

"For me, the simplicity with which I could stay and also get a bed for the night with the Spickschens was new and surprising. Only simple food was served because she did not have much money. But she never said: we cannot afford this or that. On the other hand, the recipes she created were tried out on their guests and so also on me. I remember once there was a sauerkraut casserole with some kind of fish - perhaps cod - baked with Limburger cheese. This cheese has a strong smell even when it is cold but when it was heated with sauerkraut it developed an odor as if a dead horse's body was pulled from a well. The children refused to eat it. I, as a well-bred young man, ate the good casserole although it tasted terrible.

"The important thing is that Tante Ursel was always a lady. I learned much from her. I will mention only two small examples. At home no one smoked, but all of us young adults smoked, and Tante Ursel was a heavy smoker. Once I asked her to light my cigarette. She told me, 'That is not done. You should never ask a lady to light your cigarette.' I blushed. Or, one evening I had been drinking a lot. Normally I stay peaceful, but this time for some reason I was a little off color. There was a slightly awkward silence until Tante Ursel said, 'If you cannot control your drinking you should not start it'. With that, the matter was settled."

Bergild, Ursula, Erich, Thorlef / Dannenfels 1955

Manfred Witte would be able to tell a lot more about Ursula Spickschen, her versatility, practical skills, her knowledge, her generosity and much more. For many years he corresponded with her. He stated with conviction that she has remained alive to him until this date, because she was an incredibly impressive woman.

X

Family Trees as of 2012

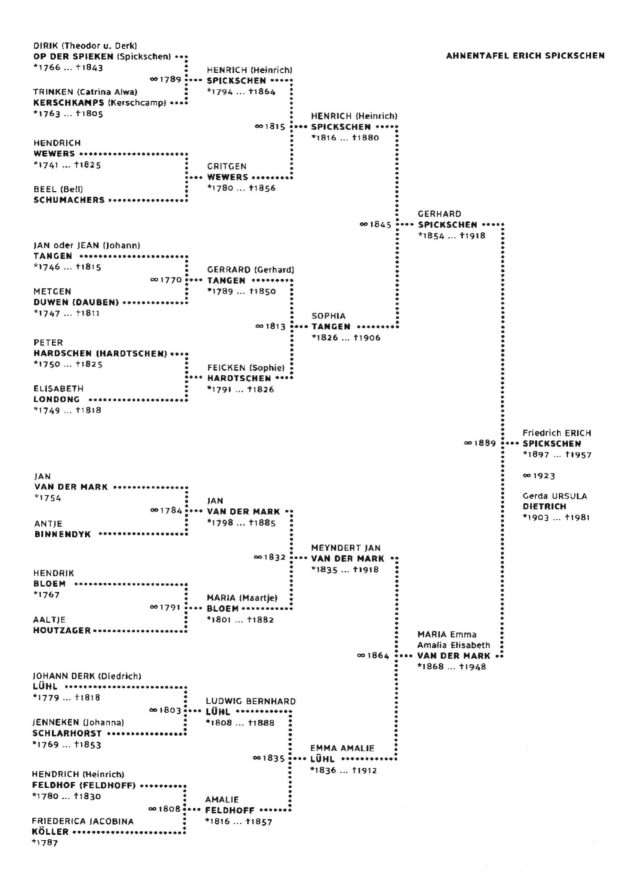

AHNENTAFEL ERICH SPICKSCHEN

DIRIK (Theodor u. Derk)
OP DER SPIEKEN (Spickschen)
*1766 ... †1843

∞1789

TRINKEN (Catrina Alwa)
KERSCHKAMPS (Kerschcamp)
*1763 ... †1805

HENRICH (Heinrich)
SPICKSCHEN
*1794 ... †1864

∞1815

HENDRICH
WEWERS
*1741 ... †1825

BEEL (Bell)
SCHUMACHERS

GRITGEN
WEWERS
*1780 ... †1856

HENRICH (Heinrich)
SPICKSCHEN
*1816 ... †1880

∞1845

JAN oder JEAN (Johann)
TANGEN
*1746 ... †1815

∞1770

METGEN
DUWEN (DAUBEN)
*1747 ... †1811

GERRARD (Gerhard)
TANGEN
*1789 ... †1850

∞1813

PETER
HARDSCHEN (HARDTSCHEN)
*1750 ... †1825

ELISABETH
LONDONG
*1749 ... †1818

FEICKEN (Sophie)
HARDTSCHEN
*1791 ... †1826

SOPHIA
TANGEN
*1826 ... †1906

GERHARD
SPICKSCHEN
*1854 ... †1918

∞1889

Friedrich ERICH
SPICKSCHEN
*1897 ... †1957

∞1923

Gerda URSULA
DIETRICH
*1903 ... †1981

JAN
VAN DER MARK
*1754

∞1784

ANTJE
BINNENDYK

JAN
VAN DER MARK
*1798 ... †1885

∞1832

HENDRIK
BLOEM
*1767

∞1791

AALTJE
HOUTZAGER

MARIA (Maartje)
BLOEM
*1801 ... †1882

MEYNDERT JAN
VAN DER MARK
*1835 ... †1918

∞1864

JOHANN DERK (Diedrich)
LÜHL
*1779 ... †1818

∞1803

JENNEKEN (Johanna)
SCHLARHORST
*1769 ... †1853

LUDWIG BERNHARD
LÜHL
*1808 ... †1888

∞1835

HENDRICH (Heinrich)
FELDHOF (FELDHOFF)
*1780 ... †1830

∞1808

FRIEDERICA JACOBINA
KÖLLER
*1787

AMALIE
FELDHOFF
*1816 ... †1857

EMMA AMALIE
LÜHL
*1836 ... †1912

MARIA Emma
Amalia Elisabeth
VAN DER MARK
*1868 ... †1948

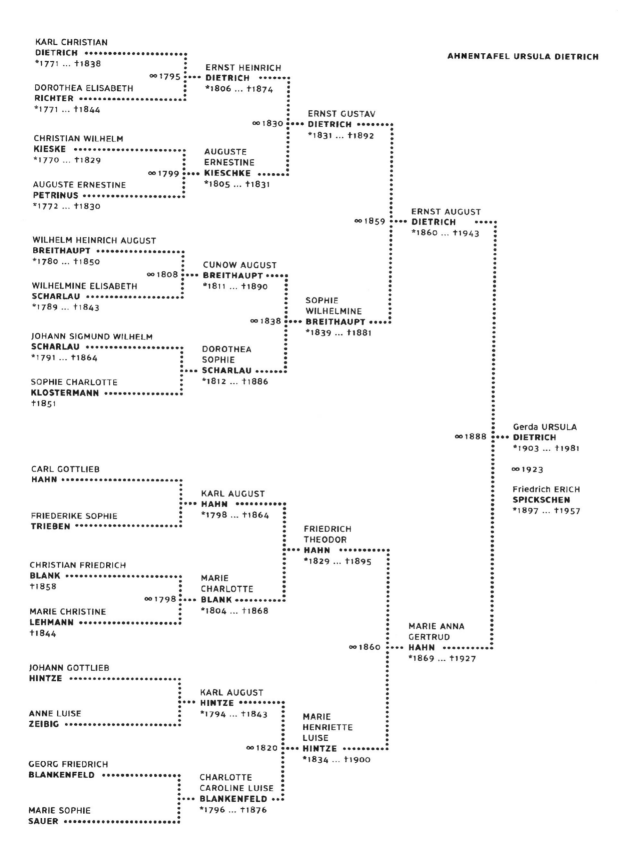

KARL CHRISTIAN
DIETRICH
*1771 ... †1838

∞1795

DOROTHEA ELISABETH
RICHTER
*1771 ... †1844

CHRISTIAN WILHELM
KIESKE
*1770 ... †1829

∞1799

AUGUSTE ERNESTINE
PETRINUS
*1772 ... †1830

WILHELM HEINRICH AUGUST
BREITHAUPT
*1780 ... †1850

∞1808

WILHELMINE ELISABETH
SCHARLAU
*1789 ... †1843

JOHANN SIGMUND WILHELM
SCHARLAU
*1791 ... †1864

SOPHIE CHARLOTTE
KLOSTERMANN
†1851

CARL GOTTLIEB
HAHN

FRIEDERIKE SOPHIE
TRIEBEN

CHRISTIAN FRIEDRICH
BLANK
†1858

∞1798

MARIE CHRISTINE
LEHMANN
†1844

JOHANN GOTTLIEB
HINTZE

ANNE LUISE
ZEIBIG

GEORG FRIEDRICH
BLANKENFELD

MARIE SOPHIE
SAUER

ERNST HEINRICH
DIETRICH
*1806 ... †1874

∞1830

AUGUSTE
ERNESTINE
KIESCHKE
*1805 ... †1831

CUNOW AUGUST
BREITHAUPT
*1811 ... †1890

∞1838

DOROTHEA
SOPHIE
SCHARLAU
*1812 ... †1886

KARL AUGUST
HAHN
*1798 ... †1864

MARIE
CHARLOTTE
BLANK
*1804 ... †1868

KARL AUGUST
HINTZE
*1794 ... †1843

∞1820

CHARLOTTE
CAROLINE LUISE
BLANKENFELD
*1796 ... †1876

ERNST GUSTAV
DIETRICH
*1831 ... †1892

∞1859

SOPHIE
WILHELMINE
BREITHAUPT
*1839 ... †1881

FRIEDRICH
THEODOR
HAHN
*1829 ... †1895

∞1860

MARIE
HENRIETTE
LUISE
HINTZE
*1834 ... †1900

ERNST AUGUST
DIETRICH
*1860 ... †1943

∞1888

MARIE ANNA
GERTRUD
HAHN
*1869 ... †1927

Gerda URSULA
DIETRICH
*1903 ... †1981

∞1923

Friedrich ERICH
SPICKSCHEN
*1897 ... †1957

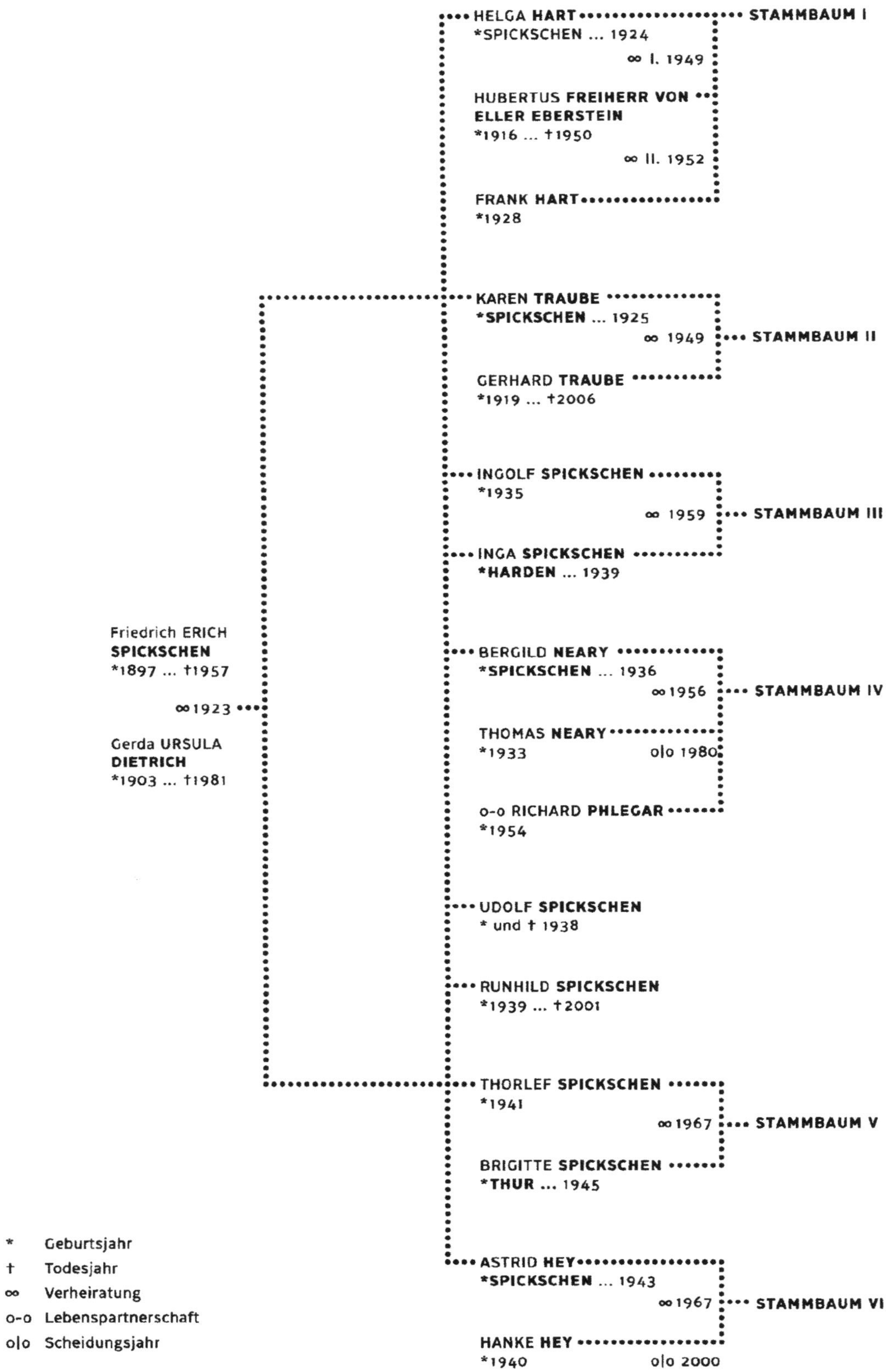
HELGA **HART**
*SPICKSCHEN ... 1924
∞ I. 1949
HUBERTUS **FREIHERR VON ELLER EBERSTEIN**
*1916 ... †1950
∞ II. 1952
FRANK **HART**
*1928
STAMMBAUM I
KAREN **TRAUBE**
***SPICKSCHEN** ... 1925
∞ 1949
GERHARD **TRAUBE**
*1919 ... †2006
STAMMBAUM II
INGOLF **SPICKSCHEN**
*1935
∞ 1959
INGA **SPICKSCHEN**
***HARDEN** ... 1939
STAMMBAUM III
Friedrich ERICH **SPICKSCHEN**
*1897 ... †1957
∞1923
Gerda URSULA **DIETRICH**
*1903 ... †1981
BERGILD **NEARY**
***SPICKSCHEN** ... 1936
∞1956
THOMAS **NEARY**
*1933
o|o 1980
o-o RICHARD **PHLEGAR**
*1954
STAMMBAUM IV
UDOLF **SPICKSCHEN**
* und † 1938
RUNHILD **SPICKSCHEN**
*1939 ... †2001
THORLEF **SPICKSCHEN**
*1941
∞1967
BRIGITTE **SPICKSCHEN**
***THUR** ... 1945
STAMMBAUM V
ASTRID **HEY**
***SPICKSCHEN** ... 1943
∞1967
HANKE **HEY**
*1940
o|o 2000
STAMMBAUM VI
* Geburtsjahr
† Todesjahr
∞ Verheiratung
o-o Lebenspartnerschaft
o|o Scheidungsjahr

STAMMBAUM I

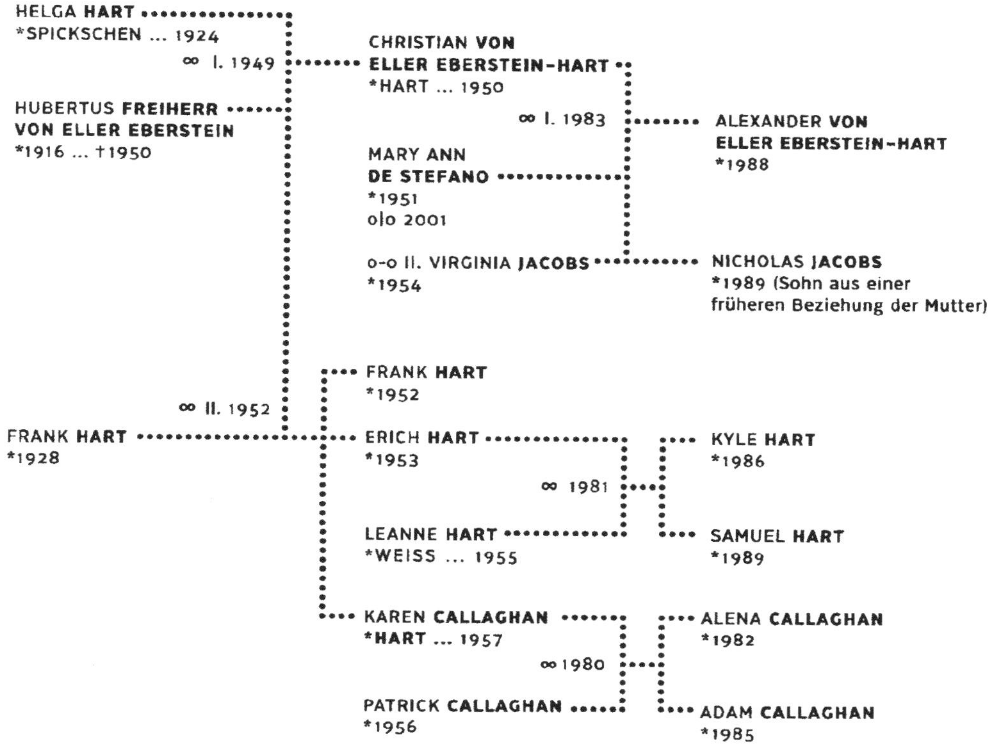
HELGA HART
*SPICKSCHEN ... 1924
∞ I. 1949
HUBERTUS FREIHERR VON ELLER EBERSTEIN
*1916 ... †1950
CHRISTIAN VON ELLER EBERSTEIN-HART
*HART ... 1950
∞ I. 1983
MARY ANN DE STEFANO
*1951
o|o 2001
o-o II. VIRGINIA JACOBS
*1954
ALEXANDER VON ELLER EBERSTEIN-HART
*1988
NICHOLAS JACOBS
*1989 (Sohn aus einer früheren Beziehung der Mutter)
∞ II. 1952
FRANK HART
*1928
FRANK HART
*1952
ERICH HART
*1953
∞ 1981
LEANNE HART
*WEISS ... 1955
KYLE HART
*1986
SAMUEL HART
*1989
KAREN CALLAGHAN
*HART ... 1957
∞ 1980
PATRICK CALLAGHAN
*1956
ALENA CALLAGHAN
*1982
ADAM CALLAGHAN
*1985

STAMMBAUM VI

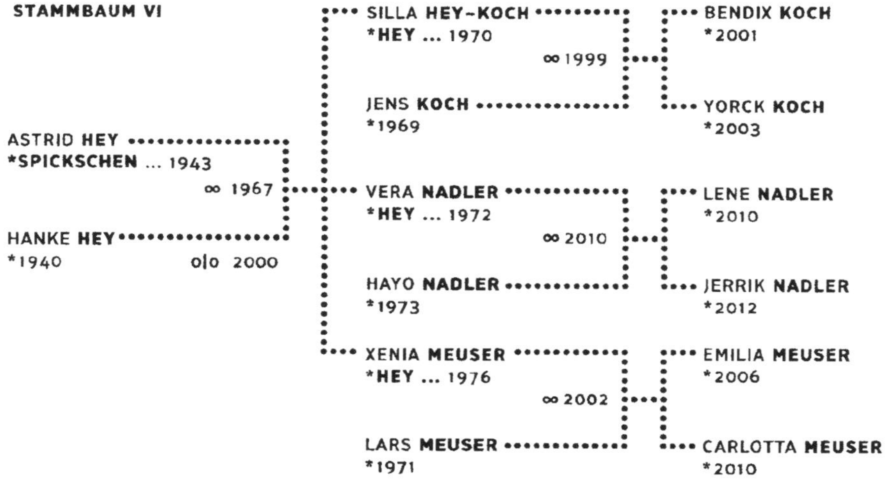
ASTRID HEY
*SPICKSCHEN ... 1943
∞ 1967
HANKE HEY
*1940
o|o 2000
SILLA HEY-KOCH
*HEY ... 1970
∞ 1999
JENS KOCH
*1969
BENDIX KOCH
*2001
YORCK KOCH
*2003
VERA NADLER
*HEY ... 1972
∞ 2010
HAYO NADLER
*1973
LENE NADLER
*2010
JERRIK NADLER
*2012
XENIA MEUSER
*HEY ... 1976
∞ 2002
LARS MEUSER
*1971
EMILIA MEUSER
*2006
CARLOTTA MEUSER
*2010

STAMMBAUM II

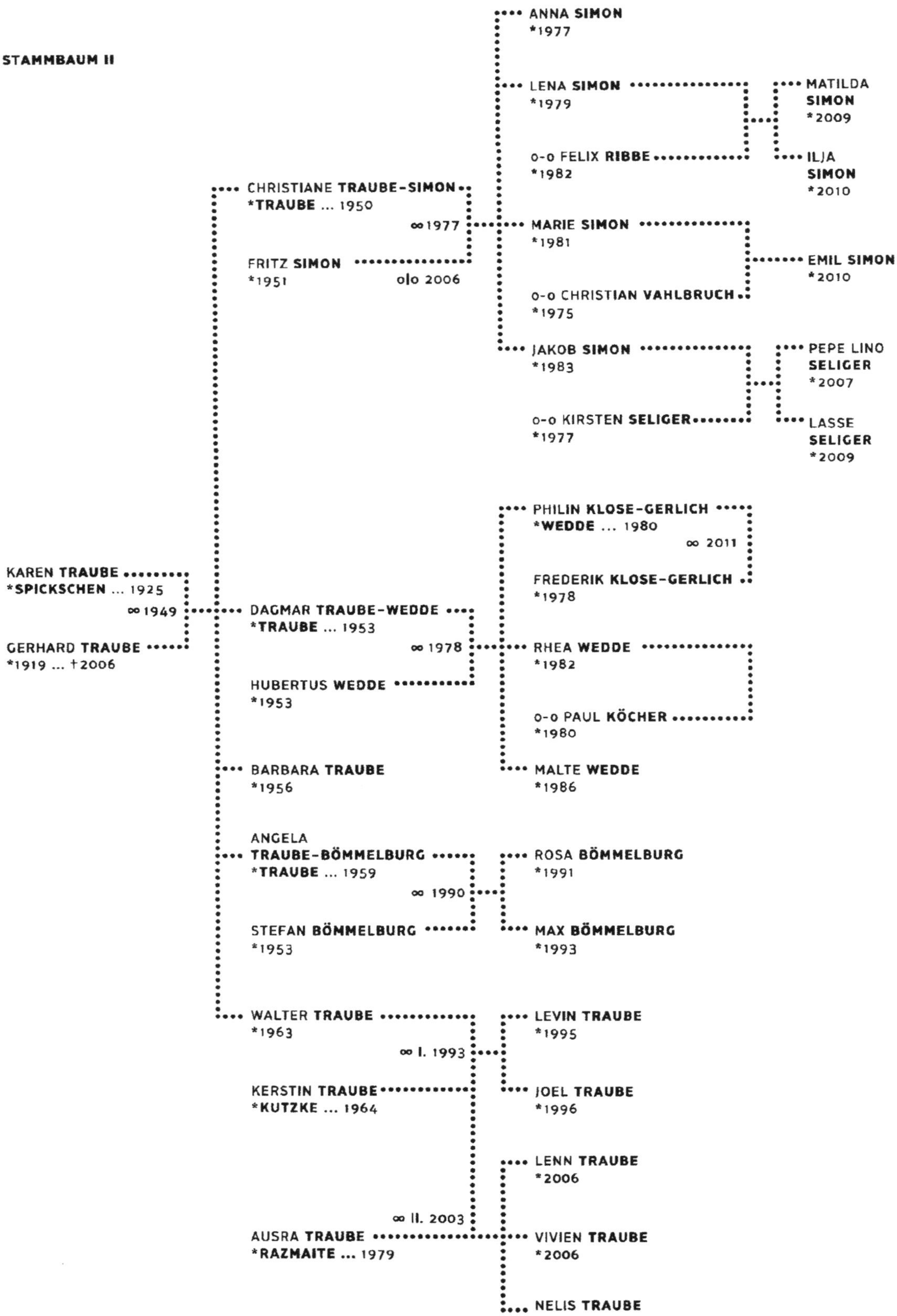
ANNA SIMON *1977
LENA SIMON *1979
o-o FELIX RIBBE *1982
MATILDA SIMON *2009
ILJA SIMON *2010
CHRISTIANE TRAUBE-SIMON *TRAUBE … 1950
∞1977
FRITZ SIMON *1951
o|o 2006
MARIE SIMON *1981
o-o CHRISTIAN VAHLBRUCH *1975
EMIL SIMON *2010
JAKOB SIMON *1983
o-o KIRSTEN SELIGER *1977
PEPE LINO SELIGER *2007
LASSE SELIGER *2009
PHILIN KLOSE-GERLICH *WEDDE … 1980
∞ 2011
FREDERIK KLOSE-GERLICH *1978
KAREN TRAUBE *SPICKSCHEN … 1925
∞1949
GERHARD TRAUBE *1919 … †2006
DAGMAR TRAUBE-WEDDE *TRAUBE … 1953
∞ 1978
HUBERTUS WEDDE *1953
RHEA WEDDE *1982
o-o PAUL KÖCHER *1980
BARBARA TRAUBE *1956
MALTE WEDDE *1986
ANGELA TRAUBE-BÖMMELBURG *TRAUBE … 1959
∞ 1990
STEFAN BÖMMELBURG *1953
ROSA BÖMMELBURG *1991
MAX BÖMMELBURG *1993
WALTER TRAUBE *1963
∞ I. 1993
KERSTIN TRAUBE *KUTZKE … 1964
LEVIN TRAUBE *1995
JOEL TRAUBE *1996
LENN TRAUBE *2006
∞ II. 2003
AUSRA TRAUBE *RAZMAITE … 1979
VIVIEN TRAUBE *2006
NELIS TRAUBE *2008

STAMMBAUM III

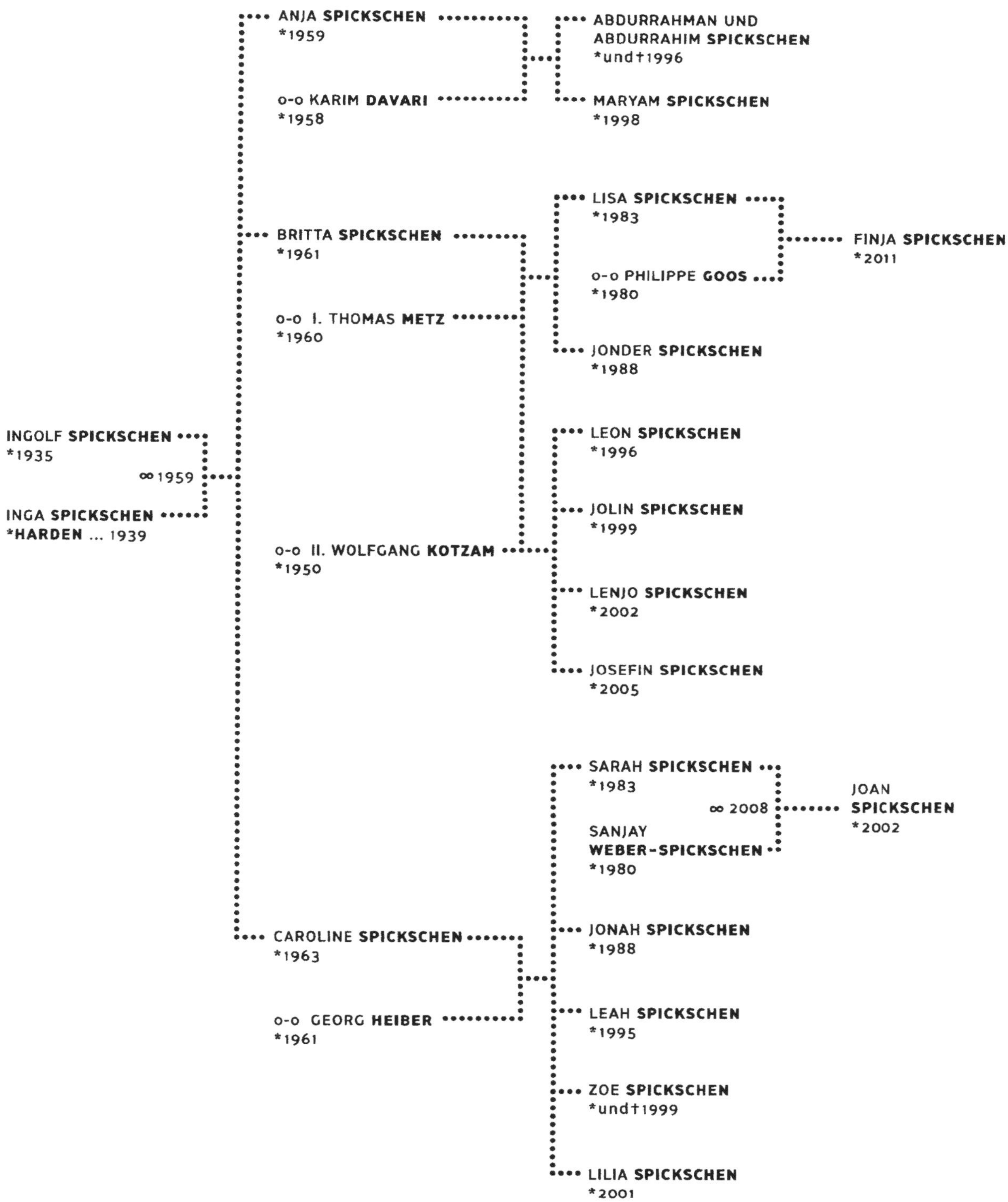
INGOLF SPICKSCHEN
*1935
∞ 1959
INGA SPICKSCHEN
*HARDEN ... 1939
ANJA SPICKSCHEN
*1959
o-o KARIM DAVARI
*1958
ABDURRAHMAN UND
ABDURRAHIM SPICKSCHEN
*und†1996
MARYAM SPICKSCHEN
*1998
BRITTA SPICKSCHEN
*1961
o-o I. THOMAS METZ
*1960
o-o II. WOLFGANG KOTZAM
*1950
LISA SPICKSCHEN
*1983
o-o PHILIPPE GOOS
*1980
FINJA SPICKSCHEN
*2011
JONDER SPICKSCHEN
*1988
LEON SPICKSCHEN
*1996
JOLIN SPICKSCHEN
*1999
LENJO SPICKSCHEN
*2002
JOSEFIN SPICKSCHEN
*2005
CAROLINE SPICKSCHEN
*1963
o-o GEORG HEIBER
*1961
SARAH SPICKSCHEN
*1983
∞ 2008
SANJAY
WEBER-SPICKSCHEN
*1980
JOAN
SPICKSCHEN
*2002
JONAH SPICKSCHEN
*1988
LEAH SPICKSCHEN
*1995
ZOE SPICKSCHEN
*und†1999
LILIA SPICKSCHEN
*2001

STAMMBAUM IV

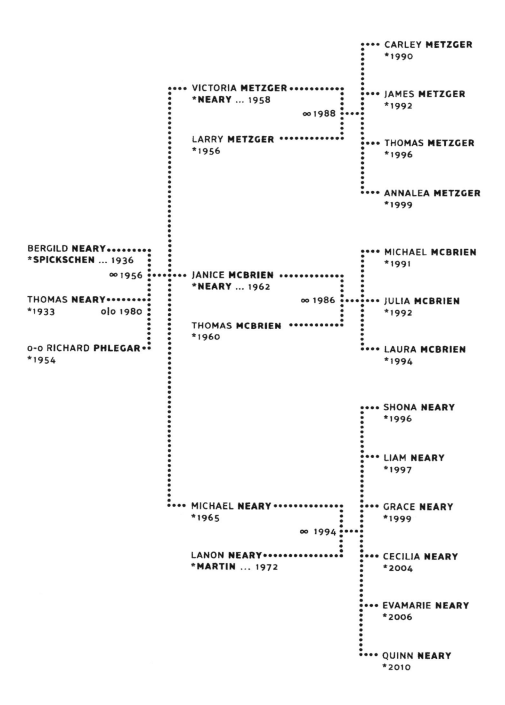

- BERGILD **NEARY** *SPICKSCHEN ... 1936
  ∞ 1956
- THOMAS **NEARY** *1933
  o|o 1980
- o-o RICHARD **PHLEGAR** *1954

Children of Bergild Neary and Thomas Neary:

- VICTORIA **METZGER** *NEARY ... 1958
  ∞ 1988
  LARRY **METZGER** *1956
  - CARLEY **METZGER** *1990
  - JAMES **METZGER** *1992
  - THOMAS **METZGER** *1996
  - ANNALEA **METZGER** *1999
- JANICE **MCBRIEN** *NEARY ... 1962
  ∞ 1986
  THOMAS **MCBRIEN** *1960
  - MICHAEL **MCBRIEN** *1991
  - JULIA **MCBRIEN** *1992
  - LAURA **MCBRIEN** *1994
- MICHAEL **NEARY** *1965
  ∞ 1994
  LANON **NEARY** *MARTIN ... 1972
  - SHONA **NEARY** *1996
  - LIAM **NEARY** *1997
  - GRACE **NEARY** *1999
  - CECILIA **NEARY** *2004
  - EVAMARIE **NEARY** *2006
  - QUINN **NEARY** *2010

STAMMBAUM V

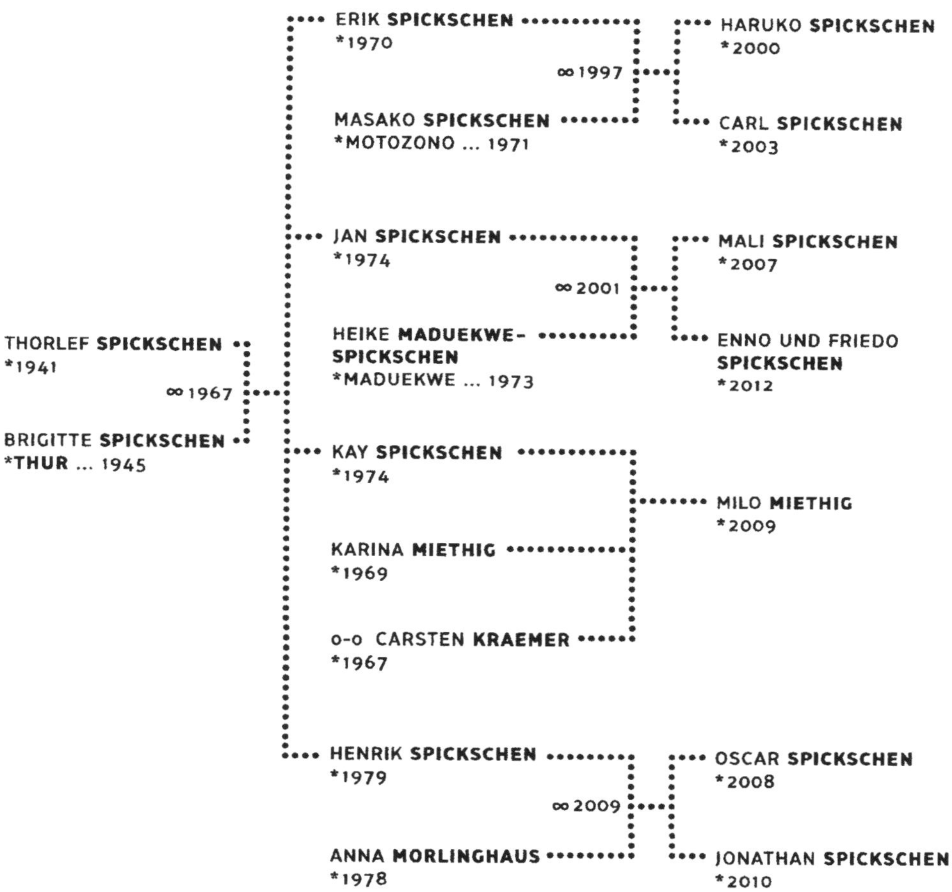
THORLEF **SPICKSCHEN**
*1941
∞1967
BRIGITTE **SPICKSCHEN**
***THUR** ... 1945
ERIK **SPICKSCHEN**
*1970
∞1997
MASAKO **SPICKSCHEN**
*MOTOZONO ... 1971
HARUKO **SPICKSCHEN**
*2000
CARL **SPICKSCHEN**
*2003
JAN **SPICKSCHEN**
*1974
∞2001
HEIKE **MADUEKWE-SPICKSCHEN**
*MADUEKWE ... 1973
MALI **SPICKSCHEN**
*2007
ENNO UND FRIEDO **SPICKSCHEN**
*2012
KAY **SPICKSCHEN**
*1974
KARINA **MIETHIG**
*1969
o-o CARSTEN **KRAEMER**
*1967
MILO **MIETHIG**
*2009
HENRIK **SPICKSCHEN**
*1979
∞2009
ANNA **MORLINGHAUS**
*1978
OSCAR **SPICKSCHEN**
*2008
JONATHAN **SPICKSCHEN**
*2010

52966942R00179

Made in the USA
Middletown, DE
23 November 2017